BOUNCING BACK — AND FORWARD

Dedicated with much love
to my two wonderful children
Tanya
and
Aryeh
who shared with me the ups and downs
described in many of these chapters

Bouncing Back — and Forward

FROM IMMIGRANT HOUSEHOLD TO CAMBRIDGE FELLOWSHIP

Stefan C. Reif

3/12/21

VALLENTINE MITCHELL

LONDON • CHICAGO, IL

First published in 2021 by Vallentine Mitchell

Catalyst House,	814 N. Franklin Street,
720 Centennial Court,	Chicago, Illinois,
Centennial Park, Elstree WD6 3SY, UK	IL 60610 USA

www.vmbooks.com

Copyright © 2021 Stefan C. Reif

British Library Cataloguing in Publication Data:
An entry can be found on request

ISBN 978 1 912676 51 4 (Cloth)
ISBN 978 1 912676 52 1 (Paper)
ISBN 978 1 912676 53 8 (Ebook)

Library of Congress Cataloging in Publication Data:
An entry can be found on request

Contents

Preface

I should begin with a user warning. Those who simply wish to read my story should dispense with these introductory remarks and proceed forthwith to the first chapter. Those who would like to know the historical background of my parents' families, and in this way to understand my ethnic origins, are invited to read either, or both, of the Appendices, summarizing the vicissitudes of the Reifs and the Rebtsovs in Eastern Europe, and after their emigration westwards. If there remain, after such a weeding process, some who would still like to suffer my personal musings about changes in interests, biography, motivation and methodology, do please read on for as long as these topics are regarded as worthy of attention.

Few writers retain wholly identical interests and totally unchanged styles throughout their careers, especially if these extend over lengthy periods. Academic writers may have their own professional conventions to which they adhere, to a greater or lesser extent, but they too are likely to make adjustments in their approach to the evaluation of other scholars' work, as well as in their choice of topics for analysis. It is now over half a century since I published my first article and a glance at how I expressed myself then, and in more recent years, undoubtedly reveals modifications of the subjects I chose and the nature of my discussions.

Required as I was to follow the German scientific methodology of my research supervisors, I began my career with a commitment to scholarly topics and to their precise literary and linguistic analysis, with only a limited attention to historical speculation, and a tendency to assess scholarship, rather than scholars. As I moved into the central period of my academic activity, various forms of historical study became more attractive to me and I became as enthused by the broader reasons for changes in texts and interpretations as by the recording of their precise details. In recent years, it has been the scholars themselves, their backgrounds and their motivations, that have stimulated my interest.

It seems that this trend towards the more personal is a characteristic of many scholars in their more mature years. It is perhaps related to the changes in one's assessment of one's own life and work. Young and ambitious academics are driven by the desire, and indeed the professional necessity, to create for themselves personae that meet the needs of their institutions, subjects and colleagues. Their backgrounds, motivations and personal preferences may therefore tend to be suppressed in favour of the image they wish, or require, to promote. When they have retired, such agendas play much less of a role, if any role at all, in their considerations, and they can concentrate on the personal, not only with regard to what they study but also in the matter of how they view themselves and their lifetime achievements.

I suspect that it is for this reason, as well as some others, that biographies of various sorts become progressively more attractive to many individuals as they reach their seniority. For such individuals – among whom I certainly count myself – there is a growing fascination with how those who have achieved success, overcome challenges, or attracted public attention, began their lives, set their ambitions and coped with obstacles, animosity and personal pain. As one reads such biographies, one comes to appreciate that, although they often have common characteristics, there are also unique, or virtually unique, elements in each of them. The early years of each person's life are controlled by families, influenced by local and national events, and guided by religious, cultural and educational considerations. Which personalities wrenched themselves free of such backgrounds and which adopted and promoted what they had inherited in their childhood and youth?

In the compilation of such biographies, there are many ideological, methodological and literary matters that need to be addressed. When I started recording my own story, I was troubled by such matters and unsure of precisely the direction that needed to be taken. I consulted a distinguished historian who assured me that I should not attempt a scholarly analysis, with detailed analysis and documentation. That would be the task of future generations. What I should do was to set down my personal impressions, and to summarize the events of my life as I saw them. I took this on board and began to enjoy the process of writing my history, describing those who were central to it, and recalling my feelings about the various developments from year to year, from place to place, and from institution to institution.

I was greatly encouraged in this by reading Hermione Lee's *Body Parts: Essays in Life Writing* which had been published in 2005. Biography was highly complex, multi-dimensional and related to numerous aspects of life in all their manifestations. In her introduction, she wisely makes the point that 'history, politics, sociology, gossip, fiction, literary criticism, psychoanalysis, documentary, journalism, ethics and philosophy are all scrambled up inside the genre'. In addition, she stresses how important it is not to lose sight of the fact that readers of biography have an insatiable appetite for stories, anecdotes and personal details and allegiances. Her remarks inspired me to continue writing my story from personal, familial and historical angles and to include many brief and, to my mind, illustrative anecdotes.

My original intention was to clarify for myself, perhaps as a kind of catharsis, the meaning of a life that is now reaching its final stage and of my responses to its numerous challenges. I also wished to bequeath to the younger members of the family the story of their forbears in general and of myself in particular. Gradually, however, it became clear to me that such a story had many elements in it that might be of wider interest. Not only were there purely personal data that might otherwise be lost; many of the events relating to my experiences had relevance for aspects of social, religious and educational history and I felt the need to record how I viewed these when they occurred.

Every historian knows that the histories of institutions more often than not reflect the views of the establishments and elites that control them. It is not rare for the writers of such narratives to promote the agendas of those who have engaged their services or, when they have themselves been active in such institutions, to present the views and analysis with which they have become familiar and comfortable. Personal reflections can complement such formal and conventional accounts and it is not unknown for them to revise and correct them. What I have written at times represents a kind of microcosm of the lengthy tale of Jewish emigration from Eastern Europe, while in other instances it sheds light on the process of training, performing and achieving that will be familiar to many academics.

It should be clear by now that what I have written here is not analytical and scientific history with footnotes but my own account of what I have seen, felt and encountered in a period of seven decades, beginning at the end of the Second World War and reaching the era of Brexit and the Coronavirus. I have not shirked from telling the truth as I see, or saw, it, but I have also been aware that writing in too direct or passionate a manner about some events and about certain individuals might cause offence and I have therefore often toned down in the text what I genuinely felt in my heart, and indeed in my mind. Those who are used to English style will in any case often read between the lines and for them at least it has not been necessary to spell everything out.

I have had the great benefit of helpful and constructive comments from those closest to me. My partner, Renate, has consistently stressed that this should be my story and has therefore acted as an invaluable filter against diluted input. My son, Aryeh, has stressed that not every reader will be interested in every topic but has encouraged me by describing the text as a compelling read. My daughter, Tanya, has paid me the ultimate compliment by assuring me that the story truly reads like a biography. My sister, Sharron, has kindly described the story as phenomenal while my dear friend, Jeffrey Cohen, chuckled his way through the chapter about our student days and declared it to be an important contribution to social history. I changed, removed and added text in accordance with their various suggestions. My Cambridge friend and colleague, Alex Wright of Cambridge University Press, has kindly agreed to allow me to cite this comment of his: 'You write very well and it was, at times, extremely moving. Throughout it was lively and engaging and you have a keen eye as well as a ready pen for the acerbic or ironic bon mot.' To all of them, I am deeply grateful for their assistance and encouragement.

S.C.R.

St John's College, Cambridge; Beit Shemesh, Israel; March 2020

Glossary of Hebrew and
Yiddish Terms

Aliyah: settling in Israel

Arvit: evening service

Aṭarah: decorated collar attached by some to their ṭallit

Barmitzvah: for a boy, reaching the age of thirteen and marking it in various
   ways

Batmitzvah: for a girl, reaching the age of twelve and marking it in various
   ways

Becher: goblet (often silver) for sacramental use

Berakhah: benediction, blessing

Bimah: reading platform at the centre of the traditional synagogue

Blintzes: pancakes filled with sweet cream cheese

Brit milah: the Abrahamic covenant of circumcision, performed on a male
   child on the eighth day after his birth, if he is in good health

Bubbe: grandmother

Chabad: a branch of Ḥasidic Orthodoxy, founded by Shneur Zalman of
   Liady, stressing the educational, as well as the mystical, aspect of
   popular Judaism, and outreach

Daven: pray

Fresser: used for a human 'gobbler' in Yiddish but for an animal's eating in
   German

Gabbay: synagogue secretary or treasurer

Gefillte fish: traditional Jewish recipe for a chopped assortment of boiled
   fish, often used as a stuffing, or fried into fish cakes

Goyim: non-Jews

Haftarah: synagogal reading from one of the Prophetic books

Ḥagim: the Jewish religious festivals, singular: *Ḥag.*

Haham: title meaning 'scholar', used specifically for the rabbinic head of
   the Spanish and Portuguese Synagogue in London

Halakhah: Jewish religious law

Ḥalutzim: pioneers, especially in early Zionism

Ḥanukah: mid-winter festival celebrating the Maccabean victory over the Syrians in the second century BCE

Ḥasidic: belonging to the breakaway sect of Orthodox Judaism developed in Eastern Europe in the eighteenth century that stressed the centrality of the ordinary, even unlearned Jew and that was led by a Rebbe rather than a Rabbi, that is, a spiritual rather than an intellectual leader

Ḥaverim: members, especially of a kibbutz, but also any Jewish society

Havdalah: the domestic ceremony marking the end of Shabbat

Ḥazan: cantor

Ḥazan sheni: 'second' or assistant cantor

Ḥeder: synagogue class

Heimishe: belong to the home, that is, the previous home in Eastern Europe, and therefore warm, traditional and loved

Ḥevra: a close-knit group of Ḥaverim

Ḥumash: Hebrew Pentateuch

Ḥuppah: canopy under which a wedding ceremony is performed and, by extension, the ceremony itself

Kehillah: congregation

Ketubah: Jewish marriage document

Kiddush: blessing over wine or strong drink before the meal on Friday evening or Saturday morning, often followed by snacks and nibbles

Kohen, plural *kohanim*: of priestly descent

Kosher: religiously acceptable food, the word *kashrut* referring to the overall adherence to this principle

Latke: a fried pancake made with grated potato, traditionally eaten on the Jewish festival of Ḥanukah

Lein: read the Torah from a scroll with the traditional cantillation

Madrich: youth leader

Maḥzor: a prayer-book for the Jewish festivals

Makolet: a small grocery store in modern Israel

Melaveh Malkah: 'taking leave of the [Sabbath] queen', that is, enjoying a social on Saturday evening

Minḥah: afternoon service

Mishige: or mishuge (the pronunciation depending where your Jewish ancestors originated), crazy

Matza: unleavened bread eaten on Passover

Midrashim: works of biblical exegesis from the talmudic and medieval periods

Minyan: the ten worshippers required for a quorum in public prayers

Mitzvah: religious precept

Parashah: pentateuchal section in a synagogal lectionary

Pesaḥ: Passover

Purim: Festival celebrating the Jewish survival in the face of Persian persecution, as described in the biblical book of Esther

Rav: Rabbi, plural: *rabbanim*, or *rabbonim* in Askenazi pronunciation

Rebbe: the Rabbi of a Ḥasidic group

Rebbetzin: wife of the Rabbi

Rosh Hashanah: Jewish New Year festival

Saba: widely used in modern Hebrew for 'grandfather'

Savta: widely used in modern Hebrew for 'grandmother'

Schnorrer: widely used in Yiddish to describe someone who begs, asks for money, or expects to receive things for nothing

Sefer Torah: Pentateuchal scroll

Semaḥot: celebrations; singular: *simḥah*

Shabbat: Sabbath (Saturday), traditionally pronounced 'Shabbos' by Eastern European Jews

Shaḥarit: morning prayers

Shammas(h): synagogue beadle

Sheitel: a wig worn by married and strictly Orthodox women, to cover their natural hair, as an act of modesty

Sheva Berakhot: literally, the seven nuptial benedictions, recited when a bride and groom have any meal in company for the first week after their marriage

Shiddukhim: marital matches, sometimes initiated other than by the couple themselves

Shi'ur: traditional rabbinic lesson

Shiv'ah: literally, seven, referring to the week of domestic mourning after the demise of a close relative

Shlemiel: The classic definition is the bungler who drops or spills something, while the *shlemazal* is the one on whom it is dropped or spilt.

Shlep: carry, or walk, with some effort and no great enthusiasm

Shmatte: literally, 'rag', but often used for clothing, and in describing the clothing trade

Shofar: ram's horn blown one hundred times in the synagogue on Rosh Hashanah

Shoḥet: the Jewish religious functionary who carries out the ritual slaughter of animals for communal consumption

Sho'ah: literarily in Hebrew 'disaster', but specifically used to describe the enslavement and murder of millions of Jews by the Nazi regime in Europe

Shool: synagogue

Shtetel: little town, with a significant Jewish population, as known by the Jews of Eastern Europe, plural: *shtetelech*

Shtiebel: a small room used for rather informal communal prayer, usually in the home of a Rabbi

Siddur: Hebrew prayer-book

Simḥat Torah: the rejoicing on completing the annual pentateuchal lectionary on the final day of the Sukkot festival

Sukkah: booth, a temporary structure, outside one's permanent housing, in which one eats one's meals (and some also sleep) during the autumnal festival of Sukkot

Sukkot; the festival of 'tabernacles' or 'booths'

Ṭallit: the shawl wrapped around the worshipper during prayer

Talmud: the extensive corpus of rabbinic traditions ranging over many centuries and finally edited in seventh-century Babylonia

Tanakh: Acronym for Torah, Neviim, Ketuvim, that is, the Pentateuch, Prophets and Writings of the Hebrew Bible

Tattele: little daddy, a term of endearment for a son

Tefillin: phylacteries, worn with the ṭallit at prayer on weekdays

Torah: Pentateuch but also the whole Hebrew Bible, and can mean the sum total of Jewish religious teaching

Tsores: troubles

Ulpan: intensive modern Hebrew language course

Wee: Scots dialect for 'small'

Yahrzeit: used by Ashkenazi Jews to describe the anniversary of the death of a Jew, usually a relative

Yarmulka: a head-covering, usuall smaller than a hat, worn by Orthodox Jews

Yerushah: inheritance

Yeshivah: a seminary for the intense study of rabbinic texts

Yiddish: Judeo-German dialect of Ashkenazi Jews

Yidden: what eastern European Jews called themselves

Yiddishkeit: traditional Ashkenazi Judaism

Yizkor: memorial service for departed relatives recited after the Torah reading on certain festivals

Yom Kippur: Day of Atonement

Yomtov: literally, 'good day', often used to refer to a Jewish religious festival
Zeide: grandfather
Zemirot: hymns sung at the Sabbath table

1

Wee Stenom
(1944–47)

Looking Back

If I look out of the front window of my rooms at St. John's College in the University of Cambridge, I can see an area that included the Norman *rue des Juifs* ('Street of the Jews') some 900 years ago, a century before the first Cambridge College was established. The church which once stood on that site – now a park and a market – was called 'All Saints by the Jewry'. The building that includes my room was built 500 years ago as part of a Christian religious foundation established to educate young men (not women, of course, at that time) in the latest ideas of scholarly humanism. The back windows of my set of rooms look out on to the site once occupied by the modest sixteenth-century Christian chapel, demolished by the imperialist developers of nineteenth-century England and replaced by a magnificent Neo-Gothic building, with splendid organs and superb acoustics, devoted to a grander version of Christian worship.

I am privileged to be part of an institution that is renowned around the world. Thousands of tourists gaze in awe at these remnants of medieval and early modern English history. Students of the sciences and the humanities make their way here from around the globe and those I meet compliment me on having a 'fellowship' in this outstanding remnant of Tudor England, of Reformation ideology, and of Victorian grandeur, now a representative of what is internationally best in contemporary learning. When I make my way through its courtyards to my rooms after dining in the splendid College hall, I often reflect on the fact that I have made a long, and at times arduous, journey from humblest beginnings.

When I looked out of my window more than 70 years ago, soon after the end of the Second World War, I could see a housing estate ('Prestonfield') built in the late 1920s by Edinburgh Corporation. That whole area in the south of Edinburgh contained large tenement buildings and little houses, a small minority with tiny gardens, all of them rented from the Corporation. There were no indications of any earlier history, other than the nearby Dalkeith Road that had for centuries led from the centre of Scotland's capital city to one of its surrounding villages. Education was represented by no more than one small primary school, less than a kilometre away, that had been opened less than a decade before.

There were no academics in the vicinity, only working-class folk, most of whom laboured hard, often early and regularly late in the day, for their four or five pounds a week. No tourists in charming Edinburgh chose to include our area in their itineraries. The achievements of such residents were basically honest, limited in scope, and not widely proclaimed. They struggled to feed and clothe their children, tended their allotments, and took two buses to the cold, austere and simple beaches at Portobello as a special treat on a Sunday or a 'day-off'. When we indulged in that 'treat', we always took with us large flasks of hot tea so that we could thaw out a little after dipping into the icy cold waters of the North Sea, or, more accurately 'the Firth of Forth'. One of the most attractive areas near the tenement in which we lived was the delightfully lush and well-maintained bowling green, for those who could afford the necessary equipment. Some locals found pleasure in football matches, by playing or spectating, some by frequenting the local pubs, and some by placing bets on the Derby or the Grand National horse-races. Women, almost always with head-coverings and aprons ('pinnies'), would sometimes stand outside their homes, with arms folded, enjoying a little gossip (a 'wee blether' in the local dialect). There were no betting shops, only an illegal 'bookie' who stood on the corner of the street opposite our building, keeping one eye on the sixpences (2.5p), shillings (5p) and half-crowns (12.5p) of his clients and leaving another wary one open for the 'polis'.

Inside But Outside

We were part of that life but also outside of it. Unlike the majority who belonged, at least formally, to the Church of Scotland, we were Jews. There were a few Jewish families of cobblers, upholsterers, tailors, and small traders who lived near us. Not all were able to go to synagogue every Shabbat (Saturday) because they often worked six-day weeks but most of them ate kosher food and attended synagogue services at least on the most important festival days. And there were hardly any who chose not to send their children to the synagogue classes to learn Hebrew, to become acquainted with the prayers and the Bible, and to learn about Jewish ideas and practices. Such classes met on Sunday morning and on four, and later three, weekday evenings for an hour or two after school. We called it ḥeder, the Hebrew word for a room, presumably a classroom, as it had been known in Eastern Europe.

The origins of almost all the Jewish families who lived in such circumstances had been in Poland, Lithuania and Russia. They, or their parents, had come as penniless refugees either before the First World War, or in the years leading up to the Second World War. By the time I was on the Edinburgh Jewish scene, there were well-established Jewish families who had opened businesses, become medical doctors or entered other professions. By and large, these more affluent families had moved away from traditional observance but, because they had the funds to contribute substantially to the costs of the local synagogue, they ran the local religious show. They might attend for a short time on Shabbat morning and then go off to tend their businesses or pursue their professions in the commercial centres of the High Street, the Bridges and Princes Street.

We did not belong to that group either. Many of the older members of our working-class community of Edinburgh, now retired from their jobs, still attended synagogue twice a day. They tallied over the prayers, chatted with each other in Yiddish afterwards, exchanged gossip and told jokes, not always of the most delicate nature, and yearned for the Yiddishkeit of the Eastern European shtetel where most had been raised. The characters, locations and troubles, later recounted in the musical 'Fiddler on the Roof', had been the reality for them. Strangely enough, they still sighed for amoleke tseiten ('times gone by'), as if it had been some kind of idyllic existence, and did not always recall the terrible persecutions that had led them to flee westwards. They had Yiddish nicknames for some of their friends, usually cruel ones that referred to some physical, mental or moral inadequacy: der Toiber (deaf), der Hoiker (hunchback), der geller Ganav (blond thief). On Shabbat mornings after prayers, they would make their leisurely walk home even more leisurely by stopping at friends' houses for kiddush, a blessing over wine to mark the Sabbath day, with an accompanying piece of herring, gefillte fish, or cake, and a bissel bronfen, a little glass of schnapps. A little boy was always given treats (usually homemade biscuits) and not infrequently plied with schnapps, especially if he had a bad cold or cough. It was widely supposed that alcohol had therapeutic effects, but who cared if it didn't?

At Home

In our home, everything was done to maintain Jewish observance, at least in so far as Zeide (Yiddish for grandfather) advised it. He never made demands but he did quietly expect Yiddishkeit to be observed. In the early years of their marriage, neither Mum nor Dad were very concerned to follow Zeide's example but they always insisted that his way was the right way and that they were simply lax. I therefore had no doubt that praying (davening, as we called it in Yiddish) was a normal part of Jewish life, as was koshering the meat, burning the liver on the open fire (to remove the forbidden blood), making kiddush and havdalah to mark the arrival and departure of Shabbat (or Shabbos, as we knew it then, in the Ashkenazi pronunciation), and preparing for Pesaḥ (Passover) every spring-time. That involved Mum (with no fridge) staying up much of the previous two nights preparing food according to the strict laws that forbad any 'leaven'. In those austere 1940s and early 1950s, much of the family food had to be prepared at home. Even for those, unlike us, who could afford to buy ready-made kosher items, few were at that time available.

All such rituals were a normal part of my young life and it was always Zeide and almost never Daddy who conducted them. Before I could read Hebrew, which I began to do when I was around five, or perhaps a little earlier, I learned to recite by heart the kiddush for Shabbat and the mah nishtanah (the four questions, or the vier kashes in Yiddish) at the seder table on the first night of Pesaḥ. Zeide gave me as a gift a little Sefer Torah (a Pentateuchal scroll with a facsimile text printed on paper) and he and Mummy made the little mantle to cover it. A favourite game of mine was walking it up and down the living room, just like the ḥazan (cantor) did in shool (synagogue) and singing the tunes I knew from there.

Although Zeide would often take me to shool with him, Mummy sometimes also came with us on Shabbat mornings when I was still a toddler and Daddy was still in the forces. She made many of my clothes for me and those included a white suit, made up of a shirt and a pair of shorts, which was especially for wearing to shool on Shabbat. The rebbetzin (Rabbi Cohen's wife, Fanny) absolutely adored me. She had no children of her own and it was a great pleasure for her (as she reminded me during a conversation in Jerusalem when in her nineties) when my mother brought me over to her and sat me on her knee for the duration of the service. I, for my part, apparently enjoyed this too since I never objected to it, nor asked to be taken back to my mother. Rebbetzin Cohen was a lovely woman, both in appearance and in character, always with charming things to say, inevitably elegant, and with time to give to all around her. This close contact with feminine elegance and charm must have left its impact on the little boy sitting on her knee.

I was the constant companion of my Zeide in my earliest years towards the end of the Second World War and in the period afterwards. Mammy

1. With Mum and Dad, 1944.

(or Mum/Mummy as I later called her) was busy running the house, earning money to supplement what she received from Daddy (Dad), then still in the military, and looking after her ailing mother. Bubbe, as we knew our grandmother in Yiddish, had obviously suffered nervous breakdowns of some sort and was eventually hospitalized in a psychiatric unit (Bangour Hospital) on a permanent basis. Mum and her sister, Bessie, visited her regularly although getting to the hospital entailed a long bus journey, almost half the journey to Glasgow. I would often go with them. Bubbe did not seem quite right to me and I could not easily follow her Yiddish, so the experience was, to say the least, a challenging one. Daddy was only occasionally home on leave. My morning routine as a toddler was to have an early breakfast while Zeide was still in shool and then to be fed little bits of his meal when he came home.

Earliest Years

I had been born at 05.15 on a Friday morning in mid-winter 1944, and I never lost my passion for early rising. My mother often told the story of how I would be fed at 06.00 in the morning and then placed in my pram one floor down, outside the front entrance to the building. There seem to have been no fears about doing this at that time but Sailor, the dog of one of the downstairs neighbours, would perform guard duty by the pram and woe betide anyone who came too near me. The milkman and the postman had to negotiate their way around the pram, and around Sailor, to make their deliveries. Incidentally, deliveries of milk and of coal were made by horse-drawn wagons. When the coal arrived, the coal carrier would shout from the street below, as he lifted the bag from his wagon, 'Coal for Rapstoff' (Zeide's surname, originally Rebtsov) and Mummy had quickly to prepare the coal cupboard for him so that he could deposit his sackful (usually two or three sackfuls in the winter). Heating and hot water were obtained via the open fire in the living room. The bedrooms had small inbuilt gas fires, rarely used because of the expense, while the kitchen and bathroom had no heating at all.

As soon as I was able to walk with him, I would accompany Zeide, sometimes on weekdays as well as always on Shabbat, to shool. One wealthy Jewish businessman went to work on Shabbat but was anxious for his son to come to synagogue and to become familiar with the prayers so he deposited him with Zeide, went to business and collected him afterwards. In shool, all the old Yidden (eastern European Jews) would make a fuss of me, pinch my cheeks, or bombard me with Yiddish expressions that I only slowly came to understand. This was especially so when I took my Zeide's snuff box to each of his designated friends and offered them, on Zeide's behalf, a schmeck tabak ('a sniff of snuff'!). Each had his own way of spreading the snuff on to the back of his hand and sniffing it up, one nostril at a time. With all the young boys, I would stand in line waiting to kiss the Sefer Torah when it was returned to the ark after the Shabbat reading (leinen). On Friday evenings all pre-barmitzvah boys (under thirteen years old) would form an orderly queue to drink from the silver becher (goblet) which contained the wine over which Ḥazan Zucker had made kiddush.

The adults at home often spoke Yiddish to each other (with Zeide and Daddy sometimes exchanging comments and jokes in Russian or Polish) but Mum insisted on talking to me only in English, or rather in the local Edinburgh dialect of English (her version of 'Lallans'). Going out walking with Zeide was a great pleasure. He dressed immaculately with a three-piece suit (complete with a watch-chain on his waist-coat) and a heavy 'Crombie' overcoat, both of which clothing items he had tailored himself. He wore boots which I helped him to put on and he marched like an old soldier, with a cane in his right hand and a bowler hat on his head. For me, and indeed for other members of the family, he sometimes made clothes, often using remnants from his tailoring jobs, or those of my mother. I remember one grey tweed coat that kept me warm as I walked out with him. I am told that it was a source of some amusement to onlookers that when Zeide did not have his cane, and strode with hands behind his back (as on Shabbos, as he called it), his little grandson mimicked the procedure.

Nobody in our area had a car (such things were only for the 'pompes', the snobs, as we termed them) and we travelled everywhere by bus, tramcar and train. The children of my Auntie Bessie and Uncle Harry lived on the Craigmillar estate (also rentals from the Edinburgh Corporation), about 4-5 stops away on the number 2 bus, so we saw them very often. Their third child, Doreen, was a favourite of my parents, and she came to stay with us at one point. I think it was when my mother was having to look after both her parents, as well as her little boy, and needed some help. Doreen was nine years older than me and when I was around two, or a little younger, she would treat me like a live doll. She was (and is) the sweetest, kindest and most loving of people and I had (and still have) great affection for her.

One afternoon she was given the task of looking after her 'wee' cousin so she took me in my push-chair and decided that she would walk me over to her mother. It would not take her more than about 30 minutes. She must have been pushing me too quickly, or perhaps not concentrating too hard on what lay ahead on the pavement, but suddenly the push-chair made powerful contact with a white stone bollard and I was sent flying, landing on to my forehead. The bruise was of course a serious one but, more worryingly, I had the evidence of a large bump on my head. Terrified of what would be said to her by my mother and grandfather, she rushed on to my Auntie Bessie who applied cold metal to the forehead and the bruise soon looked less frightening. Doreen still claims that whatever active brain I have was stimulated by that fall.

I used to play under the dining table, or in front of the fire, and Zeide sat in the chair nearby, reading or dozing. Sometimes he would rebind old books (making his glue from boiled fish bones), prepare yahrzeit lists (memorial dates of dead relatives) for friends or family, read newspapers, or some Psalms in Hebrew, or patiently help Mum with some of the tailoring and alterations that she had taken on to help ends meet. I watched him with admiration and he explained patiently and gently what he was doing and how to do it. Toys and children's books were rarities in those days at the end of the Second World War and I read one so many times that I obviously decided I had had enough of it. It was called 'Old Man Hodge' and was about Hodge's farm and the animals on it. I had obviously mastered its contents so well that I no longer regarded it as a necessary possession. I therefore one day systematically ripped it into hundreds of shreds as I sat under the table. An interesting beginning to my book career and my interest in fragments.

My night routine was to be bathed by Mum, dressed in my pyjamas and taken to bed. Having kissed Zeide goodnight, I had to do the same for my absent soldier father by way of his photograph. When he once came home on leave, he had grown a moustache, while the photo showed him clean shaven. 'Daddy got [s]pots,' I said as I saw him, and he promptly burst into tears, probably because I recognized him as Daddy, rather than because I commented on his facial features. At bed-time, Mum would hold my hand, tell me stories and sing me songs or nursery rhymes. I hated the dark so she would leave the light on in the long, dark and chilly hallway outside and sit by me, holding my hand, until I fell into a delightfully relaxed sleep.

Then Daddy Came Home

Then Daddy was 'demobbed' (honourably discharged) from the forces in the latter part of 1946 and came home. Having been in the army and the navy as an engineer for fifteen years, he had no patience for what he regarded as Mummy's molly-coddling methods with his son. Like the recruits he had trained, little Stefan should be made into a man as soon as possible. No holding hands, no sitting by the bed and definitely no light. 'No van vort und de light aut' was how he expressed the necessary instructions in his broken English. He proudly told that story on a regular basis for many years and always chuckled with pleasure at how successfully I had been managed. I had sometimes wandered into my mother's bedroom before he came home. When I made the mistake of doing so and caught them in what I much later realized was a love-making session, I was given short shrift by my father and told never again to do such a thing. I don't recall ever re-entering their bedroom and I never passed the door without fear and trepidation.

Daddy's idea of educational guidance was to deliver very hard smacks to the bottom whenever I had done something of which he disapproved, or failed to do something that he thought essential to my development. Cleaning shoes, washing in cold water without pyjamas on, and using a minimum of toilet paper were central to my early upbringing as he saw it. Doreen recalls that I once did not offer a polite 'good morning' to a friend passing by, and that earned me a beating. The smacking was itself upsetting but even more distressing was the vigour, anger and seeming lack of control that often came with it, giving me the impression that it would continue until it killed me.

There was one instance in which Daddy kept very calm and did not fly into a rage. That was when I sat playing with the hooks and eyes that Mummy was using for her tailoring work. I thought it was fun to sniff them up into my nostril and then blow them down again. One of them seemed reluctant to respond to my blowing and when he saw this Daddy quietly sat me on the chair and took a piece of wire and a torch and slowly teased out the little piece of metal. His calmness was deceptive. As soon as the operation had been successfully concluded, he subjected me to the usual punishment, forcing me at the same time, through my tears, my fears and my breathlessness, to repeat several times that I would never do such a thing again.

It could also be fun with Daddy, if he was in a relaxed mood. He would then carry me on his shoulders, or run with me in the little push-chair (or go-kart as he called it) that he had adapted from the ejector seat of a plane. He taught me how to recognize the numbers on all the Edinburgh tramcars and also the different combination of colours that went with each of those numbers (introduced, I believe, when there was an imposed 'blackout' during the war). It was a joy when he tickled me, pretended to bite my nose, and told me stories and nursery rhymes. The problem was that he was not very well acquainted with these in English and had consequently to resort to Yiddish and Polish. I objected strongly, remonstrating with him 'Daddy, not Polish, English'. But to no avail, and to this day I can remember a number of these rhymes: A A kotki dwa; A mol hot geven; Erliczka, perliczka; Shloime hamelech. A native Polish speaker who recently heard me recite one of these told me that my Polish accent was excellent. That was no cleverness on my part. Like my father, I was simply a good mimic, always a useful characteristic when learning languages. Perhaps it was that exposure to Yiddish, Polish and Russian, as well as English and Hebrew of course, that gave me a lifelong interest in languages. It is equally likely that it also had a negative effect on my early English pronunciation. I called myself 'Stenom' and not 'Stefan', finished my meal by saying 'all pitash' for 'all finished', called ice-cream 'ipee', and could not distinguish 'protestants' from 'presidents'.

Daddy would sometimes take me to the Polish Army barracks in Duddingston, a village next to Holyrood Park and at the foot of Arthur's Seat, where I would meet his old army buddies, who had fought courageously against the Nazis as part of the British war effort. They would talk to me in Polish and I had to learn to say, dzień dobry ('good day'), jak się masz ('how do you do'), bardzo dobrze ('very good'), proszę pana ('please, sir') and dziękuję ('thank-you'), and they would laugh raucously and give me sweets. But, when they kissed and hugged me tightly, they smelt strongly of the kelbasa (Polish sausage) that was generously laced with strong garlic. Neither that smell, nor their shining gold and silver teeth, were an attractive part of the experience. But Uncle 'Czeszu' (Czeslaw) Riszkowski and his wife Auntie Annie (from the Italian de Luca family, I believe), who ran an ice-cream shop about 300 metres from our home, would never let me pass by without inviting me in for an ice-cream. To this day I love ice-cream, even in the middle of winter. My son, Aryeh, finds that incomprehensible. Daddy had an impressive ability to build and rebuild things, to repair machines that had gone wrong, and to engage successfully in all manner of handiwork. He tried to enthuse me with such matters, but I was neither interested nor competent in them and this was a source of no small disappointment to him.

1947

Unsurprisingly, it was Mum who gave me my earliest introduction to the female body. On one occasion I was desperate to use the toilet while she was having a bath. She told me to come in and made no effort to cover herself up in any way. We were not a prudish family and expected each other to be relaxed about nakedness. According to what Mum told me later, I looked at her body with rather more intense interest than she had expected. She also reported to me in later years that whenever Auntie Bessie was sitting in the armchair visiting Zeide, I would enjoy stroking the tops of her legs. When she asked me what I was doing, I told her that it felt nice. My own anatomy was also proving of interest in my early years. Taking advantage of what I obviously thought was the male bond, I asked Daddy what one should do when one's penis became erect. 'Go immediately to the toilet and do a pee-pee,' he lied in reply. His razor apparently also intrigued me. While shaving, he was called away to do something and he idly left it on the table. I helped myself and began to do what I had seen him do many times. 'Daddy, me shave,' I shouted out, as I cut my lip! Another toilet story concerns constipation. When I suffered this malady, or was thought by my parents to be suffering from it, the elderly Mrs. Fielding from the ground floor apartment was summoned to assist and pressed some soapy liquid into my anus, with the required effect. Since this was not greatly to my liking, I maintained a strict bowel regime forever after, or at least made no mention of any problems I might be having. Her grand-daughter, Ellen, who was a little older than I, also taught me to beware of advice offered by older women. She suggested that we try to walk down the stone steps between our two apartments in a sack. I was to go first. Falling down most of the stairs and bumping my head were the result. 'Ellen told you to do that and you did it?', declared my mother, more in the way of criticism than of inquiry, as she cleaned me up and applied a dressing.

After a bitterly cold and snowy winter, when I learned, among other wintry lessons, that one should play with snow *without* gloves, the summer of 1947 was warm and sunny, at least in Edinburgh terms. Towards the end of the month of June I was at home with Zeide, awaiting what they told me would be a most exciting event. Mummy had gone to the Western General hospital and had given birth to a baby girl and I was told to expect her imminent arrival home. Daddy went off in the morning to collect them and I was told to sit by the window, to the right of the ubiquitous sewing-machine, so much a part of Mum and Zeide's lives. If I knelt on that chair, I could see almost all the road (Prestonfield Terrace) which led into Prestonfield Avenue and then into Dalkeith Road. I was to keep a look-out for the taxi (a rare luxury) that would be bringing back my Mum, whom I had missed a lot, my Dad, and my new little sibling. I had suffered a dreadful and debilitating bout of whooping cough earlier that year and the doctors were concerned that I should not pass this on to my baby sister. She was only 2.25 kilos and they therefore regarded her as highly liable to infection. This had not been explained to me as I awaited the return of my mother.

'Here comes the taxi,' shouted Zeide, and I was in such a hurry to get to the front door and to hug my mother that I bumped my knee as I jumped off the chair, a memorably painful experience. The rush was in vain. Instead of being allowed to hug my mother, and my little sister, I was rather unceremoniously pushed away from them both and told that it was dangerous. How I understood this I cannot recall. I just remember rushing to the door and my memory goes blank at that point. I was almost three-and-a-half years old and the previous twelve months had somehow changed the whole tenor of my life. I was no longer the apple of Mummy's eye and the exclusive centre of attraction at home. There was now a less than stable father, rather than a gentle Zeide, to deal with, and I had to share my home with two newcomers. It is hardly surprising that I took to wetting the bed fairly regularly and to sucking my thumb incessantly. Daddy's solution to the former was to smack me in the morning if the bed was wet. My response was a rather subtle one. When my little sister Cynthia and I shared a bed, I would move her on to the damp side in the morning, knowing that she would readily be forgiven for such a misdemeanor and I would be saved a beating. Daddy devised all manner of deterrents to counter the thumb-sucking, but none of them – bandages, bitter aloes, and pepper among them – was blessed with success. To this day I remember the wonderful feeling of contentment and satisfaction that the sucking brought me: a kind of escape from the unwelcome adjustments and disappointments that I felt I was experiencing.

2

Early Schooling
(1948–55)

Kindergarten

Zeide had heart trouble and required care. Bubbe was in hospital and needed visiting. Daddy earned little and Mummy was obliged to work harder at her tailoring alterations to augment their income. Baby sister Cynthia had become a heavy little girl. Were these central factors in her maternal decision, or did she think that I would benefit from an external environment, and perhaps be stimulated by it? Whatever her motivations – and she was always highly, even aggressively, ambitious for me – Mum decided when I was four that I should go to nursery school. Zeide never interfered in such decisions but I did catch the odd quiet comment from him to her about mixing with goyim, eating non-kosher food and wearing tzitzit (the fringes on a four-cornered garment worn under the shirt in observance of the Torah command in Numbers 15:38). Needless to say, I was not consulted on the matter and I was duly dispatched to meet my fate on a grey autumnal morning in 1948. Edinburgh often seemed grey and autumnal even in the other seasons. The kindergarten was attached to the front part of Prestonfield Primary School, a brisk walk of less than ten minutes from our home. You had to walk down some steep, and for little ones, rather daunting, steps from Cameron House Avenue. There was then a grassed area and a tarmac, in front of which were the folding glass doors all the way along the west side of the school, in which the nursery school was housed. That was the way I was taken by my mother to meet my fate, and that is where I felt myself cruelly abandoned.

It is difficult to judge what motivated my negative reactions to this fresh development. Perhaps Zeide's remarks and the lifestyle that he promoted and admired were not compatible with what the new educational environment had to offer. Alternatively, or additionally, Zeide, Mum and Cynthia were all at home, and I was no longer there with them. The activities to which we were introduced by the teachers, or more accurately, the nursery staff, were precisely those that I did not enjoy: handiwork,

2. With sister Cynthia, 1947.

dancing, singing, playing games. Nobody seems at this stage of my life to realize that I suffered from brown-green-red colour blindness and I sometimes had to guess what colour of item I was told to find or hold. I swallowed the food – usually tasteless soup and over-tasty cheese – with great reluctance (was it kosher?) and could not abide the fact that after lunch we were put to bed. Sleeping or pretending to sleep in the middle of the day when my brain was active felt like nothing short of torture. I did not make any friends and sat in a corner, bemoaning my fate. The staff thought that I was educationally sub-normal. In a word, I hated it all.

Mummy was supposed to collect me, at 15.00 I believe it was. Each day from 09.00 until 15.00 I looked forward eagerly to her arrival. For some reason, now long forgotten, there was one instance in which Daddy had said he would do the honours. I cannot recall why he was not at work that day. At any rate, he and his friend and sometime comrade in Polish arms, Czeslaw, were spending the day together and Czeslaw already had a car so they were able to get around Edinburgh and enjoy pleasurable activities together. So pleasurable and time-consuming were these activities that 15.00 came and went without any recall about the little bundle of miserable humanity that they were supposed to collect. Of course, there was no telephone at home and so I sat on the steps in front of my accursed torture chamber and worried that I would never again, never ever, be taken home to see Zeide and Mummy. The nursery staff were still there cleaning up and left me to my own devices. It must have been about 15.15 when the car drew up at the top of the steps and a flustered father ran down to be met by the tight and tearful hugs and bitter sobs of his little son. From then onwards, whoever took me to nursery was told, without fail, as they left 'Please be the *first* Mummy (or Daddy) this afternoon.' I truly meant it but Daddy always laughed heartily at my pathetic worries.

After a few months of seeing this profound unhappiness on my part, the family relented and I was removed from the nursery and could spend my time at home again. It must have been around this time that I began to be friends with Jack Goldberg, who lived with his parents and younger sister nearer the school than I did. We played together inside and outside and went to visit his Bubbe and Zeide, Gertie and Percy Myerthal, who lived only 200 metres from our home. She made a fuss of us both and insisted that we eat large portions of her incomparably delicious strudel. Not much insistence was required. Life began to be good again but statutory school loomed ahead at the end of August 1949. Where would that be? In the same accursed building, of course. I feared the worst and was not disappointed. Whatever intelligent and academic things, like reading and writing, that they taught me were absorbed very quickly and I was then bored. Work with paper, scissors, cloths and colours – any sort of art and handiwork – was of no interest. My fellow pupils, both boys and girls, seemed dull, and Jack, among some others, had gone to Gillespie's Boys' School at the other end of town.

Gillespie's

To her credit, Mum realized that matter could not proceed in this way and spoke to the teachers. One thought that I needed a more intensive and stimulating environment while another mentioned fee-paying schools. Mum was then talking to a friend who suggested that she try to get me into 'Gillespie's'. It did not worry Mum that entrance was selective since she was confident that I was bright enough. What troubled her were the fees of £2.50 per term. This was more than half of Dad's weekly wage. These fees were less than most fee-paying schools since Gillespie's was supported by a large endowment and by the municipal authority, Edinburgh Corporation. But even that sum was daunting for her and would have to be found three times a year. She bravely resolved that if I was offered a place, and could then develop educationally, she would work even longer hours at her tailoring alternations and find the money. Dad was somewhat ambivalent (he had been to his local school in Kalusz, Poland – today Ukraine – when he wasn't playing truant) but he was not antagonistic.

It must have been around mid-winter of 1949–50 when I was taken to Gillespie's to be interviewed and examined. The chats with the headmaster and teachers went well. The interviews were conducted in a dark and dismal hallway at the foot of some stairs. Schools were neither well-lit nor adequately heated in those days when resources were severely stretched. The arithmetic ('sums') and the English reading presented no difficulty. But then a dreaded request: 'Stefan, could you please draw a man for me?' To state that I was, and remain, totally incompetent in any form of art is an understatement. I can describe well, orally or in literary format, what I see but simply cannot reproduce it in any artistic format. I remember that I summoned up my courage and drew what can only be described a as a 'stick-man'. The woman teacher examining me asked me (in less technical language of course) why my stick-man's arm was at right-angles to his hand. Drawing may have been a challenge but dialectic was certainly not. I had no hesitation in replying: 'He fell and broke his arm'. I was offered a place at James Gillespie's School for Boys.

The next five and a half years were destined to find me in my educational element, but first there were some serious obstacles for me and my parents to overcome. We were required to wear a uniform to school and this consisted of a blazer with a school badge (Fidelis et Fortis was our Latin motto), as well as a scarf, a tie and socks, all with the school colours, red and yellow. Grey shirts, black shoes and a navy coat (a 'Burberry' we called it) were also *de rigueur*. Parents with the means could buy these at an expensive 'tailors and outfitters' in Princes Street but that presented a serious problem for my impecunious folk. Inquiries were made and they were informed that cheaper versions were available in other shops, *ersatz* copies as it were. They included a blazer without the badge, for which a badge could be purchased and on to the pocket of which it could be sewn. All that was mildly acceptable, but then we were advised that we must have white shorts for gymnastics and football (in which activities, by the way I was not, at that stage, any better than average). That was simply too much and my mother adapted a pair of my sister's underpants ('knickers') for the required purpose. No teacher said anything but a number of the boys saw through the ruse and made fun of me. I raised strong objections at home and my father went out and bought a *black* pair of shorts (much cheaper than white ones). I was the only one with black shorts but at least I was no longer the object of quite so much peer derision.

3. James Gillespie's Boys' School.

To get to my new school also presented my mother with a logistic problem. The distance was about more than three kilometres and there was no direct public transport. At first, she took me and collected me each day. We took the no. 2 bus for half the distance, then walked through Salisbury Place for about 250 metres, passing the synagogue, before catching the no. 6 tram-car for the remainder of the journey to the Marchmont area. My mother carried my heavy little sister, Cynthia, and it exhausted her. After a week, one of the women who made the same bus journey said that she would keep an eye on me and that I could probably manage the journey on my own. I assured my mother that this was ok: 'Mammy, I can do it by myself.'

And so, at the age of five-and-a-half, I was making my own way across Edinburgh, always endeavouring to give the slip to the kind woman who was supposed to keep an eye on me so that I could demonstrate my full independence. I remember the feeling very well. I was now on my own, as it were, having to 'do it by myself' so I resolved to make a virtue of necessity and enjoy the experience. The bus/tram fare was one penny (a 'penny transfer' to cover both journeys) and my mother gave me enough pocket money each week to cover all the travel costs. Out of that allowance, I did my best to save some each week and put it in my money box. Even at that early age, I desperately wanted to have a life that was free of poverty, of the kind of violent arguments I heard between my parents, of smacking and shouting, and of the feelings of total powerlessness that I saw around me. One day I would have my own house and it would be quiet, well financed, warm and friendly, but I did sometimes worry about how precisely I would arrive at such bliss.

Discipline

At school I soon learned the ropes. I loved the order, the discipline and the intensity of the studies. We were divided into 'houses': Elliot (green), Scott (yellow), Murray (red) and Douglas (blue), the names of noble Scottish families. All competitions were on behalf of one's house and the best house each year won the house cup. We had to line up in class order, two by two, outside the main entrance in Marchmont Crescent before school began. A bell then rang, and music, usually of a martial sort, was played on a loudspeaker, and we had to march all the way to our classrooms. Speaking was forbidden during that process and the punishment for breaching this prohibition was administered by Mr. Lindores, the Deputy Headmaster, a slim, wiry individual with sandy hair. He watched us as we made our way up the stairs and along the corridors and any boy who spoke was summoned to his room. All the teachers had leather belts, and he had (by virtue of his authority?) a particularly thick and strong one. The recalcitrant pupil had to offer his two hands, one folded over the other, and Mr. Lindores used his belt to painful effect, usually between one and three times, but if the misdemeanour was truly serious, it could even amount to 'six of the best'. I suffered that indignity during one march when I failed to keep quiet (not my forte), and never transgressed in that way again.

Having joined the first class half way through the year, I needed to catch up with what they had already done. I soon achieved this and greatly enjoyed the remainder of the year with Miss Macpherson. She was small, gentle, and round with a charming smile and a friendly disposition and I responded with alacrity to all her demands of me. I was soon among the academic best in the class, especially loving arithmetic, English reading, comprehension and composition, and history, and excelling in them; alas, the standards of my handwork and art in no way matched these other subjects. In my second year my teacher was Miss Grey. She was tall, thin and serious and not to be meddled with. I liked her less but continued to make good progress with what I consistently and stubbornly regarded as the serious studies. There was just one disastrous incident during my time as a six-year old in her class and I recall it with embarrassment. One could have school lunch or bring sandwiches. After a week or two of trying to eat the non-kosher meals, Zeide's training had its effect and I begged my parents to be allowed sandwiches and a flask with a hot drink. This was then the routine for the next three years. Using my schoolbag, with the flask inside, as a goalpost for our football game, meant that I not infrequently came home with a broken flask.

Having eaten my lunch at the usual time, and started the afternoon lessons, I felt the need of a bowel movement and asked to be excused. Miss Grey told me to wait until she finished a particular part of the lesson but then forgot to grant me leave. I was a little afraid of her and did not ask a second time. The result was that I dirtied my underpants and dreaded leaving school since Daddy had finished work early and promised to meet me and travel home with me. Mummy was probably visiting Bubbe in hospital. I reckoned that Daddy was bound to punish me in the usual fashion. As soon as we began to walk to the tram-car stop, I said. 'Daddy, if I tell you something, will you not smack me?' 'No, tattele ('Daddy's little boy' in Yiddish), I won't smack you.' 'Promise, Daddy.' 'I promise'. And then I told him and he laughed and told me not to worry and that he would clean me up when we reached home. I did not sit on the tram-car or the bus but knelt on the seat in each case, for obvious reasons! As soon as we got home, he stripped me off in the bath and cleaned me up, washed out my clothes, and found me clean ones. I was so relieved and deeply grateful to receive such sympathetic and loving treatment.

At that stage in my young life, I became acquainted, somewhat prematurely of course, with what was meant by preparing for one's barmitzvah. My cousin, Leon, who was twelve, dutifully came over to Zeide so that he could learn to sing at least some part of his barmitzvah portion for a synagogue appearance immediately after his thirteenth birthday. Zeide was the most patient of teachers, and Leon, though bright enough, the least receptive of pupils in this area of educational endeavour. Zeide sang the words, and Leon failed to repeat them, time and time again, lesson after lesson, visit after visit. Frustrated by this failure to achieve progress with his elder grandson, Zeide turned to me, sitting nearby, and asked me if I could sing the necessary Hebrew. I did so, without difficulty, and that was the end of the barmitzvah lessons saga of Zeide and Leon. Remarkably, Leon never held it against me and was always one of the favourite cousins, sharing his toys with me when we visited him *en famille* and remaining close to me for as long as he lived.

The headmaster at Gillespie's was Wilfred Jameson who must have been about 60 and was a veteran of the First World War. Dressed in a grey suit, he walked rather bent-over, with a severe limp, and pupil gossip had it that he had been wounded as an officer. We rarely had any contact with him, other than on special occasions in the school hall. Unlike our relationship with Mr. Lindores, we were neither in fear nor in awe of him. He seemed a composed and gentle individual, as I found out when I broke another one of the school rules. I had gone to collect something from the school office and, fearful that I would miss something, and that one of the other boys might consequently have the academic advantage over me, I was anxious to get back to my class as soon as possible. I ran along the whole length of the corridor making for the next corner where the corridor turned sharply to the right. Unfortunately for me, another pupil was equally in breach of the rules as he came hurtling around that same corner from the other direction. We clashed very heavily and I was cut and bruised above my eye.

I returned to the classroom and, given the amount of blood on my head, was immediately sent to the Headmaster's secretary, for the inevitable punishment, as I thought. She ushered me into a large room, with a long desk, some comfortable armchairs, shelves of books, and a blazing fire, keeping it beautifully warm. The headmaster sat me down and brought over his first aid kit. He cleaned the wound, applied some cream and then wrapped what seemed like yards of bandages around my head. Only then did he ask how the accident had occurred. I admitted my crime but he only smiled and 'Well, laddie, I hope you learned your lesson, and will never run in the corridor again.' I did – and I didn't. When I got home and my mother saw the copious bandages, she thought I had at least lost an eye and was highly relieved to hear that I was only cut and bruised!

Introduction to the NHS

There was another medical challenge in or around 1950. I was suffering regular bouts of tonsillitis, as well a chronic problem with nasal congestion. The solution widely promoted at that time was the removal of the adenoids. Our Viennese family doctor was Dr. Ernst Adler, a regular shool-goer in our synagogue, who had a beautiful aṭarah (decoration) around the top of his ṭallit and could recite a hafṭarah most impressively. We all had great confidence in him. In those days, family doctors did not send patients for scans, nor did they arrange for specialist consultation until they had a fairly clear idea of what was required. They really examined patients from top to toe and I often wondered at that age why Daddy crudely joked that only Dr. Adler knew Mummy as well he himself did (although I later worked it out).

Dr. Adler's wife, Dr. Regina Kapeller, had been a distinguished medical scientist in Vienna and it was through her academic connections that they obtained the visas that brought them, and their daughter Liselotte, to Edinburgh after the cruelties of the *Anschluss* had made life impossible for Jews in Austria in 1938. Around 60 per cent of Vienna's physicians lost their posts. Before the full establishment and implementation of the National

Health Service (NHS) in the UK in 1948, a doctor charged his patients for a home visit. Knowing that Zeide lacked the funds to pay, Dr. Adler would often waive the fee (was it half-a-crown=12.5 p?) when he came to see him.

At any rate, I was myself to be introduced to the NHS when I was taken to the Royal Infirmary by my parents one late afternoon for the surgical removal of my adenoids next morning, as arranged by Dr. Adler. They were allowed to see me safely into my bed and then had to leave. I remember the dour Victorian ward, with its high ceilings, the feeling of abandonment and loneliness, and the frightful medicines (laxatives I think) that I had to swallow down. I can still recall vividly the mask they placed over my nose and mouth before the operation next morning and the awful smell of what I suppose must have been chloroform before I passed out. I had my tonsils removed at the Deaconess Hospital when about fourteen but that was altogether less traumatic, unless one counts a lapse in observing the laws of kashrut. I was told by my parents that I should have the soup because it was probably vegetarian. Imagine my horror when the ward auxiliary removed my tray afterwards and asked me 'Did you enjoy your ox-tail's soup, Stefan?'

Darling Mrs. Thompson

My third year at Gillespie's (1951–52) brought me under the tutelage of Mrs. Thompson. I somehow felt very close to her and she seemed to have similar thoughts about her little Jewish charge. For the first time in that school I was top of the class. I found it all easy going, loving the lessons and adoring the teacher. I was looking forward to being awarded the class prize at the end of the year. All I needed to do was to maintain the academic momentum. When I reported my progress at home, Zeide smiled, gave me a kiss and was pleased; Daddy seemed somewhat ambivalent in his response to me, although he did boast about his son's achievements to everyone else; Mummy told me that she expected no less than this from me. I was not greatly pleased with these parental reactions but determined to continue to be best, whatever their attitude, because that is what I myself enjoyed doing. My mother, from as early as I could remember, told me that all would go well if I was 'a good boy'. I often wondered how that made sense if life so often assailed me with unpleasant challenges, but somehow that maternal lesson remained at the back of my mind and I desperately wished to believe it.

It must have been halfway through the second term, perhaps in February, when Mrs. Thompson asked me to stay behind one afternoon for a little chat. She sat me down next to her desk and said that each morning I would now have to come into school about fifteen or twenty minutes earlier than all the others, because she needed to give me some extra lessons. I had no idea of what she was planning but any additional closeness to Mrs. Thompson was welcome to me and I readily agreed. We did arithmetic, composition and comprehension, as well as history, for a few weeks, and then came the bombshell. 'Stefan, you are now ready to jump a year. From tomorrow I have arranged for you to join Miss Henderson's class. You have done very well and I am proud of you.' I was deeply disappointed to leave Mrs. Thompson's class but teachers always knew best. My parents expressed no opinions on the matter and left it all to the school.

Miss Henderson had no special liking for me, nor any close interest in me, and many of the pupils obviously resented the arrival of this little upstart from the lower class. I managed to cope with all the lessons, except the geography of Scotland. I had done virtually none of this beforehand and was thrown headlong into Grampians, Southern Uplands, Tays and Speys, firths and estuaries. I struggled, and resolved that I really loved history much more. Sport and gymnastics were also challenging, given that the other boys were almost all taller, heavier and stronger than I was, and between six months and a year older. We were always given places in the class at the end of the year and, if I remember correctly, I came tenth, out of about thirty-five, instead of first. So, there would be no prize for me. A few days before prize-giving, I was summoned to the school office and told that I was to receive a prize 'for very excellent work' and I should choose a book. I was thrilled and, incorrigible devotee of history that I already was, I chose *Scotland's Story*, written for children by Henrietta Elizabeth Marshall and well-illustrated by a number of collaborators. I later found out that my angelic Mrs. Thompson had arranged this and had paid for the volume herself. I read and re-read that volume many times and it still has a proud place on one of my more prominent bookshelves.

A Senior Junior

The final three years at Gillespie's took me into Miss Bishop's class. She was an excellent teacher but something of a tyrant. She was a large, heavy and domineering woman, with a loud and deep voice, and not easily crossed. It was her custom to address a boy in less than flattering terms: 'Get up on your hind legs, laddie, and answer the question.' She often told us that the most uncommon sense was: yes, of course, 'common sense'. She wielded a powerful tawse (leather belt) and hardly a day went by without her having to retrieve it from her drawer and make use of it. Some poor souls were belted for not achieving adequate results in their academic work; I, unsurprisingly, was belted for talking too much, or for answering back. Morning lessons began with 35 mental arithmetic questions which I always enjoyed and only occasionally got one or two wrong because I rushed to write the answer and be 'first finished'. We were taught grammatical analysis of sentences and how to identify and define their sundry parts. This undoubtedly trained me to think logically and to express myself clearly in speech and in text. During my period with her I made my way up in the class and eventually came a regular third after all the exams. Dennis Noble and David Taylor were first and second and Ian Scott was fourth. We sat at the top right of the class and those who were known, by teachers and pupils alike, as the 'dunces' occupied the final seats on the left of the last row, immediately in front of the teacher. Two special achievements of that time stand out in my mind.

There was a Church of Scotland minister who functioned as the school's chaplain. He sometimes came and took our class for a short lesson and inevitably there would be some discussion of passages in what he called the 'Old Testament' and what I knew as the Tanakh, or Hebrew Bible. On one such occasion he offered a financial inducement (it may have been a shilling, which represented for me at the time half of a week's pocket money) for any pupil who could recite a whole Psalm (I think it may have been Psalm 107) by heart to him next time he came. That was no great challenge to me, or my young memory, so I took the Authorised Version and over the next couple of evenings at home, with Mum checking the accuracy for me, I learned the prescribed passage word for word. He duly appeared and asked if anyone had taken up his challenge. I looked around, gingerly expecting there to be a host of arms raised. None were, so I offered my recitation. He was pleased with my presentation and I received my monetary prize. Some 60 years later, I heard from a fellow pupil, Richard Howard, how ironic he and his fellow pupils had found this to be. The Presbyterian cleric had found the best response in the Jewish pupil, and not among any of his own flock!

Other activities

We had always had a canary at home. However, many of them died and were replaced over the years, and they were always called 'Jackie'. One was so timid and trusting that he did not move out of the way when my mother walked into the living-room where he was fluttering around on the floor and paid for this misplaced confidence with his life. I was very familiar with cleaning the cage, replacing the water and the seeds, helping him to clean himself, and cutting his nails. Dad, who loved birds, was the expert in all this and showed me regularly how it was to be done. It was no surprise in the spring of 1955 when Miss Bishop informed us that we had to write an essay. We were always practising that activity and could usually choose our own topic. This time, however, she indicated that we had to write something about animals. Unimaginative as I was (and am), I chose to recount how a canary should be looked after. At prize-giving that year I was awarded the Margaret Burt Wright Prize 'for kindness to animals'. I chose a book about dogs and it was duly inscribed. I have it still.

On certain mornings, there was a choice of extra arithmetic or a swimming lesson. Whether because my mother could not swim, or because my father had often told me that he learned to swim by being thrown a few times into the river by two large *goyim* in his hometown, Kalusz, or maybe because my swimming trunks were not up to scratch, I was afraid of submitting myself to these lessons and did extra 'sums', as we called the subject. It was not until I was in my twenties and my daughter was born, that I made a decision to rectify this self-imposed fault in my education, and successfully did so. Maybe this fear of swimming was a reflection of an overall nervousness on my part. Later, in the final year or two at Gillespie's, this also seems to have made itself felt in constant stomach pains which had no obvious physical cause. Our doctor, Ernst Adler, decreed that I should no longer eat sandwiches at lunch-time but should come home from school for a proper meal. I therefore left each day fifteen minutes before the official break time in order to get home, eat and get back for the afternoon session. My stomach has continued to be one of my weak spots throughout my life and has always demanded an annoying degree of pampering.

Planning for Secondary School

In that final year, we did all manner of public tests that were intended to establish which level of secondary school would be appropriate for us. There were tests of intelligence and understanding as well as of knowledge and I enjoyed doing them, especially since they had to be completed in a fixed amount of time and I loved to work fast and furiously. I think it was already at this stage that my handwriting began to deteriorate. We were forced to write clearly throughout primary school. We had first to write with a pencil and then, when our copy was judged to be satisfactory, we were permitted to write it out with a pen. The pens were made of wood, with a metal nib fitted at the end, and you dipped the pen into the inkwell at the top right of your desk. Each morning one of the pupils was responsible for filling the inkwells. When I reached the final class at Gillespie's, I think that we could already by then use fountain pens.

Whatever writing implement I employed, I took to writing at a great pace and this did not improve the legibility of my hand. Further, and more serious, deterioration took place in secondary school when we had to take copious notes at speed in various classes. The options for the brightest pupils who were finishing at Gillespie's were a place at a free Senior Secondary School (equivalent to the English 'grammar school') or acceptance into private fee-paying schools such as the Royal High, Heriot's and Watson's. During that final year I already knew that most of the top ten in my class would be going to one of these latter schools and their parents would be paying their fees. For me, this was in no way conceivable since my parents simply did not have the necessary funds.

Miss Bishop advised me that there was a way forward. If I did the entrance examinations for the Royal High and Heriot's and performed extremely well, they might offer me a free place. I agreed to do that and, as one of the brightest in my class, was not apprehensive about having to do papers in arithmetic and English. There were just two problems. The first (unknown to me until later) was that the pupils already in the preparatory classes of those two schools were coached well on the kind of questions they would face in the examinations while for me the whole format and the levels were, to say the least, somewhat challenging. Secondly, my parents had to fill in a form and state whether they would be willing to send me to the school even if I did not get a free place. Needless to say, they replied in the negative. I have often wondered whether if they had somehow found the funds for one year, I might have then been awarded a free place thereafter.

At any rate, I waited for the whole summer to know the result of my examination but received no reply. My mother eventually phoned the school and was told that no news was bad news. All my bright friends from Gillespie's would be going to the fee-paying schools which were a natural continuity of that primary school, while I was destined to attend Boroughmuir, one of the best secondary schools in the city, with a good reputation, but lacking the broader educational prestige of its fee-paying equivalents. I felt miserable that my peers were going to what were regarded as the best schools while I was having to make do with what I thought was second-best. I determined not to despair but to spend much of the summer looking at the new subjects I would be studying at Boroughmuir and attempting to prepare myself well ahead.

3

Other Learning Activities
(1949–56)

Jewish Education

Edinburgh Jewish children in post-World War Two did not finish their studies when school closed around 15.00 or 15.30. On Mondays, Wednesdays and Thursdays, they had to go to ḥeder from 17.00 until 18.30, and on Sunday morning the lessons took place from 10.00 until 12.30. If Gillespie's represented a Calvinist approach to children's education, it was well matched by a similar obsession with industry, knowledge and discipline on the part of those who taught us Hebrew and Judaism on behalf of the local Jewish community. We were expected to study hard, to master the subjects and to accept the fact that any departure from the norm would be punished by the swift wrap of a ruler over the knuckles or a hard slap across the face. There were usually about a dozen (both boys and girls) in each class and one could join at the age of five and continue until about fourteen. Obviously, the numbers in each class became smaller over the years as the pressures of secular life, alternative activities and parental weakness took their toll.

The teachers were not professionally qualified as such, holding posts as synagogal clergy, studying at the local university, or simply offering their services as stalwarts of the community. The educational arrangements were the overall responsibility of the Rabbi, Dr. Isaac Cohen, but the everyday administration was in the hands of the Reverend Tony Raffalovitch who was the assistant cantor (ḥazan sheni). Although we were all expected to attend synagogue as well as ḥeder, I must have been one of the few who did so assiduously. By 1950, Zeide could no longer manage the walk on Shabbat and I became his proxy. I attended synagogue regularly and brought back all the news of who had done what that morning in the service, as well as delivering to him warm greetings addressed to me in Yiddish ('a gruss zu dein Zeide' – 'greetings to your grandpa') from many of his old cronies.

I remember well my first few ḥeder lessons which must have taken place on a Sunday morning in the autumn of 1949. The class, then fairly full, was held in a little library which led off to the right from the smaller synagogue ('bes hamedrash', as it was known in Ashkenazi pronunciation). That prayer centre was already well known to me since that is where daily prayers took place, not in the huge 'sanctuary' as the North Americans call it, which was used on Sabbaths and festivals when the numbers, at least in my early years, were large. If memory serves, Zeide had already introduced me to some of the Hebrew letters and I knew numerous blessings and prayers by heart. This gave me a head start over the others. I was the best pupil in that first class and I retained that status throughout my nine years at *ḥeder*. I might add that I consistently loved and mastered all the subjects taught there.

It was the shammas (Hebrew shammash, synagogal beadle), Mr. Samuel Rubenstein, who introduced us to Hebrew by the time-honoured (and probably by then already outdated) system of combining letters with vowels, bo, ba, be, bi, bu, go, ga, ge, gi, gu, do, da, de, di, du. These combinations were conveniently printed at the front of one of the siddurim (prayer-books) of the time which therefore served as our text-book and of course provided prayer-texts for practise when we advanced a little. Pronunciation in *ḥeder*, as in the synagogue services of that time, was unquestionably according to

4. Edinburgh Synagogue.

5. Rabbi Dr. Isaac Cohen.

the Ashkenazi tradition. Mr. Rubenstein brooked no lapses in attention whatsoever and the dialogue was known to generations of youngsters in Edinburgh: 'Verdju look?"In the book'. 'Vers di ples?"I don't know"Knak!'. That final expletive was our literary definition of the smack delivered by the (nevertheless) much-loved *shammas*.

Duncan Street

The weekday classes took place in Duncan Street school. I believe that this was an educational facility run by the local authority for handicapped children. If my sister, Cynthia, or I did not master something quickly enough, Dad would tell us that we would end up in Duncan Street School.

Dad never had ambitions to be politically or diplomatically correct. I cannot recall being taught in that building by Mr. Rubenstein so we must have graduated to the next level before we attended such weekday classes. It was Miss Mary (Mashe) Pinkinsky who then took over our Jewish education. I would get home from Gillespie's at around 15.45 and, after my main meal of the day I would be on my way, almost always by foot, to Duncan Street, which was less than two kilometres away. I was regularly accompanied by my good friend Jack Goldberg, and on the way we played all sorts of games, discussed the latest fortunes of Hibernian Football Club (then a very successful team), debated about which girls were the prettiest, tested the strength of our shoes by using them to sweep along as many leaves as possible ('How do your shoes get worn out so quickly?'), and planned the mischief we would get up to at heder. We would make our way through Blacket Avenue which in the winter evenings was cold, dark and somewhat frightening. There or thereabouts, blinded or otherwise incapacitated ex-servicemen from both World Wars resided in a special home and we often saw them as they took their walks. It left an impression, especially after I raised the topic with my father who explained, after his fifteen years in the forces, how such injuries occurred.

One evening we were playing detectives and Jack had to run across the road to take down the number of a parked car. Unfortunately, a motor cyclist was riding at speed down Dalkeith Road and, when he saw Jack crossing in front of him, he braked sharply and fell off. Distraught, Jack shouted 'I've killed him, I've killed him.' But all was well and the motor cyclist got back on his bike and continued his journey a little more gingerly, no doubt somewhat bruised, but definitely not killed. Another incident with Jack left me dentally challenged. We were fooling around before heder and showing the others just how great footballers headed goals. Unfortunately, our coordination was not all should have been and Jack headed hard into my mouth instead of into the ball, breaking two of my front teeth. My mother took me to the local Jewish dentist who will remain anonymous and who explained that under the National Health Service he could only do a minimum of work to rectify the damage. He estimated the cost of the full treatment and this was simply beyond our means. Later in my teens, that meanness on his part towards a poor Jewish family was balanced by the kind attentions of a brilliant young dentist called Harold Hart (also Jewish). Two abscesses had developed on the roots of those two teeth and Harold, under the NHS, did a superb and lengthy job of which I am still the beneficiary, and probably received a paltry sum for his splendid efforts.

At Odds with Teachers

I loved teachers who were inspiring, professional and efficient, especially if they for their part encouraged my natural industry and brightness. I responded to them and functioned as an exemplary pupil. Those who lacked such skills stimulated a kind of rebellion on my part and I then tended to be impolite towards them and even dismissive of their demands, and to inspire policies of non-cooperation in the class. It hardly needs noting that this was virtually impossible at Gillespie's where my behaviour was exemplary, except of course when I had too much to say. At ḥeder, however, Miss Pinkinsky and I were often at odds. The main part of the lesson was always devoted to reading two lines from the siddur at speed, without mistakes. I almost always achieved the best result for this, which probably bored the other pupils and led her to think that I should be put firmly in my place. She would therefore claim that I had erred or that I had not been fast enough, when I naturally thought the opposite and regaled her with my protests and objections. This riled her so much one evening that she slapped me hard a few times across my face. I planned my revenge. All the way home, I kept slapping my face until it was thoroughly swollen and red.

When I arrived home, my mother immediately asked what had happened to my face. I explained that Miss Pinkinsky had slapped it a few times. Mum decided that Dad should go and see the Rabbi about this. Dad had of course been the wildest and least diligent of students in the Kalusz shtetel and I suspect that he may have had a sneaking admiration of this kind of naughtiness on my part. His interview with the Rabbi began with his complaint about the slaps. 'But, you know, Mr. Reif, Stefan misbehaves a great deal in the class.' 'I understand. He does not do his lessons well.' 'Well, no, actually, he is good at his lessons.' 'Is he one of the better pupils in the class?' 'He is invariably top of his class.' 'Ok, many thanks, Rabbi Cohen.' When Dad reported this to me, he did so with grins and chuckles, taking more pride in this demonstration of my capacity for recalcitrance than he ever seemed to have taken in my more academic accomplishments. My annual report from ḥeder that year noted my excellence in all subjects but against the entry for 'behaviour' was written the comment 'leaves much to be desired'. More grins and chuckles from Dad. This apparently indicated to him that we did, after all, have certain characteristics in common. I always received first prize in my ḥeder class and I still have the numerous books of Jewish interest that were presented to me.

Our next teacher, Mr. Kraemer, was a more powerful figure, although his English was not of the highest standard. He was a Hungarian Jewish refugee who had served in the Israeli Army in its early days and was, I believe, studying at that time at the University of Edinburgh. I did not meddle much with him although we did manage to make fun of his pronunciation and vocabulary from time to time. We liked to hear his stories of Israel and his military exploits there. Reverend Raffalovitch – or Raffi as we called him (but not of course to his face!) – was our next teacher. A survivor of the Sho'ah, he was a fine role model and a good instructor. I remember how he showed us how to blow a shofar. Incidentally, when Zeide was no longer able to come to shool on Rosh Hashanah, Reverend Raffalovitch came to our house in the afternoon and blew the shofar for him. I marvel at the levels we managed to achieve at ḥeder. We not only learned to master the siddur and the ḥumash (Hebrew pentateuch) but also synagogal ritual, Jewish history, Zionism, Hebrew grammar, and even a smattering of rabbinic teachings.

Jealousy?

When Zeide's heart problems meant that he could no longer attend synagogue, and I had learned to read the prayers fluently at ḥeder, there were occasions when I stayed at home with him and we prayed together. We would each take a siddur in our hands and Zeide would indicate to me precisely where I had to commence and conclude. We would then each do our davening individually. I inevitably finished first and Zeide would laugh and say to me 'I have been davening for nearly seventy years and you can finish more quickly than I can. I think you must be skipping parts but that is OK. You probably skip different parts each time, so you will cover all the davening at one point or another!'

At Ḥanukah and Purim, special entertainments were organized at ḥeder and we pupils played major roles. Those of who could remember lengthy parts in plays were the leading actors in reconstructions of the stories of Esther and Mordechai, or Judas Maccabeus. There was also an annual ḥeder picnic, usually held in the countryside a few kilometres outside Edinburgh. Among the activities were races, including sprints, running in sacks, or while carrying an egg on a spoon. After I won one of the sprints (needless to say, I hated not to win), a relative of my mother, who had built up a successful business and made a lot of money at that time, complained to my parents. 'Why is it always your son who has the leading parts in plays, wins the races, and comes top of the class, while mine are dunces?' 'It's only fair', swiftly responded my father, 'Some of us have money and others have talents!' It did not make him, or me, more popular in the family.

4

Leisurely Pursuits
(1950–55)

Fitba' Crazy

Given the many hours we spent at school and at *ḥeder*, there was not a great deal of time for leisure during my primary school years from 1950 until 1955. Football, cricket, bee catching, board games, train spotting and electric trains, 'conkers' (horse chestnuts), stamp-collecting, radio and reading were my favourite diversions, plus going to the cinema, and a constant fascination with girls of course. My interest in football was kindled by the two middle-aged sisters who ran the 'Walters & Sons' shop on the Dalkeith Road, not more than about 400 metres from our home. I was often sent to one of the shops in that street to make some purchase, and even recall occasions when I, at the age of about eight or nine, recited my mother's complete shopping list to the grocer who duly brought me all the items from the shelves behind and around him, and I shlept them home in two large shopping bags. Walters & Sons were, I think, in those days described as ironmongers and dry-salters but today we would call it a hardware store.

The two women who ran the shop were fanatical supporters of Hibernian Football Club and whenever I popped in to buy something for Dad, Mum or Zeide, they would regale me with tales of the club's achievements. The late 1940s and early 1950s were the golden period for Hibs who won the Scottish League Championship three times. I became a 'fan' and can still recite the Hibs' team from around 1951 (Younger; Govan and Patterson; Buchanan, Howie and Combe; Smith, Johnstone, Reilly, Turnbull and Ormond). When I was a little older, my cousins Cyril and Eddie (and later also Doreen's husband, Maurice) would take me with them to the Easter Road stadium when Hibs were playing on a weekday evening (they also went on Shabbat) and we would stand next to the little wall surrounding the pitch. From there we could not only see our heroes from close-up but also have the additional pleasure of having muddy earth spattered on to us when Gordon Smith or Willie Ormond took a corner kick. Maurice worked at the printers who produced the match programme and he would bring an uncut proof with him. The 'boys' entrance' cost sixpence or ninepence, if I remember correctly. Little children were sometimes lifted over the turnstile. I also enjoyed playing football but was not that good. My sporting abilities improved in my teens and twenties when I was slimmer than I had been as a child, and perhaps more confident.

Unbelievable as it seems today, footballers in the 1950s received about £2 a week and thirty shillings, that is £1.50, if you were in the second or reserve team. When they retired they were delighted if they could afford a little shop or, if more successful, a pub. Jock Govan, retired Hibernian full-back, had a fruit and vegetable store just two minutes down Prestonfield Avenue and I would love to shop there for Mum because it gave me the chance of chatting to him about football. On a Saturday evening in the winter, he also sold the sports edition of the *Edinburgh Evening News* which came out an hour or two after the matches had finished with full reports on their front pages. I loved to run down to the shop, wait in line and, for a penny or two, read these reports. Managers were not to be meddled with either. An ex-St. Mirren player told me that one Saturday morning he had complained to his manager: 'Why am I in the second team this week, boss?' The reply was sharp and painful: 'Cos we dinnae have a third team, laddie.'

One football board game that was purchased for me was called 'Shoot!' Each player was represented by a little coloured button and you needed (with the aid of a larger button) to flick the ball (another button) from one player to another, and then to shoot when you got near goal. There was a goalkeeper on a long stick which you could manipulate from behind the goal. When told that your opponent was about to shoot you could try to save the shot by moving the 'goalie'. Any unsuspecting cousin who made his way to our house to visit Zeide of an evening was dragooned into playing this game with me. Doreen's fiancé, Maurice Levene, was always a willing victim and we had lots of fun together, except when I lost, when it was only he that had fun. I spent many hours practising and perfecting the necessary techniques. No computer, no files, no electronic devices, no stored memory...just a few buttons and some bits of plastic.

The Herons who lived on the top floor of our apartment in Prestonfield Terrace had a grandson who visited from England in the summer and he and I would spend countless hours in 'the back green' with a little tennis ball and a primitive bat practising our cricket. At games, when I won, I was kind and considerate and did not glory in it. Losing, however, always made me bad-tempered and disconsolate. Neither the 'English visitor' (we Scots always thought of the English as foreigners) nor I was always in possession of the necessary bat and ball and this led to one highly upsetting incident. I always saved as much money as I could right through my primary school days. When, as inevitably occurred, Mum was short of cash at the end of the week (Dad gave her £4 and kept £1 for himself, usually to distribute as largesse to all and sundry), I would lend her some from my little saving box and she would pay it back as soon as she could.

Juvenile Failures

During one summer break – probably 1953 – she sent me with a ten-shilling note (50p or £0.5 today) to Woolworth's large store at the east end of Princes Street (opposite the impressive mid-Victorian buildings of the General Post Office where one could book phone calls) to buy her some items for the house. I was hoping to play cricket with my English friend and I saw that there was a cheap set of bat, ball and wicket available for purchase, maybe for around a shilling (5p), or one shilling and sixpence (7.5p). I bought it and, when I got home, I told Mum and asked her if it was alright since she owed me two shillings (10p) from the latest loan I had made her. She was very cross and said she needed every penny that week and I should not have used some of the money. I felt guilty and distraught. On another occasion, I saved my pennies and bought her, for her birthday, a kitchen gadget that I knew she had coveted. She promptly burst into tears: 'I am not a person; I am only a scullery skivvy.'

I got it wrong for Dad too in one incident during another break from Gillespie's. On Fridays it was my custom to buy some sweets for the various members of the family, trying always to remember what each of them liked. Zeide was very partial to Fox's Glacier Mints and that became a favourite of Cynthia's too in her mature years. When Dad worked as an engineer in the Walls' ice-cream factory, he often brought home some ice-cream on a Friday afternoon when he finished work for the week. There was an atmosphere of giving and pleasing within the family. One weekday, I recalled that Daddy particularly liked one of the loaves of bread that were baked by Mr. Bialik, the kosher baker in town. I wanted very much to please him by buying him a treat. So, I took the bus into town and went to the Bialik bakery. Everything was of course baked on the premises and you therefore often bought the bread while it was still hot. The problem was that I could not recall whether Daddy's favourite was 'black bread' or 'brown bread'. I opted for the former and made my way home on the bus. When Dad arrived home, I presented him with the loaf. 'You bought me a black bread? Oh, Stefan, you know I never eat black bread, only brown bread. How could you be so stupid?' Relieved that he only shouted at me, and did not smack me, I took the bread, rushed out of the house and made the return bus journey to Bialik's to exchange the unloved loaf for the preferred one.

Hobbies of Sorts

One of the children in the immediate neighbourhood also taught me how to catch bees. There were many trees and bushes in the area in front of our house and no shortage of bees buzzing around the plants and flowers. You took an old jar, made tiny holes in the metal cover, and put some flowers inside that would attract the bees. Having duly stalked and caught a bee, you then put the cover on. Quite what the purpose of this was (since you let them go soon afterwards) was beyond me at the time and remains inexplicable to me today. I do not recall having been stung, although I undoubtedly deserved such retribution for my challenges to the world of nature. Since this hobby neither amused nor greatly interested me, I soon abandoned it.

Perhaps the problem was a lack of toys. Not only were there few toys in the early 1950s but even what was available was usually beyond the family means. My father had brought back a leather camel from Egypt and that was tucked up into bed with me. My cousin Leon had also let me have his large toy aeroplane which one could wheel around. He had himself inherited it from an elder cousin, Cyril, the son of Uncle Abe and Auntie Dolly. Sometimes at school we collected cards with football or cricket heroes on them. There was a game in the window of a local newsagent called Totopoly and Jack and I often coveted it when we passed by. He finally received it as a birthday gift and we played the game together. It was a bit like Monopoly but, like most such games, it had looked more exciting than it proved to be.

When we had spare time at school we would play 'paper and pencil cricket'. We marked a pencil with its six sides with 1, 2, 3, 4, 6 and 'out' and rolled it to see what our batsman (or bowler) had achieved. I remember England winning the Ashes in 1953 and it was usually the England and Australian teams of the day that we listed in our little notebooks and that we subjected to our paper game (Compton, Edrich, Lock and Laker; Hassett, Morris, Davidson, Lindwall). I recall playing this game at home one Sunday afternoon and Dad came over and asked me what I was doing. I explained, and he was full of contempt for such a stupid and unproductive activity. Maybe he felt that I ought to have a more interesting hobby and was driven to purchase for me the only serious toy that I ever truly loved and enjoyed, my Hornby-Dublo electric train set, a gift for my tenth birthday.

Trains

I had always loved trains. Part of the treat of going to Glasgow (apart from the kosher restaurant) was the train journey. The sound, smell and power of those old steam engines spoke to me of speed, travel and progress. I bought train-spotting books and I would go down to Princes Street Gardens, at the foot of Edinburgh Castle, and stand on a bridge there overlooking the main line from the Waverley Station that reached the far north of Scotland and the south and west of England and Wales. The steam and the soot were not very good for my clothes of course but watching and listening as the engines determinedly puffed their steamy way from stationary to speed was an adventure. My father always loved engines, especially those driven by steam, and at Waverley Station he would take me to the front cab, explain to the driver and the fireman that he too was an engineer and have a brief introduction to the massive locomotive. The Flying Scotsman and the Talisman that plied the LNER railway line between Edinburgh Waverley and London King's Cross were among the locomotives that I remember.

My Hornby-Dublo was no more than the basic set but it gave me great joy to set it up on the floor of the living room and see how fast I could make its little engine negotiate the turns of the track. I could escape from an unstable and dysfunctional background into a mini-world where I could fantasize about power, speed and control. I especially enjoyed lying flat on the floor watching the speeding locomotive hurtling towards me. I planned stations, made timetables and broke records. Inevitably the engine fell off the track and the power box had to be reset. When there were problems, Dad would always be able to solve them when he came home. This was one of the few areas where we had something truly in common. I shall never forget that wonderful purchase that he and Mum made for me. I have no idea how they managed it. They had bought me a stamp album as a gift for an earlier birthday and I would buy packets of assorted stamps in the hope (forlorn of course) that I would come upon a rare and expensive item. I still have the album and it has many German stamps from the Nazi era with the face of Adolf Hitler on them and numerous examples of stamps from British colonies, all now independent countries of course.

I could not have been more than eight or nine when I travelled alone on the train from Edinburgh to Newcastle to spend a few days with my cousin, Lawrence Schmulian. His grandmother, Rachel, and my Bubbe, Sarah, were sisters. Auntie (actually Great-Auntie) Rachel ran a women's gown shop in the Tollcross area of Edinburgh and, when Lawrence visited from Newcastle, we would spend time together. I remember that we bought cinnamon sticks and smoked them in the basement of his grandmother's shop. During one vacation it was decided that I should spend a few days with him in Pelaw, just outside Gateshead (8 Croxdale Terrace, I think), where his father was a family doctor. I was told exactly what to do, where to get off the train, the names of the family and their address but was assured that Auntie Rivka, Lawrence's mother, would meet me as I exited the platform. I followed all the instructions and arrived on time at Newcastle's Central Station, carrying my little suitcase. No Auntie Rivka. My tummy nerves began to play their usual game with me and I started to think what I should do. I would have to find some pennies and go to the nearest phone box and phone the house. Or maybe ask a policeman to help. My parents had no phone but Lawrence's certainly did. I was walking towards the nearest public phone box when Auntie Rivka came running towards me, apologizing profusely for being late, giving me warm kisses and cuddles and taking me to her car. The idea that she would have her own car intrigued me. The highlight of the visit was their television, a large wooden box with a tiny screen that broadcast a children's programme for about an hour at 17.00 and then had a break until around 20.00 or 21.00 when there were some evening programmes, exclusively BBC of course, finishing with the national anthem at around 23.00!

Other Pleasures

It was in my final days at primary school that I also began to attend meetings of Bnei Akiva, a religious Zionist movement that was run by students who were about six or seven years older than we were. One of them, Rosalind Adelman (now Landy), is still a close friend in Cambridge and another, Eddie Hoffenberg, lives in Israel and I see him from time to time. They played games with us, practised some modern Hebrew through singing songs, and told us stories of Zionist miracles in what was then still the newly-established State of Israel. As a special treat we sometimes went through to Glasgow to join the much larger groups that met there. It was around this time that Nat Gordon and I became close friends. He had been a terrible 'Mummy's boy' in his early years at

Gillespie's but had matured considerably and by then we had much in common. At ḥeder exams, I came first, Jack Goldberg second and Nat Gordon third. I don't think the others had much of a look-in. Be that as it may, our visits to Glasgow enabled us also to register for a Bnei Akiva summer camp that was held in Middleton, about twenty kilometres south of where we lived in Edinburgh. We learned that camps were inevitably uncomfortable and that was ideologically sound because it encouraged the pioneer spirit that would be needed if we later decided to make aliyah and settle in Israel. One of the madrichim (leaders) was Ephraim Groundland who later became the assistant cantor in our Edinburgh shool. I had called him 'Effy' at camp but had to be careful to address him more politely when he took up his clerical position.

The foundations were thus laid for an active association with the Bnei Akiva movement that would last at least a dozen years and that brought many adventures, much fun, numerous friendships and a welcome Zionist education and commitment. When Bnei Akiva lacked leaders, we would at times be persuaded to attend Habonim, which was a more secularly based Zionist movement. At one meeting which took place on a minor Jewish fast-day, I was unimpressed by the fact that food was served. By that time, I was at secondary school and I fired off a letter to the *Glasgow Jewish Echo* complaining about this untraditional behaviour. Such young self-importance and intolerance are not something I am particularly proud of in my more mature years but I was thrilled to see my name in print.

In the autumn of each year, the many horse-chestnut trees that spread themselves widely and powerfully over the pavements on our way to school or ḥeder would shed their round, brown, shining fruit and provide us with entertainment for a few weeks. We would choose the largest and hardest of these and drill a hole from the middle of the top through the nut. We then inserted a string which we knotted tightly at the bottom, leaving enough of the string to permit us to hang the conker in front of our friend. We would then take it in turns to try to smash each other's 'conkers'. If you succeeded once, your conker became a 'bully one', twice a 'bully two', three times a 'bully three', and so on. Not very complicated or intellectually stimulating. There was much lore about how to strengthen your conkers, some suggesting a period in a hot oven, others the application of vinegar. These competitions could also be painful experiences since you had to hold up your conker for your adversary to smash (or attempt to smash) but sometimes he would inadvertently (or perhaps even maliciously) bring the full force of his swing on to your knuckles rather than on to your conker.

Domestic Pleasures and Pains

From about the age of ten, I was permitted to join in an adult card game called 'Thousand'. Daddy, Uncle Harry and, when we were on speaking terms with him, Uncle Abe, would play a game while the women chatted and Zeide listened. They played for a few pennies and I was slowly taught how to bid, how to play my hand to extract the maximum points, and how to win. Uncle Harry would always accuse my Dad of cheating by nodding and winking, because it was the task of the others to prevent the one who had made his bid from achieving it. To that end, they had to work at least partly in liaison; hence the illicit nods and winks and Uncle Harry's complaints. My impression is that those Jews who had survived in Eastern Europe had done so not by playing to the rules but by finding ways around them. That apparently had left its effect in such matters as game playing. The adults often gave Cynthia and me the few pennies that they had won, 'for buying sweeties'.

The radio (manufactured by the Bush Company, I think) comprised a large wooden box with knobs to control volume and channel, and with a panel at the top listing the names of many places worldwide, most of which

6. Zeide with Cynthia and Stefan, 1955.

you could never hope to tune into, but which undoubtedly provided part of my geographical education. It stood on a table at the back of the living room, just behind where Zeide used to sit in his armchair. It provided news, music and sport, and I would wait with bated breath for the football results at 17.00 on a winter's Saturday evening to hear whether Hibs had won their game. The radio also provided entertainment such as Family Favourites, Housewife's Choice and Workers' Playtime. Off to school before 08.00 each morning, I of course missed most of these, except when I was unwell and stayed at home. Dad set up an extension with a speaker to the bedroom and that gave me the opportunity of listening to such programmes while I recovered from a 'flu, a stomach upset or a bad cough.

The radio was on for most of the day and I often rushed home from ḥeder so that I could listen to some adventure (was it not 'Dan Dare: Pilot of the Future'?) on Radio Luxembourg between 18.45 and 19.00, when Mum wished to tune in to 'The Archers' ('an everyday story of country folk') on the BBC Home Service, as it was then called. The SciFi series 'Journey into Space' was at 19.30 and I listened enthralled to the (as yet imaginary) tales of space travel. With the use of the short-wave option, you could sometimes access faraway places. I remember Dad often fiddling with the knobs for ages until we could faintly make out a voice saying 'This is Kol Yisrael from Jerusalem' and the first few bars of the Israeli national anthem. Dad and Zeide would shed tears when they heard this.

One traumatic event, from 1953, is associated in my mind with that radio. I came home from school as usual and was somewhat surprised that the radio was not on. When I went to rectify this, Mum said 'No, don't switch on the radio.' 'Why not?' 'Because Debbie died this morning and Zeide feels we should not have the radio on.' Debbie was one of my favourite cousins. Second daughter of Uncle Abe and Auntie Dolly (Dorothy), she had married George Benjamin a year or two before and she had, after a difficult pregnancy, hoped to have a baby that week. The baby was duly delivered but died soon afterwards and Debbie suffered from toxaemia (pre-eclampsia). The whole family expressed their support and assured her that there would be more babies for her and George to enjoy in the future. At that time, one was advised to remain in bed for a few days after a problematic birth and, perhaps as a result of such inactivity, an embolism was formed and brought about Debbie's death at the age of twenty-eight.

Debbie and George had often visited Zeide on the long Friday evenings of winter and I always enjoyed their company. On Ḥanukah 1950, they bought me *Robin Hood and his Merry Men*, a little volume (18 x 12 cm) of 256 pages by E. Charles Vivian. I was almost seven and I read and re-read that book with great joy for a number of years. Having shot his last arrow, from his deathbed through the window casement, Robin tells Little John: 'There bury me, where the good green trees will rustle over me, and the birds sing when the year is young and fresh.' I always wished that this last chapter, describing Robin's death, would somehow end differently. Family and friends would for many years afterwards always buy me books as birthday and Hanukah gifts and I became an avid reader. The range of authors was wide, including Arthur Conan Doyle, Robert Louis Stevenson, Daniel Defoe, Jules Verne and Herman Melville, sometimes in junior editions.

General Knowledge and Politics

Once, Mum responded to a door-to-door salesman by buying the eight red and gold volumes of Sir John Hammerton's *New Book of Knowledge* (I think on the basis of weekly payments). I believe that action again reflected her ambitions for me. I found it a great treat to read the entries for all manner of people, places and events. My memory was excellent and I made use of the data thus absorbed on many occasions at school. At around the age of ten I began to visit the Edinburgh Central Library on George IV Bridge. Whenever a topic fascinated me (Freud, Vatican, Holocaust, sex), I would seek out a volume and educate myself in its contents. My father had introduced me to museums and I would during the school holidays often take myself over to Chambers Street, in the University area, to visit the Royal Scottish Museum.

Early in my Gillespie's career, when I had already learned to read, I recall that we had, for a brief period, two newspapers delivered each day. This must have been a fairly 'affluent' time for some reason, perhaps around 1951. There was an interesting reason for the purchase of two newspapers, the *Daily Mirror* and the *Daily Express* (not much more than one or two pennies for each, I think). Mummy had always supported the Labour Party, seeing herself as loyal to the working class, remembering the General Strike of 1926, and being grateful for the new NHS which relieved poor families of the burden of paying to doctors and pharmacies money that they could ill afford. So, she read the *Mirror* and voted for Mr. Atlee's party. Dad had become politically right wing in the Poland of the early 1930s and had preferred the Revisionist Zionism of Vladimir Jabotinsky to the Socialist Zionism of David Ben-Gurion.

The crunch came for Dad in the post-war period when the Labour Foreign Secretary, Ernest Bevin, took a distinctly un-Zionist line and adopted a policy that meant the return of Jewish survivors of concentration camps from British Palestine to displaced persons camps in Europe, even in Germany. Bevin, who had apparently imbibed some working-class antisemitism in his youth, accused the Jews (who had just lost six million, some 30 per cent of their total number) of trying to jump the queue in the post-war wait for relief. Dad hated the Labour Party for the betrayal of Zionism that they had once championed and was an admirer (as an ex-soldier) and supporter of Winston Churchill and his Conservative Party. So, he read the *Express*. But we soon stopped both newspapers for lack of funds. At that early stage of my political awakening, I felt more in tune with Daddy than with Mummy but that was destined to change rather drastically in my late teens.

Entertainment

There were two types of cinema visits. There were children's programmes at cinemas only a bus ride away from home and there for a paltry sum one could watch the episodic adventures of some hero or another. The film would stop at a most interesting point and you were invited to return a few days later to watch the continuation. I never become one of the most stalwart supporters of this form of viewing. I developed a growing disenchantment with having my entertainment served up in instalments. Rarely in my life have I been able to watch any series on television that demanded a commitment to return at a given day, time and station each week, although I did sometimes do so during my early teenage years. The other kind of film watching was a more serious one. I would occasionally accompany my mother to the cinema while Dad babysat with Zeide and Cynthia at home, especially if there was a film that Mum was keen to see. Asa Yoelson, the Jewish cantor's son who became the famous performer Al Jolson, was the subject of two Technicolor films, *The Jolson Story* and *Jolson Sings Again* that were produced by Columbia Pictures in the late 1940s. I saw them both with my mother.

Later when Cynthia was older and could come too, Dad took us to the kind of films he liked and thought we would like too, especially those by the comedians Bud Abbott and Lou Costello. I think Cynthia and Dad enjoyed those films but I recall its having been a less than pleasurable experience for me. The absence of pleasure was compounded by Dad's methods if there was a long queue for seats. He was averse to what he regarded as the 'mishige' (Yiddish for 'crazy') British custom of waiting in queues and he would march straight to the front and buy the tickets. If challenged, he would plead ignorance of English, or simply address the complainant with a crude Yiddish phrase. I remember one film, *Abbott and Costello Meet Frankenstein,* with Lon Chaney, Bela Lugosi and Glenn Strange (1948) which was not only unfunny for me but was actually terrifying and gave me nightmares afterwards.

I also recall at least one evening when I was taken by Zeide to the Empire Theatre in the middle of the city. There was a variety show that evening with various acts and the one that had attracted Zeide most and brought him there was that of G. H. Elliott. He was a singer and dancer of the old school who would dress up as 'the chocolate coloured coon' with his face painted black but wearing a white suit. Like the 'black' impersonations of Al Jolson, such presentations were in no way racist or bigoted, nor were they frowned upon in those days before political correctness became all the rage. As with all such variety shows, there were comedians, jugglers, magicians, acrobats and ventriloquists, as well as singers and dancers. Each act was numbered and the number was shown, lit up, at the side of the stage. Zeide greatly appreciated the G. H. Elliott performance but I am not sure that I was so greatly enamoured of it.

I was undoubtedly more a product (by nature or by nurture) of Mummy and Zeide while Cynthia had been created largely in the likeness of Daddy. Given the gap of three and a half years between us, our relationship as children was bound to take some time to mature into closeness (as it did in our mid-lives) but a major obstacle to this was our totally different temperaments. She was highly volatile. She would burst into bitter tears at the least provocation and wail loudly, apparently inconsolable, for some time. She could then totally recover from this in a very few minutes and regain her equilibrium, even to the extent of laughing and joking as if nothing had happened. I learned to control my emotions (or divert them to my stomach or my head) and if I did get upset it took many hours for that emotion to subside. When my father treated me to one of his angry smacking sessions, I was distressed for hours while he would be happy to kiss and cuddle minutes later. When I went to bed that night, I would wish for either him or me to die, rather than having to face such aggression ever again. I felt cornered by this kind of violent reaction and wondered whether I could ever escape from it in one way or another. At that age, I had few options.

Moving House

One such violent incident is firmly embedded in my mind because it took place in the summer of 1954 on the day that we moved from Prestonfield to our new home in Kenilworth Drive, on the edge of the Liberton area to the south of Edinburgh. We had all been busy for days making the necessary preparations in the new house and, on the moving day itself, we delivered Zeide in a taxi after our furniture had arrived, and then set about all the tasks that were still to be completed. We were all working extremely hard, without much of a break, until well into the afternoon. I was ten and Cynthia was six and we were to share a room so that our parents could have one to themselves and Zeide could have the front bedroom with the fireplace.

I thought it would be nice if our bedroom could have a name-plate on it. On the door of the Prestonfield house, there had been a large brass plate with the name 'H. Rapstoff' on it and underneath a much smaller one in chrome with the name 'P. Reif'. I was sure that Dad would be arranging a new nameplate for himself, now that he, and not Zeide, was the householder. I checked with Mummy. She assured that this was the case. So, confident that I could use the old one, I began to see if I could scrape off 'P' and replace it with S and C, for myself and Cynthia. I had made no progress whatever when Daddy asked me what I was doing with his nameplate. When I told him that I was changing it to our names, I could see the flashing in his eyes that always preceded an explosion. I immediately reported that Mummy had authorized this, but to no avail. He went completely berserk. He twisted me over and smacked me violently many, many times, screaming 'This is what happens to you if you try to blot out your father's name. You will never replace my name with your name. Who do you think you are to do such a thing?' Not a joyous ending to the first day in our new home.

Holidays?

Holidays were not a feature of our life in those years; there simply was not enough money in normal circumstances for such a luxury. When we did get away, it would always be to spend time with family or friends in another city. It was usually cramped and invariably ended in some sort of falling-out between the families. Being sensitive to what might happen (especially given Daddy's temperament), I was never surprised when it did, but it usually spoiled the vacation. Another downside was the return visits by the said families and the disruption and inconvenience that this caused within our little Prestonfield apartment. There was a family holiday in Whitley Bay in the early fifties. I cannot recall whether we stayed with friends in Newcastle or at a cheap bed-and-breakfast. Either way, we did have fun. It was there that Dad taught Cynthia and me to ride bikes, which he had hired. 'Are you still holding me, Daddy?' 'Yes, of course, tattele.' When the question and the reply had been repeated three times, I realized that I could hardly hear his voice and, suddenly losing confidence, fell off. But I had cycled unassisted for thirty or forty metres by then and so was born a love of cycling that remains with me, especially in Cambridge, in my retirement years. Cynthia was about six and picked it up very quickly too.

When the Newcastle family did the return visit to Edinburgh, the *pater familias* and my father decided that they should spend one morning climbing up the Salisbury Crags, that is the steepest and most rocky part of Arthur's Seat, the hill of 250m that stands at the centre of Edinburgh. To my great consternation, they insisted that I accompany them. Our friend, Barnie, went first, and I followed, with Dad taking up the rear. I once made the mistake of looking behind and saw how tiny and faraway the people were on the paths below us. That terrified me, and I think that achieving the summit gave the adults singularly more pleasure than it did their unwilling junior companion.

Music

Cynthia was highly sociable; I was very eclectic about whom I chose to mix with. My Auntie Lily called me (at two-years old!) 'a little snob'. My sister would dance and sing with any group and share her views with all and sundry; I felt shy about such spontaneous demonstrations, while being perfectly happy to perform publicly if I had time to prepare and perfect beforehand. She would always wish to be taken places with me and I tried to avoid accommodating her, primarily because I knew that it would end in displays of intense emotions. She would go to Christmas parties and sing the hymns with gusto; I always felt that this was an act of Jewish betrayal. As a three-year-old, Cynthia was a daredevil and would climb on the back of furniture without regard to her safety. I always thought thrice about any physical risk. When she did that kind of thing in Bubbe's ward while we were visiting her in hospital, Bubbe became anxious and agitated, shouting in Yiddish 'Pamelech, pamelech' ('take it easy'). Cynthia's reply was 'Bubbe, my name is Cynthia, not Pamela.' In one such escapade, she broke her shoulder. She also suffered from some kind of infantile epilepsy. This would come on if she cried herself into hysteria and she would faint and wet herself where she stood. Of course, this made our parents most concerned that she should not cry too much, with the inevitable consequences on my expected treatment of her.

Our neighbours who lived one floor above us, Jack and Jessie Lanaghan, had a record player and when they played Cynthia's best-liked music they would bang on the floor and we would rush upstairs to hear the recording. Cynthia's favourite was 'My Heart Cries For You' by Guy Mitchell and she would sing along with the Lanaghans, who were much older than our parents and functioned almost as honorary grandparents. Most importantly for me, Jack Lanaghan was an avid Hibs' supporter. They were always generous to us with sweets, chocolate, books and gifts. One of their sons had died as a serviceman in the Second World War and the other (Dick) started as a 'telegraph boy' in the Post Office (delivering telegrams on his bike) and worked his way up to a senior post in the Civil Service. Many years later, Dick and his family lived near Cambridge and Lannie (as we knew her), by then an elderly widow, would come and spend a few hours with us whenever she came from Edinburgh to visit Dick. They were very respectful of Zeide's intense religious traditionalism and I cannot recall sensing antisemitic vibes from any of the families in the six-apartment building. In fact, at Passover time, I was sent around all the local families with boxes of matza for each of them. Maybe this had originated in Eastern Europe as a means of countering any libel that the unleavened bread eaten by the Jews at Pesaḥ was made of the blood of Christian martyrs.

Goys and Girls

The word 'Jew' was often used as a pejorative but it was, as it were, nothing personal. I do recall one boy who regularly used to knock my hat off my head as I walked from the bus to our home. I consistently followed Zeide's advice, ignored his jibes about 'Jew boy' and picked up my hat. One afternoon, Cynthia was with me and he did the same to her, which of course made her cry. I then lost my cool and followed Daddy's 'military advice' rather than Zeide's plea for peace. I angrily punched Cynthia's assailant a few times until he apologized and said he was only joking. He picked up Cynthia's hat and handed it back to her. From then on, he was always friendly and never bullied me again. The lesson was not lost on me.

I always had a great interest in girls and took every opportunity of looking at pictures (few and far between in those days) of scantily-clad females. I also persuaded some girls (more easily than others) to play doctors and nurses, which provided an excuse to acquaint myself more closely with parts of their bodies that were usually hidden from sight and therefore much more interesting. Any book that described even the mildest of sex scenes was a must and reading those was an exciting experience.

There were various occasions on which I (or we) persuaded a girl (or girls) to share their physical secrets with us, sometimes reciprocally. It surprised (and pleased) me that some girls, even at that early age, seemed to be thrilled by the male interest in them. One incident stands out clearly in my mind. I must have been about seven and was playing in the thick and high bushes that decorated an area in front of our apartment block. There was a girl there too and she said that she was desperate 'to do a pee' and would I turn away. I asked her if I could watch and she wanted to know what I would give her if she let me do that. I fished around in my pocket and found one and a half pence. The deal was done and I was treated to a close-up of the physiological spectacle.

5

Secondary School and Early Teens
(1955–60)

Boroughmuir School

At the age of eleven, I had been accepted for a five-year language course at Boroughmuir High, one of the city's best free schools, and in many ways equivalent to a grammar school in the English system. Interestingly, one of my brighter (and distinctly wayward) uncles had won a bursary (that is, a scholarship) to that school some 40 years earlier. Apparently, in those days fees had otherwise to be paid. The school had been founded in 1904 and had moved in 1913 to the grand and imposing building ('a brilliant polychrome Renaissance design') that I knew and enjoyed in my early teens. It had been designed by John Alexander Carfrae and was reminiscent (at least for me) of the museums constructed in various cities in the late Victorian and Edwardian periods.

We had moved house from Prestonfield to a new council estate just off the Kirk Brae in Liberton in 1954. The journey to school was therefore now almost five kilometres and I had to take two buses, for which the local authority issued a free pass, so I could save my pocket money (which I always conscientiously did). I was by then a seasoned traveller (of eleven!) and thought nothing of leaving home every morning around 07.50 to cross town and to ensure arrival in school for the start of classes at 08.50. I took sandwiches with me for lunch since the break in the middle of the day was less than an hour. I felt the need to graduate from what I thought was the childish leather school-bag that I had worn on my back at Gillespie's to a haversack that I slung over my shoulder.

My first day at Boroughmuir was around the third week of August, 1955. Uniform was advised but not, I think, compulsory, but a tie was. My blazer from Gillespie's, although a trifle worn, was navy as required, so Mum bought the badge of the new school and replaced the one from my previous school. I also had a tie in the new colours of green, navy and black. With my worn blazer and my cheap haversack, I did not look the part of a new boy, and that turned out to be a blessing. As I arrived in the lower playground of the school, where we were told to assemble, I witnessed commotions in and around the toilets. I quickly appreciated that new boys were having their heads flushed in the toilets as a 'ducking' initiation. I was not wildly enthusiastic about undergoing this gratuitous ceremony so I walked nonchalantly towards the toilets and not away from them. The boys who were leading this disgusting piece of bullying – sadly characteristic of that age – were prefects in their fifth and sixth years, with badges that showed them to be members of the 'First XV' rugby team. One of them, tall and strong, grabbed me by the shoulder and asked which year I was in. 'Second year', I disingenuously replied, and was spared the indignity.

The top two classes of the first year were 1A1 and 1A2 and I was in 1A2. There were also two or three B classes and the same number of C classes. There must have been well in excess of 1,000 pupils, boys and girls, at the school, and about a hundred teachers. My class teacher, Dr. McNeill (who taught us introductory Latin too) introduced us to all the procedures and gave us time to copy out our timetable of classes for the coming weeks. All the usual subjects were represented, together with two new languages, namely Latin and French. I had spent some time in the summer trying to acquire an elementary smattering of these two languages and that certainly helped matters. I enjoyed the literary, linguistic and historical subjects but, for sure, was not a natural scientist. Chemistry and physics were taught separately those days and presented as completely discrete topics, as indeed were geometry and algebra (and later trigonometry and calculus). No teacher at that time ever attempted to explain the broader scientific and mathematical picture. Despite that challenge, I did well in the exams at the end of the first term and did not feel the need to over-exert myself intellectually in order to do so.

One afternoon a week was devoted to rugby. Although I enjoyed sport, I could not warm to this game at all. I was short, light and with a fairly delicate frame while most of the good players were tall, heavy and muscular. We were taught how to tackle but while my tackles of them were brushed off easily by hefty and speedy movements of the arm and thigh, their tackles of me were regularly successful and I would end up in a heap on the cold, hard ground. Knowing that I could sprint well, the rugby coach shouted 'Hold the ball and run, Reif'. I followed his instructions during the first few games but was then time after time subjected to a powerful tackle by some brute or other, with much more brawn than brain. I learned to pass the ball as soon as I possibly could, leaving it to someone else to run and be upended. I invariably got home with a pounding headache after 'games afternoons'. Once, the headache became really bad and I suffered nausea

7. Boroughmuir High School.

for 24 hours. Mummy sent me to see Dr. Adler who promptly diagnosed migraine. Classical migraine has remained with me my whole life although it now finally seems to be easing. Various medicaments were prescribed at sundry stages but it was only with the arrival of the triptan drugs that migraine became truly manageable and bearable. Before that, it was the most awful experience and put one virtually out of action for at least 24 hours.

Another bugbear at high school was the art class. The teacher simply did not wish to accept my impressive degree of incompetence in the subject and was determined to show me how I could master at least a simple form of artistic reproduction. I co-operated with him as best I could and felt I was actually making good progress. For the examination I had to draw a picture and, following his guidance, I thought I had done brilliantly well, even welcoming the fact that I was not after all so bad at art. I felt truly proud of my picture. For my pains, I received the mark of 14 out of 50 which altogether ruined my overall average, which was compiled from all one's subjects. I never forgave the art teacher and dropped the subject as soon as I could find a persuasive excuse for doing so. But in Latin I received 100 per cent, which was a mark virtually unheard of in the UK schools of that day. That marginally consoled the failed artist and the inadequate sportsman. I was relieved still to be, despite the art master's best efforts, among the top few in my class.

Abdominal Problems

As I now appreciate, I needed to be challenged and driven in order to exert myself to the maximum; otherwise I would do the minimum and spend (waste?) time on other things. At that stage, I could do my homework while listening to the radio and conversing with my family. Given that we all occupied one small house, and that the coal fire warmed only the one main room, there was not much choice. Where a teacher was strict and demanding, and I liked her or him and the subject, I would do well. If such conditions were absent, so too were my concentration and ambition. I think it not an uncommon feature of male adolescence. The new year of 1956 was, however, destined to challenge me in a number of ways, beginning with abdominal pains on Wednesday 29 February.

I arrived home from school that day and told my mother that I had some pains in the gut. She assured me that it was probably constipation. I struggled to school the next day so she thought that things could not be that bad. When I got home, I was in more pain so she suggested I take a laxative, which I did, but to no apparent effect. Dad went to the doctor's surgery and reported the situation but somehow the message appears never to have reached Dr. Adler. Friday was worse at school and after I got home, and during Friday night I was crying in severe pain. Auntie Bessie lived nearby so Mum went around to her home and asked her to take a look at me. She had eight children and was a fairly good judge. Her verdict was that the doctor should be called immediately. So, Mum walked down Kirk Brae in the dark to the nearest phone box (about a kilometre away) and called Dr. Adler. On being told the symptoms, he said he would be there in about 20 minutes. He looked at me, felt my abdomen, checked my pulse and blood pressure, and said I should be hospitalized at once with a suspected appendicitis. He would call for an ambulance from his house telephone as soon as he got home. On the way out, he turned to my mother and said 'I hope for your sake, mother, that we are in time.' Hardly surprisingly, this left Mummy in a dreadful state. I think Dad was at work that evening attending to some mechanical breakdown. Within half an hour I was on my way to the Edinburgh Royal Infirmary and a short time afterwards I was wheeled into the operating theatre for emergency surgery.

The next I knew I was in a bed in a surgical ward, with Mum and Dad, and I think Auntie Bessie, sitting around me and chatting. They welcomed my return to consciousness and told me that I would now be fine. I had suffered a perforated appendix, peritonitis and pus in the abdomen. I would be in hospital for some time and I should not worry about the various tubes making their way from my abdomen into large bottles by my bed and the drips into my arm. I was being treated with penicillin, streptomycin and pethidine. I especially remember the stench from the bandaged wound and the poisoned fluid oozing out of me. I fell asleep again and awoke to the noise of their conversation which annoyed me intensely and I told them so. My angry reaction cheered them up since they saw in it an indication of the return of my wilful and determined character. They went home to tell Zeide, who had been reciting Tehillim (Psalms) all night, that the news was good and I would be alright.

It was not so simple. The pain for the first few days was excruciating and I begged them for more pain killers which they could not give me until the four hours were up. The family was a little more worried on Sunday and Monday since I seemed less myself than I had been a few hours after the operation. I had no dressing gown so my Zeide had applied his tailoring talents to good effect and made me one for use in the hospital. By about Tuesday or Wednesday I was able to get up and gingerly walk a few steps. It was an exhausting and painful exercise. The doctors and nurses were amazingly efficient and kind and I learned a good deal about how hospital wards worked. Attentive and interested as I became when I felt a little stronger, I observed how some elderly people behaved before and when they died, how the nurses were terrified of the ward sister, and how she in her turn was in awe of Matron and her inspections. The consultant surgeons came in with their juniors around them and chatted to me, explaining my case to their minions, and thereby also educating me.

My cousin, Doreen, was to be married on 13 March to Maurice Levine and my absence from their wedding really disappointed and upset me. All the family members were busy that day so they arranged for some friends who were not involved in the wedding to visit me that afternoon. But, once they had gone, I lay back on the bed and wept that I was alone in the hospital while my beloved Doreen and Maurice were being married. I sobbed myself to sleep and was awakened by shouts around me in strong Edinburgh accents of 'Wha' a byoo'iful bride!' The bride (and beautiful she indeed was) and her groom had come to visit me and I loved them even more for that.

During my second week in hospital I began to worry about catching up with school lessons and it was arranged that details of what to do, and the necessary books, would be collected by my father and brought to the hospital. When the doctors came to examine me, and saw what I was studying, they tried to offer some assistance, sometimes even successfully. I so admired them that for a while I decided I might after all wish to study medicine. I gradually realized that this was not the quickest way to recognition, success and financial security, especially if you were from a poor family, and the idea slipped away. By the time I was sent home after about three weeks I had lost a considerable amount of weight (thankfully, my chubbiness never returned), was still fairly weak, and the wound had still not wholly healed. I had to go back to the hospital a number of times to have copper sulphate (bluestone) applied to the wound, presumably to keep any infection at bay.

I finally struggled back to school and attempted to catch up with what I had missed. I think that I managed this in all but the physical sciences. I am not sure whether that was because the technical data and the experiments were difficult to reconstruct on my own, or because they were not my natural areas of competence. I did get a chemistry set but, once one had used up each of the materials included, the game, and the educational value, lost their significance. At the end of the year I had dropped some places in the class but was still in the top 25 per cent of between 30 and 40 pupils.

Again Hospital but a New TV

Some weeks later, the family were treated to another shock and more hospital visits. Dad suffered a severe concussion from an accident at work and was in the Royal Infirmary for about a week. He was strong and fit and recovered well and fairly quickly. The problem, for him, was that he had arranged the purchase of our first-ever television set, a Pye Invicta. He was to go to the store and make the payment, and the television would be delivered a day or two later. When he left the house for work at around 05.00, Dad would often be home before 16.00, so he assumed he could get there before the shop closed. We were all excited about this new form of entertainment and greatly looking forward to it. Now Daddy was in hospital and we reckoned another disappointment was imminent. I cannot remember why Mum could not go and pay; I think maybe she had a daily job as an alterations tailoress at that time and simply could not get away.

When we went to visit Dad in hospital on the Sunday afternoon, he was feeling better and said there would be no question of postponing the payment and the arrival of the television. Mum would give me the money in cash – I think it was £110 – and I would travel by bus across the city after school and make the payment. I was, after all, twelve, and perfectly capable. I cannot say I was not nervous when I undertook the task. I was, after all, carrying what amounted to the equivalent of about ten weeks' wages. It was successfully completed and television became a part of our evening life. The mid-1950s saw a gradual improvement in the standards of working-class families. It was then that my parents acquired their first fridge, washing machine and telephone.

Difficult for Zeide

That same year – 1956 – had been difficult for Zeide. He had always loved all the traditional dishes of the eastern European shtetel, including cholent (a kind of ghoulash cooked overnight on Shabbat), kigel (potato pudding), and tsimmes (meat cooked with sweetened carrots), all of them made with lashings of chicken fat. When my mother would skim the fat off the top of the chicken soup, he would say in Yiddish 'Annele, du varfst avek der beste zach' ('Annie dear, you are throwing out the best part')! He had had a heart condition since 1950. I well remember the day he was diagnosed. I was with my mother and Auntie Bessie at the Royal Infirmary and as they walked from the hospital to the bus stop, they were talking about the six weeks the doctors had given him to live. His six weeks had, with Mum's great care, become six years, and he had reached the age of 86.

Now the doctors were denying him his favourite foods and this was depressing him terribly. Healthy meals were no pleasure, nor did he enjoy all the pills he had to take to keep his heart in order. While, previously, he had had a zest for life, a cheerful outlook and a lively sense of humour, he now became morose, miserable and resigned. Mum and Dad were, as always, very solicitous of every aspect of his well-being. I was during those months learning my barmitzvah portions (of which more anon) and I did my best to cheer him up by reciting those for him. This was undoubtedly an act of filial piety but I matched it with some very adolescent arguments against our traditional religious practices, indicating to him that I might not always follow these, even if I did scrupulously do so at that time. I believe that he saw me and Cynthia as the family's future carriers of the banner of Yiddishkeit and my remarks must have hurt him, at least as much as the barmitzvah portions pleased him. His own children, like the majority of their generation, had not brought him much joy in the matter of traditional Jewish observance.

Most mornings I would walk up the stairs from our house to the street and, before turning right to walk to the bus-stop on my way to Borougmuir, I would look up to his window. He was often already there, in ṭallit and tefillin, davening shaḥarit (saying his morning prayers), and he would smile and wave to me. On the morning of Wednesday 21 November, almost two weeks before he was due to celebrate his 86th birthday, he did not appear, because, as I found out later, he had not felt very well and had decided to remain in bed a little longer. When I got home from school, Mummy told me that Zeide had died that morning and that Daddy and I had to go to a cousin's house nearby. We were kohanim (of the Jewish priestly caste) and could not remain at home with a corpse in the house. I showed no emotion, not that afternoon and not in the evening.

My Zeide had been with me my whole life and I wanted to accompany him to his last resting-place. I was told that the Rabbi had said I was, at the age of twelve, too young for that. Whether it was the Rabbi, or, as I suspect, family members other than my parents who were perhaps jealous of my closeness to Zeide, I shall never know. But I was terribly disappointed. Doreen was given the task of coming and looking after me and my sister Cynthia, while everyone else went to the funeral. Still no tears and they all thought I was totally heartless. As soon as they had gone, I went upstairs, locked myself in the bathroom and sobbed the most agonized sobs for many minutes. 'Zeide, Zeide, how can it be that I shall never see you again? I am so sorry I argued with you about religious things. Zeide, Zeide, my Zeide, please always look after me! I shall miss you forever. How will I cope without your calmness and love?' And I have never stopped missing my Zeide from then until today, over 60 years later.

Specializing

By the summer of 1957 it was becoming clearer which subjects I would continue to study in my final, important school years, leading up to what we called our 'highers', as our leaving certificates ('matura') were dubbed in Scotland. They would provide the key to university entrance. I had by then demonstrated that my talents in conducting scientific experiments and analysing data in physics and chemistry were no more than adequate, probably better than half the class, but not more than that. Mathematics had presented no major headache for me until I met Miss McHardy. She obviously felt that I was a little too big for my boots, as she would have put it, and, to mix my metaphors, that I needed taking down a peg or two. I declined to co-operate with her in her project to improve my personality and took every opportunity of contradicting her and doing the precise opposite of what she had demanded. She disliked me and I returned the compliment with enthusiasm. It hardly needs to be said that my level in mathematics, and my approach to the subject, suffered.

One Monday morning I was delighted to see a young and pretty woman in Miss McHardy's place. It was difficult for a male adolescent to concentrate on the mathematics (which she taught very well), rather than on her attractiveness, but I did my best to impress her and to excel in her class. Now maths seemed much more interesting. Alas, she was there only as a temporary substitute teacher for a few days. Miss McHardy returned to the daïs and our feud resumed. Since mathematics was not a subject one could or should drop at that stage, that was foolish of me (and of her too). Luckily, an excellent mathematics teacher called Mr. Anderson restored the equilibrium for me in subsequent years so that I had no problem with the final examinations. I mastered algebra, trigonometry and calculus but never really understood the overall mathematical relevance of the diagrams and theorems we learned in geometry.

Learning a new language, translating foreign texts into reasonable English, analyzing literature, whether poetry or prose, mastering the intricacies of grammar and writing essays were a joy for me. They somehow allowed me to express my inner personal propensities in a way that the natural sciences and mathematics never did. So, it was decided by my Latin and French teachers that I should be given the extra challenge of mastering Greek for the leaving certificate. History had always been a favourite subject and I would also specialize in that. By that time, my Hebrew and Jewish knowledge had progressed in leaps and bounds and was ultimately to become more important than my school subjects, albeit destined at the same time to be influenced by them.

6

Ḥeder Influences and Barmitzvah (1954–56)

Rabbinic Role Model

I remained on the roll at ḥeder until I was about fourteen or fifteen. My final years there were under the tutelage of the spiritual leader of the Edinburgh Hebrew Congregation, Rabbi Dr. Isaac Cohen. He was for me a role model of gigantic proportions. I found him always a superb and learned teacher, a kind and sensitive mentor, and an interesting preacher, whose Welsh accent (he was born in Llanelli) seemed to make his words that much more mellifluent. He was also something of a dandy, being always superbly dressed (in suits made for him by my Uncle Abe), slim and sporty, and on days other than Shabbat he would briskly march his way home down Minto Street, swinging his umbrella and using it as an elegant walking-stick. I kept an eye on him and would often engineer it that I could walk with him part of that way, since he lived half way towards our (new) home in the south suburb of Liberton. We would chat and I treasured his every sentence. I had, probably because of Zeide's religious commitments, often expressed the idea, when a small boy, of becoming a Rabbi. If I could become someone like Rabbi Cohen, that would be the most wonderful achievement. As I saw it, he had authority, dignity, status, style and polish.

I thrived in his ḥeder class and although at one point he joined my class with that of those who were a year older than I, I still managed to win the first prize each year, much to their chagrin. I raised the topic of studying for the rabbinate with him and he advised me that I should contemplate studying at Jews' College, the Orthodox Rabbinical Seminary in London, and taking a degree at the same time at the University of London, as he himself had done some 20 years earlier. I studied with him for the Schools Certificate in Jewish and Hebrew knowledge of the Central Examining Board under the auspices of Jews' College. Studying some Talmud was a requirement and he, and his Rebbetzin Fanny (née Weisfogel), on whose lap I had comfortably sat a dozen years earlier, hosted me for lunch on many a Shabbat, after which he would teach me the relevant texts. It was at their table that I was introduced to salads, napkins, manners and presentation. It was in their home that I first saw a PhD certificate, Rabbi Cohen proudly showing me what he had obtained at the University of Edinburgh. Paradoxically, some 50 years later in Jerusalem, he was preparing a volume on an aspect of that dissertation that he had developed further and sought my academic advice on its contents. When the Cohens left for Ireland, where he had been appointed as Chief Rabbi to succeed Immanuel Jakobovits, I was (quietly) heartbroken and wondered how my Hebrew studies would now progress.

Novice

During the academic year 1958–59, I myself began to teach at the Edinburgh Ḥeder, being given responsibility for the beginners' class. I also taught two handicapped children how to read Hebrew in the privacy of their home (a highly affluent one to my working-class eyes) at the other end of Edinburgh. In addition, at around the age of sixteen I agreed to supervise the milking process at a farm in Biggar, 30 miles south of Edinburgh, so that the community could be sure that the milk was 'kosher for Passover'. I had to go twice since the first time I went I overslept at the pub where I spent the night and could not get to the farm in time for the 06.00 milking. The traumatic effect of waking up late on that occasion remained with me for the rest of my life and I never overslept again!

In my late teens I also undertook to lead the synagogal services in Aberdeen on the three days of Rosh Hashanah and Yom Kippur (New Year and the Day of Atonement), the holiest days in the Jewish calendar. I spent the nights in an apartment above the synagogue and, on Rosh Hashanah, I had my meals with Phil and Sarah Orkin, in whose home I could be sure of kosher fare. They were academics and had two sons. The atmosphere was consequently an intellectually challenging one, which I much enjoyed. With all these sources of employment, I learned a good deal about how to interact with people and institutions. I also acquired some income of my own, of which I saved as much as I could.

I have always maintained that anyone who can teach in a communal ḥeder (at least as they were in those days) can teach anywhere. The children came under protest, they were frequently absent, they misbehaved outrageously (as I myself had done of course), and the aids, if they existed at all, were no more than chalk and blackboard. I started the process of adjusting to this daunting task in Edinburgh and continued to acquire the necessary skills when I later taught in London. I learned how to create and maintain interest and enthusiasm, how to channel the talents of the brightest and noisiest of the children, and how to plan a lesson, or set of lessons. All of this had at that stage to be without guidance from above. Rabbi Jacob Weinberg had by this time taken over as communal Rabbi and the Reverend Abraham Brysh was the synagogue cantor and ran the classes. He very kindly agreed to continue teaching me Talmud and we used to meet on a Shabbat afternoon in his home to study the texts relating to the field of legal damages (neziqin) that I would have to master for the Schools Certificate. We would then walk on together for the afternoon service at the synagogue. I also owed him another great favour that he did me on the day of my barmitzvah.

Barmitzvah

His older relative, Berl Zucker, originally from Danzig, had been the ḥazan at our shool from my earliest days. I do remember his predecessor, Rev Levinson, but only as an elderly and retired individual who sat on the bimah behind his successor while the latter conducted the services. Unlike today, retirees were not regarded as surplus to requirements (like old household utensils) but were allowed to maintain their standing and to receive honours as if they were still in post. Rev Levinson's son was the choir master in the synagogue and, when his daughter was to be married, he asked a group of us in ḥeder, whose voices he tested and approved, to come along for a few sessions (in what little spare time we had) and to learn how to sing in a choir so that we could perform at her wedding. We were promised a treat, perhaps a visit to the circus or similar entertainment. She was duly married, we duly performed in a competent, some said impressive fashion, and the choir master duly forgot to reward us in any way.

It was Rev Zucker who not only performed the circumcision rite on all of us local Edinburgh boys when we were eight days old but who also prepared us for our barmitzvah portions in the few months leading up to our thirteenth birthdays. Along with Alvin Warner, the grandson of the shammash, and my friends Jack Goldberg and Nat Gordon, we trudged along every Sunday morning to the barmizvah class that he held at the dining room table of his apartment. Mrs Zucker always gave us tasty biscuits. It was a typically old and dour black tenement built in the first part of the nineteenth century on one of the main roads (Clerk Street) leading south to Newington, and it always felt cold and damp. The staircase leading up the two flights seemed even colder and damper and certainly darker. There we learned the notes and their names and the two different ways of

8. As barmitzvah boy, December 1956.

cantillating the Hebrew texts, depending on whether it was a pentateuchal piece read from the unpointed Hebrew in a Torah scroll written by a scribe, or a prophetic passage (hafṭarah), usually read from a printed edition, with vowel points and musical notes in the text.

Most boys learned to read the final section of the former text, and the whole prophetic portion that followed it. Each Shabbat had its own specific readings. Zeide had wished to teach me the whole Torah reading but was simply not well enough at that time to do so. I therefore followed what all the others did and, under Cantor Zucker's tutelage, mastered my two biblical readings, and the blessings to be recited before and after their recitation, or rather, intonation. The system was that we first learned the theory and then we all learned the passages to be sung by the boy whose barmitzvah occurred next. So, we studied and mastered a few different readings while we attended the class. I should add that Ḥazan Zucker was not very well during those months of our tuition. We must have been among his last pupils. The synagogue was therefore actively pursuing the matter of locating and appointing his successor.

On the Day

A candidate, Cantor Abraham Brysh, a holocaust survivor in his thirties, originally from Kleczer in Poland, with a pleasant voice, a friendly manner and a charming wife and two little daughters, who was a relative of Ḥazan Zucker, was invited as a guest ḥazan for Shabbat 29 December 1956, the Shabbat of my barmitzvah. Since my mother had lost her father only a few weeks earlier, we had no serious celebrations. This was probably no bad thing since I recall clearly that, even before Zeide died, nothing had actually been settled. In any case, if ever I wished a matter to be taken in hand, I knew I had to initiate the necessary progress myself. At twelve, I was already completing official forms for my parents. Be that as it may, less fuss was made of such *rites de passage* in those days. So, all we did was to have a kind of running buffet after Shabbat in our home, and family and friends popped in, most of them with small gifts of course. Apart from the liberal selection of fountain pens which every barmizvah boy received in the 1950s, I remember an excellent English dictionary (Nuttall's) that I still use. It was given to me by George Benjamin, who had been married to my late and much lamented cousin, Debbie, and was still close to the family.

So, to the synagogue on the Shabbat morning. Before leaving I was made to drink a mixture of raw egg, honey, lemon juice and hot water. This was supposed to improve my voice production. I cannot guarantee that it did. I was always nervous about performing in public and suffered terrible 'butterflies' in my stomach. But, in every case, once I started, everything turned out fine and I enjoyed what I was doing. On that occasion too, I was gaining in confidence as I sang my portion from the large Torah scroll in front of me and had reached the final verse. 'Va-Yeḥezaq', I began. The shammash, Mr. Rubenstein, immediately corrected to 'Va-Yaḥazeq'. I knew that my vocalization was right and he was wrong, so I repeated 'Va-Yeḥezaq' and he stubbornly repeated 'Va-Yaḥazeq'. In the next second or so I was debating to myself whether to follow his correction, even if I knew it to be wrong, or to repeat the correct version a third time. Luckily from behind me I heard Rev Brysh say out loud 'The boy is right. The boy is right.' Vindicated as I was, I went on to a triumphant finish.

The incident had not unnerved me too much and I performed very well in the lengthy hafṭarah. But it did teach me a lesson. When in life you know for sure that your proposed course of action is right and those in authority around you insist on your doing something else, stand your ground as much as you possible can. Rabbi Cohen made much of the 'Va-Yeḥezaq' episode in his sermon to me. He stressed the need for 'strength' (which is the basic meaning of the word) in all that one tackles. Yes, indeed, determination as well as strength, I thought then, and still think so now. My parents' explanation was that someone had planned this challenge against my competence. They often indulged in such conspiracy theories if events did not turn out quite as they wished.

There was another challenge for boys who had performed well with their barmitzvah readings in the synagogue. On the Sunday of Ḥanukah, the lighting of the candles in the synagogue, as well as leading the afternoon prayers (minḥah), were undertaken by a boy of thirteen or fourteen. This was another excellent introduction to conducting synagogal services and one that stood me in good stead for what I later had to do as a student in London. Of course, I had to overcome serious panic attacks whenever I undertook such public performances but I learned to keep going and to wait for the nervousness to pass. Standing on a high stool in front of the ark, where the scrolls were kept, at the far end of the huge synagogue building, and reciting the blessings over the lighting of the Ḥanukah candles, in front of hundreds of congregants, loud enough for all to hear, was daunting. For me, at least, leading the prayers from the bimah at the centre of the synagogue, from where you could concentrate on the large cantor's siddur on the desk and ignore all those around you, was less nerve-wracking. But public performances were to become more and more central to my life in the years that lay ahead.

7

Final Years at Boroughmuir
(1958–60)

Strategy for Departure

Two important personal developments had occurred by 1958. After Zeide's death, I had again become positive in my attitude to religious traditions. I attended synagogue regularly, always took time off school for early Shabbat on Fridays and for all festivals, and participated with all the other kohanim in the priestly blessing recited in unison in front of the ark on festivals. With his encouragement, I had made up my mind to follow Rabbi Isaac Cohen's example and to study at Jews' College in London and at the University of London. That would mean leaving home and returning only during the vacations but that idea was not only in no way daunting; it was highly appealing. I had a passionate desire to get on and do well, as I saw it, and to be independent in as many ways as possible. I had therefore to achieve two things. I had to obtain a good leaving certificate from school and to pass the Schools' Certificate examination in Hebrew and Jewish studies arranged by Jews' College. That would permit me to begin my studies in London.

My final subjects at school were English, French, Latin, Greek, History and Mathematics and one could choose to do these at the 'higher' level or the 'lower' level. I have no doubt that I could have attained the higher level in all six subjects had I applied myself diligently. I began a correspondence with Jews' College and was informed that the University of London would not accept even the 'highers' (as they were called) as anything other than 'O' level equivalents and I would have to take two 'A' levels in addition, in order to obtain entry to a degree course there. If this facility was not available to me in Edinburgh, I could join Jews' College for a preparatory year, increase my knowledge of Jewish studies, and study for these two 'A' level certificates, preferably in Classical Hebrew and English Literature. Two considerations came to my lazy, adolescent mind. Why study for 'highers' if they counted only as 'lowers' and why risk failing and obtaining nothing? My teachers pressed me to do 'highers' in at least five of the subjects so I compromised and took the more advanced exams in English, Latin and History and the others at the lower level.

Teachers Remembered

I learned a great deal from my teachers in those three major subjects. Mr. J. C. Kidd was the teacher of Latin and I adored him. He was a tiny, jovial, and highly knowledgeable individual who took great care with those who were interested in his topic and left the others to do as best they could, or to misbehave if they preferred. He loved his subject, had (I believe) studied at Oxford, and provided outstanding insights into Latin prose and poetry, as well as Roman history and culture. He guided us, and encouraged us in the attainment of impressive levels of unseen translation and Latin composition. I came to realize how important it was to translate into a foreign language and not just from it. To explain how the scansion worked in Latin poetry he would skip and jump on the daïs between the blackboard and the classroom desks, indicating by his leg movements the short and long beats. He had a lively sense of humour and recognized in me something of a kindred spirit – a bright boy with ideas, a cheeky personality and an ambition to do well academically. We truly hit it off personally as well as educationally. I always valued his personal advice as well as his pedagogical guidance. By comparison, my Greek teacher was rather dull but we covered the ground as necessary and I truly enjoyed tackling difficult passages in Greek for translation into English, and composing Greek prose. By way of my study of Latin and Greek, I laid the foundations of a sound approach to the close analysis and understanding of ancient languages and texts, as well as an awareness of the importance of historical background for mastering these cultures.

The standards of teaching in English and history were also impressive, now that only those who had chosen these subjects were continuing. Miss Orr (if I remember her name correctly) was a well informed and dynamic teacher of English literature. She may have been tiny in height but she was assuredly not to be trifled with and she always provided excellent guidance. We read novels, poems and essays, as well as plays by Shakespeare. We learned many passages by heart (a wonderful exercise for the mind and the memory) and were taught how to analyze such literature and how to write essays about it. My history course changed dramatically when I moved into Mr. Macadam's class in 1958. I had never had trouble in mastering dates, names and developments and thought that I knew how to write about them. The first topic he set us was an essay: 'To what extent was the Elizabethan

9. With Classics teacher, Mr. J. C. Kidd.

period a golden age in English history?' I competently amassed all the facts that I could muster from the literature suggested and wrote a very detailed essay, expecting to be given a high mark. Those who studied in other countries (and other periods?) should be aware that in the UK outstanding marks were rarely more than around 80 per cent, and brilliant ones were not a great deal higher. My essay was returned to me with a mark of 9/25, that is 36 per cent! I asked to see Mr. Macadam and suggested that he must have erred in his assessment since I thought I had covered all the ground. 'You did cover the ground, Reif, but you did not discuss and answer the precise question that I asked.' That was a salutary lesson in essay writing.

Mr. Macadam, a severe character and a chronic sniffer, also achieved something else. No pupil ever misbehaved in his class and you could almost hear a pin drop while he marched up and down his daïs and dictated his historical impressions. On the first day of the academic year, as pupils trooped into his classroom for their first session with him, he would pull in a boy from the corridor for some alleged misdemeanour and belt him soundly in front of us all, before he had even greeted us. That settled the problem of discipline for the whole year. In our final year we had to choose a topic and write our own study of it. I opted for Benjamin Disraeli and received a high mark. My theme was the degree to which his original Jewishness (or, more correctly, that of his father's family) had left an impact on the man who became Prime Minister, and on his political achievements. We learned to admire the works of G. M. Trevelyan of Cambridge in English History and of H. A. L. Fisher of Oxford in European history.

No courses were ever given on any topic after 1914. When I asked about this, I was told that events of 40 years earlier could not yet be properly understood; they were therefore in the realm of current events and could be written about by journalists but not by historians. The teacher of Religious Knowledge was a Church of Scotland minister and it was from him that I first heard about the documentary hypothesis, according to which four authors, classified as J, E, D and P, had each written different parts of the Pentateuch, and that the four sources had later been edited together. I found books to read about this theory and discussed it with Rabbi Cohen, while he was still in Edinburgh, and was therefore not altogether surprised or shocked when encountering the theory again during my undergraduate Hebrew studies.

My maths teacher, Mr. Anderson, rescued the subject for me, after the depredations of Miss McHardy. Although I never really mastered the nature of geometry, which I foolishly thought of as a kind of arithmetical geography, he raised my level to what it had been before the damage done by McHardy and I began to enjoy all other aspects of the subject, including calculus. He too tried to convince me to take the higher level but I resisted the temptation of having to work too hard. The same thing applied in French. Speaking, reading, writing and analyzing the language presented no problem and I enjoyed learning poems by heart. I so excelled in the subject that my teacher complained to me that in my 'mocks' I had done so well that the headmaster, Mr. R. L. S. Carswell (or was it his deputy?), wanted to know why I was not being entered at the higher level. Perhaps she told him my reasons; if so, he was probably unimpressed, and rightly so. All the school exams leading up to the final Scottish Leaving Certificate examinations in the spring of 1960 were successfully negotiated, as were indeed my finals. I recall with a smile to myself the inherent pessimism of the Scottish examiners who always instructed at the beginning of each question: 'Write your answer (or fair copy of an answer)...'

Recognition and Recreation

In both my penultimate and final years at Boroughmuir I was awarded the school prizes for Latin and Geek. In my final months I even wrote something for the school magazine but cannot now recall whether it actually appeared in print. I also joined the school choir and, under the tutelage of Dr. Cassells, we performed on major occasions such as the annual concert and the prize-giving. We sang classical pieces which I enjoyed, although I must admit that my taste at that time, and for a few years afterwards, was more attuned to Top of the Pops that was broadcast on the radio on Sunday afternoons and featured the records that were proving the most popular with my generation. Cliff Richard, Marty Wilde, Tommy Steele, Little Richard and Roy Orbison were among the contemporary 'pop' favourites. By the time I finished school, my taste had extended to Tchaikovsky, Beethoven and Holst. I think I would have loved to learn to play but there was never sufficient money for lessons or instruments.

On the recreational front, a few of us managed to find time every day in the school's short lunch-break to walk up to the grassy and hilly area called the 'Links' and to manage a game of five-a-side football there. The games afternoons no longer involved obligatory rugby but we had a choice of either football or hockey. I was upset to hear that the football places had all been allocated and I would have to play hockey. After a few games, and some good coaching, however, I really took to the game. Unlike what I had narrow-mindedly imagined, it was not a game only for weaker individuals but demanded speed, stamina and talent. I made the centre-forward position my own and enjoyed scoring goals from there. My cousins would still take me to weekday football matches and, now that I was older, this included games in Glasgow (75 kilometres away). On one such occasion we went to Hampden Park and were among over 100,000 spectators. It was an amazing experience, but a little frightening when I got carried off my feet as we made our way to the exit and I could do nothing but be transported outwards and downwards by the force of the crowd. Such huge crowds were later banned after the disaster of 1971 when hundreds were either killed or injured by such spectator force at Ibrox Stadium, the home of Glasgow Rangers.

One match, Celtic v. Hibs, was at Celtic Park in the impoverished East End of Glasgow and we arrived so late that the only place left to stand (we always stood in the 'terraces' in those days) was among the Celtic supporters who were (and are) among the most devoted and partisan in the game. I was warned by my cousins not to emote in any way or I might find myself seriously assaulted and waking up in a hospital bed. That spoilt the game for me, especially when Hibs scored (they ultimately lost, I fear) and I had to keep totally mum, as if I were a disappointed Celtic fan. In 1955 Dad bought me my first (second-hand) bike for ten shillings (£0.50) and I greatly enjoyed it. During school holidays I would have races with friends or plan trips and picnics to parts as distant as 7 to 8 kilometres!

Cheekiness, humour and outward self-confidence were always an essential part of my personality. Those that loved me or enjoyed my antics usually forgave this or even chuckled at it but I have no doubt that others were resentful and even vengeful. That was given expression at a birthday party for a good friend of mine when some other 'friends' managed to play a game that involved blind-folding me and whirling me around many times until I was thoroughly dizzy, fell over and smashed my head on the wall of the room. End of party for me; beginning of vengeance for them. But the close family was more forgiving of my naughtiness.

My Auntie Bessie was very proud of the fairy cakes she made. Pretending to be from a major flour manufacturer I sent her a letter saying that an agent would be calling on her to sample her cakes with a view to awarding her a prize. She told my mother all about it (in my hearing – I could hardly keep a straight face) and then on the expected day of visitation she cleaned her house very well and made a lovely selection of fairy cakes. There was a knock on the door and she welcomed the visitor and began to show him the fairy cakes before realizing that he had come for quite something else. I must say she saw the funny side and loved me no less for my practical joke. When my cousin Doreen was pregnant, I wrote a letter suggesting that she come for some free napkins for the new baby. She sent her husband Moshe (Maurice) to the false address I had given and was very cross with him when he arrived back empty-handed, calling him all sorts of names for his incompetence. I owned up when she told us the story and I promised I would buy them half a dozen nappies for the new baby – which I subsequently did when little Aaron (called after my Zeide) was born. But they too forgave me my shocking waywardness.

After Zeide

After Zeide died we could finally get away as a family and the four of us spent an enjoyable holiday in London in the summer of 1957. We did all the usual tourist attractions and I took photographs with my Brownie 127. Alas, I carelessly left it (or perhaps had it stolen from my bag) on the 'Tube' during one of our travels and it was never recovered despite a number of visits to the 'Lost and Found' office of London Underground. It was not uncommon for me to forget things in my early teens; that happened once with my watch and another time with my football boots. Dad, who had bought these for me, was (justifiably) unimpressed. My second camera a while later always jammed when I was moving on the film and that was frustrating. One had in those dim and distant days to remove the film from the camera and take it to be processed and printed. We as a family had a very relaxed time and, although we of course stayed with family, we also managed to have a lot of fun. I felt enormously attracted to the great, sprawling metropolis that seemed to have everything available at all times, and wondered if I could one day actually live there.

We travelled to see various family members who lived in and around London. One day was devoted to a visit to the Bascoe family, relatives of my father through the marriage of one of his aunts, who lived in Tenison Avenue, in Cambridge, a short walk from the railway station. I especially remember the goldfish pond in their garden and how charmingly welcoming they were to Cynthia and me. I think their son and daughter did university degrees and at least one of them became an academic. Typically, my parents chose to sit and chat with their cousins and not to see the sights of Cambridge. I had no idea then that I would one day be able to rectify this omission on numerous occasions when living there and entertaining family and friends.

Interesting Young Women

Being at a mixed school, I had many opportunities for interacting with girls. Only few of the boys, even if they were bright, were academically serious and to be friendly with them one had to pretend to share their disdain for scholarly pursuits. Thus it was that I tended to gravitate towards the girls for serious discussions of academic progress, school pursuits other than field games and politics. There was one attractive girl called Elizabeth who was an ardent socialist and I had many an argument with her about the degree to which the state should assist those in need. I pointed out that both my parents worked extremely hard and received nothing other than what they had sweated for and that was how it should be. She dismissed such a view as heartless and pointed to those who really were unable to do so. The Conservative government was at the time that of Anthony Eden and then Harold Macmillan ('most of our people have never had it so good') and I defended the 1956 Suez Campaign while she criticized it strongly.

Another girl, also pretty, with the unusual name of Ariel, worked as a volunteer in the school library and I took every opportunity of joining her there and we chatted much about nothing much. I used to also walk her to her bus afterwards. But, since these girls were not Jewish, it never occurred to me to advance the relationship in any serious way. I was still active in the religious Zionist Bnei Akiva movement and went to summer camps on an annual basis so that I built up connections with boys and girls from other Jewish communities. When still at ḥeder I had often walked home one of the girls in my class and that helped me to understand how to engage with the opposite sex. There were also some parties with friends from the Edinburgh Jewish community that contributed to my broader sex and gender education.

This natural and growing interest in girls continued throughout my teens and into my student days. For those many youngsters of today whose standards are somewhat different from those that we had in the fifties and sixties, it may come as a surprise to know that flirting and 'petting', as it was then called, were regarded as major sexual indulgences and by no means all relationships advanced to that level. Those that did had likely been in existence for some time. In one case, I was rather taken aback by an approach from an older woman who had been friendly with my parents. I was at the time about sixteen, I believe good-looking, and certainly lively and cheeky. She had been a few years younger than her husband who had suffered from a heart condition for a number of years. When my father, as was his custom, asked him about whether his ailment interfered with his sex life, he replied that he would in any case rather have a plate of steaming soup.

A few months after her husband died, she – let us call her Miriam – asked me to pop into her house and do some sort of maintenance work for her. I obliged and, when I finished, she made me cup of coffee and some biscuits. I cannot recall how she managed to raise the subject, but she informed me that women have all sorts of differently shaped breasts, some longer, some rounder, some larger, some smaller. Then Miriam added 'My breasts are average size and they are pear-shaped.' My teenage testosterone level being what it was, I certainly felt aroused but was a little embarrassed and afraid of making the sort of the suggestion that she was apparently inviting, something like 'Would you like to show me?'. I finished my coffee and dashed home quickly. It was probably a good thing that I did, or who knows what kind of complications such a relationship would have landed me in. Three or four years later I might not have been so able to resist the temptation.

Signs of Maturing

My relationship with my father underwent something of a change. This may partly have had to do with one incident that occurred when I was fourteen or fifteen. Cynthia was standing next to me and I pulled open a drawer rather too quickly and it hit her bust. She squealed and made a fuss (later acknowledging that she had exaggerated) and Daddy came running over ready to hit me for hurting my sister. I was by then taller than him and perhaps almost as strong. I intercepted his hand with my own and said 'Dad, don't ever hit me again. If you do, I may hit you back and I would not want to do that since you are my father and deserve my respect.' He never again raised his hand against me although it has to be said that he found ways of conducting psychological warfare that were equally hurtful and upsetting. I began to help him do jobs around the house and I identified with him more than I had previously. That meant more criticism of my mother and that was perhaps a little unfair on my part. Mummy and I had always had a close relationship and a mutual understanding but my male development seemed to lessen the importance of this for me, at least for a few years. It was Dad who paid the entrance fee of £5 for my Schools Certificate examination organized by Jews' College and when I saved up almost enough money to buy myself a Baby Hermes portable typewriter, he chipped in with the remaining amount. I believe the cost was around £15.

I negotiated with Jews' College that I would enter in October 1960, to do the 'A' levels required and then to proceed to a degree in Semitic languages with the emphasis on Hebrew and Aramaic. The British government had announced a couple of years earlier that conscription to the armed forces of eighteen-year-olds would end by 1960 so that one of the obstacles to my plan was removed. In addition, I was successful in obtaining a full scholarship from Edinburgh Corporation. I filled in all the forms concerning the income and assets of my father and mother, and Dad signed them. Their income was certainly low enough for me to be awarded the full amount and my grades were also impressive enough to permit the award. The news that my parents were expecting another child, due to be born almost seventeen years after my arrival, and thirteen after Cynthia's, was more than a little unnerving but, after I chided them in what I thought were appropriate terms, I came to terms with the development, unaware then that the new arrival would add immeasurably to my life and that of Cynthia.

I passed the Schools Certificate examination arranged by Jews' College and there was a wonderful side-effect. A wealthy donor, Henry J. Levitt, had endowed a travel scholarship to Israel for any pupil of the Edinburgh Hebrew Congregation classes who successfully obtained that Certificate and I was awarded the scholarship to enable me to participate in the trip being arranged by Bnei Akiva for the summer of 1960. I would therefore see Israel for the first time and strengthen my links with the religious Zionist movement during the trip. I left school for the last time at the end of June 1960, wearing the red rose that was the traditional sign of a school-leaver, and feeling excited and optimistic about the road ahead of me.

From Zeide I had learned calmness, gentleness and a love of Yiddishkeit and the State of Israel, but I grew to realize that there were always those who might take advantage if one did not back up such commitments with strength and determination. From Mummy I learned unselfish love, fairness and ambition but grew to realize that if these did not include an assiduity to protect the ones you loved they were only partially beneficial attributes. From Daddy I learned energy, industry and the capacity to tackle every daunting challenge but grew to realize that, if such characteristics were not balanced by stability and self-control, they could be destructive rather than creative. From all three of them I learned decency, generosity, active concern for the elderly and needy, and intense loyalty to one's family, community and friends.

I thought I could now begin a fairly independent existence and make my own way in life. Naively, but importantly for my self-confidence, I believed that my degree of success would ultimately depend only on me. I had a lot to learn about the challenges and realities of life.

8

Israel and Leaving Edinburgh
(1960)

Youthful Journey

In the first half of 1960, during my final months at school, I made full use of my portable (and manual of course!) typewriter in corresponding with Jews' College, through its Principal Rabbi Dr. Isidore Epstein, with regard to my upcoming arrival in October, and with Bnei Akiva about the summer trip to Israel. The latter correspondence was conducted with Trevor Wise, who was one of the movement's organizers in London and would be our madrich for our visit to the Jewish state. The payment for the six-week trip was about £100 and I was able to meet that cost through the Levitt Scholarship that I had won. We received detailed instructions of what to bring. The problem was, as always, that neither my parents nor I (in spite of the money I had saved from my teaching privately and at the Edinburgh Ḥeder) could afford to buy anything other than the cheapest versions of what was required, whether a large rucksack, hiking shoes or working clothes. We went to army and navy surplus stores and managed to acquire my (less than basic) needs fairly economically.

The travel to London was included in the cost so that those coming from distant parts, like myself, would pay no more than those coming from the English capital itself. Bnei Akiva was at that time closely associated with Ha-Poel Ha-Mizrahi which was the religious Zionist wing of the Israeli labour movement; hence the socialist principle that was of advantage to me. Israeli governments since 1948 had always been dominated by the Mapai (Labour) party and moderate religious groups consistently participated in the coalitions that it put together and headed. There was also a stipulation (perhaps also motivated by such principles) that spending money should be limited to £20. That was a relief to me since I could just about manage that sum from my savings and the contribution (of £5, I think) that my parents made. I knew that my frugal habits would mean that I could work out exactly how to manage on that sum and still bring home some presents for the family. There were of course government currency restrictions in place at that time and one had to buy travellers' cheques from the bank and have the details entered into one's passport. What I did not appreciate was that most of the London members of the group, from vastly more affluent homes than my own (which meant the majority of them), brought sums greatly in excess of the stipulated amount, and were consequently much less inclined to be as frugal as I had to be. I always found excuses not to indulge myself the way a few of them did, without revealing the true financial reasons.

Kitted out as necessary, or almost as necessary, I set out in the final week of July for London, travelling by train, with a voucher provided by Bnei Akiva ('youth and group travel') from Waverley Station in Edinburgh to London King's Cross. Fortunately for me, the headquarters of Bnei Akiva was at that time at 345 Gray's Inn Road, just opposite King's Cross Station. If I recall correctly, they had kindly organized a night's stay with one of the members of the group before our departure for Israel next day. I was the youngest of the group, a year younger than most of the others and even almost two years younger than some. Although there was some ribbing about my age, I was able to hold my own in most respects and soon made friends with my new travelling companions. There are some of them with whom I remained close during my student days in London and with whom I am still friends today and see from time to time, a number of them in Israel. In a not uncommon development of their later university careers, a few drifted away from Zionism and/or Judaism. I was soon leading the davening when invited, participating in the intense ideological discussions and singing the latest pop tunes in the communal showers with Lionel Rosenfeld and Alex Deutsch. I also had a girl-friend for a short time and that again helped me to understand how to relate to the opposite sex.

Travel to Israel was not by a direct flight of under five hours from London to Tel Aviv but took a week by sundry means. We travelled from London to Newhaven by train, then boarded the ferry for the long crossing to Dieppe. A train took us to Paris where we changed stations and travelled on to Marseilles. There, we were able to board the SS *Artsa*, one of the old boats that had been minimally reconditioned by its owners Zim, and that haltingly and noisily made its way to Naples. We spent a few hours there before sailing on to Haifa. I learned there how not to bargain in a market. Anxious to buy a sun-hat for Israel, I confidently offered only 50 per cent of the price that the vendor had suggested. He promptly accepted and I realized I should have started at 25 per cent, not 50! Accommodation was in the belly of the ship in highly uncomfortable bunks and as we moved further into the warmth of the Mediterranean, many of us decided to sleep on deck. That was fine except when we encountered powerful storms as we sailed around Crete. Meals, such as they were, were available at two sittings and I recall that during one such storm, I bravely made my way to the dining room believing that, unlike my companions who were bunk-bound, I could manage to eat something. I took one look at what was on offer and rushed over to the end of the deck to engage in a lengthy bout of sea-sickness.

Sights of the Holy Land

It was early morning on Tuesday 2 August, when we spotted in the hazy distance the Israeli coastline. It was 9 Av, the fast day that commemorates the destruction of the First Jerusalem Temple by Nebuchadnezzar of Babylonian in 586 BCE and the Second Temple by Titus of Rome in 70 CE. We had prayed and recited lamentations on deck the previous evening and that morning, and were already emotionally charged. Seeing the Carmel range of mountains and the city of Haifa gradually clearing in the distance brought tears to the eyes of many of us. I thought of how generations of my

10. On the boat to Israel, 1960 (back row, extreme left).

family had earnestly (but hopelessly) prayed for such a moment, and how so many of them had perished at the cruel hands of antisemites for the want of their own homeland. I felt deeply privileged that I was myself to set foot on the soil of the Holy Land within a few hours. My father had of course visited Haifa many times as a sailor in the 1930s and 1940s, when the British exercised their mandatory rule over what they called Palestine, but I was now about to enter the independent State of Israel, then only just twelve years old, but already with a sound democratic system, a powerful army and impressive educational and cultural institutions.

The formalities on disembarking took some time, as they inevitably did then (and even do sometimes now), and we were all very tired and hungry (still obviously fasting) by the time we boarded the coach and were taken up the steep Carmel Hill to the hotel. It was bit cooler up there than it had been in the port and I was delighted to be staying in a hotel. I think that this was the first time I had ever spent time in a hotel and for me, even if it had only three-star status, it was unadulterated luxury. We had the afternoon service in the hotel and then rested until the fast was over and we were able to drink lots of water and eat a meal that we were by then all awaiting with some desperation. Dinner and breakfast were fairly basic, as one expected in those early days of the State, but we were never left hungry, neither then, nor during the whole trip.

We had four weeks of activities ahead of us, mostly involving early mornings and late evenings, hard work, intensive sight-seeing and ideological discussions. The object of the trip was to strengthen our Judaism, our Zionism and our knowledge of Jewish sources and spoken Hebrew, to introduce us to the simple and industrious Israeli lifestyle, and not to provide us with a holiday. Most of the participants had just finished school and were about to commence university courses and they did hope to enjoy the trip as something of a vacation and not only as an educational experience. This led to tensions between our madrich, Trevor, the Israelis (ex-Israeli army) who assisted him, on the one side, and us teenage participants on the other.

Tensions

This tension made itself felt in our first bout of almost a week's work on the land. We were taken to Kibbutz Saad, a Bnei Akiva kibbutz established in 1947, very near the Gaza Strip, which had been occupied by the Egyptian army in the Israel War of Independence. Set in a desert area and with very high temperatures, it had been destroyed during that war and been subsequently rebuilt. The ḥaverim (members) were serious, industrious and very ideologically motivated and they did not have a good deal of patience for those whom they saw as spoilt ḥutsnikim (Jews of the Diaspora). They put us in old shacks that had been built a dozen years earlier and were only retained for visiting youth movements. The nets were full of holes which meant that we were hot, bitten and exhausted each morning when we set out for work at around 05.00.

We had to pick apples and, after a couple of hours of back-breaking effort, we walked back to the dining hall for breakfast. Israeli breakfast in those days was not what it became in the hotels of later years. On the large and long tables at which we sat in the communal dining room (or, rather, shed) there were bowls containing boiled eggs; chopped tomatoes, peppers and cucumbers; slices of bread; leben, which was fermented milk common in the Middle East; and jugs of sweet tea and *ersatz* coffee; none of which was quite what we were used to the UK! When we grumbled in any way about any aspect of this treatment, we were informed by the kibbutzniks, or our leaders, in no uncertain terms that things had been much worse in earlier years and we were very fortunate in what was available to us. We felt suitably chided and resolved to try harder to be ḥalutzim (pioneers).

We toured all the usual sites that were then available in the tiny area of Israel (called 'the Auschwitz borders' by Abba Eban) that represented the temporary ceasefire lines established after the 1948–49 War of Liberation. Getting around those limited areas meant doing massive detours and there were of course famous historical sites that were simply not open to us because they had been occupied by the invading Arab armies of Egypt, Jordan and Syria. When staying overnight on some kibbutzim we were warned that we were only a short distance from enemy territory from where attacks were sometimes made on the Israeli residents and we often heard the barking of the guard dogs along the fences.

Jerusalem and Other Cities

The most disappointing of all our visits, for me at any rate, was the short period we spent in Jerusalem. Almost the whole area that was historically and emotionally central to Jews and Judaism had been conquered by the Jordanian Legion in 1948 and no Jews had been permitted to remain, had they even wished to do so. We walked up a grassy slope overlooking the Old City and could see some of its ancient buildings and walls and the Jordanian sentries conducting patrols along their lengths. We were strictly warned to keep our heads down and not to take photographs, or the Jordanian snipers might take offence at such aggressive Jewish behaviour.

Western Jerusalem was still under-developed, with almost no air conditioning, poor road connections and only a few hotels. Shops closed at lunch-time so that the owners could have a siesta during the hottest hours. The whole economy was still a highly socialist one. In what large stores there were, there was a complicated procedure for choosing, paying and collecting, each stage of the purchasing process having to be separately negotiated. I understood this better when I visited the Soviet Union about a quarter of a century later. I had no friends or relatives to invite me for Shabbat but I found myself the guest of one of the directors of the Israel Broadcasting Service who had been brought to Israel in 1936 on the very boat (SS *Polonia*) on which my father had served as one of the engineers.

On Sunday morning we had to find our way back to Tel Aviv to rejoin the group, the members of which had all stayed in different locations for Shabbat. I arranged to meet one of the girls at the road exiting Jerusalem where hitchhikers usually gathered and, given the uncomplicated nature of the roads at that time, this was easily done. We found a heavy and rather ancient lorry that took us on board and made its very slow way down to Tel Aviv. Quite how we found the agreed meeting places I can neither recall nor understand. We travelled to Eilat, which was no more than a primitive port with a few shacks, and we had places at the youth hostel. It was, however, more comfortable, and cooler, to sleep on the beach.

As we were often told, we were not part of a package holiday and we had to work for our bread (such as it then was). To do that we were taken to another kibbutz, this time in the Galilee, not far from the Kinneret Lake. The members of Kibbutz Lavi were much warmer towards us than those on Saad. It had had been established in 1949 by members of our own youth movement, Bnei Akiva, who had come from the United Kingdom, some of them previously rescued from Nazi Europe by the *Kindertransport* system that had brought them to safety but left most of their parents behind to perish in Nazi concentration camps. They had friends and family in common with many of our group and they had retained some of the British culture with which we too had been reared. We were thrilled to see Corn Flakes on the breakfast table, a rare sight in Israel in those days. We worked at picking cotton and the temperatures were not as high as they had been at Saad since Lavi was a few hundred metres into the hills above Tiberias. Our accommodation was also marginally better.

Homeward Bound

At the end of August we had to begin our return sea voyage. The SS *Theodore Herzl* (launched in Hamburg in 1957) was certainly an improvement on the SS *Artza* and, although we had more storms around Crete, Sicily and outside Marseilles than we had had on the way out, the boat seemed to cope better with them and to be more stable. Unlike the *Artza* which would soon be out of commission, the *Theodore Herzl* sailed on with the Zim Company for almost ten years more. We were all exhausted but we had built up a warm camaraderie, become more attached to religious Zionism, to the Holy Land and to the young and struggling State of Israel. A number of us promised each other that we would work together in Bnei Akiva when we started our university courses.

It was towards the end of the first week of September that I arrived home in Edinburgh and that gave me only two weeks until the Jewish religious holidays began. I had to quickly make all the preparations for my projected departure to Jews' College and the University of London after Sukkot ended in mid-October. Some of my clothes and equipment would do for future camping in Bnei Akiva while other items had served their purpose – almost out-served their purpose – and could be thrown out. My mother had opened a Post Office account for me some years earlier and had taught me how to save money and deposit it there for when I truly required it. I made sure I had some money to start me off in London. My account had in it the grand sum of £29.19s.6d.

The final day of the Jewish religious holidays in 1960 was on Friday 14 October and Mum went into labour a day later. She was admitted to the same maternity hospital where she had given birth to me in 1944, the Simpson Memorial Maternity Pavilion, managed by the Edinburgh Royal Infirmary and part of the large complex of hospital buildings in Lauriston Place. She had a similarly difficult birth and Sharron Adele came into the world on Sunday evening, 16 October. I visited Mum and Sharron a day or two later to welcome the new addition to the family and to say goodbye to them both. I was off to London on 19 October and would see them again at the first College vacation two months later.

9

Undergraduate in London
(1960–64)

New Vistas

There were at that time student flights from Edinburgh to London at a considerably reduced fare and I had booked myself on one of them, then operated on propeller planes by British European Airways. It was my first-ever flight. Turnhouse Airport was being rebuilt and expanded into the Edinburgh Airport of later times and the flights were temporarily relocated to East Fortune, a former RAF base a few miles east of Edinburgh on the North Sea Coast, whose runway had been extended to accommodate larger aircraft. My father came with me on the coach to East Fortune and saw me off, slipping into my hand another pound note as he did so. In those halcyon days, you showed your ticket and walked on to the tarmac and up the steps to the aircraft. I had one heavy case with me which contained my clothes, some Hebrew books and the usual ṭallit and tefillin for prayers, as well as some washing and shaving equipment. The flight took about 75 minutes and there was then a shuttle bus from Heathrow to the Gloucester Road Terminal where I could connect with the London Underground and take the Circle Line to Baker Street. From there I walked about half a mile to Jews' College at 11 Montagu Place, just off Montagu Square, arriving just before the case became too heavy to carry any further, and just in time for supper with a few of the other residents.

The building, in an elegant part of the West End, was a superb one and had been purpose built in 1957. It had offices and a well-stocked and efficiently managed library on the ground floor, a beautiful little synagogue and a spacious meeting hall (with table-tennis table and some comfortable chairs and tables for relaxing) on the first floor, lecture rooms on the second floor, and bedrooms for about twenty students, with a large set of toilets and showers, on the third floor. There were two apartments on the fourth floor, one occupied by Hannah and Harold Levy who were the Matron and Warden, and the other by the Poulsons, who were the caretakers and in charge of the cleaning. Also on the fourth floor was a splendid squash court.

Catering was done in the basement by a refugee from Vienna after the Nazi takeover of 1938, Miss Valerie Aarons, who managed the kitchen there and prepared all our meals, with a little assistance. There were numerous small tables, each for four. This building was to be my educational base for eight years and my London residence for five of those.

My room was comfortable and well heated. It had a single bed, a working chair and desk, an arm-chair, a bookcase, and a sink, with a shaving point. I was thrilled with my new surroundings and full board was to cost me £5 a week. My student grant, apart from paying the fees, allowed me around £300 for living expenses so there would certainly be a need to find other sources of income. Laundry was extra and, after seeing how much it cost me during the first two weeks, I opted for the local launderette where I could, usually accompanied by one or two fellow students, wash and dry all my clothes. Mum had wisely taught me from an early age to do this kind of thing, as well as to iron, to sew on buttons, and to cook (and clean up afterwards!). At the end of the corridor there was a little kitchen that we could use for basics, as well as an ironing board. The view from my window was not the most inspiring, taking in the adjacent building and the College car park, but I felt I had little to complain about.

Being already then a fairly routine person, the tight College timetable suited me very well. We were expected to attend synagogue services in the little shool on the first floor. They would usually begin at around 07.15, allowing us to get to breakfast by about 08.00. Inviting colleagues to lead, or participate in, the services, arranging for others to prepare the Torah readings, and ensuring that enough of the residents attended in order to ensure a minyan (ten, for the quorum), were the duties of the gabbay, or synagogue secretary. I duly took my turn at fulfilling this function a few months after my arrival and I have two specific memories which still bring a smile to my face. One of the residents had a real problem about waking up in time for davening and I agreed that I would hammer on his door enough times to ensure his participation. When asking me to undertake this task, he advised me that there would be some occasions when he would simply not respond and that I was to be sure to use all possible means for arousing him from his nocturnal stupor. One morning he simply would not respond to knocks on the door, to shouts, and to severe shakings. I could think of only one other method and poured some cold water over his head. That did the trick but he was singularly unfriendly for the following few days.

The other occasion concerned Mr. Poulson, the caretaker. He had been a regimental sergeant-major in the regular British Army. That became obvious from the manner in which he always shouted his suggestions, marched around the College in a very upright fashion, and told students very frankly what he thought of any behaviour that he regarded as below the required standard. He would also keep us informed of any developments that he thought we should know about, especially if those occurred on a Shabbat when religious laws denied us access to our radios. When Hugh Gaitskell, then leader of the UK Labour Party, died on 19 January 1963, Poulson came down to our rooms to tell us.

Whatever his many qualities, delicate and polite language was not one of them. The adjective that he most commonly used was based on the well-known army word beginning with f and concluding with k. He did not use it as a swear word but merely to give stress to his statement. Occasionally the Chief Rabbi, Dr. Israel Brodie, would appear, unannounced, in the College synagogue for a service and Poulson knew that those who had not managed to get up in time might be found wanting by the leader of Orthodox Jewry who was also President of the College; and that this would not augur well for the future development of their careers. One morning I was just locking my room and leaving for the service when Poulson came rushing into the corridor shouting at the top of his voice 'Get up, you lazy lot, get up; the f——-n Chief is here downstairs'. The Very Reverend Chief Rabbi of Great Britain and the Commonwealth must undoubtedly have had many delightful epithets applied to him in the course of his long service to the Orthodox community, but Poulson's usage was surely innovative and unique.

Daily Routine

When we went down to have breakfast, Miss Aarons was waiting for us at her hatch between the roomy and well-equipped kitchen and the spacious dining room. There was porridge or cold cereal, toast and poached eggs, and ample amounts of tea and coffee. Miss Aarons was there for most of the meals. When she had time off, Mrs Levy, the Matron, would cater. Neither of these two formidable women was naturally relaxed, friendly or cheerful. Typical students that we were, we were insufficiently appreciative of their efforts in our early years and only as we matured did we learn that a kind word and an appreciative gesture would go a long way to improving our relationship with the culinary providers. We could all mimic Miss Aaron's Viennese accent: 'deez gos hier, and dat gos der, und der you are, mein dear'! There were many occasions when I was busy teaching in the later afternoon and arrived back at College well after the time for supper.

Miss Aarons always kept my supper warm for me and welcomed me kindly, especially after I learned to be polite to her.

A close friend of mine from College days (still close today) has referred to what he called my wicked sense of humour. This was given expression one morning at the breakfast table. There was a resident student who made a point of adding about six spoons of sugar to his morning 'cuppa'. He performed this action as a kind of theatrical performance, smiling at us broadly as he scooped teaspoon after teaspoon of sugar into his cup, bouncing and down in his chair, and loudly counting out the numbers as he did so: 'That is one, that is two, that is three...' I could not resist the temptation to respond to this. Before he arrived, I cleaned out the sugar-bowl and replaced the sugar with salt. We then 'innocently' got on with our breakfasts as he arrived with his tray and began his ritual counting. We smiled gently in response but the smiles turned to raucous laughter when he tasted his cup of tea and spat it out all over the table! The sugar was still added on subsequent mornings but the ritual was somewhat more subdued.

There was coffee and cake (for which we paid a small sum) each morning at around 11.00, between lectures. Similarly, there was tea and cake in the afternoon. These were the occasions at which the students could meet those of the opposite sex and a number of shiddukhim (matches) were engineered that way. No girl was studying for the Rabbinate at an Orthodox seminary at that time but there were a number of girls doing the teacher's course for which they had to study for the University of London's ordinary (not honours) degree in three subjects. I shall come back to this later. The table tennis table was also a place for rendezvous between girls and boys. One of my close friends had suddenly to run away from one game of foursomes involving him, myself and two girls. Later I went to his room and inquired why he had disappeared. He explained that the bouncing up and down of the girl playing opposite him had greatly distracted (attracted?) him and he could not therefore continue playing!

Fun and Games

In the evenings after supper we would go over lectures or prepare for new ones, play a game of table tennis, or listen to music. I also learned to play and love squash and spent many a happy hour on the fourth floor. We arranged some games with other teams and when I saw that I had been paired with someone about fifteen years older, I was confident that my youth and my energy would overcome him. Sad to relate, I learned that he was vastly superior to me and stood in the middle of the court dictating the game while I crazily ran around trying to find a way of returning his superbly placed shots.

Rowing on the lake at Regent's Park was another of our relaxations, as was playing cricket on that beautiful green site. Cricket would generally take place on a Friday afternoon in the summer when Shabbat did not begin until late. We put together some money to buy equipment. We would sometimes go to one of local pubs for a beer or take the tube into the centre of the West End to see a play or a new film. That is where I saw such classics as *Ben-Hur*, *Dr Zhivago* and *Lawrence of Arabia*. There were late-night movies at the Classic Cinema in Baker Street and they would be screened from midnight until 02.00. I particularly remember the powerful impact made on me by Elia Kazan's film *Splendour in the Grass* starring Natalie Wood and Warren Beatty. Being very near such places was a great thrill for me, provincial boy that I was, and I also thought it a great treat to walk down to Marble Arch and shop at Selfridges, buying birthday presents for the family at that famous store. For my parents' twentieth anniversary I bought a silver kiddush becher and inscribed it to them from Cynthia, Sharron and myself. Now that my parents are gone, I follow their example and regularly make kiddush from that becher.

Another 'treat' was to buy books. We would take the 'tube' (the underground train) to either the Jewish Memorial Council (JMC) bookshop in Woburn House, near Euston Station, or to Aldgate East in London's (then still very Jewish) 'East End'. In the former location, we had the advantage of a serious discount and it was there that we purchased many of our standard text-books. The woman who attended to our bibliographical needs and wrapped the books for us did so with a cigarette permanently in her mouth and the ash often dropping on to the books and the packages! In the latter location, we could enjoy a kosher salt beef sandwich at Bloom's and then walk around the Jewish bookshops. My favourite was that of M. L. (Moshe Leib) Cailingold. The owner had a wonderful collection of items that were rarer and much less standard than those of the JMC, and one could browse for long periods among the dusty shelves. When one found such a rarity and expressed an interest in purchasing it, Mr. Cailingold, a religious Jew from eastern Europe (Warsaw, I think), would try to discourage (yes, *dis*courage) its sale. It seemed that he preferred to leave it in his shop to keep him company. If we succeeded in making the purchase, we would take back our spoils to College with feelings of great glee. So it was that the number of books on our shelves grew and grew and the nucleus of each of our personal libraries was built.

Choosing girls to take to West End treats was also a regular activity for me and some of my more forward student colleagues. I met a succession of outstanding young women in my College years, always falling in love with them long before they felt ready to fall in love with me. Somewhat paradoxically, when some of them did eventually reciprocate emotionally, this induced a kind of panic in me. My passions then immediately cooled and I tended to opt out. Perhaps my early childhood had trained me not to rely on anyone's affections, to shy away from emotional dependency and to manage 'by myself'. I have often asked myself whether this had to do with the intense relationship that I had with my mother until my father came home from the forces and how I had to learn to be independent of it and demonstrate that I was not emotionally involved. As I recall, each of the young women attracted me in her own way. Some were lively social companions or interesting intellectual colleagues, while others had especially pretty faces, elegant shapes or beautiful hair. Perhaps unsurprisingly, I did not fall for any who were spiritually inspiring or religiously dedicated.

One recollection is related to the matter of beautiful hair. One girl, who was very proud of her long and sexy hair, attracted me greatly, teased me mercilessly, egging me on but always pulling back and proclaiming her lack of serious interest. We baited each other like puppies and kittens for many months until matters reached a head when we were having a coffee together one evening. She said something gratuitously unpleasant and I told her not to do that again. She said she would do so whenever she wished and I responded by declaring that if she did, I would pour my coffee over her hair. 'You wouldn't dare', she countered as she repeated her criticism; but dare I certainly did! I believe it was from that point that I fell out of love with her and she fell more in love with me, but all to no avail. Immature posturing on both sides, I think.

The front door at College had two keys; the lower one could be opened with our ordinary key but only until 23.00. If you were returning later than that, you had to obtain a late key from the Matron. That way, she knew if you were perhaps overdoing it. Of course, if one forgot, or chose not to, obtain such a key, there was an alternative strategy. You shouted up at a succession of College windows with lights on, in the hope that a friend would come down and let you in. Not unexpectedly, neighbours trying to sleep at around midnight were not greatly thrilled with this procedure and sometimes made complaints to the College.

Miss Aarons tended to be a little generous with the oil and the fat that she used in certain dishes. If you squeezed a piece of fried chopped meat with your fork, this generosity immediately became apparent. Some of us blamed the indigestion that we occasionally suffered on our College diet and sometimes we would skip lunch and go off to one of the three kosher snack bars that then plied their business in Baker Street. You could buy a salt beef sandwich for 2s/6d (12.5p) or a liver sandwich for 2s/- (10p). To save money, I usually opted for the latter, reserving the former for a special treat when the financial situation permitted. Immediately after lunch, at 13.45, we gathered in the synagogue for the afternoon service (minḥah) and supper was similarly followed by arvit (the evening service). Talking of lunch, I should mention that some of the teachers would come and eat in the dining room but they usually did so at separate tables. In fact, when in 1960–61 the controversial issue of the possible appointment of Louis Jacobs to the College Principalship was at its peak, I distinctly remember one lunch-time when the Principal Isidore Epstein ate at one table, the Chief Rabbi Israel Brodie at a second, and Louis Jacobs at a third! I shall shortly write more about this controversy.

Shabbat meals were fairly good and we would sing zemirot (Shabbat hymns) at the tables. On Shabbat morning we generally did not organize our own minyan but went to a variety of different shools that were within easy walking distance of the College. That way, we could hear great (and mediocre) preachers and ḥazanim and sometimes enjoy a lavish kiddush. We often went up to the fourth floor to have another kiddush kindly provided by Harold and Hannah Levy and to chuckle at Harold's idiosyncrasies, but also to imbibe some of his worldly wisdom with glasses of his Scotch. At supper on Friday evenings, one of the students would offer some comments on the weekly Torah reading. I had only been there two or three weeks when I was called upon to perform this latter function and what I managed to produce was fairly basic, but then I was not yet seventeen and only in the preparatory class.

Some of the older students had a little fun at my expense by referring to my young years, my weekly rather than daily shave, and my beginner's status. When I took on responsibilities in the Jews' College Union Society and proved my mettle by carrying off prizes at the end of each year, they became a little less condescending. I should add that I obtained distinctions in some of my examinations. On Motsae Shabbat (Saturday evening) we often organized a Melaveh Malkah ('saying goodbye to the Sabbath queen') in the College dining room. There would be a guest speaker, discussions and refreshments, and, in addition our own student body, there were often a large number of students from other institutions who were active in religious Zionist movements such as Bnei Akiva and Bachad. Again, something of a marriage bureau.

Studies and Students

Those of us who were at Jews' College in the early 1960s think of it as one of the College's liveliest and most productive period in its history, and we were intellectually and religiously stimulated not only by the classes we took but also by each other. This was especially true among those who were resident. Some at the College tended to be more pious, others less so, but there was a common commitment to the kind of modern Orthodoxy that included an open mind, consideration of those who were less knowledgeable and/or not so observant, an enthusiasm for study and teaching, and a love of the land of Israel and its modern State.

Among those whom I particularly remember and knew well were Raymond Apple, who ministered at Bayswater and then Hampstead before returning to his native Australia and excelled there as a leading Rabbi; Cyril Harris whom I got to know as the bombastic Glaswegian Rabbi of Kenton Synagogue (where I taught, and later headed, its ḥeder classes), and who went on to be Chief Rabbi of South Africa; Abraham Levy from Gibraltar who assisted the Haham Solomon Gaon in the Spanish and Portuguese Synagogue and ultimately became its Principal Rabbi; Irving Jacobs whose brilliance as a teacher became almost legendary and who ultimately became Principal of Jews' College; and Jeffrey Cohen who combined impressive scholarly abilities with outstanding pastoral skills and devotedly served London's largest synagogue, Stanmore, for some twenty years. I often muse on the fact that Abraham, Irving, Jeffrey and I have managed to retain our independence of mind, our modern interpretations of Judaism, our love of historical Jewish scholarship even in those circumstances when it might have served our careers better if we had followed alternative and more dominant trends in the academic, educational and communal worlds. We probably each paid a price for remaining true to ourselves and what we learned at the Jews' College of almost 60 years ago but I suspect that not one of us would have wished it otherwise.

Jeffrey Cohen had studied at Gateshead Yeshivah (traditional rabbinical seminary) and had come to the College a year before I did. I was sixteen and he was twenty when we met. He generously took me under his wing and became my mentor and advisor in many different ways. We not only played squash, table tennis and cricket together, and went for kosher sandwiches in Baker Street, but he also encouraged my learning process. We would meet in his room most evenings for an hour or two and work our way through basic biblical and rabbinic texts. Although he was older, more mature and more learned than I, he never called rank but treated me with the utmost kindness. When he and Gloria were married in Manchester in the summer of 1963, I was given the honour of being his best man and of delivering a speech, and they would then often invite me to spend Shabbat with them in their home in Hampstead Garden Suburb where Jeffrey was the Youth Minister. He and Cyril Harris performed the wedding ceremony for Shulie and me in 1967 and he and Abraham Levy did the same for my daughter Tanya and her husband Anthony in Cambridge in 1991. Jeffrey and Gloria remain today among my dearest friends.

We were even almost arrested together in February 1961. Jeffrey had arranged a twenty-first birthday party at the home of a friend and invited many of us from College to join him for the celebration. The problem was that we needed more cushions so that the revellers could sit on the floor at the party. Thinking out of the box, as youngsters often do, we opened one of the windows on the third floor and threw some cushions from the College down to where colleagues collected them and whisked them off to the party. Unfortunately, some neighbours spotted this process and thought that we were burglars illicitly removing furniture from Jews' College. I am not sure whether they actually called the police but we certainly got a serious ticking off from Poulson and Hannah Levy.

Another dear friend was Mayer Nissim. Mayer had been born in Aden in 1941 and educated there at Selim School under the headmastership of Abraham Marks (later CEO of the Board of Deputies of British Jews) who had inspired him to come westwards in language and culture, and for his further education. Mayer was a fluent speaker of Arabic and Hebrew. The Jewish community in which he was reared had been warm, traditional, Zionist and broad-minded. They were Yemenite Jews who had benefitted from the presence of the British who had controlled, with Ottoman acquiescence, what came to be called the Aden Protectorate after their conquest of the area in 1839. In 1960 when Mayer arrived at Jews' College, Arab nationalists in Aden were gradually growing in strength and in fanaticism and threatening the British presence, as demonstrated by later events (and indeed the current situation). His aim was to complete his 'A' level requirements and then to study for a University of London degree in Hebrew and Arabic, and after some tribulations he achieved this.

Mayer was highly intelligent, generous, good-looking and physically very fit. I greatly valued what was almost always his balanced approach. He could have had his choice of female companions but he and Ruth Cohen had fallen in love from his early days in London. Her parents were not altogether thrilled with his non-Ashkenazi background and this caused innumerable problems and many tensions. We became close friends and spent many hours in each other's rooms talking about every aspect of life, as well as playing games, going to the pool, and trying to solve our respective romantic problems. He spent one Pesaḥ with me and my family in Edinburgh and everyone grew to love him. He even tried to teach me to swim but my success in this had to wait for another few years. Mayer's intention was always to settle in Israel and when he finally married Ruth Cohen in the late 1960s, they made aliyah.

Other friends at College included Peter Ebstein from South Africa, Michael Rosen (son of Rabbi Kopul Rosen) from Carmel College, Elkan Levy whose father was a well-known minister/cantor in the United Synagogue, Yaakov Grunewald, Martin Balanow whose father was a Rabbi in Glasgow, and Joel Rockman whose father led the Catford and Bromley community. Only Rosen and Grunewald later became Rabbis. Rosen was intensely active in the promotion of Jewish education and spirituality in Jerusalem and Grunewald was a successful and much-liked spiritual leader of the Pinner Orthodox Synagogue in London for some 35 years. Elkan

11. With fellow students Peter Ebstein (centre) and Mayer Nissim.

went on to study law and ultimately became President of the United Synagogue in London. Other contemporaries who went on to the rabbinate were Freddie Werbel from Sweden, Moishe Golomb from Australia, and Lionel Chiswell and Harvey Cohen from Liverpool. Francis Treuherz was destined for a career in education but diverted to homeopathy in which field he has made an international name for himself.

I knew of course from the beginning that I would have to find sources of income to supplement my student grant. I went to see Dr. Isidore Fishman, who was then the Director of the London Board of Jewish Religious Education and responsible for the appointment of teachers for all the synagogue classes throughout the United Synagogue network in London. He was a kindly and learned man whose handshake one never forgot. It was like trying to take hold of a soft, damp rag. He found me a post at Wembley Synagogue, then headed by Rabbi Myer Berman. I found the organization of the classes there sadly wanting and soon transferred to Kenton where I worked successfully with Cyril Harris and where I became headmaster in later years when I was a graduate student. I taught there on Sunday mornings and on Tuesday and Thursday evenings. On Mondays I gave private barmizvah lessons. All those teaching commitments took place many miles away from Jews' College and I had to travel by tube and then walk a fair distance at both ends. London had pea-soup fogs in those days and I remember one evening getting lost a few times on the less than two-kilometre walk from Kenton Synagogue via Shaftesbury Avenue to the Preston Road underground station.

On Shabbat I also undertook to prepare the occasional Torah readings for Raymond Apple at Bayswater and also to take the children's service in that synagogue and there was an honorarium for doing this. Raymond and his charming spouse, Marian (from the distinguished rabbinic family of the Untermans), would sometimes kindly invite me for lunch with them. The first time I did the leining in his shool I projected my voice very well and put all my intensity into making the text meaningful. Raymond congratulated me on my competence but wisely advised me to take it more slowly and more gently in the future or I would have no energy to do anything else that day. In addition, I applied for and obtained an Aria Scholarship. This fund was established when Aria College in Portsmouth was closed in 1857 and grants were given from it to promising Jews' College students. For most of my undergraduate days I had to be busy with teaching as well as learning but it did help see me through the financial challenges of those days. The teaching experience was also invaluable. One certainly learned the hard way how not to teach.

Lecturers

Who were our teachers at Jews' College and how did I relate to them? My first contact with some of them was when I was interviewed on my arrival. If I am not mistaken, Dr. Epstein asked me a few gentle questions to get me started and then handed me over to Dr. Jacobs and Dr. Zimmels. The former wanted to know what parts of Talmud I had studied and I seemed to parry his not very demanding questions without any serious difficulties. Dr. Zimmels and I seemed not to hit it off right from the start. He asked me about Jewish history and I answered all his questions. He then wanted to know the origin of the Fast Day of Gedaliah. I explained the situation that had led up to the assassination of the governor Gedaliah by groups opposing his pro-Babylonian regime. 'But was he Jewish?', asked Zimmels. I thought I must have got it wrong and thought I had better correct it. 'No' I stammered in ignorance and lack of confidence, 'maybe he wasn't'. Zimmels was clearly unimpressed with me and I always felt the same way about him. The apologetic and modest style that he seemed to cultivate was in fact not reflective of his true character. He did not take kindly to any challenges or any disagreements on the part of his students and, if you persisted in crossing him, he could be fairly vindictive. He once wrote to my parents threatening to withhold an academic report from my grant provider if I continued to oppose him. He called me, in biblical terms, an 'enticer and misleader'.

Zimmels's background had been doctoral studies at the University of Vienna but, whether because of bad experiences during the Nazi period or for some other reasons, he always presented to us the position of a rigidly Orthodox Rabbi rather than a broad-minded but observant scholar. He had an encyclopaedic knowledge of Jewish history and he collected important data in a number of volumes relating to Ashkenazi customs and halakhah. As one of his colleagues put it, he was a *Zusammensteller*, a compiler, rather than an analytical historian. His lectures were informative but deadly dull and his powers as an administrator unimpressive. As a student body we were astonished when the College appointed him Director of Studies and then Principal. Of this, more later.

Louis Jacobs was the College Tutor and taught us Talmud. He was an interesting and exciting teacher. As one who had long been in the yeshivah world, he loved and lived the texts and argued in the traditional Talmudic style, using his hands a good deal and marching around the room. I did sometimes have a problem with his Mancunian accent and I wondered for a long time what 'boods' were, in the botanical context. He was considerate, kind and tolerant and had no problem with any challenge that we might throw at him. His weakness was that he had a bee in his bonnet about Pentateuchal criticism and took every opportunity of arguing that one could be Orthodox and still accept the documentary hypothesis about the origins of the Torah. Like all those who newly convert to an idea, he became a missionary for it. He had become aware of such critical theories only as a mature adult already serving as an Orthodox Rabbi and, to my mind, the shock somehow left a deep impression on him. I objected to his views at that time, adopted them later, and finally concluded that speculative historical and literary theories should not be used to challenge traditional beliefs, nor can such beliefs be employed to confute scientific ideas. They simply operate on different planes.

Louis would have made a wonderful Chief Rabbi, or Principal of Jews' College, but the decisions about his future became wrapped up in communal politics, as much as, if not more than, in theological trysts. Epstein did not wish to resign; Brodie had an eye on leading the College himself; the chairman of the College Council, Sir Alan Mocatta, wished to see a more liberal and moderate form of Orthodoxy; the editor of the *Jewish Chronicle*, William Frankel, made use of the controversy to promote his newspaper as well as his preference for Conservative over Orthodox Judaism; and Louis himself was perhaps too honest, erudite and outspoken to realize that quiet diplomacy and a mild indulgence in dissimulation might have taken him further than a reliance on supporters who had their own varied agendas. That said, Louis and his wife Shulamit were the most charming of individuals and, unlike most of the College teachers, they actually invited the students to their home. I was truly saddened when he resigned at the end of my first year. When I did well in my exams that summer, he wrote me a charming letter in which he expressed his confidence that I would become a foremost Rabbi and scholar. I hope that I have proved him at least 50 per cent correct.

We all loved Mr. Eli Cashdan and he often said to us 'Boys, boys, I love you all'. He taught us Hebrew Bible and for him this was in itself an act of love. He explained the grammar carefully, summarized the various commentaries – ancient, medieval and modern – and made it a lot of fun for us all. He was excellent at that aspect of his teaching and inspired us to enjoy and appreciate the scriptural texts. He also had to lecture on Comparative Semitic Linguistics and here he was on less firm ground and we had to do a fair bit on our own. But, given that this is so often the case in university courses, it was hardly fair to expect him to spoon-feed us as he did with the biblical texts. In class, Jeffrey and I, and a 'day boy' (as it were) called Stephen Roth would keep up a lively banter with Mr. Cashdan. Stephen, who was rather small and round, subsequently called himself by his Hebrew name, Simha, and became a conservative Rabbi in Israel, sadly dying in his sixties. He loved opera and would often sing famous arias to us, including 'Nessun Dorma' almost three decades before it became so popular when used, in Pavarotti's rendering, as the theme for the FIFA World Cup soccer tournament in 1990. When Jeffrey and I tried to emulate his example, Stephen always stressed that the final word of the libretto when repeated a third time at the end of the aria was 'vincer' and not 'vincerò', with what kind of musical or linguistic justification I have no idea. He also arranged for the student body to go to Sadler's Wells to see a production of *Tosca*. That was my first real exposure to a musical medium that became of major importance to me in later life.

Two lively exchanges spring to mind. We were once dealing with a passage in Isaiah 20 where the prophet describes how Egyptian and Ethiopian prisoners will be led off by their Assyrian captors naked, barefooted 'and with their buttocks uncovered'. In the next verse there is a reference to 'kush mabaṭṭam' and Cashdan asked us to suggest a meaning. I immediately and flippantly piped up 'Clearly, given their state of undress, it means "kiss my bottom!"' The whole class, and Cashdan, choked with laughter for a number of minutes. When we studied Isaiah 54:8, there was a reference to God's limited degree of anger expressed in the Hebrew phrase 'shetsef ketsef'. I suggested to Cashdan that he should henceforth use this expression to refer to Stephen (Roth) since it was translated as a 'little wrath'. More explosions of laughter. There was massive amount of biblical Hebrew text for us to cover with Cashdan for the Hebrew course, both at 'A' level and for the degree, and we completed it all, despite the fun and the hilarity, or maybe because of them. Although he was more devoted to teaching than to scholarly publication, Cashdan nevertheless produced some first-class translations of rabbinic texts that came to be widely appreciated and used.

Naphtali Wieder was also an inspiring teacher but in a wholly different way. He was intensely private, aloof, conscious of his dignity as a scholar, demanding of respect and never hesitant to employ his acerbic humour to belittle students whose standards were not what he expected (or even when they were). Though born and reared in the Hassidic environment of Sighet in Northern Transylvania, he had sought broader intellectual pastures in Berlin in the 1920s and had become a devotee of scientific inquiry into Jewish history and literature at the famous Hochschule für die Wissenschaft des Judentums. He spent the Second World War years in Oxford and made much of this opportunity to exploit the rich liturgical content of the

Bodleian Library and to cultivate friendships with other refugee scholars, among them Alexander Altmann, Chaim Rabin, Paul Kahle and Jacob Teicher. Appointed to lecture at Jews' College in 1947, he saw it as his role to re-mould students in his scholarly image rather than to produce communal functionaries. Unsurprisingly, only a minority could cope with his demands and his style. His scholarship was impeccable and his lecturing style magnificent. To be his student one had effectively to suppress one's own feelings and opinions in favour of what the master regarded as the ideal. He was the College's finest scholar, who made seminal contributions to the study of midrash, liturgy, Dead Sea scrolls and Karaism. He taught us Talmud almost every morning for about two hours and woe betide anyone who stumbled over the text. 'Control me, sirs', he would declare when he wished us to follow him in the reading of a text. There was no way that anyone would have dared to suggest that this was a Germanic use of the verb and not an English one.

Similarly, he once required us to translate a well-known hymn into Classical Hebrew. By way of introduction, he read us the first two lines 'Soon thou wilt come to thine eternal home', pronouncing 'come' exactly as he pronounced 'home'. When we sheepishly suggested an alternative pronunciation, he dismissed this out of hand, angrily explaining that the usual pronunciation had to be sacrificed for the sake of the rhyme. Who were we, native Brits and benighted juniors, to dare to contradict the Master? He regaled us with all his innovative research on the textual history of the prayers, introduced us to the critical study of midrashic texts, and guided us in the understanding of Hebrew grammar and the composition of Classical Hebrew prose. When we composed what we thought was an amusing student rag, he contemptuously defined it as puerile. After some two decades at Jews' College, he taught at University College London and then at Bar-Ilan University in Israel.

Rabbi Dr. Ernest (Ephraim Yehudah) Wiesenberg was a warm, caring and hospitable teacher with a remarkable reservoir of Semitic knowledge, as well as profound rabbinical learning and wisdom. He maintained a successful and popular presence in the communal, as well as the academic, world, and succeeded in combining the piety and unworldliness of the mystic with the rationalism and absent-mindedness of the scientific scholar. Born in the Slovakian city of Košice when it was still part of the Austro-Hungarian Empire, he had, in common with so many other scholars of Wissenschaft des Judentums in Central Europe, to acquire a familiarity not only with Yiddish and Hebrew, but also with Hungarian, German and Slovakian. He obtained his rabbinical diploma from Rabbi Joseph Horowitz of Frankfurt am Main in 1937 and, by the time that he settled in London in 1935, he had completed his matriculation studies in Vienna.

After studies at Jews' College, and the award of a BA and PhD from the University of London, Wiesenberg was appointed lecturer in the department of Hebrew at University College, London, in 1949 and promoted to a readership in 1963. Among the Jewish fields in which he specialized and published were the calendar, astronomy, religious law and liturgy, and his most significant contribution was probably his annotated edition of *Abraham Maimonides' Commentary on Genesis and Exodus* (London, 1958), an important Judaeo-Arabic source of the thirteenth century. When we were his students at Jews' College in the West End of London, he would often invite one of us (or sometimes two) to join him and his family for Friday evening dinner in Golders Green, a Shabbat walk of almost two hours. When the invitation was during the summer, and Shabbat came in at around 21.15, prayers took until around 23.00 so that it was often after 02.00 before we got home to the College. There was a charming and loving atmosphere in his home and he, and his wife and children, made us feel part of this. He represented for many of us a brilliant combination of devoted family man, learned Rabbi, outstanding scholar and caring teacher.

There were other more occasional teachers who left an impression on me during my years at Jews' College. Reverend Leo Bryll was an excellent musician, a fine cantor, and a charming and kind teacher. He taught us how to lead services with the correct melodies on the various Sabbaths and festivals of the Jewish calendar. Only a few of us took the trouble to attend his Friday lectures but those of us who did so derived considerable benefit. Although a leading cantor in his own right, he stressed the importance of using cantorial skills only on special occasions, and simply following the established traditional tunes on a more regular basis. Whenever, and wherever, I led the services in subsequent years, I attempted to follow his wise counsel.

Our abilities to hone our skills as public speakers were greatly enhanced by Harry Johnson who was an expert in all the ramifications of oratory. His aim was to encourage us to deliver our remarks in a clear fashion, to ensure that our audiences saw our faces, heard and understood our voices, and to avoid the 'ums', 'ahs' and 'ehs' to which some speakers are prone. Various communal Rabbis also attempted to teach us homiletical skills and of these the one I recall with the most affection was Dr. Isaac Levy of Hampstead Synagogue who rightly decried those who would address congregations with any forms of pomposity, arrogance or spiritual superiority. We also enjoyed lectures by a leading professor of educational psychology whose name escapes me at present. She taught at the University of London's Institute of Education and was a leading figure in her specialization.

We also exploited the educational opportunities provided by lectures given by visiting scholars at other institutes of the University of London such as University College and the School of Oriental and African Studies. I recall attending a series of inspirational public lectures by the distinguished American scholar of Bible and Archaeology William Foxwell Albright of Johns Hopkins University in Baltimore, subsequently published under the title of *Yahweh and the Gods of Canaan*. He contrasted the religious traditions of the Hebrews with those of the Canaanites and what we found most refreshing was the manner in which he took issue with some of the theories propounded by Julius Wellhausen and his followers that were somewhat less than friendly to Judaism and its history.

Cecil Roth came from Oxford on a weekly basis to teach us how to use Jewish sources for the writing of Jewish history. It was a privilege to hear one of the world's leading Jewish historians, although it must be admitted that Mr. Johnson would not have been greatly impressed by Dr. Roth's manner of delivery. In the first lecture I heard from him, he challenged us to state where the famous eleventh-century rabbinic scholar Isaac Al-Fasi (known as the 'Rif' in traditional circles of Jewish learning) had originated. Grossly ignorant as we were, we had no clue and he proceeded to enlighten us that in Arabic 'al-Fasi' meant 'from Fez' and to explain the importance of the Islamic influences on the Jews of that period.

Academic progress

My period as a holder of offices in the Jews' College Union Society taught me much about student politics, professorial sensitivities, bureaucratic hypocrisy and the unreliability of some colleagues. The College had proposed that some of us who were resident in the College should move out to make way for younger students, some of whom were doing courses other than the strenuous and demanding one in which we were engaged. We took exception to this and made our demands known to the Council, threatening to organize a student strike if the proposal was not abandoned. As the Secretary of the Union Society, I had the task of formulating and sending the letter. The officers and committee all agreed its content but, because I had signed it on their behalf, I was regarded as the arch villain. Dr. Zimmels blamed me for the troubles, and one of the College bureaucrats passed a copy of the letter to the *Jewish Chronicle*, remaining silent when I was accused of what was seen as an act of betrayal against the College. Equally silent were my student colleagues.

I did not overly exert myself in the first two years of my degree course but the situation changed in my final year and I recall precisely why. My close friend Jeffrey Cohen came into my room in the summer of 1963 to announce proudly that he had just achieved a 'first-class honours' result and to invite me to do likewise in the subsequent year. That challenge, and my awareness that if I wished to advance to postgraduate degrees I would need a 'first', drove me to adopt a more industrious approach in the final year of the degree. Our BA Honours course at the University of London was centred on the Semitic languages, and there was an option to take various combinations. Jews' College students were instructed to take the Hebrew and Aramaic combination which demanded a knowledge of Hebrew and Jewish Studies from the biblical to the modern period. Not only were we examined in the critical study of biblical, rabbinic and medieval texts but we also had to demonstrate competence in literary history and comparative Semitics.

The final examination in the 1960s consisted of nine three-hour papers. We completed four of those papers on a Thursday and a Friday, four more on Monday and Tuesday, and the ninth on Wednesday morning. It was a test not only of knowledge but also of stamina and composure. We had to travel by underground from Baker Street to Euston Square and from there walk to the University of London's examination halls in Gordon Square. Neither the journey nor sitting with hundreds of other examinees were very relaxing experiences. One morning I felt so nervous and panic-stricken, and my stomach was churning so much, that I entered a pharmacy and asked for some help. The pharmacist gave me some pills and assured me they would calm me down. I later realized that they were nothing more than antacids but they had the required psychological effect.

During the third examination, one of the students began to shout that he was going blind, no doubt another manifestation of examination neurosis. There was also an 'oral' some weeks later, when the London examiners and an external examiner could discuss your papers with you. The external examiner for me was Professor David Winton Thomas of Cambridge and I enjoyed all but two of his questions. One was why my comparative Semitic grammar was less outstanding than my other papers and the other was why I had failed to read one of the Hebrew words correctly in an unseen midrashic text. I manoeuvred my way through these challenges and was later told by one of my examiners that I had achieved an overall percentage of 87. In Cambridge that would have been called a 'starred first'. I happily reported to Jeffrey that I had done what he had invited me to do but of course said nothing about the specific mark.

By this time, I had made up my mind to do whatever I could to become an academic and to follow the example of Naphtali Wieder, of whom I was greatly in awe. The rabbinate was no longer appealing for a number of reasons. Firstly, I felt much more comfortable lecturing from a daïs than preaching from a pulpit. I had the impression, rightly or wrongly, that the former had more chance of making an impact than the latter. I also found the act of standing in the pulpit a very lonely and nerve-wracking experience. What is more, I had concluded that I was simply not sufficiently pious or spiritual enough to inspire others with religious guidance. I therefore determined to write a doctoral dissertation as quickly as I possibly could. The notion of applying to Oxford or Cambridge appealed to me but the College was very anxious to retain the services of Dr. Wieder who was undoubtedly nonplussed by the appointment of Zimmels to the principalship. They therefore appointed him director of a newly-established department of postgraduate research and I was encouraged to stay and be his first student.

Travel and Transport

Many times during the vacations of my student years, I led groups of Bnei Akiva youngsters at camps under canvas in summer or indoors during the winter. This involved imparting to them the values of religious Zionism and a love of the Jewish homeland. It was good practice for a budding teacher or lecturer. That was in my late teens and early twenties. Earlier than that I participated in hiking tours with my contemporaries. I recall walking (and blistering of course) from Strasburg in France to Basle in Switzerland and from Dinant in Belgium to Luxemburg City. I gave courses at what was called Seminar Torani in Holland (I think I was twenty or twenty-one) and have distinct memories of the thrill of realizing how girls of about seventeen became attracted to their 'lecturer' but at the same time recognizing that one should under no circumstances take any inappropriate advantage of such a status. I also clashed with the Rabbi and Professor from Israel, Dov Rappel, who led that camp and wished me to stay on longer than the period to which I had originally agreed. I was adamant that I had to leave because I had purchased tickets for concerts and plays at the Edinburgh Festival and had a girl-friend coming to join me. He lectured me on ideology and I parried with statements about personal choice. Interestingly, it led to mutual feelings of respect and years later he challenged me not only to identify textual variants in medieval Jewish liturgies but also to attempt explanations of why they had occurred. I attempted to do just that in my later publications.

Having used the underground many times for my first two three years in London I graduated to my own form of transport in 1962. Mr. Poulson's son was selling his Puch 150c.c. scooter and I thought this would distinctly improve my ability to get around the capital much more quickly. I made the purchase, arranged the insurance and reached my teaching locations much more quickly. There were two minor problems and one more upsetting one. In the winter months, I fell off the scooter a few times on the icy roads but my young and supple muscles and bones took this punishment in their stride. I also coped with the fact that the carburettor sometimes choked, soon learning to dismantle the relevant part and blow it through. The upsetting problem involved my first criminal record. I had in Edinburgh often borrowed my father's 50c.c. moped and was therefore well able to ride my newly-acquired scooter. I had not yet taken the test and had no right to take a passenger.

One Sunday morning a fellow teacher at Kenton synagogue classes asked if I could spare him the journey by 'tube' all the way from the West End by giving him a lift on my scooter. I kindly but foolishly agreed and we were stopped by an assiduous young policeman, keen on making an arrest. Appearing before the Marylebone magistrates, I was fined £20 and banned from riding for three months, a grossly unfair punishment when compared to what others received elsewhere for the same misdemeanour. By this time in my political development I was moving towards a socialist or even anarchist commitment. That act on the part of the legal authorities convinced me that the police and the courts were unfair and dishonest institutions, especially since the policeman's evidence was partially untrue. I did not have the courage to contradict him, fearing (probably rightly) that this might add to my punishment.

I soon wished to exchange the cold, the frost, the slippy roads and the padded jackets that were the bugbears of the motor cyclist for a more comfortable form of transport. The ideal would have been the purchase of a Mini but I simply did not have enough funds at that point for such an investment. I therefore made the mistake of buying (for £185) a well-worn Heinkel three-wheeled 'bubble car' while at home in Edinburgh in the summer of 1963. I took my father with me to examine the body and the engine, although I must admit that I did not really want to hear what he, as an experienced mechanic, had to say. 'Remember that if you buy a second-hand car, you buy someone else's tsores' is how he expressed his advice. I duly ignored it and suffered a year of mechanical breakdowns, a welter of replacement parts, and numerous, excruciatingly slow journeys between Edinburgh and London. Two of those journeys ended up in garages on the way, and trips to the nearest railway station to catch the train to London.

Home in Edinburgh

I also of course spent time at home with my parents and sisters in Edinburgh. During term-time in London I wrote, or rather typed, a lengthy letter to them almost every Thursday evening or Friday morning and, the postal service being what it then was, they almost always received it the next day, on Shabbat morning, and replied on Sunday. Mum would also sometimes send me a parcel of all sorts of 'goodies' that she had prepared for me and I would share these with my fellow students. In my early years at College, I would take advantage of a superb service provided by British Railways. If you purchased a ticket from London to Edinburgh, you could, for the princely sum of five shillings and threepence (about 26p in today's money), ask for 'PLA', that is, 'passenger luggage in advance'. Your suitcase or, in my case, a large trunk with all my belongings, was collected from your London student's residence and delivered to your Edinburgh home.

While at home, I was able to look after my little sister Sharron on many occasions. I took her with me on many a trip and babysat her when my parents went to the cinema or theatre with tickets I had purchased for them. She was not the easiest of little children and it demanded considerable bouts of energy and patience to maintain any equilibrium with her. My friend Mayer spent Pesaḥ with us in Edinburgh around 1962 and he was a real hit with Sharron, with Cynthia, and with my parents. When I took girls out for the evening, Sharron would demand to come with us, but I, or at least my Mum, drew the line at that. But the relationship with Sharron grew and flourished. She accompanied my parents to one of my College prize-givings (Cynthia had already left home, I think) and when I received my prize, she ran forward and shouted, much to everyone's amusement, 'I want a prize too!' I also learned from Dad how to service a car in the days when units were not sealed and it was a relatively easy process to clean, lubricate or replace them. I helped Mum in the kitchen, especially on Thursdays and Fridays and developed quite a skill in the preparation of chicken soup, gefillte fish, chopped liver, chopped herring, and roasted chicken and potatoes.

I remained close to my friend from school and heder days, Nat Gordon. We would often eat in each other's houses and on Shabbat we would take long walks together and discuss the various ways in which we were planning to change the world, political, religiously and socially. He became active with the Liberal Party and I became involved with the activities of the Labour Party. This drove no wedges between us since we both saw ourselves as radical reformers and, like most young people, had no inkling then of how our attitudes would change in the course of the subsequent decades. Nat was also with me on one of my ill-fated journeys by 'bubble-car'.

Another major influence was my mother's eldest brother, Uncle Abe. I would spend many an evening with him at his home in Forest Road, around the corner from the massive complex of grey and grim Victorian buildings that constituted the Edinburgh Royal Infirmary. He was a master tailor who had learned his craft from his grandfather, Shneur Zalman, and his father, my Zeide, Aharon Rapstoff, commencing his apprenticeship with them at the age of ten! While he made suits for his customers (and chain-smoked cigarettes), I would ask him for his views on life, love and literature. He advised me to read novels by Dostoevsky, which I duly did, explained to me the nature of romantic love as he saw it ('think of the woman who would be most ideal for you and then marry the next best thing'), and recounted his military adventures during the First World War at the Battle of the Somme, during which he was seriously wounded, and after his return to France to serve another term there until the armistice. He was an autodidact who had absorbed information widely from his many learned and professional customers (with whom he chatted at length while he measured and fitted them) and from his wide reading. He was also an active Freemason who had served as Master of his Lodge and was an accomplished public speaker. Auntie Dolly would prepare tea and strudel for us and then retire to bed, leaving us to what she saw as our male pursuits. It was often nearly 02.00 when I got home.

It was during one of my vacations that he told me about his forthcoming hernia operation. He had refused the offer of staying in hospital overnight and insisted that he would be fine if they sent him straight home. I offered to be there, in his home, to help him and comfort him when he arrived, and he, and Auntie Dolly, readily agreed. I was consequently there when the ambulance staff brought him into his bedroom, and party to the insults he heaped on all and sundry for the excruciating pain he was in. 'Bloody butchers they are, oh, the agony of it, my God, the pain, how could they do this to me, heartless medics, cruel surgeons and unfeeling nurses.' So it continued for some time, while I tried to comfort him. I did not remind him that he had determinedly opted to come straight home. Nor did I honestly understand what he was experiencing until over 50 years later when I myself underwent a hernia operation and suffered awful pains for between one and two weeks. Young and immature as I then was, I still had a lifetime of learning and of experience stretching before me.

10

Maturing as a Graduate
(1964–68)

Road to Research

Five years passed between the exciting award of my BA degree by HRH Queen Elizabeth the Queen Mother, who was then Chancellor of the University of London, at a ceremony which I attended in person in the latter part of 1964, and the capping and gowning of the doctors of the same university which, to my regret, I was unable to attend because we could not afford at that stage in 1969 to travel from Glasgow to London for the event. Those years saw the emergence of a young scholar from the chrysalis of his research studies, his success as headmaster of the Synagogue Classes at Kenton Synagogue (then Middlesex), an early form of academic recognition by the University of London, a marriage that was destined to be happy, fulfilling and productive in numerous ways, and a first university appointment.

The summer of 1964 had gone well. I had learned to drive in London in the previous few months but, expensive as it was, I could afford no more than the basic eighteen lesson and there was nobody among my friends or family who could take me out for practice. After those eighteen lessons I failed my first driving test in London and then went to Edinburgh for the summer vacation. There I took a few more lessons (less expensive than in London) with a very good woman instructor who determinedly insisted that I had to do precisely what I was told. I did exactly that, and to my great glee, passed my second test and was finally able to purchase my first brand-new car, a Morris Mini, for the princely sum of £425. I made the deposit and signed a contract to pay it over three years. Although there were some minor problems from time to time (which, with Dad's assistance, I could resolve), I loved my little Mini, as did my female friends.

I then enjoyed the first of three relationships with girl-friends that were more serious and somewhat lengthier than those of my undergraduate years and that were to occupy me from then until I was married in 1967. I learned not to run away too quickly from these girl-friends and spending lots of time with them undoubtedly taught me how to build sound and enjoyable connections with the opposite sex. My close friends, Jeffrey and Gloria, kindly invited me to spend happy Shabbatot with them on many occasions in Hampstead Garden Suburb and I gave a regular Friday evening lecture to some of the youth while I was living in that area in 1966-67. I also agreed during those years to give Torah lessons and academic lectures to many groups and this taught me how to relate to an audience, how to attract their attention and their interest, and how to bring topics alive that might otherwise seem somewhat dry and dull.

First, then, I had to navigate the academic year 1964–65, my first as a postgraduate student. The normal procedure was that one had to complete the MA before one undertook research for a doctoral degree. If one was a successful enough student, one could dispense with the MA stage but that could be done only at the end of one year, or was it perhaps during one's first postgraduate year? I therefore had to spend the first few months attending MA lectures, some of which did not interest me at all. At least two of the courses were taught by Dr. Zimmels and our relationship had not improved since my undergraduate days. My way of dealing with these was to absent myself on occasion. My frustration at not being able to proceed with research on a full-time basis meant that I did not make the most of that year. What I did very much enjoy were the courses and seminars given by Menahem Levin, an Israeli educator who was in London as the emissary of the Torah Department of the Jewish Agency. He was an inspirational guide to pedagogy, as well as an enthusiastic teacher of modern, spoken Hebrew and we learned a great deal from him. I also used his up-to-date methods in my running of the Kenton Synagogue classes, and found them helpful and productive. I also practised speaking modern Hebrew with him and other Israeli colleagues and visitors.

One of the reasons for being less industrious in my studies in that year 1964–65 was that I had moved out the Jews' College residence to share a luxury home with my close friend Mayer Nissim. His mentor in Aden had been Abraham Marks who owned a delightful apartment in an expensive area of Maida Vale, no more than a ten-minute walk from the Spanish and Portuguese Synagogue in Lauderdale Road, where our friend Abraham Levy was building his career and working with the Haham, Rabbi Dr. Solomon Gaon. Mayer and I had lots of fun together that year while he was still engaged on his first degree and I was supposed to be occupied with my MA. Coming home late one evening from some entertainment or another, we were suddenly confronted by strong arc-lights, and a voice from a loudspeaker that told us to 'just keep walking'. It was Otto Preminger directing a film that starred Laurence Harvey and later became a box office hit by the name of 'Bunny Lake is Missing'. There is a two-second shot of Mayer and me walking home in Maida Vale that night and that is clearly the reason why it was so widely acclaimed. In many ways, that summarizes the year, more entertainment based than academically industrious. Being in that area, we were sometimes invited to Shabbat lunch with the local Rabbis and synagogue dignitaries, including the Haham. I think he was fond of us both and we greatly welcomed his warmth and friendship. Our apartment was on the eleventh floor and I often walked all those flights on Shabbat. When someone was already going up in the lift, I permitted myself to join them. This was destined to have an effect on my later career, as I shall explain in due course.

In 1965 I was finally registered for the PhD degree under the supervision of the lecturer whom I greatly admired, Dr Naphtali Wieder. As a result of my excellent BA results, I successfully obtained a three-year graduate award from the Scottish Education Department. It is a happy reflection on the educational priorities of government departments in the 1960s that I received total financing for eight years of full-time study, partly because of my parents' modest incomes, but also in response to the levels of my academic achievements. I am often asked how I came to choose the subject of my doctoral dissertation. The answer is that I did not choose; Dr. Wieder did.

I was sitting in the College library checking some literature when he summoned me to follow him to the end of the corridor where we could talk without disturbing any of the readers. He indicated to me his view that my impressive competence in Hebrew language and grammar made me suitable for research on a manuscript of considerable importance for the history of those subjects in the sixteenth and seventeenth centuries. I was to prepare an edition of MS 37 in the collection of the London Beth Din (housed then at Jews' College Library under the competent and watchful eye of Ruth Lehmann), a text and commentary on the prayer-book of the Ashkenazi rite written by Shabbethai Sofer of Przemysl early in the 1600s. I did some preliminary reading of the little that had been published on the subject to date but the research got under way more seriously, and intensively, only later in 1965. By then, I was again operating at a good academic level and enjoying the challenge of deciphering the text of the manuscript, and understanding its significance in the light of other linguistic, liturgical, educational and communal developments in Polish Jewry in the previous centuries. I was at that stage no more than twenty-one years old.

I greatly enjoyed visiting a number of major research libraries, as well as working conscientiously in Jews' College Library, and often spent the morning at the British Museum, consulting Hebrew manuscripts and early printed editions of the Jewish prayer-book. I became immersed in my topic and excited about the new data I was uncovering and the fresh interpretations that I was developing and promoting. It seemed to me that an academic career beckoned, but I had little idea of how I might ensure a successful arrival. When my father met Dr. Wieder and asked him if I would become a fine Rabbi one day, he was told 'not just a Rabbi, Mr. Reif, a Chief Rabbi'.

When my former mentor, Isaac Cohen, then Chief Rabbi of Ireland, visited Jews' College, he tried hard – even desperately – to persuade me to opt for a rabbinic career, but by then I felt that a university post would suit me incomparably more and I strongly resisted his overtures. Naively, I argued that the world of academia would demand of me less politics and less compromise, and would allow me to pursue the search for truth, knowledge and historical understanding in a much purer form than anything I could do communally. How foolishly innocent these views were about the world of higher education, as I would learn, sometimes to my cost, and on other occasions even to my advantage, in the course of the subsequent years.

Discovery and Finance

During a research visit to the Bodleian Library in Oxford, I experienced the maiden thrill of discovering a manuscript that had been virtually overlooked by my scholarly predecessors, bound up as it was with a printed prayer-book. Corresponding with the Library's Curator of Oriental Manuscripts, seeing the item reclassified and renumbered, and obtaining a microfilm of it, were all exciting developments for me. It was even more sensational an event for me when an article that I had written describing, editing and annotating that Oxford manuscript was accepted for publication by the editors of the *Journal of Jewish Studies*, then based at University College, London, and published in the English capital. In 1967, my three-year award from the Scottish Education department would come to an end and I knew that it would require one more year of research and writing to complete my dissertation. I therefore applied for a postgraduate award of the University of London. These were highly competitive awards given in the fields of humanities, sciences and medicine, and one had to make a case about one's research, have the support of one's teachers and undergo an interview with two senior scholars.

I was thrilled to be told that I had made it through to the interview stage and was invited to attend at the School of Oriental and African Studies, there to be grilled about my academic work by Professors Ben Segal and Edward Ullendorff, both of them on the faculty of the School. These two gentlemen had not only reached the pinnacles of success in their fields of Semitic Studies but had also previously served as officers during the Second World War. I felt very much like a young recruit being tested by senior commanders. Segal probed and challenged, questioned and inquired, but with undoubted fairness and a certain degree of charity. Charity to budding young scholars who had not been his students was not among Ullendorff's characteristics. He seemed sharp, cynical and personally distant. Although I parried all his aggressive lunges, I feared that I might not have impressed him sufficiently. I was therefore relieved, and more than a little delighted, to receive notification a few weeks later that funding would be provided for one, or possibly two, years. My inquisitors must have reported well on me since out of the blue a letter came a few months later informing me that I had won the top humanities postgraduate research award of the University of London, the William Lincoln Shelley Studentship, for 1967 until 1969.

With my income from Kenton, and from giving various courses and lectures in the Jewish communities of north-west London, I was thus fairly well established financially, at least compared to what I had seen during my days at home. The only condition that had been placed on my award was that in addition to being supervised by Dr. Wieder at Jews' College, I had also to register in 1967 at University College and have Dr. Siegfried Stein as my other research adviser. Stein was Berlin born and bred and Wieder had spent most of the twenties and thirties in the German capital and had come to England to escape the Nazis. Stein was a great stickler for detail and accuracy and preferred to worry a scholarly topic to the umpteenth degree for an inordinate amount of time than to proceed swiftly to publication. His standards were high, even if his productivity was somewhat less so. I recall travelling back to north-west London with him from a meeting of the Society for Old Testament Studies at a conference centre of King's College London in Clapham Common. He spent much of the 45-minute journey trying to explain to me why it was highly significant that Leopold Zunz in the mid-nineteenth century had on one particular occasion used the word vielleicht (German for 'perhaps') indicating that great scholar's caution, and demonstrating thereby his own similar tendency. Stein was always kind and helpful, and instrumental in instilling in me the need for detailed analysis and historical criticism, as well as the close textual comparisons that Wieder favoured.

Wieder was himself a brilliant researcher and critical analyst and I learned a great deal from him in related areas. He combed through the many pages I prepared and put aside about a third of them. 'This is too much. You will use these later.' Disappointing though it was at the time to see the result of some of my labours excluded from the dissertation, I came to realize later in my career that my teacher and supervisor was correct in this connection. In another connection, he was less correct. His style of academic writing (unlike his lecturing ability) was stiff, dry and formal, reflecting his decade and a half in the German capital and his higher education there. He therefore did not like my looser and more British style and insisted that I change this. As he dictated in one instance: 'One must write: "Noteworthy is…"'. I often deferred to his wishes (where I could not avoid it), but felt that I was writing like Wieder and not like Reif. I think it fair to say that it took me the best part of a decade to recover and to revert to the kind of style that I had developed during my years at high school in Edinburgh under the tutelage of some excellent teachers of English language and literature.

Shulie Arrives

After my year in Maida Vale, I returned to Jews' College residence in 1965 and was there until 1966. Now, however, I was among the senior students, not only engaged on work for a higher degree, and with a standing as a successful educator, but also with the ability to catch the eye of the opposite sex with a welcome degree of success. My girl-friends were now tending to be with me for longer periods and I was clearly approaching the age when I might consider a more permanent attachment. As in Puccini's famous opera *La Bohème*, much of the flirting between the students took place at the coffee shop, in this case the refectory at Jews' College, where many tables were filled with young women and men not entirely averse to finding companions of the opposite sex.

As well as those studying for the BA honours degree in Semitic studies, there were also those who were taking what was called the BA general in three subjects, with a view to then training as teachers. To our great delight, many of them were bright and attractive young women. In my more mature role, I tended to hold court at coffee time and a group gathered around me intent on hearing all the latest gossip, discussing the current news and, of course, flirting. During the previous year or two I had had two regular girl-friends (consecutively, not concurrently, I might add). I had therefore not paid too much attention to a very intelligent, attractive and shapely young woman by the name of Sulamith Stekel, nor she indeed to me. Matters were destined to change drastically for me and her in the course of the academic year 1965–66.

Sulamith had been the German/Austrian equivalent of the Hebrew name Shulamit so that is how her father registered her and how she had come to be known as Sully. But for me the Hebrew original Shulamit (from Song of Songs) was more beautiful and therefore more appropriate and I decided I would call her Shulie. She had been a brilliant pupil at the preparatory school of South Hampstead Girls' School and had won a free place at the upper school. Things had gone wrong for her when the narrowness of curricular arrangements at the school had prevented her taking for 'A' level the subjects she loved and in which she excelled. The alternatives were not greatly to her liking and she passed only one of three. She had therefore come to Jews' College to do the additional 'A' level needed for a university course and had chosen Classical Hebrew. By the summer of 1965 (when she was nineteen) she had, under the tutelage of my friends Jeffrey Cohen and Irving Jacobs, who were now teaching at the College, succeeded in that examination and had started her BA course with a view to taking up teaching. During her first year at Jews' College she had still suffered from the loss of confidence engendered by her problems at school, as well as by her parents' tendency to stress only their children's inadequacies, rather than their qualities and their achievements. Strange as it seems today, that was seen in central Europe of pre-Second World War days as the ideal way of rearing children and encouraging them to do well. Needless to say, it often achieved the opposite effect. But now she found herself a popular young woman who was inundated with invitations to go out. By the time we really began to notice each other at coffee, she had begun to believe again in herself.

We exchanged glances, winks and smiles over the coffee table and I told one of my College friends that I felt confident that if I asked her out she would agree, in spite of the fact that she was at that time seeing another young man, a younger colleague of mine who was fairly besotted with her. The crunch came when she prepared a delicious birthday cake and told us that we should share it since our birthdays were both in January! That displeased him no end and when, a few days later, we went on a College outing to Stratford-on-Avon in a hired coach, she was my girl-friend, and not his, by the time we were travelling home. That evening he told me that my behaviour had been despicable; my response was that all was fair in love and war. Shulie was going through a bad patch at home because her father was fighting a prosecution for an alleged breach of the Companies' Act and there was considerable tension and nervousness in the family. I supported her as best I could, which was more than could be said for some of her less immediate family and friends.

The truth is that, in addition to being intensely and mutually attracted, we provided each other not only with love but also with precisely what was needed. She gave me calmness, order and security, and I gave her confidence, admiration and a bolthole from a difficult environment. I had always to assure her that she was a totally rounded person who could cope with all manner of problems and find solutions, and that she was what is known in German as geschickt, that is, multi-talented. She had to assure me that I could be a success in the academic world despite my under-privileged background and lack of powerful patronage. She taught me to a be a little more sceptical about people and their motivations and I introduced her to a Jewish working-class world that was totally unfamiliar to her but that she slowly (and perhaps only partially) learned to cope with.

I had become a little lax with some of my Orthodox observance in my postgraduate years and it was Shulie and her strong commitment to traditional but tolerant Orthodoxy that drew me fully back into the fold. I developed a very close relationship with her family and felt especially at home with her parents. Elly was honest, direct and undiplomatic and although it took me a little time to warm to her Viennese reserve, I grew to respect and admire her many qualities and her tolerance of a difficult marriage. Edmund (Muni) was by origin from the same Galician background as my father but he had had an upbringing in sophisticated Vienna and a university education which had put him one generation ahead of Dad. But the humour, the intensity, the industry, the family loyalty, the ability to survive major misfortunes, and the refusal to be anything other than himself, whatever the cost to him and others of refusing to compromise, were characteristics that were wholly reminiscent to me as the son of Pinḥas Reif.

Shulie and I, when we were not studying, spent most of our time together and greatly enjoyed each other's company. I even took her canvassing with me for the Labour Party in the constituency of St Marylebone, held then by Quintin Hogg (Lord Hailsham). We did not have much luck in identifying Labour voters in that area and one woman took the trouble to quote to me a maxim that has been attributed to Winston Churchill but seems to have predated him. 'Young man', she said, 'Anyone who is not a socialist at the age of 20 has no heart. Anyone who remains a socialist after the age of 40 has no head.' I was very cross with that comment at the time (I was 22) but began to understand it very well and sympathize with it totally some 25–30 years later! Perhaps more importantly, Shulie and I exchanged our first, exciting kiss on the dark staircase of a tenement in Mr. Hogg's constituency. The swing to Labour in that 1966 election was almost 3 per cent but, if I am not mistaken, it was somewhat less in St Marylebone!

I was, however, not yet ready in the spring and summer of 1966 to commit totally and even went out occasionally with other girls, just to maintain my independence, perhaps also because I was still afraid of being rejected in love. Shulie knew this and also knew that making a fuss about it might frighten me off. She decided to be patient. During the long weeks of the summer vacation, when I was in Edinburgh and she in London, I fully expected her to find another boy-friend and to inform me from afar that all was over between us. I even wrote to her along these accusatory lines on a regular basis. She was hurt by this and obviously not yet able to understand the deep psychological reasons for my lack of confidence in female loyalty and affection. I was perhaps half-hoping to be rejected again so that I could avoid having to commit and having to risk all.

Commitment and Marriage

But commit and risk I did, when we got together again in October 1966. It became clear to us, and to all our family and friends, that this was now the real thing. She acquired teaching experience by taking a class at Kenton and we would travel there together on a Sunday morning. When I was at home in Edinburgh for short periods, I would drive my Mini overnight from there to London on Saturday night. At that time, there were only a few short sections of high-speed motorway and the journey could take up to ten hours, especially in inclement weather. I would arrive early on Sunday morning, have a quick shower, daven, and eat breakfast, before picking Shulie up and going off to teach and administer at Kenton!

During that year, 1966–67, I shared an apartment in Ossulton Way, in Hampstead Garden Suburb, with my friends Mayer Nissim and Peter Ebstein, so that I was not very far away from Highfield Gardens in Golders Green, where Shulie lived. I spent Shabbat with the Stekels and attended, with Muni, an early morning shtiebel (a service held without formality usually in the home of a Rabbi or communal leader). I took to the fast and furious services like a duck to water and have preferred that kind of minyan ever since, although it has not always been possible to find one quite as quick. Elly was a great cook and Muni's mother, Sarah, an outstanding baker. They of course spoiled me and I loved it. I would play games with members of the family on Shabbat afternoon, demonstrating how bad a loser I could be. Unlike Muni, and Shulie's brother, Ronnie, to whom I also grew fairly close, I did not boast when I won but, again unlike them, I was certainly petulant and bad-tempered when I lost. Shulie needed to teach me how to cope more graciously with inconsequential defeat.

My parents and sister Sharron (Cynthia was by then in Toronto) were due to be in London in January 1966 for a family wedding. This seemed like a grand opportunity of introducing the families to each other. The Reifs came over to Highfield Gardens on a Thursday evening and I was expected to pop the question and make the announcement. I lost courage at the last minute and had to wait for the next meeting of the two families on the Sunday to take the plunge. Both families were overjoyed and plans were made for a swiftly arranged engagement party in the Stekel home soon afterwards, in March. With much of the catering done at home, few formalities and a relaxed atmosphere, it was truly a lovely and happy occasion. We made plans to get married in the autumn. Shulie was not keen to continue with her studies but preferred to undertake full-time kindergarten work. Since she always loved little children (for her, the attraction was especially in the fact that there were no sides to them, and what you saw was what you got), this suited her well and brought us some income.

I was hoping for another research award for 1967–69, which I subsequently received, and the Kenton teaching and headmastership would also bring in the remainder of what we needed for a simple life. I hoped I would complete my doctoral dissertation in 1968 and then perhaps find some form of academic or educational employment. Between the two of us, if I recall correctly, we had savings of less than £2,000. We therefore concluded that we should have a small wedding, rent a modest apartment, buy some simple furniture, and live according to our limited means. We even checked out a small but comfortable apartment for rental in a relatively inexpensive section of Highgate.

Muni was decidedly not of the same mind. He had just lost his court case and had to pay a hefty fine and everyone was expecting him to be bankrupt. 'How will it look to all my business associates,' he argued, 'if I make a small wedding for my daughter, and if the young couple have to rent a modest little place to live? They will decline to do any business with me and I shall l never recover from these setbacks.' When the Six-Day War broke out in June, we saw this as a wonderful excuse to have a small wedding. We could argue that we would rather give the money to support Israel. To no avail. He had used up all the family money, including the substantial endowments in the name of his two children, and had borrowed extensively. Ever the supreme optimist, Muni would now take on even more debt to make a large wedding but would later recover financially and it was his intention (alas, never fulfilled) to ensure that the family members were reimbursed.

So, preparations were made for a large wedding at the Brent Bridge Hotel between Hendon and Golders Green. Where Shulie and I were able to follow our own preferences was in the matter of the ḥuppah (wedding ceremony). After strongly pressing our case, we were permitted to have our friends as the officiants and to relegate all the right-wing Rabbis whom Muni felt he had to honour to less central roles. Jeffrey Cohen was the Youth Minister in Hampstead Garden Suburb and was able to arrange for our ceremony to take place there, led by himself, by Rabbi Cyril Harris of the Kenton Synagogue with whom I had worked for a number of years, and by a cantor with a lovely voice, Shem Terry, who was studying at Jews' College too.

If the Highgate option was a non-starter for Muni, and we (and he) had limited funds, what were we to do? A new apartment block, High Mount, had just come on to the market in Station Road, Hendon, a much more walkable distance from the family home in Highfield Gardens and, for that reason alone, much favoured by my future father-in-law. The cost of a tiny apartment, with a small fitted kitchen, roomy lounge and reasonably sized bedroom was £6,200 and he would somehow ensure that a deposit was made and a mortgage was arranged. It was not an easy time to find a mortgage but Muni finally persuaded the Bristol & West to underwrite the risk, assuredly with himself as guarantor. The accommodation was indeed beautiful and we managed, with our savings, to buy the little amount of furniture that was needed.

Just how we would be able to meet the cost of the hefty monthly mortgage was not discussed. Press-ganged into accepting the arrangement, we made the purchase and hoped, as impecunious and optimistic as Mr. Micawber, that something would turn up. What indeed turned up were the incessant bills and a few months after the wedding we realized that we simply could not afford the cost of the lovely flat that we were occupying. We would have to think of some alternative. Meanwhile, the legal costs of making the purchase constituted another headache. In the presence of Muni, the lawyer presented us with a bill for over £300. I looked at Muni and he looked at me. 'I am grateful to you for doing it at a reduced price,' he said to the lawyer, 'and I am sure that Stefan can write you a cheque for that amount.' With no more than about £800 left in my account, and with feelings of frustration and resignation, I wrote the cheque.

Wedding Woes

And now to the wedding day itself. All went well until the ḥuppah was over. Our friends had done us proud in every respect at the ceremony and it was time for everyone to make their way to the banqueting hall. I should add that I was very jolly throughout the religious formalities and this seemed somehow to antagonize Muni. 'This is not an occasion for levity,' he harshly informed me. The reminder of the day was not as Shulie and I would ideally have wished it and there was indeed not much levity in it for the two of us. We were whisked off in the bridal car (actually Uncle Bert's large Cadillac) and were able to spend the traditional few minutes together and have a little snack before joining the guests. Having made our entrance into the reception hall, we were surprised to see that neither my parents, nor Shulie's grandmother, had arrived. Shulie's cousin, Sammy, had been given the responsibility for ferrying them over from the synagogue to the hall but his father, Bert had apparently instructed him to take some Rabbis first. Without my presence there to ensure that matters were smoothly handled (as had been the case with previous meetings between the two families), my parents were left behind, almost last to leave. The only extenuating factor that prevented them from seeing this as a calculated and personal snub was that Shulie's grandmother was also waiting with them. By the time they arrived, they were, to put it mildly 'not happy bunnies' and they lost no time in informing me of how they felt. I felt powerless and distressed.

There must have been around 300 guests, only about 50 of whom were from the Reif side. We had pleaded with my father-in-law not to allow a long list of super-Orthodox Rabbis to recite their platitudes but he felt obligated to indulge them and the result was again a painful one. They heaped praise, some of it in Yiddish, on the Stekel family and had virtually nothing to say about the Reifs, whom they did not know of course, although one of the rabbinic eminences must have had some second thoughts about this since he added, at the end of his lengthy oration, a sentence along the lines of 'and I am sure that the groom also comes from a good family'. My Uncle Abe was one of the later speakers and he tried to rectify the situation and indicate the impressive eastern European background, the traditional values and the industry of my grandparents and parents. Sadly, this only served to consolidate my parents' impression that they had been slighted.

I should add that prior to the wedding one of my cousins had managed to find newspaper reports of my father-in-law's court case and 'thoughtfully' regaled my parents with this salacious information. Ignorant of the true situation as they were, some of my mother's family were under the

12. Marriage to Shulie, 1967.

impression that I was marrying a millionaire's daughter and they found new ways of indulging a long-standing jealousy and resentment of me and my achievements. If all this was not enough to prevent Shulie and me from actually enjoying ourselves, she was also nervous about damaging or staining her beautiful wedding-dress. There had been insufficient money to buy such a beautiful garment and she had therefore hired it. The condition was that if there was as much as a speck on it, it could not be returned but would have to be purchased outright. By the time we reached the West End Hotel that we had managed to book for ourselves for two days, we were exhausted and disappointed and wholly conscious that our parents had truly not taken the trouble to ensure that it would be our 'happy day'. They had been primarily concerned with themselves. It was a lesson that we tried to absorb for future reference.

Happiness Alone

There were only two weeks left before the Jewish New Year festivities so we had only two lots of sheva berakhot to celebrate with family and friends before we could finally get away from it all and enjoy each other's love and company. We certainly could not afford anything very expensive by way of a honeymoon so we travelled in our little Mini across to Holland and spent a week or so in Scheveningen, near the Dutch capital, The Hague. We relaxed, loved and laughed a lot, and saw many interesting parts of the country. We did, however, soon have to return to our teaching duties, as well as to our family commitments. Shulie had had an amusing experience on the Sunday before our wedding. She had told her class at Kenton that she was getting married and they had all wanted to know to whom. When she replied 'to Mr. Reif', they inquired incredulously whether she meant their very own headmaster, Mr. Reif. On receiving this confirmation, one of them shouted out 'Oh, your poor thing!'

So it was that we spent the year of 1967–68 as a young and happily married couple in the luxury flat that we could not afford. Shulie assisted at a kindergarten and I made progress with my dissertation. We both continued to teach at Kenton Synagogue classes. We managed to meet the costs of our groceries with the £5 that she earned at the kindergarten but that meant eating at least one, if not usually two, weekend meals with Muni and Elly in Highfield Gardens. That was no hardship but it did make clear to us that our financial situation was less than wholly solvent and that we could not continue in this way for any serious length of time. We helped each other to cope with the domestic responsibilities and there were of course the usual shocks to overcome. We had mini-explosions in the kitchen when we did not quite know how to deal with pressure cookers or when Shulie forgot to cut the potatoes that she was baking in the oven.

We found some little pellets in one of the fitted kitchen cupboards which turned out to be mice droppings. These little rodents had no respect for the degree of luxury of the buildings, insouciantly making their way up from the ground floor via various shafts and pipes and finding some delicious treats awaiting them. The *Hendon Times* made no less a meal of this story about the luxury flats than the mice had made of the chocolate that they had fortuitously discovered in one of our food cupboards. Members of both families visited us regularly and it was a special pleasure to have my little sister Sharron with us to stay. She has the happiest memories of that occasion to this very day. I also remember sitting at my desk working on a chapter of my dissertation when the news broke in August 1968 of the Russian invasion of Czechoslovakia and the end of the Prague spring and the more liberal Dubček regime. It certainly made me more than a little suspicious of Soviet socialism. With some welcome help from Muni, we exchanged our 1964 blue Mini for a 1967 maroon one.

Now What?

I also needed some serious encouragement from Shulie in my academic adventures. I had completed a draft chapter and submitted it to Dr. Wieder. No more than glancing at a few lines, he returned it to with an air of contempt, declaring 'This, sir, is beneath criticism.' I sat at the chapter for hours and could find no more than a few minor matters to amend and I asked Shulie to look at it for me. She confirmed that it all seemed perfectly in order and convincing, as well as being well composed. It was with fear and trepidation that I handed the 'revised' item to Dr. Wieder a week or two later. I heard nothing from him. When I gingerly broached the subject with him, his reply was simply 'Yes, yes, this is alright. Carry on in this way.' I realized, with important support from my new wife, that this was simply the master's way of keeping me under control and ensuring that I would

13. Professor Naphtali Wieder, 1905-2001.

strive for the highest levels. Similarly, when I found a large amount of relevant source material for my topic, I reported to Dr. Wieder that I was drowning in the data. His reply was: 'You will drown, sir, or you will learn to swim.'

Following the Pesaḥ holiday of 1968, Shulie began to feel nauseous in the mornings and, after a visit to the doctor, we were thrilled to be informed that the next generation was on its way. We thought we would keep the news to ourselves for just a little while but were frustrated in this endeavour by an incident during the walk home from Golders Green to Hendon one Shabbat afternoon. Shulie simply could not avoid the inevitable result of an awful attack of nausea and spewed the results into the gutter beside the pavement, not very far away from the Hendon Adas Synagogue where we often went to daven that year. We knew that somebody was bound to have seen this, drawn the obvious conclusions and resolved to make some comment to Elly. We therefore immediately phoned both sets of parents that evening to pass on the news that they were to become grandparents. This was warmly welcomed of course but the transmission of the information had been made not a moment too soon. The next morning a neighbour phoned Elly to report what she had seen the previous day on Brent Street. Once the weeks of nausea were over, Shulie felt very well and the pregnancy proceeded without incident. The new arrival was, however, destined to take place many hundreds of miles away from Hendon.

Although I still had one more year (1968–69) of my William Lincoln Shelley award, I began to apply for academic posts. Hoping that I could finish my dissertation within a year, I had made up my mind to opt for an academic career, and both Shulie and I came to the conclusion that moving away from London would probably not only solve our economic difficulties but also give us the opportunity of being ourselves, building our own lifestyle and making decisions more independently. Two of my older colleagues, Irving Jacobs and Jeffrey Cohen, were now teaching at Jews' College and I half expected that I might also be offered at least a part-time post. Chief Rabbi Brodie would have none of it. It had been reported to him that I had been seen on a Shabbat entering the elevator at Stuart Tower in Maida Vale during my year in that apartment block and, without any explanation being requested, that was enough reason to veto any appointment.

In fact, given our clashes over the years, I cannot imagine that Dr. Zimmels would ever have contemplated the possibility of having me on his academic staff. He thought, probably correctly, that I would not be prepared to toe his theological line. At University College, there were also developments in funding and in appointments but Siegfried Stein, although one of my supervisors, saw me as a Wieder product and ultimately preferred to appoint those whom he saw more genuinely as his own students. I thought that my abilities, my achievements, my energy and my personality would be enough to win me an academic position, not realizing then how much patronage mattered, nor appreciating the degree to which appointments committees had their own agendas.

I duly made four applications that year for an academic appointment. In two cases, I was not even invited for interview. In a third, I was interviewed and felt that I had won over at least some members of the committee. Sad to relate, at least for me, there was an internal candidate who had more support than I did. It was said that he was nearer to the completion of his doctoral dissertation than I was. In fact, he spent so much time teaching in that university that he never did complete it. The fourth post was advertised as a lectureship in Modern Hebrew in the Department of Hebrew and Semitic Languages at the University of Glasgow. Money had been raised by the Memorial Foundation for Jewish Culture in New York, the Cultural Attaché of the Embassy of Israel in London, and the local Jewish community. The idea was to complement the teaching of Biblical Hebrew with some classes in rabbinic, medieval and modern Hebrew. In the first two areas I felt wholly competent but in the third I had studied assiduously with Menahem Levin at Jews' College but it was not my research field. I read up everything I could lay my hands on about modern Hebrew literature and was delighted to be called for interview. After the results of the previous applications, I was a bit dismayed. If I had not been successful with jobs that were suited to my qualifications, how could I expect to be appointed to one that was less suitable? These doubts notwithstanding, I was happy to be on a short-list.

My day in Glasgow went well from beginning to end, and feelings of dismay slowly gave way to those of elation. As well as being interviewed by some of the leading professors in the faculty of humanities, I met the newly appointed Professor of Hebrew, John Macdonald, the cultural attaché at the Embassy of Israel (I think it was then the novelist, Aharon Megged), the representative of the Glasgow Jewish community, Dr. Berl Cutler, himself a local physician (a popular family doctor in a very disadvantaged area of east Glasgow) but with an active interest in ancient Canaanite and the Ugaritic inscriptions of the fourteenth pre-Christian century. At the end of an exciting day, I was able to telephone Shulie and report that I would be teaching at the University of Glasgow from October 1968 and that we would be moving north a few weeks earlier. My parents, who lived in Edinburgh, were overjoyed at the prospect of seeing us, and our expected addition to the family, on a regular basis since we would be living only an hour's journey away. My parents-in-law were proud of my achievement but a little disappointed at the distance from London to Glasgow that would now separate us. At the same time, it took some of the pressure off Muni. It did not matter too much to him if we lived a modest life 400 miles away from north-west London where none of his friends and business colleagues could be witness to our less than affluent status.

11

Belonging to Glasgow
(1968–72)

Moving North

In the summer of 1968, Shulie and I travelled for a day to Glasgow and found a house at 37 Whitton Drive, Giffnock. It was in an area of south Glasgow that was heavily populated with Jews, many of them committed to such activities as synagogue attendance, communal arrangements, religious education and Zionism, and some devoted to all these. The advantage of Whitton Drive was that it was, like Graffham Avenue nearby, a less splendid street, although still off the Braidholm Road, and near Kilmarnock Road, and the prices were therefore less than in other parts of Giffnock. We made an offer of £4,600 and were delighted to be able to finalize the deal. House purchases in Scotland were (and are) much simpler than in England. The market being then very depressed, we could not sell the London apartment and were therefore forced to take a bridging loan against the deeds of the apartment to enable us to buy the Glasgow property. The University of Glasgow had an arrangement with Glasgow City Corporation whereby newly-appointed faculty members could obtain a mortgage from the Corporation at a reasonable rate. We took advantage of this and were all set for our move.

One of our major concerns was to ensure excellent conditions for the birth of our expected baby towards the end of December. My mother's first cousin, Abe Goldberg, was the only other academic in the family. He was the son of her mother's sister, Rachel, and was at that time the Regius Professor of Materia Medica at the University of Glasgow. I had known him when I was a small child and he was a medical student, and I was certainly somewhat in awe of his brilliance and his success in carrying off numerous prizes. I rang him and asked for his advice. He explained that there was an excellent maternity department at the Queen Mother's Hospital in Yorkhill near the River Clyde in Glasgow. Two groups of people were entitled to be treated there: the local folk who lived in a fairly run-down area nearby, and those who worked at the University of Glasgow. The academic in charge of the department was promoting and developing the then fresh notion that having a baby was not a disease and that it should be treated quite differently from other medical conditions. He pioneered and championed novel ideas, including diagnostic ultrasound tests, little lounges where prospective parents could sit and chat, and classes to explain to them how to deal with the delivery and their new offspring. His name was Ian Donald and he was Regius Professor of Obstetrics and Gynaecology in the University of Glasgow. Abe advised us that Shulie should register with his department.

In the late summer of 1968, we left our Mini in a special parking lot at Euston Station. It was to join other cars being ferried northwards on the same train on which we were travelling ourselves. We could retrieve it soon after our arrival at Central Station in Glasgow and drive it to our new home. We booked 'sleepers' (overnight accommodation) but the noise, the excitement, and the narrow bunks that we occupied, as well as Shulie's inability, six months pregnant as she then was, to get into a comfortable position, meant that we did not sleep very much. Our removals van had picked up our possessions, such as they then were, in London a day or two before, and we had arranged to meet the van on its arrival at the house in Glasgow.

My parents came through from Edinburgh to help us and to feed us as we sorted out our new home. For the first day or two we ate with them, either what they brought us, or at their home in Edinburgh, and we sorted out our new home as best we could. The house had a sloping front garden, a fairly long back garden, and a garage at the side, adjacent to the back-garden. Inside there were a kitchen, a dining room and a lounge downstairs, and two large bedrooms and one tiny one upstairs. There were a number of major problems. We had only the furniture from our small luxury apartment in London; we had to prepare a bedroom for the new arrival; I needed a little study in which to work and where to keep what was then still a rather small collection of books; and we were very short of money. Neither set of parents was able to assist us, and we therefore had no choice but to rely wholly on our own resources.

Paying Bills

We had both been educated by our parents that hire purchase (paying by instalments with added interest) was an invidious choice of transaction by which to buy anything. One paid much more than the original cost, the goods were not yours until you had paid off the debt, and it was cheaper to borrow money from the bank. Alas, we could not do the latter since we were at the limit of our borrowing capacity because of the mortgage and the bridging loan. So, we swallowed our pride, ignored the principles dictated by our families, and bought about £120 of furniture on what was at that time in Scotland called 'the never, never', i.e. you *never* stopped paying. In fact, within little more than a year we had paid off the debt. Having dealt with the acquisition of furniture, the two of us then got busy with renovating the house. We painted and decorated it ourselves, we put up all sorts of shelves, we outfitted the kitchen as best we could and we prepared a room for the baby. Shulie, in her seventh month, knelt on the floor with me in the rear bedroom (overlooking a large green area and a rugby pitch), fixing linoleum ties to the floor of the baby's room. Shulie made lovely nursery curtains for that room, and we put together whichever items we could in preparation for the arrival. My father gifted us a selection of tools to add to the little tool box we already had.

Shulie and I coped with most of the necessary handwork but I did have problems with some of the electrical wiring and we had to pay for an electrician to do some of the less simple work. His attendance to complete some electrical work in the house created a major problem of language and comprehension. I had arranged for him to set up a time-switch which would enable us to have the lights coming on and off on Shabbat as we needed them. Knowing that Shulie's understanding of Glasgow dialect was not quite all it should be, I explained to him what I wanted and off I went in our Mini to the University. An hour or so later I received a frantic call from Shulie. He was asking a question and she had no idea whatsoever what he meant or how she should reply. 'Put him on to me', I suggested to her. 'Wha' are ye askin ma wife, Bobbie?', I inquired. 'A dinnae ken if I should fix a cu-oo', he replied. 'Aye, Mr, will ye be wantin' sometimes to cu i' oo'?' It dawned on me that his reference was to a cut-out switch that Shulie would have known as a by-pass. I duly advised him that we did indeed require such a switch, and Shabbat observance was thus rescued for us by Bobbie the Glaswegian electrician.

That winter I also began to cultivate the back garden and we soon had a wide selection of vegetables that I had planted there and that we could use enthusiastically in our cooking from as early as the spring of 1969. Giffnock Synagogue was a fifteen-minute walk away and I enjoyed going there, especially since they had an alternative minyan downstairs which was quicker, less formal and greatly to my taste. The synagogue was very well run by Dr. David Granet and Mr. Philip Jacobson, both lovely people, with whom we became friendly. Dr. Granet was in fact our family doctor. The

Rabbi was Jeremy 'Rooky' Rosen, the son of the late Rabbi Dr. Kopul Rosen. He was very learned in Jewish religious law, held a Cambridge degree in philosophy, and was an excellent speaker and a very popular individual. His brother Mickey had been one of my fellow students in Jews' College and his younger sister Angela later came to Cambridge to study. He was a young, handsome bachelor at that point and, unsurprisingly, very much in demand in Glasgow social circles. He welcomed us very warmly (once having us over for a dinner which he prepared and hosted with a local girl-friend) and had all sorts of ideas of how we might assist the community. He had an MG sports car and I remember well one visit that he paid us. His car made that wonderful throaty noise as he parked it in front of our house. He did not open the gate but jumped athletically over it. As he left an hour or so later, I saw my neighbour glancing at him through her window. She came into our house a few minutes later to ask who that gorgeous man was. When we told her that he was our Rabbi, she immediately retorted 'If he could be my Rabbi, I would be happy to convert from the Church of Scotland to Orthodox Judaism!'

New Boy

After our major and broadly successful efforts to get the house into order, I had to report to the University in order to plan with Professor Macdonald exactly what and when I would be teaching. John Macdonald was a gentle and friendly individual who had recently been appointed to the chair of Hebrew and Semitic languages at Glasgow. His specialization was in Samaritan studies and his approach to the Hebrew Bible was a linguistic rather than a literary or theological one. He had little knowledge of rabbinic traditions or of medieval and modern Hebrew and was therefore very enthusiastic about having me in his department. That first day with him was a real education for me, in a rather unexpected way. I arranged to meet him in his office on the ground floor of the department of Hebrew and Semitic languages which was attached to the faculty of humanities and located in a house on South Park Avenue, very near the University Library, the main offices of the University and the two main roads running through the area of Hillhead, all of which effectively constituted the campus. As planned, I arrived at around 09.30 and we chatted about my academic interests, about scholars we both knew and about how Shulie and I were settling down in Glasgow, until about 10.00. He then explained that we should go over to the College Club (for faculty members) where we could have a cup of coffee together. It was almost 11.00 when we returned to his office and we spent about ninety minutes talking generally about the courses I could give. The choice was very much up to me. He then invited me to join him for lunch in the College Club. I found some items that I could eat with a clear Orthodox conscience (Orthodox Judaism was more relaxed in those days than it is today) and he introduced me to various members of the University who were also lunching there.

When we returned to his office at around 14.15, he took me to the other rooms in the building and introduced me to the faculty and administrative staff of his department, as well as of the department of Old Testament, also based there but attached to the Faculty of Divinity. That day, and indeed on some subsequent visits to the department, I met a scientifically serious but congenial John Mauchline, a dry and somewhat suspicious James Martin, and an iconoclastic Robert Carroll, among the 'Alttestamentlicher', and William Barclay who was a distinguished scholar of the New Testament and a major media personality at that time. That took until nearly 15.30 when he suggested that we had both had a busy day and should make our way home. When Shulie asked me about my day, I reported precisely how industrious and productive it had been!

In October 1968 my first term as a university teacher began, and I felt pleased and challenged. In the course of the next four years I taught various courses in Biblical and rabbinic texts, and in modern Hebrew literature. My university students were those taking a first degree in Hebrew or in Old Testament but there were also mature students who came to hear my lectures simply as auditors, with no examinations to worry about. I, from my side, could teach them whatever I wished and took the opportunity of brushing up on such modern writers as Bialik, Tchernichovsky and Agnon. I have to admit that I do not recall the names of the undergraduates but I do remember those 'auditors', mainly from the Jewish community, who sat in the Modern Hebrew classes. Two of the most regular attendees were the sisters Dorothy Isaacs and Esther Mellick, originally from a learned and observant Jewish family in Sunderland, the Bermans. They were both qualified teachers and very keen on Hebrew literature and they responded well to my teaching and to the progress that we made. They also became close friends to Shulie and me during our stay in Glasgow and indeed for many years afterwards.

One of the other participants in the modern Hebrew class, although on a less regular basis, was David Daiches Raphael. He was a distinguished scholar of moral philosophy who was at the time Edward Caird Professor of Political and Social Philosophy at the University of Glasgow and went on later to Reading, and then Imperial College, London. He had a quiet and thoughtful manner but he knew, and sometimes demonstrated, a fair amount of knowledge about Jewish religious thought. I had a personal link to him too. His wife, Sylvia, was the daughter of Rabbi Dr. Salis Daiches who had officiated at the wedding of my parents in Edinburgh and who had himself been no mean student of philosophy. David had added his wife's maiden name to his own.

John Macdonald ran an Akkadian seminar for faculty and graduates at which we all read cuneiform texts and Berl Cutler provided a similar service for Ugaritic. We greatly enjoyed the camaraderie as well as the scholarship that these seminars generated and it undoubtedly broadened my Semitic education and my interest in the Ancient Near East. There were also meetings of the Glasgow University Oriental Society and I was privileged to deliver a paper to its members, which was subsequently published in its transactions. My closest colleagues in the department came to be Robert Carroll, who was there when I arrived, and Robert Gordon, who joined our department, soon after I did, to replace James Martin who had left for St Andrews. The two Roberts and I had much fun together since we shared a sharp and radical sense of humour. I was still at that stage politically to the far left and this gave me much in common with Carroll. At the same time, I was religiously committed, a commitment that was well understood by Gordon who was himself a devout Christian.

Friends and Groups

My closest personal friend was a scholar with whom I had attended the Hebrew Classes of the Edinburgh Synagogue some 20 years earlier. Alexander Broadie had distinguished himself as a student of philosophy at Edinburgh and Oxford and was by then a young lecturer in that subject at Glasgow. We renewed the friendship we had had as youngsters and took to meeting regularly to play squash. This went on throughout my time in Glasgow until Alexander had to undergo a serious operation and was therefore no longer able to exert himself to the degree demanded by that game. I should add that Shulie and I often entertained these students, colleagues and friends at home during our time in Glasgow. Like her mother, she became an excellent hostess and a superb cook and baker. I learned very soon after we married that my best role in the kitchen was to be, at best, the *sous-chef* and to respond efficiently to her requests for menial assistance and to the need for clearing up afterwards.

Two other seminars with which I was associated in Glasgow were held in domestic rather than institutional settings. There was a group of professionals, mainly in their fifties and sixties, who met regularly in each other's homes to discuss topics of Jewish interest. They included Berl Cutler and Ralph Steen (another local physician), other medics, teachers, lawyers and business people. They were all fairly learned in Jewish matters (usually Zionists but mostly not very Orthodox) so that one could usually be assured of an efficient and interesting presentation, as well as a lively discussion afterwards. As was fairly customary in those days, it was a men's club. The wives sometimes went out to their own social commitments but not before preparing some delicious snacks for us to enjoy after our intellectual exertions were completed.

That group had been established for many years but while we were in Glasgow a younger set of professionals, led by Paul Vincent, decided that they wished to emulate the example of their seniors but with women involved too and with a broader and even more radical agenda. I joined that group too and spent many happy evenings with both sets of what I suppose we are entitled to call the local intellectuals. These two groups were an accurate reflection of the Glasgow Jewish community's pride in its identity, interest in its history and commitment to maintain at significant levels its Hebrew and Jewish knowledge and understanding. There were also more Orthodox circles with which we were friendly but most of them were inclined to be suspicious of the historical approach. They preferred the traditional learning methods of the yeshivah world where Talmud was studied as it had been for centuries with the emphasis on how Jewish religious law came to be played out and little, if any, reference was made to linguistic, literary, cultural or theological history. The joke in yeshivah circles was that they knew what the talmudic teacher Rava said, while we who had studied in a rabbinical seminary and university knew what colour of trousers he wore.

Tanya's Arrival

All those activities were well under way by the time that we had to face the immediate prospect of becoming parents. Shulie was due towards the end of December and, almost on time, on Sunday evening 22 December she began to have labour pains. All had been arranged with the Queen Mother's Hospital so we made our way there and she was examined by one of the obstetricians. He thought that there was still some time to go and that she might be more comfortable at home. So we returned, empty-handed, as it were. The pains occurred on and off between Sunday evening and Tuesday evening, when they became a little more severe and we finally checked into the hospital. Poor Shulie, she was by this time exhausted and the labour pains still dragged on the whole day of 25 December until our beautiful little daughter finally made an appearance, with her daddy present as was then permitted at that progressive hospital, at 21.24 on Wednesday evening. The doctors had constantly promised Shulie all day that they would ensure that she had a Christmas baby. We did not feel that we wished to hurt their feelings by saying that this was not the first thought on our minds. We had prepared everything at home and, within a few days, mother and baby daughter were in Whitton Drive and we were now a real family. The timing had been brilliant since all this had occurred during the University's Christmas vacation. By the time I had to teach again, matters were fully under control. Shulie, being Shulie, had established a fairly good routine for her and Tanya. We both liked the name Tanya but Elly's mother had died a few months earlier and so we thought it appropriate to add one of her names (she was Golda Miriam) so that our little girl became 'Tanya Miriam'.

Sources of Income

We had hoped that the Glasgow appointment, in addition to being an academic blessing, would bring an improvement in our financial situation. In London our total annual income had been around £1,200 and, when we saw that the salary being offered in Glasgow was £1,470, we felt that we would be able to balance the books without difficulty. We had failed to take account of the need for a bridging loan, the demands of a new house and a new baby, and, above all, the slice of our income that would be taken by the Inland Revenue. We had paid very little tax in London because most of my income was from my studentship and now my university salary slip at the end of the month showed a net receipt of less than £100. We were therefore earning less and spending more. I could not bear to see the huge overdraft on our bank statement which took account of the bridging loan. To make me feel better I asked the bank to open a separate loan account, which of course made no financial difference but it did make for less depressing reading! We realized that we would need some other income and to that end we responded favourably to a request from the local Jewish community for Shulie to teach in their synagogue classes on Sunday mornings. In addition, she took on some private teaching which also helped.

That brought us a connection with Baruch and Nehama Epstein and their children. Rabbi Rosen had appointed him as Giffnock Synagogue's director of Jewish education and, given our background as teachers in

London, he thought that we could work with Baruch in various ways. Baruch was a remarkable character. With his long dark beard, his frock-coat and his wide-brimmed black hat, he looked the image of the eastern European yeshivah Rabbi but he was in so many ways totally different from what that external appearance would have led you to expect of him. He had studied many years in a distinguished yeshivah in Jerusalem and was therefore very learned in Jewish religious law. He had also functioned as a communal Rabbi in outlandish places. In addition, however, he was fully at home in art, music, handiwork, various languages, and, perhaps above all, obsessive pipe-smoking. He had been brought up in a secular home in Sweden, with almost no Jewish observance, and his pre-yeshivah education had been broad and multi-cultural. He would often expatiate on the wonderful nature of non-kosher cuisine and how tasty all the forbidden foods had been. He inspired many youngsters but was not always equally successful in maintaining relations with their parents who were suspicious of him and not entirely sympathetic to his radical ideas and uncompromising Orthodoxy. Baruch had all manner of novel ideas about how to teach, often involving aids such as games, booklets, boards, questions and answers, and diagrams, at a time when most teachers simply taught a lesson and expected children to absorb its content.

Rabbi Rosen left Glasgow in 1971 to become Principal of Carmel College, the Jewish 'public school' that his father, Rabbi Dr. Kopul Rosen, had established near Oxford, and Baruch joined him soon afterwards. But for most of our time in Glasgow we worked together and while Shulie taught for him on Sunday mornings, his wife Nehama looked after our daughter and, later, our son too. Nehama was from a Swiss family and, as one would have expected, her family was not enamoured of Baruch and his ways. Nor, I imagine, would they have approved of the ramshackle, untidy and not very clean house that he and Nehama ran. When Tanya was about two years old, she accompanied Shulie on a brief visit to the Epstein home in Graffham Avenue to speak to Nehama. Nehama was in the kitchen so Shulie sauntered in with Tanya in her wake. The little two-year-old took one look at Nehama's kitchen and cried out 'What a mess!' To her credit, Nehama laughed and said 'She is right; it is a terrible mess.'

Religious Commitments

In the early part of our stay in Glasgow we often spent the Jewish festivals with one of the two sets of parents, either in Edinburgh or in London. When it was the former, Shulie had to put up with a standard of Orthodoxy that was not quite as high as that to which she was accustomed, while in the case of the latter I had to tolerate the strictest form of Orthodoxy that was characteristic of the circles in which Muni and Elly operated in Golders Green. Our own home in Glasgow followed a religious practice that was somewhere between the two and suited Shulie and me. Once Tanya was with us, we decided to change our pronunciation of Hebrew from the Ashkenazi to the Sephardi so that the children would in due course find it easier to deal with modern Hebrew. Observing Shabbat and the ḥagim and eating kosher were *de rigueur*. Some incidents come to mind in connection with observance. There is a tradition not to eat meat for the week before the Fast of Av which commemorates the destruction of the first Jerusalem Temple in 586 BCE and the second one in 70 CE. I was aware that some codifiers opted for less stringency in this respect and so I did not mention to Shulie in one of the first years of our marriage that we had entered that non-carnivorous period. So, we sat down to a meat meal. For some reason the issue of the calendar came up and she was horrified about my laxity. How could I possibly allow us to eat meat on those days? I received the impression that for her it was almost like eating on Yom Kippur.

We did not use the telephone on Shabbat but had an arrangement with the family in Edinburgh and London that, if there was a real emergency, they should phone three times, with only a minute or two between each call. On my return from synagogue one Saturday the phone rang and we ignored it. It then rang again. Once more, no response from us. When we heard the third ring, we became nervous and jointly decided that there must be an emergency. I answered and the voice of Berl Cutler at the other end piped up 'Oh, I thought you didn't answer the phone on Shabbos!'. Muni and Elly had sold their large house and moved with Savta into an apartment in Melvin Hall, on the Golders Green Road. When we were staying with them for one of the ḥagim – I think it was Rosh Hashanah – we had finished early but there were many other worshippers, mainly of the very Orthodox type, who were still making their way home up and down Golders Green Road, all of them of course suitably attired. Tanya was on the balcony watching the Jewish world go by and stated with great astonishment 'Look, a Baruch. Another Baruch. And another Baruch...'

And Then There Was Aryeh

It was during our Passover visit to London that our second child was conceived. I was somewhat surprised that Shulie was so relaxed at that time about family planning arrangements and only afterwards did she admit that it had been her hope all along to have another child soon after Tanya. By the summer, we knew for sure that we were to have an addition to the family. Elly had always repeated the mantra that she had learned from somebody whom she clearly admired. 'Having one boy and one girl is a gentleman's family.' When we broke the news to her, she took me aside and with a very straight face – a 'mother-in-law face' one would have to admit – she said 'You know, Stefan, nowadays there is no need for couples to have babies every year.' I don't think she ever believed Shulie when she told her that it was all planned. Experienced as we now were, we knew what we had to do to prepare for no. 2, who would sleep in a carry coat for the first few weeks and then move into the children's room. The obstetrician told Shulie that her baby would be born in the middle of January and she countered with the view that her calculations made it more likely that the birth would take place at the end of January. Like many physicians, he nodded and ignored her.

Shulie reported for a check-up in mid-January and they were concerned that the baby was showing no signs of arriving, or even contemplating an arrival. They suggested that they might have to induce. Shulie once more expressed her view that the end of January was more correct than the middle and they again took no notice. By Friday 30 January they were determined that there was to be no further waiting and that they would induce Shulie before lunch-time. Since Shabbat was around 16.15, and I had promised to be at the birth, it was going to be a rather tight affair. In addition, I had to look after Tanya and asked my neighbour to take over that duty when I was called. I received the summons at around 2.00 pm and by the time I got to the hospital the birth process was fairly advanced. I joined the group around the expectant mother and saw only women. Assuming (as one did in 1970) that they were all nurses, I asked if no doctor was to be present for the birth. One of the women looked sternly at me and replied 'I *am* a doctor!' So Aryeh was born in the Queen Mother's Hospital, Yorkhill, thirty minutes before Shabbat which gave me just enough time to make telephone calls to the grandparents and to sort out Shabbat arrangements. My friend Alexander Broadie baby-sat with Tanya after I put her to bed and I was able to get over to the hospital to visit Shulie and to see my new son.

On Sunday we made plans for the brit milah (circumcision) to take place on Friday, on his eighth day, and Elly booked to arrive on Wednesday by air and to bring with her lots of kosher food from London for the celebratory meal. Aryeh, however, had other ideas. When I met her at

Abbotsinch Airport, as the Glasgow airport was still widely called, it was with the news that we would have to eat some of the goodies and freeze the others, because my little son had changed colour, to yellow, and was suffering from new-born jaundice. The ritual was finally completed on Sunday 9 February and the name given was Aryeh, after my paternal grandfather, Dov after Shulie's maternal grandfather, and Binyamin, after my Auntie Bessie. Bessie (Yiddish name Buna), my mother's sister, had died a day before Aryeh was born and been buried only a few hours before he entered the world. When I registered his birth, the friendly official asked what 'Aryeh' meant and I replied 'a lion'. He then inquired about the meaning of 'Dov' and I said 'a bear'. He must have thought how crazy these Jews were since he did not ask about the meaning of the third name!

I looked after Tanya while Shulie was in hospital and she and I became very close in that week, so close, in fact, that when Shulie came home Tanya kept running to me rather than to her and this upset Shulie a little. On the Monday, while mother and baby were still in hospital, I took Tanya with me to Edinburgh to visit the family who were sitting shiv'ah (seven days of domestic mourning) for Auntie Bessie and although she was only thirteen months old she loved the company and they all adored her. She was a very sociable little girl, but this was not an example followed by her newly-arrived brother, who tended to be very impatient with company. When the family and/or friends became too much for him he would achieve the peace and quiet that he craved by retiring to his bed and sucking his thumb.

We soon had to acquire a Silver Cross double push-chair and Shulie would wheel them in that splendid contraption to the local supermarket and the other local shops. Glasgow passers-by would often look at the little ones and say what 'bonnie wee bairns' ('beautiful little babies' in Scots dialect) they were and it was not uncommon for them to put some silver, say a sixpenny coin, into the push-chair. One woman stopped to admire the two little ones and to offer Shulie some advice: 'Remember that this is the happiest time of your life and make sure that you enjoy every minute of it.' Shulie certainly did. She was a superb and devoted mother to Tanya and Aryeh and she just loved dealing with them, especially at that pre-school age. She would undoubtedly have welcomed more children and I fear that it was I who was not enthusiastic about this.

Young babies and the whole business of dealing with them did not appeal greatly to me but that was not the main concern. I felt that we were obligated to do whatever we could for our children and to set them up so that they had a better start than we had had. I hoped to be able to do this for two but saw no way of taking on such a responsibility for four. To say that our incompatible views about the ideal family number caused tension would be an exaggeration but she felt in some way deprived and I, although committed to my view, felt more than a little guilty. I became more tolerant and contributed more when our children were older and, interestingly, their teenage years presented me with less of a problem than it did Shulie. I could not abide the illogicality and tantrums of tiny tots while she had little patience with teenage moods and complexities.

Another Challenge

If we may now return to earlier months, before Aryeh joined the family, it was during the academic year 1969–70 that I took on a new educational responsibility. I needed additional income, as well as a closer relationship to the wider Jewish community, and the philanthropists who were supporting and running the Glasgow Jewish Board of Education needed someone to take charge of the Glasgow Hebrew College. The major and most active philanthropic figures at that time were Efrem and Melech Goldberg who owned a large departmental store in the middle of the city, with numerous branches around central Scotland. Efrem's son, Mark, was also coming more into the picture, and Shulie and I became friends with him and his wife, Linda, the daughter of Dr. Ralph Steen.

Glasgow had a generous supply of traditional Lithuanian Rabbis who occupied the pulpits of at least seven shuls at the time. Most of them were devoted to the Glasgow Yeshiva headed by Rabbi Shapiro, or at least to the educational methods and Talmud-centred study represented by the yeshivah world. The less religiously Orthodox but no less educationally committed Board of Jewish Education ran the Glasgow Hebrew College. It had been founded in the 1920s by an outstanding educator called Nathan Morris and had taught its students a broader Hebrew, Jewish and Zionist curriculum than that of the yeshivah, even extending to Ivrit be-Ivrit, that is, teaching the pupils modern Hebrew by way of speaking that language and not merely studying its literature. By 1969 it needed some fresh blood and some novel ideas and I agreed to take over as its principal. In the three years that I served, we had some excellent teachers and some outstanding pupils and I believe that an educational impact was made on the wider community.

Calderwood Lodge, the only Jewish primary school in Scotland, had been opened in 1962 and its places were then still almost fully occupied by Jewish pupils. I worked closely with its headmistress, Pauline Gaba, and some of its teaching staff. In drawing up the Hebrew College's curriculum, planning the classes and guiding the teachers, I tried to apply the methods that I had learned at Jews' College from Menahem Levin and from our professors at the Institute for Education of the University of London. In order to encourage the senior pupils to take up (at least part-time) teaching within the Jewish community, I organized an educational workshop and had local Rabbis, teachers and educators come and share their knowledge and experience with the senior pupils who were in their mid- or late teens. These latter then had to contribute articles to a booklet that I produced (*Glasgow Hebrew College, Educational Workshop 1970-71*). I should add that some of the pupils also baby-sat for us at times.

Dr. Reif I Presume

My own tertiary education had been neatly rounded off by the completion and submission to the University of London of my doctoral dissertation on the prayer-book of Shabbethai Sofer of Przemsyl in the late spring of 1969, when I was 25. In those days, one typed out one's work with at least one carbon copy and making changes was no easy matter, involving whiteners, new carbons and the re-planning of pages. There was also the matter of ensuring the safety of one's work. Shulie often joked about those occasions when the dissertation accompanied us on our dates for fear that the sweated scientific labour of some three or four years might somehow be lost, misplaced or stolen. When all was done, I took it to a local Glasgow typist. She was paid by the page and that is the reason why it extended to over 600 pages and not some two-thirds of that size, as it could and should have done. It was during the first academic term of 1969–70 that we had to travel from Glasgow to London for my oral examination. We made the journey by car of course since we had so many of Tanya's baby items to take with us and it was in any case a cheaper way to travel.

We stayed with the Stekels in Melvin Hall. Shulie was in the sixth or seventh month of her second pregnancy and well enough to look after Tanya without difficulty. The three of us made our way by car to Gower Street, since the oral examination was to take place at University College, where Dr. Siegfried Stein, who was chairing the examination committee, was departmental head. The other examiners were to be Dr. Naphtali Wieder and Dr. Jacob Leb Teicher, Lecturer in Rabbinics at the University of Cambridge. We parked nearby (no real problem in Bloomsbury in those days) and Shulie agreed to walk around with Tanya in a push-chair while I attended for examination. In the days before mobile phones, we arranged that, when my viva was completed, I would simply walk around the area until I found my wife and daughter and could tell them whatever news there would be.

I came to know Teicher much better when I took up an appointment at Cambridge some four years later. He was a very learned scholar of rabbinics, with a traditional background in talmudic studies, but had also received the more scientific and historical education of an Italian university and rabbinical seminary. He was a wholly original thinker with brilliance in the study of Jewish and Islamic philosophy. He preferred novel rather than established viewpoints, declared as spurious manuscripts that many regarded as authentic, and refused to accept that the Dead Sea Scrolls belonged to the Second Temple period of Judaism. He dated them much later. Whatever his final views of any topic, his process of analysis was always stimulating and worthy of attention. During my oral examination, I answered various questions about my dissertation and took the opportunity of explaining my impressions of Polish Jewish culture in the sixteenth and seventeenth centuries.

All was going very well until Dr. Teicher began to make his own, very personal suggestions, about some of Shabbethai's comments on the prayers. At first, I took issue with his novel interpretations and then I saw that Wieder was indicating to me with a barely perceptible but clearly intended sideways shake of his head that it would be wiser not to dispute. I followed his guidance and began to express my gratitude for Dr. Teicher's interesting and thought-provoking remarks that I would examine closely and, where necessary, add to my dissertation. This was diplomatically the right thing to do although I must admit that, in the end, I made only two or three minor adjustments, with gratitude duly expressed to my Cambridge examiner. The examiners dismissed me but told me to wait outside and a few minutes later they told me informally that I would be awarded the doctorate as long as I made those (minor) amendments suggested by Dr. Teicher.

Many months later, Wieder confided to me that the examiners' report was an excellent one and would stand me in good stead in my career. Well, yes, maybe, as I was later to find out. I located Shulie and Tanya somewhere in Gower Street and imparted to them the good news. I am not sure that my ten-month-old daughter fully appreciated the significance of the development but, when she saw how happy her parents were, she also smiled! Mr. Reif was to be Dr. Reif. There was great elation among all the close members of the Reif and Stekel families. Either during that visit to London or a later one, we were invited to the Wieders for a coffee and my august teacher told my attentive wife how unfortunate she was to be in the

UK and not in Germany or Austria. In those countries, not only would her husband now be Herr Dr. Reif but she would be Frau Dr. Reif!

Rabbi Gottlieb

Mention of Austria reminds me of my relationship with a Vienna-trained Rabbi in Glasgow. When I arrived in Glasgow, I was warned to steer clear of the controversy between Rabbi Dr. Wolf Gottlieb, who was the spiritual leader of Queen's Park Synagogue, and head of the Glasgow Beth Din, and Rev Dr. I. K. Cosgrove, minister of the Garnethill Synagogue. Growing up in Edinburgh and reading, as we did in the family, the Glasgow Jewish newspaper *The Jewish Echo*, I was aware of the tensions between these two distinguished rabbinic personalities and took care not to tread on their toes. In fact, I maintained amicable relations with both. I had been in Bnei Akiva with one of Dr. Cosgrove's sons, John, and my teacher of Tanakh, Eli Cashdan, was the brother of Mrs Dorothy Cosgrove. It was, however, to Rabbi Gottlieb that I grew close during my Glasgow period.

When I became Principal of the Glasgow Hebrew College, I asked to see Rabbi Gottlieb because I knew that he had played a major role in Jewish religious education in London in his younger years. He welcomed me very warmly and was most helpful. Perhaps the Ḥasidic background of my father's family in eastern Galicia was a factor since he himself had also been born in 1910 in that strongly Ḥasidic area, some 50 kilometres west of Tarnopol. His image as an uncompromising and strict interpreter of Orthodoxy was one that he had acquired in Glasgow but was not a reflection of his education, background or personal warmth. He had moved to Vienna in 1921 and had studied at the Vienna Rabbinical and Teachers' Seminary (Israelitisch-Theologische Lehranstalt) and at the University of Vienna, as well as being an accomplished violinist. He had been a highly active religious Zionist and college principal, saving many of his pupils after the German-Austrian *Anschluss* of 1938 by arranging for them to go to Palestine.

I studied Talmud texts with Rabbi Gottlieb in Glasgow on a weekly basis and found in his approach that combination of Ḥasidic warmth and scientific criticism with which I was thoroughly familiar and to which I was personally partial. My friend Alexander Broadie joined me for this shi'ur. Sadly, at that time, Rebbetsin Betty (Bracha) Gottlieb (the sister of Chief Rabbi Rosen of Rumania) was terminally ill and it was clear that this was heart-breaking for the Rav. I can still remember some of the important insights that he offered into rabbinic thinking and the Ḥasidic anecdotes and sayings that he relayed to us. ('When you are welcomed into the next world you will not be asked why you were not Moses or Abraham, only why you were not yourself.') He even kindly came to speak to my students at the Hebrew College when I arranged my educational workshop. After retiring in 1976, he lived in Jerusalem and prepared an edition and commentary of Obadiah Sforno's sixteenth-century pentateuchal commentary for Rav Kook publishers.

Family Visits

Once the financial situation had improved, our personal lives became more enjoyable. With two adorable and well brought up little children, a large circle of friends, beautiful countryside to visit within a 30-minute drive, and an active Jewish community, we felt comfortable and settled. The Stekels visited from London, with Muni's mother, known to our kids as Savta, and the Reifs, including Sharron of course, drove, or took the train from Edinburgh, only a little over an hour away. ('Is Savta their Sharron?' little Tanya once asked about the Stekel trio). Muni had an important business associate in Glasgow and would occasionally fly up for the day to have a meeting with him. One incident immediately comes to mind since it demonstrates that I was still something of a young hothead.

I had collected Muni from the city where he had had his meeting and was bringing him home for a meal before driving him to the airport for his return to London. As we made our way south on the Kilmarnock Road, I was doing about 35 miles per hour. Muni, as was his wont, offered some advice. 'You know, the limit is 30 here and you are doing five over the limit.' Not wishing to take advice from my know-it-all father-in-law, I increased speed and said 'And now I am actually doing 40!' Needless to say, at the next turning in the road a policeman waved me down and issued a ticket. To his great credit, Muni said not a word. He didn't have to. On at least one occasion (when Muni and Elly were travelling), Savta came on her own to spend time with us in our Glasgow home. She was then almost 80 years old but was still lively, active and good company. She was a superb baker and she taught Shulie how to make the family's favourite cakes and pastries. Once, when she was making blintzes, Tanya stood on a stool next to her eyeing the whole process. As she watched she began to sing to one of the nursery tunes she had been taught by Shulie: 'blintzes, blintzes, more blintzes, more blintzes.'

When my father came to visit, he would often bring an item to add to my tool box or advise me how to tackle a particular do-it-yourself problem.

14. Shulie and Stefan with Mum, Dad, Cynthia and Sharron, 1967.

I still have (and sometimes use!) a car battery charger that he purchased for me almost 50 years ago. Sharron came fairly frequently on her own and developed a very close relationship with Tanya and Aryeh. We did our best to treat her as one of the nuclear family and to give her a good time. This brought her great pleasure at that stage of her life but some angst later when she resented the fact that she was not actually one of our children but my little sister. She had her own bed on the landing outside our bedroom and I recall one incident when she was suffering from attacks of nausea. Tanya came to her bedroom door to see what was going on. 'Please don't send me to bed again. I want to watch', she exclaimed.

It was while we were in Glasgow that Cynthia informed us that she was going to marry Kalman (Karl) Bielak and that she very much wanted the ceremony and the dinner to be held in Edinburgh. She also asked my mother to make her wedding dress, quite a challenge for poor Mum. Kalman's parents would come over with them for the family festivities. I remember well the day they all arrived at my parents' home in Edinburgh. I welcomed Kalman and, in my usual, naughty style, expressed sympathy that he was going to have to put up with my sister! He told me in a rather serious fashion that if I wished to get on well with him, I should not make such remarks. I quickly back-pedalled and bore the lesson in mind as often as I could, but perhaps not as often as I should. I helped to organize the ḥuppah and the dinner party, including the seating arrangements. I recall that I suggested that Muni and Elly would probably enjoy sitting next to the Adlers since they were both originally from Vienna. I think that it worked out. I also had to make some payments here and there in spite of our less than affluent circumstances. I was anxious to help my parents and therefore did what I could. Sharron and Tanya enjoyed their special roles as bridesmaid and flower-girl. The date, 21 June 1970, was also the date of the World Cup Final between Brazil and Italy and guests kept leaving the dinner and popping into the hotel bar to check the score. I think it was Uncle Abe during his speech who announced, for those who were anxious to know, that Brazil had won 4–1.

With the Kids

There were Jewish shops not far away in Giffnock and also some that still operated in the old Jewish 'ghetto' of Gorbals, almost seven kilometres to the north and nearer the city centre. One of these was still being run by the son of a baker from Edinburgh who had been a friend of my grandfather. He was Bob Plancey and my mother had been a close friend of his sisters Gertie and Freda. An older sister (Minnie) was the Bubbe of my friend from school days, Jack Goldberg. Bob and Ray's son, Alan, studied at Glasgow Yeshivah, became a Rabbi and had a successful career as a much-loved spiritual leader in Boreham Wood, sixteen kilometres north of central London, and then as a helpful Jewish chaplain at Luton Airport. Alan and I always regarded each other almost as family.

For Pesaḥ and Rosh Hashanah we usually made our way to Edinburgh or London but, children's health being what it is, that could be a risky proposition. I think it was in 1970 or 1971 when both kids were suddenly suffering from some infantile ailment and we had to cancel our Pesaḥ visit to London at the last minute. We had placed no order with our local grocer for special Pesaḥ food. We quickly bought what we could but what was no longer available was purchased for us in London by Elly and a boxful of those groceries was taken to Euston Station to be conveyed by train and picked up by us at Central Station in Glasgow. Crisis averted.

At about that time, Chabad came to Glasgow. Not everyone was keen on this development but the Chabad Rabbi and leader, Chaim Jacobs, was such a delightful person, that the community as a whole came to love him.

His children were brought up in the city and I believe that a son of his now runs part of the Chabad project there. In my early days in Glasgow I got up at about 06.30 or 07.00 and did my davening at home. Once I was the Principal of the Hebrew College, I felt I should attend the daily minyan in Giffnock shool and so I began to rise a little earlier. One of the teachers at the Hebrew College was Monty Greenspan and his father also liked to go to shool each morning but was finding the walk a little tiring. I gave him a lift each morning and therefore started the day with more than one mitzvah. Our close friends, Jeffrey and Gloria Cohen, joined us in Glasgow in 1970–71. He became the spiritual leader of Newton Mearns congregation, a little further south than Giffnock, and studied for his doctorate at the University of Glasgow. He later took over the Hebrew College when we left Glasgow. It was a great pleasure for both families to be able to spend time with each other.

Numerous friends were physicians and I remember two particular incidents relating to dietary health. We were feeding eggs to Tanya when one of those physicians was visiting us. He introduced us to what was then the fairly new concept of cholesterol and warned us to avoid high intake of items that would produce an excess of fatty deposits in our blood. On another occasion, Shulie was trying to feed Tanya who was unwell and would not eat. Shulie was coaxing her but with no success. Dr. Granet popped in for a routine visit (as family doctors did in those distant days) and saw what was going on. 'Mother. Mother, do you have an appetite when you are feeling unwell? Leave her alone and when she is hungry she will eat.' In the final year of our stay in Glasgow (1971–72) we exchanged our four-year old Mini for the second-hand Hillman Minx of friends who were leaving Glasgow for the USA. That was not a good move and I wistfully recalled more than once my father's lesson that buying second-hand cars was like buying someone else's 'tsores'.

In that final year, Tanya began to attend the Jewish kindergarten nearby and was beginning to develop a delightful Glasgow accent when we left the city. Aryeh was still at home and delighted to be there with his Mummy. Like Tanya, he loved to listen to stories, poems, nursery rhymes and music and, long before he went to kindergarten in Cambridge, he was reading some of his nursery books from beginning to end and turning the pages at the correct point. Visitors were greatly impressed that one so young could read but of course he had simply memorized the content. He could perform as well as his elder sister but not to order. If family and friends wished to hear a performance, they received one from Tanya but Aryeh, when invited, usually replied 'No, don't want to'. When Aryeh was about two he sat down at the piano one Shabbat and began to play, or rather, to pound the keys. Very tolerantly and kindly, Shulie said 'Aryeh, we do not play the piano on Shabbat.' His immediate and confident reply was 'Yes, but I do.' Shulie also started teaching the children to recognize the Hebrew letters, using the global method (via whole words, not individual letters) that we had promoted at our Educational Workshop.

Back to Israel and Academic Progress

Although deeply committed to the Jewish state and its then still early development, Shulie and I had not visited Israel for a number of years. I had last been in 1960 and she in 1964. In 1970 we both had the opportunity of rectifying this and updating ourselves on what was going on in the Holy Land. There was a teachers' group from around the UK which was to spend two weeks in Israel in the spring of that year and the lay leaders and funders of the College agreed that it would benefit me and the College very much if I participated. They would pay half the subsidized cost of £100 and I would pay the balance of £50. This was still a great deal of money for me and I when I had to make the payment I went to the bank and drew the necessary notes, not I might add from a machine, but from a teller, as matters were conducted in those days. I hung my coat up in the University Club while I had some lunch, forgetting that the cash was still in my pocket, and when I returned it had, to my considerable consternation, been stolen. I telephoned my friend Berl Cutler and told him I could no longer afford to take part in the trip because of the theft. Within minutes I received a call from his Board of Jewish Education colleague, Dr. Ralph Steen, telling me that I should go ahead with the trip and that the balance would be met by a donation. To his day I feel indebted to these people for their kindness and for such a display of confidence and support.

Although it was difficult to leave Shulie and the children behind, I had a very successful fortnight, learned a lot about Jewish education (both theory and practice), updated myself on developments in Israel and made some new pedagogical friends, including Dr. Bernard Fisher of Liverpool. We were addressed at the Hebrew University of Jerusalem by Professor Haim Hillel Ben-Sasson, who taught medieval Jewish history, and I was brave enough to challenge (deferentially) one of his interpretations, which seemed to me somewhat narrow, and even a little parochial. He was not greatly pleased and my Israeli friends later told me that senior academics in Jerusalem were not used to having to justify themselves in any way to younger scholars, even if the challenge was made in a polite fashion. I also managed to spend some time with my College friend, Mayer Nissim, who had made aliyah and was living with his wife, Ruth, and children, in Jerusalem.

I suggested to the University and to the College that I would like to return to Israel for the month of September, 1970. I wished to develop various educational and academic contacts and to update my knowledge of modern Hebrew. I believe that both institutions contributed to the cost but this time I took the family and of course we paid for their travel ourselves. We rented an apartment in Ben-Zion Street in Kiryat Moshe where many distinguished members of the National Religious (Mizrahi) circle were then resident. We also took the opportunity of visiting Elly's cousin, Willie (Zeev) Low (Lev), already a distinguished and internationally recognized scholar in the field of microwave physics, as well as an ordained Rabbi who contributed in a major way to the suggested solution of halakhic problems via scientific knowledge and innovation. He later established what became popularly known as Makhon Lev (Jerusalem College of Technology). His eldest son was a senior member of one of the crack units of the Israeli army and involved in a number of high-profile and successful ventures.

On the first morning in Jerusalem we took our double push-chair, with the two children, for a walk to the local makolet to buy some groceries. We were no sooner down the stairs and out the front door when a woman stopped us and addressed Shulie in Hebrew in a somewhat accusatory tone. 'Ima, Ima, bli kova'im beḥom kazeh?' ('Mummy, mummy, no hats for the children in such hot weather?') It was indeed a hot September and we quickly absorbed the lesson. Tanya took to the heat but Aryeh was perhaps too young for this major change of temperature and was not too happy during our stay. The only cereal widely available in those days in the young state was a gruesome concoction called Shalva, a kind of tasteless popcorn. Undaunted, Tanya ate her way through it but, after a few mouthfuls, inquired whether it was 'poddits or coddits', i.e. porridge or corn flakes, both of which were familiar to her from Glasgow.

Shulie and I took the opportunity of visiting our friends, Mayer and Ruth, and their two little children. Mayer, as native Arabic speaker and a university graduate in that language, was by then employed as a ketsin mimshal (administrative officer) in the West Bank government, liaising between the Israeli government and the local Palestinian Arab sheikhs and their families, such as the Jabaris in Hebron, who were the mayors of the various cities. Mayer knew all these local mayors and introduced us to three of them and they all welcomed us most warmly, even sending out for bottled drinks which we said we preferred (being actually afraid of a cholera outbreak that had occurred not very long before). It seemed that Moshe Dayan's policy of normal relations between Israelis and Arabs was working well. Sad to say, all those older and wiser families were later overthrown and the current impasse owes much to the fact that their pragmatic and moderate views were replaced by more intense Palestinian feelings and policies. Mayer took us to the natural pool in Sachne where he and Shulie swam and I realized that I would soon have to rectify this failure on my part if I wished to have future fun in the water with my children. Sadly, it was to be the last time I saw Mayer.

Since 1968 we had met various scholars and writers who had visited Glasgow and were able to renew some of these acquaintances during our visit, as with Dr. Yehuda Friedlander who taught Modern Hebrew literature at Bar-Ilan University. Perhaps even more importantly, we took the opportunity of introducing ourselves to a number of leading academic figures at the Hebrew University, such as Ezra Fleischer, Chaim Rabin and Ezra Zion Melamed. This would prove useful at a later stage of my career when I was initiating new projects in Cambridge that were greatly in need of Israeli contacts and support of one sort or another. When friends of ours saw the double push-chair they begged us to leave it with them in Israel since no such thing was available, or was available only at a grossly inflated price. We did so and they paid us the price of a new one, which we promptly purchased on our return to Glasgow a few days before Rosh Hashanah.

Before the Michaelmas term started, I went over one Monday morning to the University pool and asked one of the swimming instructors if he could teach me to swim. He said he could and was true to his word. By the end of the week I could report to a delighted Shulie (who loved swimming) that I could now go swimming with her and the children. She had mentioned to me a few months earlier that she was determined to take the children swimming as soon as possible, perhaps a salutary warning about what I needed to do. It is not easy to learn to swim in your twenties but I accomplished it and have enjoyed the sport even since.

By that time, I had been able to spend much of my day at the University of Glasgow in the University Library, doing research and preparing articles for publication. I was no slouch in this connection and successfully submitted three or four items to scholarly journals. Shabbethai Sofer, the meaning of Hebrew words, especially in the light of rabbinic Hebrew, and medieval Hebrew grammar were among the topics I tackled. Andrew Macintosh in Cambridge published an article in which he took insufficient account of the work of medieval Hebrew philologists. I published a rejoinder and we not only became close friends but he turned into a keen enthusiast for the study of their work. I also published more popular items in the *Jewish Echo*. Already at that stage I was becoming slowly aware that academics could benefit from exposure to the wider world represented by the media. I also began to write scholarly reviews.

Shuddering Halts and a Restart

The possibility of what might have been a few more years of contributions from me and Shulie to Glasgow Jewish education was brought to a shuddering halt by an interview with two local philanthropists. From their viewpoint they were proposing better financial management but for me it was an example of educational short-sightedness. It had occurred to them that the same philanthropists were now contributing to the cost of the University lectureship and the College principalship. Why could the two posts not be merged into one and the total remuneration reduced? I told them that I was not in favour of this but received the distinct impression that it would not be more than a year or so before their proposal was foisted upon me. I did not have the patience to put up with a less than satisfactory arrangement even for a short time and I returned home from that interview to tell Shulie that we would soon be packing our bags and seeking greener academic pastures. Precisely how and where was not clear but my mind was made up that we should move on. I felt that I had energy, ideas and the necessary talents to achieve something major in the academic world but I had to find somewhere that we would allow me to do just that. Little did I then appreciate that energy, ideas and talents were precisely those characteristics that were often resented by mediocre colleagues with institutional power.

For about a year and a half between the end of 1970 and the late spring of 1972, I conducted correspondence with three institutions regarding a possible academic appointment that would take me away from Glasgow. I had attended my first conference of the Society for Old Testament Study in Oxford in 1970 and introduced myself to John Emerton who had in 1969 been appointed Regius Professor of Hebrew at Cambridge in succession to David Winton Thomas (my BA examiner). I knew that there were some posts coming up for appointment at Cambridge and I spoke to him about those. He encouraged me to apply and I received the impression (perhaps wrongly?) that I would have a reasonable chance of being considered. John Macdonald was convinced that Cambridge would snap me up. I duly applied but meanwhile two Oxford graduates (as Emerton himself was) were also among the applicants. It seems that Emerton was keen to have them appointed. I was interviewed for one of the posts and have it in writing from the appointments committee's secretary that they valued my qualifications highly and only regretted that they did not have two posts to offer.

Many years later it was leaked to me by a somewhat inebriated academic (today no longer in the land of the living) who was present that the committee was divided and that Emerton was firm and resolute until his preference was agreed by the others. When asked whether Dr. Reif was not an accomplished young scholar, he responded 'Yes, perhaps altogether too accomplished.' I was deeply disappointed at the time but I gradually came to the realization that there were likely to be numerous factors involved in such decisions and a failure to be appointed was not necessarily an indication of one's inadequacies. I shall have more to say about my interaction with John Emerton when I write about my Cambridge years. I felt miserable that John Macdonald's optimistic prognostications had proved unjustified but ultimately resolved to look forward rather than back. I had at the back of my mind the idea that I would somehow one day prove my worth to Cambridge. Quite how I would do that was not at the time apparent to me but I determined that if a future opportunity arose, I would not be found wanting.

Another iron in the fire, or, if you like, another bread cast upon the waters, concerned Tel Aviv University. It was still at that time a newish academic centre with a more open mind about its appointments than the Hebrew University of Jerusalem. A distinguished graduate of the latter, Aron Dotan, had been among the early appointees to lectureships at the newly established Tel Aviv University and by 1970 was head of its department of Hebrew language, associate professor, and an acknowledged expert in the development of Hebrew grammar and Masorah. I knew that Tel Aviv was anxious to make strides in those fields and thought that my research and publications on the work on Shabbethai Sofer might be of interest. I began a correspondence with Professor Dotan that seemed promising but appeared to me to have fizzled out after some weeks. Unfamiliar as I then was with Israeli academic procedures, this was in fact a misinterpretation on my part. When he met me a year or two later at a conference, he asked me why I had gone elsewhere and not waited for Tel Aviv to make its decision. He explained (somewhat too late of course) that in Israel such matters always take months to resolve.

Assuming that nothing would come of my approach to Tel Aviv, I looked at even more distant climes. I had seen an article in the *Jewish*

Quarterly Review by Abraham Katsh, the president of Dropsie University in Philadelphia, and an eminent Hebraist, that dealt with the non-standard pointing found in some Hebrew manuscripts. Since that had been one of the areas in which I had specialized during my doctoral studies, I wrote a response and had it accepted for publication. I therefore thought that I might have a chance of some sort of appointment under Katsh at Dropsie. To my surprise and delight, I was offered (in a letter from President Katsh) a post as Assistant Professor of Hebrew Language and Literature at the princely salary of $12,000 per year with another $1,000 towards our removal expenses. My appointment was to take effect from 1 September 1972 and so we set about making arrangements for our departure from Glasgow and our move to the USA. What seemed like an exciting prospect loomed before us. Young as we were, we were unafraid of all the new challenges that this would present; on the contrary, we felt that it might be the beginning of a more settled period for us as a family and of a tenured academic appointment in the development of my career. Little did we understand at that point the urban setup in the USA, the situation at Dropsie, and the nature of American Jewish scholarship.

We were also under the impression that, given their common language, the UK and the USA had a similar culture. We soon appreciated that there was much about the UK that was European and much about the USA that was not. Our first encounter with American bureaucracy was at the American Consulate in Edinburgh where we had to attend in order to obtain our visas, mine for working and Shulie's for accompanying a working spouse. We went there with the two little children, as instructed, and were told to fill in the forms on the table. We went through the list of questions, ticking the boxes, and made solemn declarations along the lines that we were neither physically nor mentally deficient in any way, nor members of the Communist Party. We dutifully completed two forms and handed them back to the officer in charge. 'What about the children's forms?', he demanded, somewhat impatiently. I looked at him quizzically, stating that they were only 2 and 3 years old. 'You are required to fill in forms for each of them', was the peremptory reply. I have never been one for missing the opportunity of a humorous response so I immediately stated that I could not guarantee that they were not members of the Communist Party. My humour was not greatly appreciated. 'Do you wish to co-operate sir? If not, you will not be able to obtain the necessary visas.' And so, on behalf of Tanya and Aryeh, I completed the forms and answered all the questions, struggling to suppress my conviction that I was participating in something of a farce.

12

In and Out of Philadelphia
(1972–73)

Shipping and Flying

My teaching at Dropsie was scheduled to begin on 1 September and we knew it would take us a few weeks to settle into our new home in North America. We therefore arranged for our departure from Glasgow to take place in mid-July, 1972. We easily sold our home, cancelling the mortgage and being left with the sum of £6,200 that we had received from the sale of our original apartment in Hendon. We deposited the funds in our building society account where the rate was around 5 per cent and moving upwards. More of this financial management (mis-management?) will be noted later. The local Glasgow removers, Brewer and Turnbull, came and packed all our household goods into a 20-foot container, Shulie thoughtfully making sure that the children's favourite toys were the last things to be placed inside so that they could be the first items to emerge at the other end. We were amazed at just how much that container could contain. Once the container was gone, we bade farewell to our neighbours and our house and Shulie shed a few tears over the home where we had truly become an independent family with our own domestic arrangements, educational activities and Jewish lifestyle. We drove to London to stay with the Stekels until we could fly to Philadelphia and arrange for the delivery of our container to our newly rented home at 1625 West End Drive in Overbrook Park. We left the Hillman Minx with our father-in-law to be sold by one of his garage contacts.

That rental, initially for one year, had been pre-arranged by Tamar and Uzi Adini. Tamar's father, Sammy Low, and Shulie's mother Elly, were first cousins and the Adinis, although both born in Israel, had been in Philadelphia for a number of years. Uzi had degrees in Jewish studies and in education and had obtained a doctorate at Dropsie College. He was teaching at Gratz College (for training Jewish teachers) where he ultimately became Vice-President. Tamar had a similar educational background and was teaching at Akiba High School. They and their two young daughters were out of town organizing some Jewish summer camps when we arrived but they had very generously arranged for us to have access to their home, to borrow their second car, and to finalize the rental deal with the 'realtors', a new word for us who knew only of the somewhat clumsier English expression 'real estate agents'.

We went straight from the airport to their home in north-east Philadelphia, all of us of course suffering from jet lag. Tanya, aged three, and Aryeh, aged two, behaved beautifully, as they had done on the long flight (I think it was on TWA, one of the largest American airlines of those days) and we managed to find bedding for them and settle them down. It was a horribly hot and humid Philadelphia summer evening and we had been told about the air-conditioning, a device we had never seen in our lives. We managed to switch it on but not to control the temperature so we froze for most of the night until somehow I got the hang of the system of adjustment. The forecast was horribly unchanged in the morning and we wondered how we could possibly put up with such weather conditions. Luckily, the meteorological situation did improve after a few days.

When faced with a long list of essential matters to deal with, Shulie and I were never inclined to procrastinate so we had our breakfasts and drove over to Overbrook Park to sign the rental documentation at the office of the realtors. We had chosen the area of Overbrook Park because it had an Orthodox shool, some Jewish schooling, kosher shopping and relatively easy access to what was called 'Center City' and to Dropsie. Shulie had packed some of the basics so that we could survive and make the children fairly comfortable for a few days, while we did all the necessary shopping. We found one of the local supermarkets and were overwhelmed by its massive size and the huge range of products on sale. The children were equally overwhelmed when we took them a few weeks later to Toys R Us and they had money from their grandparents to spend on themselves. There were just so many toys to choose from that they both declined to opt for anything and needed to leave quickly. We felt the same way that July morning but we did manage to buy the basic groceries, including, of course, items stamped with 'OU' (for Orthodox Union) to indicate that they were kosher. We also learned that if one came late in the evening to some supermarkets, they were usually selling off at low prices items that they did not wish to keep until the next day.

The next stop was the port of Philadelphia to obtain clearance for our container which had by then arrived by sea from Glasgow. Armed with all the necessary documentation, we found the container arrival area, and located the office and the officer who would deal with us. It should not be forgotten that in those days there were no GPS systems and one really had to use a map and work out how to reach one's destination without much help from any device or individual. The officer scanned (with his eye, I might add!) our list of household goods and offered us a choice. 'I can either charge you a standard rate by my estimate, or we can go through the whole container and decide precisely how much tax you should pay.' We opted for the standard rate, which was under $100, and booked the arrival of the container for a few days later. We returned to the parking lot to find that we had a puncture on one of the tyres (or should I say 'tires'?). I found the jack, inserted it into the relevant part of the car undercarriage and started to turn the screw. To my astonishment the car did not lift, only the metal support descended into the tarmac! I realized that I had to locate and use a plate to hold the metal support and then succeeded in changing the wheel. All this was done in a temperature of about 85 degrees Fahrenheit (29 Centigrade) with help from Shulie and with two tired and overheated little children waiting in the car. I should add that those two little kids had to shlep everywhere with us since we had nobody with whom we could leave them.

USA-Style

Day after day we made all our arrangements. Two of the largest stores in Philadelphia at that time were Gimbels and John Wanamakers, both of them in the centre of the city. We parked (not so difficult in those days) and made our way there to buy such essentials as a bunk-bed for the children and some other furniture to add to the basic provision already in the rented property. All this could have been done relatively easily had we had accounts there. We soon realized that we needed to open accounts and so trundled along to the accounts department to do just that. When asked about our current mortgage, our other credit cards, our debts, and our overdrafts, we proudly declared that we did not owe anything to anyone. For us this was a source of pride; for the accounts department a clear indication that we had no credit rating and could not be offered an account! We managed to open a bank account and obtain a local Pennsylvanian credit card (soon to be told that it would not be accepted in any other state of the Union!) and somehow sorted out the credit rating by obtaining faxed letters from my father-in-law (or from his various property companies) that made all sorts of declarations about our credit worthiness. We still had little idea of what to buy where. I saw the need for a light summer jacket and tried on a few in a large men's clothes store. Each seemed much too expensive to me and when I indicated my budgetary reservations to the salesman, he asked me where I was from and I told him that we had just arrived from the UK. 'Well, sir, you better know that in the USA you get nuthin fir nuthin'. A lesson we soon absorbed.

We also needed a car. We drove to various huge showrooms and the two cars we liked best were in the Renault and Ford 'small compact' ranges. After driving a Renault, we went to the Ford dealer and test drove the Pinto, which we liked slightly better. Wishing to negotiate the price, I told the salesman that we had just driven a Renault and were thinking of buying it. 'No such car in the USA, sir', he confidently declared. I said I was quite certain I had driven the Renault, one of the French range, pronouncing it as one should as 'Reno'. 'Ah, you mean, a Renault' he said, pronouncing it fully, with each letter expressed, as the Americans did and do.

Our international driving licenses would do for a short time but we thought it best to take the test, which involved reporting to a test range where we had to drive through, over and under various obstacles, and demonstrate that we really could drive. That presented no challenge at all and went well for us both. We were then told we had to memorize all the data in a little booklet and would be asked ten questions. We opted to do so there and then. I concentrated on what I thought were the really important points while Shulie wisely memorized everything. She went first and got ten out of ten. When I was asked about what I thought were sensible questions I knew the answers but I had not bothered to absorb items such as the number of yards that one should leave between one's parked car and a water hydrant! I got seven out of ten, the minimum required to pass. Another important lesson: prepare according to the syllabus not according to what you personally think is important in it.

First Impressions at Work and at Prayer

Once we were fairly well settled, I had to make my way in our new Ford Pinto to Dropsie in North Philadelphia, to 'check-in', as it were. The building was a grand one from the beginning of the twentieth century. I was soon to appreciate that the academic grandeur of the institution could also be dated to many decades earlier. I was still, however, optimistic and enthusiastic. I introduced myself to the president, Abraham Katsh and his office staff, and to the few faculty members who were there in August. I also popped into the financial office to ask how I might obtain the $1,000 that had been promised towards our travel expenses. The financial officer disclaimed any knowledge of this and said that I would receive a $1,000 a month from the end of September and nothing more. I asked to see the President who supported that statement until I showed him his own letter with the promise of the travel expense. 'Ah yes, I remember now', he said as he telephoned though to the financial office and instructed them to issue a cheque to me for the sum agreed. That troubled me a little but there were many more troubling developments to come later. Meanwhile, I cheerfully pressed on and set up my two courses of four hours each for the whole year ahead, covering various aspects of Bible and Hebrew studies, with the emphasis on the medieval Jewish commentators.

The local Orthodox synagogue (Beth Hamedrosh) was only a few hundred yards from our rented home and I made my appearance there alone, on Friday evening, and with Shulie and the two children on Shabbat morning. The two children sat with me but were not far from Shulie either, since the seats were arranged in a semi-circle, the outer ring for the women and the inner ring for the men. We were warmly received and we had a chat with the Rabbi, Meir Cohen. He was born in Israel, a good speaker of modern Hebrew, with an impressive knowledge, a good oratorical style and a lovely sense of humour. He advised us that we should not rely on the local kosher meat but should order from Scranton, which was 200 kilometres north of 'Philly', as they mostly called the city. The meat was indeed of a high quality even if of course more expensive but Rabbi Cohen was now our Rav so we followed his advice throughout our time in his kehillah. From other members of the community we heard that it was not wise to drive the way I had done in order to get to Dropsie since the nearby section of North Philadelphia was a run-down area renowned for drugs, killings, thefts, bars and numerous funeral parlours to cater for its many deaths. We should use the expressway. It was upsetting to see such areas in what we had thought of as affluent North America. There were also hints from new friends about committing oneself to an institution and a President whose reputations were not, in the opinion of many locals, all that they might be.

Some other incidents occurred in connection with Rav Cohen and his congregation. Rosh Hashanah was in early September that year, so that we were attending the yomtov (or ḥagim) services quite soon after our arrival. In order to obtain a seat for what they called there 'the holidays' (Jewish festivals), one had to make a payment and also declare in synagogue one's gift to the congregation. Each person stood up and pledged a specific sum, saying that it was in honour of his family, or in memory of his parents, in the hope of a healthy year, or in recognition of the Rav. I declared that I would give a gift but without mentioning the amount or making any link with anyone or any ambition. The congregational leaders and the Rav looked a little surprised and even disappointed. When I arrived at the office the next day to make all the payments for the year, including a donation, the Rav happened to be there. He told me how impressed he was that I was the first to do so and to be so generous. He had thought that the non-mention of a sum meant that I would give virtually nothing. I explained that matters in the UK were a little more discreet than in the USA.

In Glasgow, we had converted a garden shed into a sukkah each autumn and now we had to decide what to do in our rented house. Having checked Sears Roebuck's printed catalogue (no onlines then!), we decided to buy a small tin shed that we had to put together ourselves. We set it up on our little terrace and were able to enjoy the Sukkot festival as it is traditionally celebrated. That DIY tin shed was our sukkah in Cambridge from 1973 until 1983 and somehow managed to survive the rigours of the British weather.

There must have been a regular attendance on a normal Shabbat of between 50 and 60, many of whom were observant, but the membership was much larger and most of them were less committed to Shabbat and kashrut. What was immensely important for them was the recitation of yizkor, the memorial prayer, for close relatives, that was recited on various festivals, and they attended in large numbers for that part of the service only, especially on Yom Kippur. The synagogue officials therefore stopped the service at that point and a few of the leaders went to the synagogue hall downstairs where they had arranged a yizkor-only service, precisely for such congregants. It took only a few minutes. Once that was over, they all went home or perhaps to their businesses. We had neighbours who had their own special way of celebrating the solemn fast day of Yom Kippur. When we made our way home for the break between the services in the afternoon, we saw a large group of family and friends standing on the terrace in front of their house with drinks and (impressively unkosher!) canapés. 'Happy holiday' they shouted over at us, as we struggled home with our empty stomachs and pounding headaches.

I got into conversation with the Rav about whether it was permitted, in strict rabbinic law, to drink non-Jewish wine. I argued that nowadays, unlike it talmudic times, there was no danger of its being used for any sort of idolatrous purpose and he countered that it was still forbidden. Knowing from the kiddush events that we had shared on Shabbat mornings that he was a keen whisky drinker, I then pointed out that many whiskies were matured in sherry casks and so had absorbed some of what he called forbidden wine. He was taken aback, a little perturbed and even somewhat downcast at this challenge. A week or two later, he came back to me with some counter arguments that he found convincing. As Blu Greenberg, who was an early champion of Orthodox Jewish women's rights, once stated 'Where there is a rabbinic will, there is a halakhic way.'

Kindergarten

We thought that Tanya would enjoy a local Jewish kindergarten and registered her for one that was, in its religious orientation, more right-wing Conservative than strictly Orthodox. The latter institutions tended to be less tolerant of personal variation than the former and at that time we were still of a liberal outlook on such matters. Shulie thought that Aryeh should stay at home with his Mummy for one more year and she enjoyed having him with her and continued to educate both children in Hebrew and English, as she had done from a very early age. Tanya soon came home able to 'pledge allegiance to the flag' but she never quite repeated the word 'indivisible' in the correct fashion since she had no idea what it meant, and no teacher appears to have explained the content to the children, merely taught them the declaration by heart.

Tanya was a very bright, precocious and pretty little girl who socialized well and she appeared to enjoy the classes and came home happy. It was obvious to Shulie that Aryeh was of a different social mettle and would need to have an alternative form of education when his turn came. There was a swimming pool not far away and Shulie walked the children over there so that they could enjoy the water. It also occurred to her that Tanya might be ready for swimming lessons. As a conscientious parent, she arranged for a local instructor to give Tanya some lessons. He told Tanya that she had to put her head under the water and she expressed strong objections to doing so. 'If you do not put your head under the water, you will not learn to swim.' Tanya's response was to march out of the water saying 'Ok, then I don't want to learn to swim.' Obviously, she was an opinionated young woman. Many years later she confided in me that she was a little suspicious of that instructor's physical attentions.

Friends and Family

We made friends by way of the community and also the various educational personnel with whom we became acquainted, including some from Temple University, University of Pennsylvania and Gratz College. Uzi and Tamar, whom we saw a number of times, were not our only family there. We also had the grandson of my father's Aunt Rose, Jeff Brown, and his wife and child with whom we made contact since they lived not very far from us. The next time I saw Jeff was in London 46 years later! We met and befriended the Brauners and the Tigays and were invited to their homes. All of them were astonished at the degree to which our children could behave, especially at the table during meals. There were others who consistently made the statement 'We must have you over sometime' but there was rarely any follow-up. It was like the question 'How are you?' for which nobody ever expected a real answer.

My parents had moved to Toronto a few months earlier and were pressing for us to visit them. We were short of money for the first month or two, so that when we decided to travel to Canada for a long holiday weekend in the late summer we booked tickets on the Greyhound Bus. The journey was about eleven hours, with various stops, a truly exhausting experience, but it was fairly cheap. At one of the stopping points, the driver, who was black, offered to help Aryeh to get down the steps. The poor little boy was not yet very familiar with that colour of person and burst into tears. Later that year he did see black workers emptying our garbage and when he saw a very well-dressed professional black American passing our house he declared to Shulie that he had just seen a funny looking garbage man. He gradually became more relaxed with black Americans as we encountered them in many of our activities. I had to coax him to use urinals with me on our various journeys and, when I had finally succeeded, we stood next to a large Afro-American, all three discharging our urine. As we were making our way to the sinks to wash our hands, Aryeh, who was bright, aware and had a sharp eye, turned to me and exclaimed quite loudly 'Daddy, that was the biggest penis I ever saw'! Our black friend seemed by no means offended but smiled appreciatively.

My parents were both working at that stage and were doing well, at first living in Karl and Cynthia's basement (not a happy experience), but then moving into a very comfortable rented apartment in a thoroughly Jewish area of Downsview, within easy walking distance of my sister Cynthia and her husband Karl and their little boy Yakov, then just over a year old. Cynthia was pregnant with her second, Simha, whom we saw on our later visits. She was an amazing hostess producing meals as if she was running a large kosher restaurant in the East End of London or the Lower East Side of Manhattan, with masses of choice for each course and nothing designed to keep one slim. Twelve year-old Sharron had an especially difficult time in the basement but enjoyed it more after they moved. She was also greatly thrilled when we and her little nephew and niece came to visit. My father took us to various interesting sites during our first visit and was very good with the children. He seemed at that stage of his life to be mellowing.

For our next visits with them, we drove by car and were therefore able to go out and enjoy some exciting places, including Niagara Falls of course and various delightful museums in and around Toronto. We took the children to many museums when they were little and the upshot of those visits was a determination on both their parts as adults rarely to visit museums! I had no idea that I was not permitted to park my car outside their apartment block overnight and I found a parking ticket on my car next morning. Since it was for only $2 and I was in any case returning to Philadelphia, I was told by the family to just ignore it. For a few years I fully expected not to be allowed back into Canada each time that I arrived at Lester Pearson Airport! My parents and Sharron attended an Orthodox shool but also sometimes joined the Bielaks when they later left the Chabad Lubavitch shool (which was not women-friendly enough for Cynthia) and became active in the Conservative synagogue just a couple of hundred yards from their home. They were, at that stage, one of a number of religiously observant families who attended that synagogue and ultimately they became very close to its Rabbi, Philip Scheim, with whom I also developed close relations. On later visits to Toronto from Cambridge, I would sometimes give lectures at his synagogue.

Academic Industry

Between September and January, I worked very hard at Dropsie, teaching my courses and supervising some of the doctoral candidates, as well as continuing to prepare and publish scholarly papers. I also gave lectures in more popular contexts in the city of Philadelphia, earning some much-needed extra dollars. I added considerably to my experience of all those academic activities and became a popular advisor and mentor to many students. I occasionally meet students from those distant days who remember, with pleasure and gratitude, the sessions they had with me. Perhaps some of them politely decline to remind me of one winter morning when I appeared in the lecture room with a strange pair of shoes. I had risen early to get to work, while it was still dark and Shulie and the children were fast asleep. I had felt for my shoes without any light and was glad to find one right shoe and one left. Unfortunately, one was black and one was brown and I noticed only when I was halfway through my lecture! I kept my feet under the desk for as long as I could.

15. Dropsie College, Philadelphia (University of Pennsylvania).

The quality of the student body, drawn from all over the world, was varied but I soon realized that the attractiveness of the institution was waning, its reputation falling and its funding reducing. This was not only because of the competition from Temple and 'Penn', and because so many universities were now establishing courses in Jewish studies, but also because an independent graduate school, with what had become (already from the days of the Great Depression 40 years earlier) a very limited endowment, simply no longer had the capacity to provide everything that graduate students need and demanded. I retained my standards in assessing research work presented to me and had to point out very frankly to those whose efforts were below the required level that they would have to do better. One of them who had repeatedly failed to meet the target suggested that I should come over to his home where he and his wife would be delighted to entertain me well over a whole evening. This was my first experience of such an offer (but not the last approach of the kind in my long career) and I resolved to steer very clear of any such temptation. From then on, including my time in Cambridge, I tended to leave my door open when seeing any young female student on her own.

A very promising young scholar in Assyriology who was later to have a distinguished career in that field at Cornell, David Owen, warned me that the institution was not being efficiently run and that the president was not always to be relied upon. It took a while for me to appreciate how true this was but in the meantime Dr. Katsh, with whom I had apparently hit it off, offered me the additional post of Academic Dean with all the responsibilities that entailed and a welcome increase in my salary to $15,000. Despite Dave's wise warnings, I could not resist the challenge and did all I could to meet the demands of the job. I was given secretarial assistance and on the first day that I required such assistance I telephoned the office and asked the young woman who had been assigned to me to come over to my office and to bring with her some stationery, some pencils and pens of various sorts, and a rubber. I received a call a few moments later from the head of the secretarial office (who, it was rumoured, had received her appointment courtesy of the affair she was having with one of the board members) inquiring what I had asked for. When I reported my list to her, she explained that what I needed was an eraser, not a rubber, since that latter expression in the USA meant a contraceptive! 'Two nations divided by a common language', as George Bernard Shaw is reputed to have put it.

I also took responsibility for the library which had a remarkable collection of Judaica and Hebraica, including a fine collection of manuscripts, including some 500 Genizah fragments, not my first encounter with Genizah material as a research source but my first opportunity of seeing some 'face to face'. Katsh told the librarian, a helpful but very junior appointee with little authority or experience (and probably not well paid), that he had to sell off some of the duplicates. I myself immediately made a reasonable offer for a few of these but insisted that I obtain a receipt for what I bought and at which price. This proved later to be a wise precaution.

What of my Colleagues?

The Dropsie faculty was still at this stage fairly impressive. In addition to budding young scholars such as Owen, Richard Steiner (who went on to a highly successful career as a Semiticist at Yeshiva University in New York) and myself, there were some well-established and even internationally renowned professors. They were mostly elderly and, as retirees, could probably be paid a pittance by president Katsh. The brightest star in its firmament, as Dropsie saw it, was Solomon Zeitlin who was by then in his eighties but still teaching rabbinics. He was highly knowledgeable and a prolific author (even if somewhat uncouth) and was totally convinced that the Qumran scrolls were not from the Second Temple period but from the early medieval centuries. Like Dr. Teicher in Cambridge, he expended great energy in defending this hypothesis in spite of the growing evidence against him. He also edited the *Jewish Quarterly Review* which was published out of Dropsie, and he was assisted in this by Leon Nemoy, by then in his seventies. Nemoy had been a notable Arabist and Hebraist and curator, at Yale, and had come to Dropsie after retirement. He had suffered a stroke and was unable to speak, having to write notes to you in response to any inquiries. Solomon Grayzel, also in his seventies, was a charming scholar who had produced many books and articles, widely read and enjoyed, on Jewish historical topics.

For me, the most exciting senior colleague to meet was Theodor Gaster. He then lived in New York and taught at Barnard College and used to come as a visiting scholar each week to give some courses in comparative religion, a topic in which he had excelled. When I introduced myself to him, he realized that we had both studied at Jews' College and the University of London, even if there was a gap of some 40 years in our ages, since he was then in his late sixties and I in my late twenties. We chatted about many personalities and institutions that we both knew well in London. His father, Moses Gaster, had been the Haham of the Spanish and Portuguese Synagogue in London, a fine scholar of Judaica and a leading Zionist, in whose home the first draft of the Balfour Declaration had been drawn up. Theodor, born in 1906, was called after Theodor Herzl who had died in 1904. His maternal grandfather, Michael Friedländer, the Principal of Jews' College, had also been an eminent and prolific scholar. Professor Gaster invited me to go out and have lunch with him and I felt very honoured. He asked me if I kept kosher and when I said I did and chose a tuna salad, he bellowed out that he would have a ham sandwich and he was sure that this would cause his late father to turn in his grave.

I pretended to be amused but was somewhat upset by that statement. I later found out that he had crossed swords many times with his father as a young man and had moved far away from his family's standards of Orthodoxy, even if he had in fact inherited and maintained its high scholarly levels. Theodore Gaster was certainly a lively and interesting conversationalist and I subsequently enjoyed reading some of his publications. I recall that Miss Sarah Zausmer was one of the Dropsie secretaries. She had been secretary to Abraham Neumann, the previous president, for many years and greatly resented the new incumbent of the post whom she regarded as a *parvenu*. She insisted on referring to us all, not as Dr. or Professor but as Mr., as they apparently did in Harvard. She gave the impression of being a very unhappy lady but, somehow, she remained in post. Maybe she knew some unsavoury secrets.

By the time that the Christmas break occurred, I knew that I would wish to stay at Dropsie only for as long as it took to obtain another post. Dr. Katsh had been very hospitable and had invited Shulie and me to his home, there to be warmly welcomed by him and his kind and friendly wife, Estelle. I was a little surprised to see that under the glass that protected the coffee table on which we had our drinks and snacks there were authentic Genizah fragments, introduced to me by him as his 'private collection'. He had done important work in obtaining microfilm copies of Genizah fragments from the Russian collections but I have no idea from where his 'private collection' had originated. Genizah fragments were occasionally offered for sale by auction houses and their earlier provenances were not always clear.

Dim Prospects and Diverse Aspects

I attended various scholarly meetings and conferences and attempted to make myself known to various leading scholars. By and large they were uninterested in a young non-American academic and usually brought the conversations to swift and abrupt ends. Nahum Sarna of Brandeis, originally also from Jews' College and the University of London, was kind and chatted a bit to me, as did Professor Alexander Altmann, who was interested to hear that I was a student of his sometime colleague and friend Naphtali Wieder, but remained wholly aloof during our brief conversation. When he learned that I had studied only a limited amount of Arabic (and Syriac, I might add) for my first degree, he seemed unimpressed and moved away. Similar experiences had given me little hope of breaking into what seemed to me to be a rather parochial scholarly market in the USA.

As I was becoming disillusioned about the academic prospects for me in the USA, so Shulie was growing despondent about the way that children were generally brought up there, about the run-down city centres that we had seen, and about the values, or lack of values and caring, in many contexts of the American lifestyle. She was also not very happy about the rented accommodation in which we lived. Her feeling of discomfort was aggravated when we went down into the basement and found a large number of cockroaches, our first experience of that North American hazard. I took on the responsibility of cleaning them out and then purchased a spray to keep them at bay for the remainder of the year. We were also informed that the previous owner of the house had committed suicide in the bath. After that gem of information had been shared with us, visits to that bathroom were never quite the same.

Shulie's parents, Elly and Edmund, visited during the seasonal vacation and invited Shulie and me, and of course Tanya and Aryeh, to join them for a couple of days at a rather grand New York hotel before they returned to London. Edmund suggested that I make the bookings from Philadelphia and he would pay for them when he reached New York. I did this before they arrived and was absolutely clear on the telephone about the need to have adjoining rooms. We thought that in this way we could take turns to pop out while the children were asleep.

When we arrived at the hotel, Edmund and I approached the check-in desk and asked about the two room bookings. Yes, indeed they had been made, but on two different floors. I stressed that I had asked for adjoining rooms and been told that this had been arranged. 'I am afraid I have no available adjoining rooms', I was told, and my arguments and complaints seemed not to touch the clerk at all. My father-in-law had been standing by and now took over. He pushed a ten-dollar bill across the desk and asked whether there might be adjoining rooms available if he returned in half-an-hour or so. 'There is no need to wait half-an-hour', said the brazen clerk. 'I can do that for you immediately, sir.' I then received a gentle lecture from Edmund about how the world worked. 'Az man schmiert, foort man' was the relevant Yiddish saying, meaning that if one greased the wheels one's travel was easier, that is to say, bribery gets you everywhere. Young, idealist, socialist and liberal intellectual as I then was, I fumed but I later took the message to heart in the broader world. I never applied it in any way in the academic world, remaining aloof from such 'schmieren', neither offering nor receiving it which, on reflection, probably did not make me too popular. We had fun in New York and Tanya never forgot her first sight of ice skating. We returned to Philadelphia having taken my in-laws to JFK airport and the kids were in tears about the departure of their lovely grandparents.

Before leaving London for Philadelphia a few months earlier, I had mentioned to Edmund that we had deposited the money from our house (£6,200) in our building society account. He poured scorn on the measly return we would obtain from such a deposit and suggested I leave him a power of attorney and he would make sure that we would receive a much better return on our funds. Shulie, who had experienced the bad as well as the good of her father's financial activities during her childhood and youth, was more than a little cynical and suggested that we think twice. When he phoned a few weeks after we left for Philly and said he had the chance of buying stock that would definitely be a 'winner', I discussed it with Shulie who remained sceptical. I thought that Edmund must know what he was doing and persuaded Shulie that we should give him the go-ahead. By the time we saw him in New York, the money had increased considerably. During a phone-call in January he reported that it had now doubled. I meekly suggested that we might then perhaps sell and take our profits. 'Don't be foolish; it will triple soon', was his reply. That remained to be seen.

Cambridge Beckons

The next few weeks saw some remarkable developments that were destined to change our young lives once again. In the latter part of January 1973 an advertisement appeared in the *Times* (of London) inviting applications for appointment as an 'Assistant Under-Librarian' to be responsible for the Taylor-Schechter Genizah Collection at Cambridge University Library and to teach some rabbinics at the Faculty of Oriental Studies. I subsequently found out that Dr. Henry Knopf had left this job to make aliyah to Israel and to join the library staff at Bar-Ilan University. Edmund knew that we were not greatly enamoured with our situation in Philadelphia and telephoned to ask if I might wish to submit an application for this appointment. Shulie and I discussed it at length. The annual salary was less than £3,000, the status was that of junior lecturer, the post was primarily library-based though also faculty-attached, and the Cambridge Jewish community was no bastion of Orthodoxy. On the other hand, I felt confident that I could prove my worth, obtain promotion, make an impression in the Faculty, and win my academic spurs, so to speak, in an internationally-renowned academic centre of excellence. Otherwise, we could soon leave Cambridge for greener pastures.

Alas, these ambitions of mine were, through no fault of mine, neither easily nor swiftly realized, as will shortly become apparent. Nevertheless, I was 29 and, full of hope and energy, with outstanding support from my wife, was ready to embark on this challenging task if they would appoint me. Edmund telephoned the news to the University Librarian, Eric Ceadel, stating that there was no way that I could meet the deadline for all the necessary paperwork since letters then took about a week. Having spoken to John Emerton, the Regius Professor of Hebrew, who was familiar with my work, my publications, my qualities and my personality from previous encounters, Ceadel agreed to extend the deadline and, anxious to have me interviewed by an appointments committee, agreed to meet the cost of all my fares from Philadelphia to Cambridge to attend the interview.

While I prepared my paperwork and my journey, Eric set up a meeting of the appointments committee for mid-February and arranged for some of the orientalists at the Library and the hebraists at the Faculty to be present. I did not wish Dropsie to know anything about this and so I reported that I would have to miss some lectures that week (and that I would make up for them in earlier and later weeks of course) because I and the family had to be absent for a few days. All four of us travelled to the airport in Philadelphia, ostensibly setting out on the same trip together, but Shulie and the children flew to Toronto to be with my parents while I flew to London to spend the night with Edmund and Elly before the day of the interview. On the big day itself, Edmund dropped me off at King's Cross Station and thought me overly anxious and nervous when I insisted on catching a train an hour earlier than the one that would get me to Cambridge in time for the various meetings set up for me. This was a wise move since the train I caught broke down halfway to Cambridge and we had to wait for a replacement. I therefore arrived just in time.

Guys in Gowns

The result of my previous interview at Cambridge had been depressing for me but, banishing this from my mind, I determined to convince them that I was the man for the job. I was met at the entrance to the University Library by Margaret Manning, Eric Ceadel's secretary, who took me for coffee, showed me around the vast and imposing (if rather severe) building and then introduced me to the various librarians who were responsible for the Hebrew and Arabic materials. They were Don Crane, Wilf Lockwood and Jill Butterworth who operated from a rather cramped and old-fashioned looking office. They were friendly but I got the impression that they would at no stage sympathize with those major ambitions that lay behind my application. Rather, they showed me all the humdrum activities that I would have to undertake. Learning how to catalogue Hebrew books, keeping account of Genizah publications, responding to inquiries from scholars about the Genizah fragments – none of this seemed wholly attractive to me but my view was (how innocent!) that I would soon rise above such levels of bureaucratic and bibliographical procedure. Before having lunch with Mrs Manning in the unimpressive staff tea room, I was taken into the manuscripts stacks behind the Manuscripts Reading Room to be shown the great Genizah treasures themselves.

I noted that there were 32 large crates full of 'raw' unconserved fragments (each later proving to contain over 2,000 items) and that most of the items already on the shelves needed better conservation and improved storage systems. Some conservation and microfilming were being done but at a slow rate that would take many decades to reach completion. My office was to be a small room with few facilities other than a telephone. Whatever nagging doubts all this created in my mind, the interview lifted my spirits and restored my optimism. Those impressive (or apparently impressive) Cambridge dons with their gowns, their posh accents and their academic power, created an atmosphere of scholarly significance and importance. Both they and I seemed to enjoy the encounter and it went exceedingly well. They wished to know why I was willing to take a cut in salary and status to undertake this task and I answered, in all honesty, that I saw it a rare opportunity to deal with one of the world's greatest collections of Jewish manuscripts.

I later understood that there had been other applicants but it seems that they had decided to interview only me that afternoon. The chairman of the committee was the Master of Fitzwilliam College, Edward Miller. He had studied at St John's, and John Emerton was a Fellow of that same College. Charles Taylor, who had brought the Collection to Cambridge, with Solomon Schechter, had been Master of St John's College. Dr. Miller's final remark to me was to thank me for coming and to say that he himself thought that I was 'tailor-made for the job'. 'No. sir', I replied, 'not tailor-made, rather Taylor-Schechter made.' There was a pregnant pause while they recovered from my 'No, sir' and understood my humour. The members of the committee then burst into laughter, thanked me for coming, and I was told to wait for a few minutes.

Eric Ceadel promptly emerged to say that the committee wished to offer me the appointment and explaining that they would also reimburse the cost of my moving back to the UK. This would be done as soon as I sent the receipts but if I stayed only a year, they would wish to recoup two-thirds of the expenditure, and if I stayed only two years they would wish to recoup a third. I thought this was normal procedure but later found out that, believing me to be over-qualified for the job, they suspected that I might be using the appointment simply to get back to the UK at another's cost! For my part, I accepted this and asked him to increase the annual salary to over £3,000. He agreed to put that to the committee and let me know. They duly agreed. John Emerton had arranged to spend the remainder of the afternoon with me and to take me over to the Faculty to meet some of the members and to plan what I would teach in the coming year so that he could draw up the necessary syllabus for publication in the University's official weekly *The Reporter*. He also indicated that after three years my appointment would become tenured and he would then try to get me membership of St John's College so that I could have the right, during term-time, to dine there once a week with the Fellows.

On my way back to London, I felt elated. I had made it into a bastion of academic brilliance (and soon to membership one of its most prestigious colleges) and now I would show them just how successful I could be. Had I been 49 and not 29 I would probably have seen all the obstacles and never have made the application, or perhaps declined the offer once I had seen those neglected crates and the state of the whole collection; but I was still a very young person and that gave me the confidence to believe that I could overcome this massive challenge, establish my personal scholarly reputation, and possibly also make academic history while I did so. Back in the Stekel apartment in London, I telephoned to tell Shulie and the children that they would soon be living in the rarefied atmosphere of a world-famous academic centre.

Back in Philly

I knew that I could not keep the information secret for long and so I asked to see president Katsh and told him of the Cambridge offer and that I was of a mind to accept it because my wife was missing England and her family. He accepted this but, feeling the need to justify my desire to leave, later hinted to colleagues that I had to leave because I had removed duplicates from the library. When that was reported to me in Cambridge some months later, I showed the conveyer of the slander my receipt for the purchase of the duplicates. I have kept it to this day. Before we made our plans for another transatlantic move, I had to finish my courses by the end of May, examine and grade students, and try to give as much guidance as I could to those writing dissertations.

There was one jarring note in this charmingly cheerful symphony. Edmund (always keen to lead from the front) had given my parents the impression that he had engineered our move back to the UK, rather than simply telling me about the advertisement. They were upset and felt I was abandoning them in North America for the Stekels in the UK. I wrote a justified but unnecessarily angry and rather puerile letter of criticism to Edmund and he was so offended that did not make contact with us until I had telephoned him and apologized. He was equally puerile and kept my letter in the drawer of his study table where I found it 22 years later, after he had died. He often mentioned that he and I had always got on together except in that one incident.

My appointment was announced in the *Jewish Chronicle* in London and I received congratulations from many scholars and best wishes for my success. At the same time, some were not slow in telling me that Cambridge had neglected its Genizah Collection and its complete Hebrew codices for many decades, that it would be difficult to rectify all this neglect in the course of one career and that I simply would not have the wherewithal to do that. Knopf also wrote to explain the job to me, at least as far as he had carried it out, and that too was somewhat depressing, given the possibility that I might have to be no more than a cataloguer and a message boy for visiting or corresponding scholars.

I nevertheless drafted my plans for my first few months and took close advice from Professor Shlomo Dov Goitein who was the leading figure in the study and publication of the documentary Genizah and my teacher, Naphtali Wieder, who had made major use of the Cambridge Genizah Collection over a period of two decades. They suggested a lengthy list of *desiderata* and offered some helpful and positive advice to balance the discouraging and pessimistic comments made by a few less senior figures. For his part, Ezra Fleischer of the Hebrew University of Jerusalem, with whom I had started a regular correspondence, in his congratulatory letter, compared my moves from London to Glasgow, from Glasgow to Philadelphia and from Philadelphia to Cambridge to the constant migrations of the Hebrew scholar and exegete, Abraham ibn Ezra, in the twelfth century. I was not sure whether to read this as humorous, critical or flattering.

Making the Most of It

We made the most of the remainder of our time in Philly, hoping, as we did, that we might soon be in more comfortable surroundings. We again had an enjoyable time in Toronto, spending the Passover holiday with my parents, Sharron, and with Cynthia and Karl, who had meanwhile added little Simha to their tally. Again, my mother spoiled the kids with some of their favourite foods while my father bought them treats and arranged for outings. We again motored all the way to Toronto but this time it was not as pretty as it had been in the North American fall when we had driven through the beautiful countryside of New England with its magnificent autumnal colours. Aryeh was at that time an avid and devoted sucker of his thumb which was constantly becoming infected. We tried all sorts of remedies to stop this but to no avail and in response to our discouragement of his sucking habit he decided to punish us by having a revolt against moving his bowels. We abandoned the thumb campaign and tried to bribe him to perform as normal by promising him a little metal model car that he greatly coveted. We did not succeed and his strike continued for over a week! Perhaps it trained him well for when he served in the Israel army some seventeen years later and was busy on manoeuvres in the desert and away from his base!

The tendency of North Americans to over-eat was exemplified for us on one occasion when we took the children for an ice-cream treat in Philadelphia. We asked for two small ice-creams and the quick-fire response was that they had nothing small, only three sizes, namely, 'regular, large and for the big fresser' ('gobbler' in Yiddish). One family trip to the beach in Atlantic City, New Jersey, ended in something of a disaster for Shulie and me and taught us an important lesson. Although the sun was shining, there was a cooling sea breeze, the temperature did not seem so hot and we therefore took every care to keep the children's heads and bodies protected but did not treat ourselves to the same level of caution. They were both fine when we got home while Shulie and I were badly burnt and nauseous. We felt dreadfully unwell all night long and could find nowhere comfortable to put our severely damaged skin. This was useful training for what not to do when we often visited Israel in later years.

We went to spend a few days with Shulie's aunt and uncle in Peekskill, Westchester County, on the Hudson River, just 50 miles north of New York City. Elly's sister, Dina, had married her sweetheart Benno in Vienna after the *Anschluss* in 1938, which made life impossible for Austrian Jews, and the couple had fled to the USA. They had both been advanced in their medical studies but, while he could finish and serve as a medic in the US army, she could not face starting again from scratch, as the USA medical authorities demanded. They were highly intelligent, cultured and liberal, more European/American than Jewish in many ways, and they made us very welcome. Benno was always up early in the morning in order to go to his office and deal with drug addicts that he had among his patients and he therefore fed Tanya and Aryeh their breakfasts. He told us how surprised he had been that they had also eaten the kind of things he liked for breakfast, like spicy eggs with pepper! Brought up to be polite little children, they had usually said 'yes, please' to everything that they were offered, especially by relative strangers. Benno and Dina were not kosher but she knew what was required, having been brought up together with Elly in a strictly Orthodox home in Vienna, and she kindly purchased and prepared for us accordingly.

On the way back to Philly, from one of our visits north, we had a tyre puncture at 65 miles per hour while I was driving in the fast lane. I could only just keep the car under control without even thinking about moving right to the hard shoulder. So I stopped in the fast lane, put my sign up 50 metres behind me, and left my lights flashing as I fixed the tyre, with Shulie's help. The car was simply too hot to sit in, as it was early summer, so we settled the kids on the grass verge between the two highways and told them that they dare not move. In those days, well-brought-up children obeyed orders. My son, Aryeh, today describes this as regimentation! When I was half way through the replacement of the tyre, a police car with two officers drove up behind me and parked with its flashers on. I thought that this was wonderful and that they might come and help me. No such chance; they simply sat in their air-conditioned patrol car and watched. At least when we slowly started to pull out they did the same so that we were protected from the fast traffic in the rear.

On another visit to New York, I went to hear a long (very long) presentation by the Rav, Rabbi Dr. Joseph Ber Soloveitchik. My friends in Philly were very devoted to 'the Rav' (Rabbi, par excellence) and said I really must take the opportunity of listening to him. His kind of approach was, however, simply not to my taste at all since my training had been primarily that of the historical and linguistic style of the central European *Wissenschaft des Judentums* while his yeshivah preference was for the spiritual and moralistic traditions of the eastern European, especially of Volozhin, in spite of his impressive university education. I was therefore a little disappointed and my Philly friends were disappointed with my disappointment.

Another Container-Full

And so almost exactly one year after a container had been unloaded for us in Philadelphia, another was being loaded for the journey to Cambridge. Again, Shulie ensured that the children's favourite toys were packed last. In the weeks before our scheduled return to the UK, Edmund had been busy trying to locate a home for us. We had indicated that it needed to be within walking distance of the synagogue in Thompson's Lane, that it should have three bedrooms, a study for me to work in and a good working kitchen. Edmund made contact with Ros Landy (née Adelman), who lived in Cambridge with her husband Barry, and who had known me well in Edinburgh where we had both spent out childhood; but she knew of no obvious house that was for sale.

Eventually, Edmund located a small, fairly new, terraced house in Manhattan Drive that might fit part of the bill. It was about a hundred yards from the Brunswick Bridge over the River Cam. He reported that it was fairly small but met the other criteria, except for the presence of a room that could function as my study. He had therefore asked a carpenter who worked for him on a regular basis to extend the small dining area towards the tiny back garden and to build some shelves there. The cost of the house was £11,000 (they now sell for more than 30 times that sum) and we suggested that he use the invested money which should easily cover the whole cost. Strangely, he waved aside this suggestion without explanation and stated simply that the money was there for the house and not to worry. It was not until many months later that he confided that the whole investment had been lost and he had had to find ways of replacing it for us.

It was a warm July morning when we touched down at Heathrow and Edmund picked us up and took us back to the Stekel home. We were all tired but he was anxious to show us the new house and so we left the children behind with Elly to sleep a little and we drove off to Cambridge. In those halcyon days one could still drive through the city and as we did so we saw some of the beautiful old buildings that would soon become very familiar to us and the children. We passed the large expanses of trees and luscious green grass known as Jesus Common (beside Jesus College) and Midsummer Common (because of the fair that began in the middle ages and is, to the chagrin of residents close by, still held there), and the River Cam, parallel to the road leading to the area where we would be resident, with many long house-boats, some of them prettily decorated, moored along its banks. So finally, in a state of exhaustion, we parked outside 9 Manhattan Drive.

Tiny House and Super Car

We made an inspection and found John the carpenter still working on the extension. That extension was to trouble us with leaks of rainwater during our stay there but at least there would be a place for many of my books. The remainder of my library, which was then not so large, would fit elsewhere in the house. The kitchen was long and narrow but reasonably functional and there was a tiny garden at the back and only a narrow strip of grass which ranged across a few of the terraced houses at the front. As Shulie was fond of putting it, 'as you opened the front door, you fell up the stairs!' We knew that we would have to stay some ten days in London until our container arrived and until we managed to buy and receive all the necessary kitchen utilities. I could see that Shulie was not thrilled but Edmund put this down to her tiredness after the all-night journey.

When we were on our own, back in the Stekel apartment, she confided in me that she really did not like the house at all. I looked on the bright side and argued that it would be fine for us until we could afford something better and we would at least be able to move to Cambridge and get ourselves organized before I started work on 1 September and the children, or at least Tanya, started nursery school. She was four and Aryeh three at that point. Shulie was not convinced but put up with the situation. The truth is, as she admitted when we finally left for a much nicer house some eleven years later, that she truly hated that house through all those years.

I had to buy a car fairly quickly especially since we had to travel back and forward to Cambridge. I asked about the car we had left with Edmund and he got cross, asking if I did not trust him. I abandoned the inquiry and only many years later did it emerge that a car dealer had sold it for him and did the money finally reach us. For the first few journeys we borrowed Elly's old Hillman Minx which Shulie could drive without difficulty but which I never quite mastered and drove only when I had to do so. In the matter of the new car, I owe it to my father-in-law that he was most supportive. He asked me what I would really like to buy. I explained that we were, for the first time, since we were married, not financially under great pressure and we could afford to buy a reasonably good car. I ideally wished to buy a white MG BGT, a beautiful little sports car that was not much more expensive than a family saloon. Her told me that if I had the money I should go ahead and buy it without feeling guilty, adding that 'one never regrets what one has bought; only what one has not bought'. And so, through one of his Welsh car dealer friends, we got a good price and we both loved RFF 298M. The children sat on the bench at the back and we had special belts fitted for them. I have to say about that car that it was the only car of the many cars I have driven and owned through my life that I truly loved.

We drove to Felixstowe, went through all the same procedure as in Philly, chose the same flat rate option and arranged for delivery. We did not pay for unloading and so we were given between 30 and 60 minutes to unload the container ourselves while the driver sat in his cab and had his lunch. We placed everything on the grass verge, the children happily played with their toys, the weather remained pleasant and one of our more elderly neighbours, Mrs Phillips, wished to have our assurance that the contents would be taken into the house soon (!). John and Carole Miller (he was the son of the Dr. Miller who had chaired my appointments committee and was, like his father, a historian) lived two doors away and were very friendly and helpful. John and Jane, the children of Dorothy and Gurdip Dosanjh (who was, as he once put it to me, 'a Punjabi Sikh in disguise') were soon playing with Tanya and Aryeh. By the end of the afternoon we were in our new home, reasonably well settled, and ready for our newest adventure. I did still have all these nagging doubts about quite how I would tackle all the problems facing me in the University Library but gamely resolved to set about my tasks as soon as possible. My nagging doubts proved to be an underestimate of the difficulties.

13

Bricks Without Straw
(1973–84)

Induction

By the middle of August, we had settled into our new home and arranged for Tanya to begin her English primary education at the Brunswick Primary School, a few hundred metres from our house, across the pedestrian bridge over the River Cam. We were undoubtedly in a physically beautiful ambience that we loved, except when the Cam overflowed one winter and came up to within 20 metres of our house. I was ready to face my responsibilities at Cambridge University Library and I arranged a meeting with Eric Ceadel, the University Librarian, that is to say the Director of the University Library, but expressed in understated Cambridge academic terminology. I told him I would start working very shortly and he was rather taken aback, assuring me that my salary would not begin until 1 September. I explained that I was anxious to see what needed to be done and did not mind adding a few days of *pro bono* activity before my official appointment took effect.

The University Library that I joined in those days was a very different place from what it is today. Men had to come dressed in jackets and ties, women in skirts and not trousers; porters wore uniforms; there were still on its staff a number of serious scholars with international reputations, at least two of whom, if I recall correctly, were Readers (Associate Professors) in the University; there was more concern for manuscripts and books and their availability than enthusiasm for the imposition of up-to-date bureaucratic procedures. Computerization was still a long-way off and to operate a lift (elevator) one had firmly to close a cage door and an inside door before choosing a floor. Members of the University were recognized by the porters at the front desk and staff were known to the custodians of the rear entrance, and all were simply nodded through.

Very soon after my appointment, all those newly-appointed to posts in the University were summoned to a meeting – an induction meeting I think they called it – at the University Centre at the foot of Mill Lane, on the edge of the River Cam. A retired professor had been given the task of addressing us about how things worked in Cambridge. Given that he must have commenced his academic career in the 1920s, his notions of Cambridge workings were not perhaps as up-to-date as they might have been. For example, he explained that our salaries would be paid monthly and not three-monthly as had been the case in earlier years and (to my astonishment at least) he added that he wondered why that had been necessary and whether many University officers were really so dependent on their University income! Another comment proved to be right on target. He explained that in Cambridge if you wore a hat well for the University, you would be rewarded by being given more hats to wear! The underlying assumption was that those who failed to wear the hat allotted to them would be spared any further demands. How true I found that to be over the decades.

It seemed to me that the first things I had to do at the Library were to compile a short guide to the Genizah Collection, to draw up a list of academic, administrative and financial *desiderata* that would occupy me for a number of years, and to make an impact on the Anglo-Jewish community. It quickly became apparent that only a minority of my colleagues at the Library appreciated these plans. Most of them saw my task as the continuation of the *status quo* that I had inherited from Dr. Henry Knopf and made it clear to me that the comprehensive treatment of the Collection was not for one man or one career but would take many decades, even perhaps centuries. Such antagonism made itself felt in a reluctance to assist in my efforts, and even at times in a determination to thwart them. The head of the Map Room, Roger Fairclough, was a man of honour, political principle and kindness and he invited me and Shulie to join him and his wife for dinner one evening. While we enjoyed their kind hospitality, he warned me that I would not only encounter opposition to my grand schemes but also might at times catch a whiff of antisemitism. He remembered that when Dr. Knopf was appointed, there had been some who had not been slow to point out that the University Library had not previously engaged Jews on its staff.

Such warnings notwithstanding, I drew up my list of what needed doing and asked to see Mr. Ceadel again. I explained the urgent need to increase the speed of the conservation and microfilming, set up an extensive programme of cataloguing and publication and employ a number of senior and junior researchers. It was also essential for us to compile a full bibliography of published research on the Cambridge Genizah material, expand the study of the Genizah texts at the Faculty of Oriental Studies and arrange co-operative projects with leading academic institutions around the world. I was much pleased when he offered his hearty endorsement of my plans. So encouraged, I pressed on with my critical inquiry: 'And how much of a budget do I have for these purposes?' 'Budget? No, I am afraid there is no existing budget for these endeavours, worthy as they are.' 'Well, what is to be done about the funding, Mr. Ceadel?' 'That, Dr. Reif, is why we appointed you', he replied, and with a gentle and friendly gesture, led me to his door. I would clearly have to find ways of raising external funds to finance all my Genizah projects. If Cambridge was my Everest, I had now reached the foothills and could, if I still so desired, begin my climb; but there were no maps, no companions and no equipment.

Eric, as I later came to call him, proved to be a reliable support and a helpful guide over the next six years. As a young and bright classicist, he had been taught Japanese in the context of British Military Intelligence between 1942 and 1945 and had subsequently become Lecturer in Japanese at the University's Faculty of Oriental Studies and a Fellow of Corpus College. He had proved himself an admirable administrator and had served on various important University and College committees before being appointed to lead the University Library in 1967. He was serious and industrious, arriving first in the Library in the morning in his aged Morris Minor and among the last to leave, late in the evening. Humour, relaxation and amiability were not among his central interests and he genuinely could not understand why staff in the Library would oppose any policy of his when he could prove its value, logic and need. For their part, those who did not wish any changes to be made and were happy for the Library to remain in the 1930s, when some of them had first joined its staff, detested him and his plans to drag them into the present. He almost always communicated by brief handwritten (or sometimes typed) memoranda and he remained true to what he had written and decided. If he accepted your suggestions, he gave them his wholehearted support and encouraged you as best he could. Despite his love of orderly administration, he had been a successful and productive scholar and teacher and always admired scholarship, especially if it was combined with energy and innovation. We grew closer over the years and even dined in each other's homes, when it was good to see him relax a little and soften his brittle exterior.

I learned a good deal from Eric Ceadel about how to administer efficiently and how one's success and drive for progress and change, even if wholly sensible and justified, would not always be welcomed by one's colleagues. I always thought of him as an individual who could rise above the petty contempt to which he was subjected. Most of the time that was true but a few days before he died, he confided in me that he too felt hurt at times, and frustrated with the negative responses that his industry and energy had generated. Although he was supportive, he could also say 'no' when he thought I was pressing too hard. In 1974, I received the offer of a professorship at $20,000 for eight months' teaching a year from a major university in the mid-west of the USA. I reported this to Eric in the hope that it would encourage him to offer me an improvement on my paltry salary of around £3,000. He explained to me that the general principle at the University of Cambridge was that when anyone mentioned that they had received an offer elsewhere, the response should always be 'Congratulations and good luck with the new appointment.' I felt suitably chastened and not a little deflated, although Shulie was fairly clear that she did not wish to return to the USA, only to go to Israel if yet another move beckoned. I have the feeling (and am even a little disappointed) that the University policy that Eric enunciated is no longer in place but that was certainly the situation in the 1970s. When I suggested that we establish all sorts of lectures in the Library relating to Hebrew manuscripts, he responded by stating that he had neither desire nor need to duplicate what should be done in the Faculty of Oriental Studies.

On the other hand, when the post of Keeper of the Oriental Books at the Bodleian Library in Oxford came up in 1977, he encouraged me to apply and thought I would be able to do an excellent job there and modernize what was in his view a rather moribund set up. I made my application and was summoned for interview. From the questions asked, and the remarks made, it was clear that the committee was going to argue that I was a scholar and not a librarian, and they duly appointed a staff member from within. This was going to be a recurrent theme for the next 20 years. It often happened that a committee that was considering me for appointment or recognition demonstrated a reluctance to acknowledge that any serious academic specialist could also function as a punctilious librarian and bibliographer, a lively teacher, an efficient administrator and a competent fund-raiser. There is, for some absurd reason, a great suspicion of those who claim to be able to do more than one thing at a time in their professional lives, especially if they seem to succeed. The result is that those who appear to achieve this in the academic world are sometimes regarded neither as genuine scholars, nor serious librarians, nor impressive administrators, nor successful fund-raisers. Perhaps the explanation lies in feelings of inadequacy, jealousy and resentment on the part of less accomplished and industrious individuals.

Fund-Raising

It should not be forgotten that in the 1970s the idea of fund-raising for the humanities, as distinct from areas such as natural science, medicine and engineering, was neither widely valued, nor deemed essential for future development. The thought was still that the University, or the Government, should foot the bills. I recall one of my colleagues at a committee meeting making a reference to me as an 'academic entrepreneur'. Some decades later, the master of a Cambridge College who had been consistently supportive of my efforts in the Library and in the Faculty introduced me to a guest at a reception as the scholar who had not only rescued the Cambridge Genizah collection and brought it into the limelight but also as one of the first scholars in humanities to have succeeded in raising external funding in order to do so. It was a generous comment on his part and brought home to me just how innovative such an approach had been in the early 1970s. It should also be remembered that the western economies in those years were not in a good state and that it was not therefore an easy time to attract monetary gifts for educational projects.

When the first major financial awards were made early in 1974, with the Leverhulme Trust and the Pilgrim Trust leading the way in appreciating what needed to be done with the Genizah materials, I proposed to Eric that the Library should establish the Taylor-Schechter Genizah Research Unit and that I should be asked to direct it. He was wholly enthusiastic and the Library Syndicate approved the proposal, without, I might add, voting any budget or additional salary. I was once asked by a colleague many years later how much extra money I had earned through my innovative development of the Genizah Research Unit. He would not believe it when I responded with the phrase 'not a single penny'!

Progress, Promotion and Antagonism

A steering committee was set up with representatives of the University Library and the Faculty of Oriental Studies and it was agreed that it should meet once a year and report progress. In fact, it soon became clear that major progress was being made each year but that committee proved to be a way of keeping the Faculty on board and having them feel that they were part of developments. Eric also agreed that I should become a member of the Faculty Board of Oriental Studies which is in fact the overall management body of the Faculty and I sat on that committee for many years. I learned much about the manner in which the University proceeds, or is at times reluctant to proceed, and about the pettiness that is not entirely absent in some colleagues.

Eric may have told me that I could not bargain about my status and salary but (in typical Cambridge fashion) he found a way of using the next 'under-librarianship' that was vacated by retirement to the benefit of the Genizah project. In 1976 I was promoted to Under-Librarian, the equivalent of a full and tenured lectureship. Eric also arranged for me to move into a more spacious and updated office. There were mumbles and grumbles among some of the staff in the Library and one female member took to stealing the letters arriving in my mail box and hiding them behind books in distant parts of the Library! It sometimes took 20 years before they were discovered and returned to me. A scheme had to be devised by which my letters were placed in the drawer of a senior figure from where I could collect them. Although identified, during the time when John Oates directed the Library after Eric's death, as the major suspect, the woman concerned received neither sanction nor punishment, merely a warning to desist from her malpractice. Despite such pathetic but obstructive animosity, which only later came to light, Eric was convinced that I was worthy of the promotion he had arranged for me and that certainly helped me to overcome some of the problems and to feel that there was a degree of acknowledgement, at least in certain circles, of what I was trying to do. But it was certainly tough going most of the time.

Eric also laid the foundations of another project that I was destined to see successfully completed. Cambridge University Library was the only major research library in the world that did not have a catalogue of its Hebrew manuscripts, that is, the complete codices, not the Genizah fragments. Attempts had been made to fill this lacuna for a century and a half, starting with the first Lecturer in Talmudic and Rabbinic Literature, Solomon Marcus Schiller-Szinessy, who had dealt with the biblical material and left behind him, at his death in 1890, hand-written descriptions of the remainder. Herbert Loewe, who taught Rabbinics at Cambridge in the 1930s, had prepared a handlist that was never published. Jacob Leveen, formerly in charge of the Hebrew manuscripts at the British Museum in London (now the British Library) was at that time working on such a full catalogue but he was concerned to say everything there was to say about each and every item and Eric feared that he would never compete the task. Indeed, he thought that Leveen (no great fan of Ceadel's) was anxious to continue the project for the rest of his life. He was at that time in his early eighties. Eric asked me to take responsibility for the project and I shall, a later chapter, write more of how this was brought to a successful conclusion.

Eric had thus found various ways of demonstrating that that he valued my abilities and my industry and I always tried to respond to his confidence in me with more effort and additional achievements. The climax to this relationship came in 1979. At three meetings with him between early March and the end of May, the University Librarian expressed the view that I was yet to have been granted the status and the remuneration that he felt I deserved. He thought that one way of rectifying this was to offer me the Deputy Librarianship of the Library, that is, the position of his second-in-command, which would be combined with the directorship of the Genizah Research Unit. I could choose whichever areas of the Library administration appealed to me and such an arrangement would ensure that I would remain in the Library, be adequately compensated for my efforts, and complete all the projects I had commenced. He felt that he could win over the Appointments Committee and the Library Syndicate for his plan. We spoke for the last time about this at the beginning of the final week of May and the matter was due to be discussed at the Appointments Committee scheduled for 6 June, at which I was to be available for interview.

Alas, Eric died at the early age of 58 five days earlier, on 1 June, and those who were not inclined to favour his ideas or his management style were undoubtedly relieved, if not overjoyed. 'It is not surprising,' one colleague said to me, 'given the long hours he worked'. John Oates took over the running of the Library as a stop-gap measure and one year later sent me a hand-written note in which he reported that the circumstances were 'very different from those of a year ago' and that my name would not now be included in the short list of candidates to be interviewed. I had assumed as much in the course of the inconsiderately silent twelve months that had elapsed and no longer expected anything from the temporary regime headed by Oates (with whom I never enjoyed a close relationship), nor indeed was I optimistic about what I could expect from the permanent regime that was expected to follow within a year or so. In connection with that permanent change, I was ultimately to become pleasantly surprised. I have often wondered how things would have turned out if Eric had lived another few weeks and I had been appointed as his deputy. I would then have had to run the Library on his death and I am not sure if that is what I would ideally have wanted.

Faculty Involvement

If Eric was my mentor in the Library, it was John Emerton who drew me into the work of the Faculty and forged the connection between me and St

John's College. It will be remembered that he played an important role in recommending me for the post at the University Library and he worked closely with Eric Ceadel on arranging that appointment and on encouraging and supporting my efforts to establish the Genizah Research Unit and to ensure that it flourished. A short time after I was appointed to my Cambridge position, he wrote to say how pleased he was that I would be joining them in Cambridge. From then on, he ensured that I played an active role in the teaching programme of the Faculty.

In addition to lecturing on rabbinic texts, I also gave College supervisions (tutorials) on various papers for the Tripos (as the undergraduate course is known in Cambridge), sat on a number of committees relating to Hebrew and Jewish studies, examined for the Tripos, and gave occasional lectures in the Faculty of Divinity. It was John who, with the active co-operation of Andrew Macintosh, arranged for me to become a member of St John's College in 1976, after I was admitted to the degree of MA of the University of Cambridge. Then, as now, those who are given tenured appointments at Cambridge and have degrees from other universities are made academically 'kosher' by the award of a Cambridge MA. This gives them the formal status of a senior member of the University.

In addition to working closely with those who taught Hebrew studies at that time (including John Emerton, Sebastian Brock, John Snaith, Nicholas de Lange and Avi Shvitiel), I also made the acquaintance of other orientalists. Jack Plumley taught Egyptology but was an Anglican pastor by origin and conviction; Bob Serjeant was Professor of Arabic but, unlike some, was not an active and one-sided politician of the current Middle East; Susan Skilliter had worked in the University Library before being appointed as lecturer in Turkish and this gave her an understanding and a sympathy for what I was trying to achieve there; and such a sympathy was also apparent in Michael Loewe whose father had been a distinguished scholar of Judaism and whose brother Raphael was teaching at University College London and very much encouraged and lauded my efforts in Cambridge.

I also came to know some of the leading scholars in the Faculty of Divinity. Donald McKinnon was a charismatic Scottish character whose expertise was in the philosophy of religion. He always had something to say and he did so in a totally idiosyncratic manner. I especially recall his reference to what he called the crofter's prayer 'O that the peat would cut itself and the fish jump in at the door, and we could lie in bed all day, O Lord, for evermore.' Charlie Moule's gentle manner, sense of humour and friendliness belied the fact that he was internationally renowned as a leading scholar of the New Testament. Henry Hart was a superb and much-loved

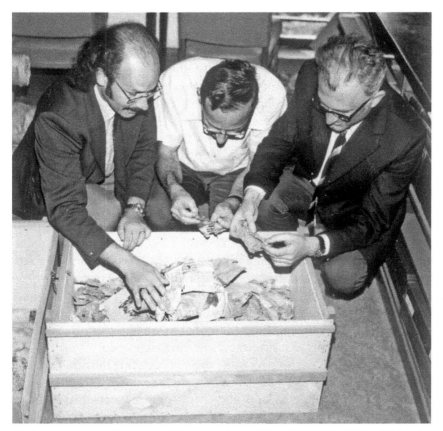

16. Sorting fragments with Israel Yeivin and Ezra Fleischer, 1974 (Cambridge University Library).

teacher who would introduce a speaker by doing no more than stating his name and his subject and would offer his thanks at the conclusion of the lecture in a similarly abbreviated fashion. German scholarship of the kind I knew from my own teachers was represented by Ernst Bammel and, like them, he was not the relaxed and affable type. He would never have told me himself but many decades later I heard from a leading American professor who had been a graduate student of his that Bammel had forecast in the 1970s that I 'would have a powerful impact in our field'.

Lecturing and Supervising

Some of my students went on to work in the academic, educational and ecclesiastical fields but the majority moved into other professions. I enjoyed teaching them and I believe that most of them related more enthusiastically to Hebrew language and literature as a result of my efforts. One of my favourite supervision topics was Classical Hebrew prose and poetic composition, which was a subject examined in the Tripos (the undergraduate degree). A student was given a piece of English text, prose or poetry, and asked to translate it into the kind of Hebrew to be found in the biblical books. I sometimes amused myself and horrified them by choosing something like that morning's editorial in *The Times*. It was an excellent training in appreciating the original language and literature of the Hebrew Bible and in meeting the challenge of translating from one cultural milieu to another.

One student was anxious to have some supervisions specifically with me and, when I suggested a meeting at eight o'clock, he responded by stating that he attended College dinner at that hour. I indicated to him that I did not mean 20.00 but 08.00, apparently an unknown hour for him! We fixed the supervision and he turned up at 08.10. I asked him why he was there and he told me that he had come for a supervision. I explained that I had waited until 08.07 and then started working on something else. If he wished to fix another appointment, I would be glad to see him then. Needless to say, neither he nor any of his colleagues was ever late again.

A young woman was so busy with her acting career at the theatre of the Amateur Dramatic Club in the University that she neglected her Hebrew studies and was in danger of failing her Tripos exams. I was asked in about February to take over her supervisions and to attempt a rescue. At first, I got nothing but cheeky and flippant responses so I challenged her with a selection of difficult passages from the Hebrew Bible. This reduced her to a tearful admission of her inadequacy and to a request that I assist her in putting things right. She finally worked hard, as I suggested, and received a very respectable degree in her final examinations, before proceeding with her preferred profession 'on the boards'. One girl came from a family of Reform Jews but her studies moved her in the direction of greater observance and today she belongs to an ultra-Orthodox community in Israel. Melvyn Ramsden was so good at Hebrew grammar that I asked him to teach our children that subject while another, Ian Gamse, was an excellent reader of the Torah in the synagogue and helped our son to prepare for his barmitzvah. Both registered to do doctorates with me but abandoned that aim when they departed Cambridge for professional commitments.

Soon after my arrival in Cambridge, John Snaith, who taught Classical Hebrew and Aramaic in the Faculty, suffered a dreadful accident on his motor-bike, and I was asked by John Emerton to lecture on some of his texts. If I recall correctly, they included the first chapters of Genesis. In one of those early years in Cambridge, I served as the Chairman of the Examiners for the Faculty. That was, to say the least, a challenging experience, given that not all my colleagues were prompt with their marking and with reporting the results and there were various last-minute arrangements to be made as a consequence. I made serious and wholly justified demands of some of the more recalcitrant members which achieved the required result as far as the work of the committee was concerned but did not enamour me of the relevant backsliders.

Emertonian Pros and Cons

John Emerton was always most hospitable, both at College before I myself became a member, and in his home, where his wife Norma made every effort to ensure that Shulie and I could eat the meal that was prepared. When unsure, she always checked beforehand and there were never any embarrassments in that connection. We also had them over to our home on numerous occasions, both in order to meet visiting scholars at sherry receptions, and also for dinner parties to which we invited those with whom I most closely worked. Shulie always prepared delicious meals and made sure that they were all very well looked after. They knew about kosher food but one guest insisted (against our culinary religious custom) on having milk with her coffee after a meaty meal and some serious diplomacy was required in order to sort that out. As a member of the College with dining privileges, I could not in my own right book rooms, arrange functions, or access certain parts or services of the College. Whenever that was necessary, both John and Andrew Macintosh were helpful.

I began to play squash with Andrew, who was by then a close friend and scholarly colleague, but he soon concluded that he should find me a more evenly matched partner, and that partner turned out to be Julius Lipner who taught Indian Religious at the Faculty of Divinity. He and his wife Anita became close friends of Shulie and me, and Julius and I played squash regularly for some 30 years, as well as interacting professionally and socially. I gave regular lectures on Judaism over many years to Julius's students in comparative religion at his faculty. On the matter of sporting activity, I also remember many a pleasant evening playing cricket (as wicket-keeper) for the University Library team. Shulie and I also attended local concerts and theatre productions on a regular basis and, when finances permitted, occasionally treated ourselves to a trip to a London show or concert.

To understand John Emerton's approach to me and how his support could sometimes be limited, one needs to bear in mind that he was, in addition to being what a colleague has privately called 'a fairly evangelical Anglican', a champion of Old Testament critical theory, as created and developed in Protestant Germany in the latter half of the nineteenth century, and he saw his study of the Hebrew Bible very much in that context. He was more progressive than some of his colleagues in that he found the comments of the Jewish exegetes useful and often asked me to explain how they had understood some difficult passages. He would then make brief reference to their comments in his articles. On the other hand, he was more than a little afraid that a broader vision of the study of the Old Testament might one day win recognition and that the theologically and christologically-angled views of the 'higher critics', which were not always very friendly towards rabbinic Judaism, might have to give way to a more ecumenical kind of scholarship, or to an approach that was more clinically linguistic and historical.

John would always recommend me highly for anything to do with rabbinic texts, the overall history of the Hebrew language from the Second Temple period until the modern age, and the critical study of Jewish religion. He was, however, less than enthusiastic if he saw any threat to his own scholastic 'holy of holies'. There was to be no treading on the toes of Old Testament scholarship as he interpreted it. When any relevant appointment seemed to be moving away from the direction that was acceptable to him, he would argue his case powerfully and stubbornly in the relevant committee, ultimately ensuring an appointment that satisfied him. He also had a tendency (on his own admission) to accord more credence to applications and references coming from Oxford or Cambridge, rather than from any other academic institutions. That may sometimes have been justified but certainly not always, and he slipped up on occasion in this connection. There will more about this in a later chapter.

Bureaucratic Contrariness

Those individuals who ran the more bureaucratic aspects of the Library's work did everything in their power to demonstrate that I was not be treated any differently from any other member of the staff, regardless of my scholarly accomplishments, my Faculty commitments, my drive to attract major funding and my success in rectifying the Library's neglect of its Genizah material and its major Hebrew codices over many decades. If I wished to have time off for Shabbat and the Jewish religious festivals (ḥaggim), I would have to compile a list of those hours or days taken as leave and details of all the time worked in lieu. Even if I came in much earlier and left much later than most others, I should still be available for lunch duty to cover areas of the Library when other officers went to lunch. When preparing materials about the history of the Genizah and Hebrew collections, I should not necessarily expect any assistance from staff members who knew where to locate the relevant data. During my first few days in the University Library, one of the most senior librarians specifically declined to offer me any such assistance.

The problem was our differing images of the job I was doing. I saw myself essentially as a scholar of some years' standing who had effectively been seconded to the University Library to undertake a unique task of international significance that needed scholarship, as well as many other abilities, in order to be completed in the course of one career. They saw the job as one of numerous others within the Library that should in no way be given any priority, and they deeply resented any attempt to stress its special urgency and importance. I should immediately add that, in addition to Roger Fairclough whom I have already mentioned, Arthur Owen, the head of the Manuscripts department, and his assistant Peter Gautrey, David McKitterick, of the Rare Books department, and Glynn Parker, head of Accessions, did not follow such a policy but were most helpful and friendly, as were, in due course, Dorothy Owen and Elizabeth Leedham Green of the University Archives. I also had a passing acquaintance with Peter Fox who was a cataloguer of German books before leaving for Dublin to become Deputy Librarian of Trinity College in 1979 and would later come back to Cambridge to direct the University Library. My relations with the porters, the tradesmen and the cleaners were always excellent. I always made a point of expressing my appreciation of what they did for me and they seemed to value my industry and my devotion to the Unit's projects.

Determination to Publish

I was determined that my duties at the Library and in the Faculty should not prevent me from continuing to publish scholarly material that was sometimes, but not always, connected with Genizah materials. During the first decade of my time in Cambridge I managed to publish one lengthy monograph, seventeen articles, twenty lengthy reviews and numerous short notices, all in reputable academic journals. It was not easy to find the necessary time for preparing these publications. With the co-operation of Eric Ceadel and my Faculty colleague, Gordon Johnson, later to be president of Wolfson College, I had a revised version of my doctoral dissertation accepted for inclusion in the Faculty's series published by Cambridge University Press.

Those who are used to today's methods of preparing material for publication should be aware of what had to be done in those distant days some 40 years ago. Preparing camera-ready copy involved setting English and Hebrew texts separately and pasting them into each other. These texts had to be printed on to a thick and glossy white paper, especially prepared for the purpose. Photographic plates then had to be prepared for the press. This was a highly laborious process and at times bits of Hebrew would fall on the floor and have to be retrieved. Authors, photographers, printers and publishers were all involved and lots of careful checking needed to be undertaken at all stages. I was highly relieved to see my volume *Shabbethai Sofer and his Prayer-book* finally in print in 1979.

Another volume that required close involvement on my part was the Festschrift for Erwin Rosenthal, a fine scholar and gentleman who had emigrated from Nazi Germany in the early years of the Hitler regime. When *Interpreting the Hebrew Bible* was published in 1982 to mark his 75th birthday, Erwin confided in me his view that it would never have appeared without my efforts. In the late 1970s, John Emerton had approached me and inquired whether I would be willing to edit with him a volume in honour of Erwin and I gladly agreed. I learned from the experience that junior partners in editing projects often have to do the bulk of the work and that the names of their august seniors usually appear first. I tried to avoid this particular tendency in my own senior years.

Doing a good job of editing is a thankless task. One receives no kudos if it is done well – nobody seems inclined to note the fact – but the critical comments flow if there are any inadequacies. I had to do much of the hard graft but I was very fond of Erwin and undertook it gladly. From my earliest days in Cambridge, Shulie and I had made regular evening visits to the home of Erwin and Elisabeth in Chesterton Road and had become very close to them. In a very old-fashioned set up, while Elisabeth and Shulie drank tea and chatted downstairs, Erwin and I would go up to his study 'to deal with academic matters', as he put it. This involved sharing an outstanding bottle of Mosel Auslese or Spätlese and a fine cigar. I sat for many evenings listening to the story of his life so that I could compile a biographical appreciation of him for that volume.

John and I took great care in the scholars we approached and the topics we approved and I believe that the result was not only greatly to Erwin's liking but also represented a welcome collection of important essays. Erwin occasionally invited me to dine with him at Pembroke where he was Fellow and it was there that I learned, not from him, but from our fellow Hebraist who was then the Dean, Dr. Ernest Nicholson (who later held a chair at Oxford), how to drink copious amounts of alcohol without getting drunk, at least not too drunk. In those days, college catering took little account of personal preferences and the first time Erwin asked me to join him and I told him about my kosher limitations, his catering manager at Pembroke would not co-operate and forced him to disinvite me!

Erwin was the author of numerous important publications in the field of medieval Jewish and Islamic thought. He also published three books on Islamic philosophy which are still widely regarded today as essential reading for students in the field. In addition to his Pembroke fellowship, he had a University readership but he was never appointed to a personal chair at Cambridge, or a fellowship of the British Academy, and this rankled painfully with him. I suggested to him that personal jealousies on the part of leading hebraists and arabists might play a part in such unworthy treatment but little did I realize until later in my own career the absolute truth of that sad assessment.

Functioning as a scholar, as well as curator and editor, also meant making my presence felt in all those areas in which scholars were active. This could of course be done in Cambridge via all the learned societies in which I participated, including the Old Testament Seminar, the Society for Near Eastern Studies, and the Theological Society, where I took on various tasks, as well as offering lectures from time to time.

Activity Abroad and Reviewing

As mentioned earlier, I also greatly enjoyed my lecturing and supervising. Cambridge was, however, only one important academic centre and it was obvious to me that it was necessary to make some sort of personal impact in other such centres around the world. I therefore welcomed opportunities to lecture at conferences and to speak about the Genizah Collection around the United Kingdom and Ireland, in mainland Europe, in North America and in Israel. As anyone who has been an active scholar knows, such involvement can in itself be a demanding and exhausting exercise. It may therefore easily be imagined how much more energy and devotion are needed when one is also running a massive research project in all its aspects.

During my various visits to Israel in the 1970s, I had built relationships with all the leading scholars in fields relating to the Genizah and to my own favourite research subject of Jewish liturgy. I developed particularly warm relationships with Ezra Fleischer and Yaakov Sussmann, in spite of the fact that they themselves rarely saw eye to eye in matters concerning the planning and running of teaching and research at the Hebrew University. I shall shortly mention more about this. When Mordechai Friedman organized a conference at Tel Aviv University in 1977, and invited me to attend, I swiftly took the opportunity of spending a week or so in Jerusalem. At the conference itself it became clear to me that most of the Israeli scholars, as indeed those from other countries, were interested in supporting me and my work primarily because it would ensure for them personally a greater availability of Genizah texts.

I spent a few days in New York in 1977 and, during that and later visits, met a number of Genizah scholars there, especially at the Jewish Theological Seminary, but also at New York University, particularly Larry Schiffman. At the Seminary I was able to develop or expand personal relationships with Menahem Schmelzer, who ran the library there as well as teaching various courses, a man of fine scholarship but also of great charm, integrity and warmth; with Louis Finkelstein, as well as with Gerson Cohen, his successor as Chancellor, and Ivan Marcus. The Seminary scholar most closely associated with Genizah texts was perhaps Moshe Zucker and it was a pleasure to make his acquaintance, although I have to admit that his treatment of original Genizah fragments left more than a little to be desired. After showing them to me, he crushed them into an already full drawer under his table, not the best way to ensure their safe conservation!

What I did not know then was that a young boy of about ten had, despite his objections, been cajoled by his mother to come to one of my lectures in New York that year. He told me some 45 years later that he was so impressed by my presentation that it influenced him to take a deep interest in academic Jewish studies. He is today a leading American-Israeli Orthodox Rabbi with a major international reputation who plays a central role in sorting out matters of personal religious status in Israel. At the Jewish Museum of the Diaspora in Tel Aviv, a permanent exhibition about the Cairo Genizah was mounted, with the Unit's close co-operation and assistance. In 1978, I returned to Philadelphia to deliver some guest lectures and to meet again with some of my academic friends from earlier days.

Whenever I was asked in the early years of my academic career to write a review of a scholarly book, I read it through punctiliously and made copious notes. I was then able to assess (fairly, as I believed) the value of the whole publication and make numerous suggestions about what could have been more accurately done and what was simply erroneous.

Unsurprisingly, this did not make me the flavour of the decade among some of my colleagues and by the latter part of the 1970s I apparently had something of a reputation among them. On at least one occasion the editor of a journal wrote and asked me to limit certain criticisms which, though academically justified, would be better left unsaid, because it would otherwise damage his relations with the scholar whose book I was reviewing. This annoyed me greatly but led to a growing awareness on my part that progress in academic life for those with the necessary abilities and qualifications could come via two routes.

One could be very careful about never criticizing those with the power to assist or hinder your career, attach oneself to one of those as your mentor, and obtain swift recognition and advancement. Alternatively, one could be direct, adhere to one's scholarly integrity, and call a mistake an egregious error when the opportunity arose. Some 25 years later, a visiting scholar from Israel confided in me what he had been told about me in 1977. 'Old Yarntonians [from the Oxford Centre for Hebrew Studies then based at Yarnton Manor, outside Oxford] articulated your name with fear and trembling, as if you were the Bin Laden of Jewish studies; I was therefore pleasantly surprised to find you an amiable person with no protruding fangs.'

14

Raising Funds and Conserving History
(1973–84)

Publicity

Working on my own, I made a large number of applications to various foundations, compiled and printed my little booklet about the Genizah and arranged for one of the editorial staff, Meir Persoff, and a photographer, to prepare a feature for the *Jewish Chronicle*. I also made contacts with individual philanthropists, especially in London, and – an unusual initiative at the time – began to welcome groups to see some of the fragments and to hear lectures from me about their significance. I delivered about 140 popular lectures in eleven years to an average audience of 50, thus conveying information about the Genizah manuscripts to some 7,000 people. A well-illustrated and attractively-written feature by Meir Persoff appeared in the *Jewish Chronicle Supplement* in London in December 1973, a little over three months after my arrival at the Library. I also did whatever I could to have my booklet noticed in scholarly publications. Whenever I sensed interest on the part of anyone with financial wherewithal, I asked for a personal meeting and travelled to London to his or her office to explain what I was trying to do with the Genizah collection, drawing parallels for them with the exciting discoveries of the Dead Sea Scrolls.

Of course, I did not mention how the University had effectively neglected the collection for over 60 years, nor how much I was working virtually on my own, since that would undoubtedly have been unproductive for the fund-raising effort. I had to stress just how anxious the University now was to give the collection its due attention. I also sent notes to radio and television producers in the hope that some might express interest in what was, and is, one of the world's greatest and most extensive collections of medieval literary and documentary treasures. I should say that I received no administrative help whatsoever from anyone in this connection. I was told by Miss Waller who ran the General Office in the Library that if I submitted copy to her, letters might be typed within three or four days, but

I decided to bring in my own old manual typewriter and do it all myself so that I could send things off with the utmost speed.

When the Unit's externally-raised funds permitted it, I was able to employ a part-time secretary and that helped greatly. Sonia Peacock and Sandra McGivern in the first two decades, and in later years, Sarah Sykes, were among the longest serving and the most industrious and loyal of those who served in that capacity. I also began compiling lists of published books and articles that made mention of Genizah fragments and to make plans for the publication of a set of catalogues, once I could find researchers to assist with their compilation. It should also be noted that those were the days before bureaucrats dictated everything that was done in university departments. I would take the train to London (or drive if I had to) and then present the relevant vouchers to Miss Yorke of the University Library's financial office who would immediately refund the expenditure in cash from a tin box. The lengthy and tedious process of proving one's bona fides by filling out forms to obtain permission, submitting details and justifications afterwards, and waiting for weeks for reimbursement was a pleasure yet to be experienced by 'academic entrepreneurs'.

Finding Funding

I have to admit that in my earlier years I had developed what can only be described as an unfair assessment of wealthy businessmen, communal leaders and administrators and their intellectual capacities. Maybe it was also related to what were then my pronounced and youthful left-wing political views. I soon learned to think otherwise in both connections. Many of the managing directors and chief executives of companies and organizations whom I met had sharp minds, as well as biting wits. You could in no way fool them and you had to be well prepared in your presentations. I remember one such driving force in a major international company whose secretary told me that I should come to see him in London. One of his meetings that morning finished at 10.59 and the next started at 11.01. He would give me five minutes between these two meetings. I arrived at his office with a five-minute talk about the Genizah that I had carefully prepared and stopped talking exactly on time. He picked up the telephone, told his secretary to delay the next meeting for a few minutes and instructed me to carry on in more detail.

Cyril Stein and his wife Betty became important supporters of the Unit for many years and close personal friends of Shulie and me. He arranged dinner parties with leading commercial, political and educational personalities and played a central role in guiding my efforts to establish a regular income for the Unit. Of course, there were always a few who wished to give the impression of knowing more than they did. One such poser heard me lecture at a dinner party in London and suggested to me afterwards that I should simplify the presentation. Some two years later, I used almost precisely the same lecturing style at a different venue and he suggested to me afterwards that the presentation should not be so simple!

My earliest contacts with Chief Rabbi Immanuel Jakobovits had been none too friendly. He had been appointed as Chief Rabbi in London in 1967 and I had gone to my lectureship in Glasgow in 1968. I heard that he was considering who should be appointed as Principal of Jews' College and I wrote to him strongly suggesting my teacher and research supervisor, Naphtali Wieder. He on his part wished to have someone more akin, as he saw it, to the yeshivah world, and ultimately brought Nachum Rabinovitch to London from Toronto. Rabbi Dr. Rabinovitch was neither a product of, nor an enthusiast for, the approach of the *Wissenschaft des Judentums* that had been championed by Wieder and transmitted to his students, and I made my feelings clear to the Chief Rabbi.

When it was suggested that I enlist his support and that of the executive director of his office, Moshe Davis, I was somewhat apprehensive that I might have become *persona non grata* to Rabbi Jakobovits. It turned out that this was not the case and he visited Cambridge, once alone and on another occasion with a large group of fellow Rabbis, saw some of the Genizah treasures and became enthusiastic about encouraging support among his many wealthy contacts in the London Jewish community. He was especially interested in the eleventh-century fragments of Jewish prayers. He and Rebbetzin Jakobovits (later Lord and Lady Jakobovits) generously agreed to host some dinner parties in their home at 85 Hamilton Terrace, in a splendid area of St John's Wood not far from Lord's Cricket Ground. These events led to an important increase in the number of foundations and individuals committed to making regular contributions to the Unit's funds.

I recall two particular evenings in Hamilton Terrace. The first time I gave a lecture there, I brought a slide projector and my slides, and we needed to set up all the equipment for screening the show. Remember, of course, that these were the days of actual slides, and not the computerized representations that we use today. The distinguished and learned Chief Rabbi of the British Commonwealth of Nations crawled around on the floor to ensure that all the leads were correctly attached and linked to the electricity supply. I had objected strongly to this and said I could do that myself but Chief Rabbi Jakobovits insisted that he was the host, I was his guest, and he was anxious to assist me. On another occasion, I took Eric Ceadel and John Emerton with me to the Chief Rabbi's home. As is appropriate in Orthodox Jewish circles, Rabbi Jakobovits recited a very short grace before the meal, to which we all, including Eric and John, recited 'amen'. At the end of the meal, before my presentation, the Rabbi indicated that he would now recite the grace after meals. Eric and John both clasped their hands together and bowed their heads. What they did not know was that the traditional rabbinic grace after meals goes on for a number of pages and they waited some five or six minutes before they could say 'amen' and resume their normal postures.

Cyril Stein had suggested that we should go and see Sir Marcus Sieff, of the noted Jewish family that had been both marital and business partners of the Michael Marks who had founded Marks and Spencers (M&S) stores (originally a penny bazaar in Manchester) in 1884. Sir Marcus was then chairman of M&S and we went to see him and his son David in their flagship offices in Baker Street, in London's West End. He was a great supporter of Jewish educational projects and of Zionism and I stressed the connections of the Genizah with the history of the Jewish communities in the Holy Land in the medieval period and the importance of these documents for understanding broader Mediterranean Jewish history at that time. He expressed interest and for many years we received an annual donation from his charitable foundation.

What intrigued me was not our scholarly discussion but the snack that he arranged for us. He ordered tea and suggested that his assistant bring a selection of the latest biscuits that M&S were newly promoting in their stores. When we had drunk our tea and eaten our biscuits, he was most anxious to solicit our views, one by one, without exception, on the quality and tastiness of the company's new biscuits. Sir Marcus was not too grand to take a close personal interest, as the family had done for almost a century, in the products that they were marketing. I was greatly impressed. Another philanthropist made an annual donation of £1,000 and then asked if I could assist his son's application to come and study in Cambridge. He suggested that, if his son was accepted as a Cambridge student, he would feel even more indebted and attached to Cambridge and would increase that donation considerably. I am glad to say that I did not take the bait and was relieved that, even without any filial presence in Cambridge, he still continued to support our work in the original sum.

SJC and USA

John Emerton had suggested that St John's College might be able to fund some of our work and I therefore invited its Senior Bursar, Chris Johnson, to come and see the Collection and chatted with him about its needs. Chris was a graduate of Oxford and Cambridge who had turned from research in physics to College administration. He had been Senior Bursar and Fellow at Selwyn before coming to St John's. As well as being a delightful personality and an efficient administrator, Chris was known to be a good judge of what was genuinely deserving of financial assistance from the College. I was consequently delighted that he thought the Unit worthy of College support for a number of years. I am glad to say that my personal friendship with him remained in place for many decades after that initial professional connection, ending only with his death in 2019.

Raphael Levy was the grand-nephew of Solomon Schechter through his mother and had for many years been an active and successful fund-raiser for Jewish charities in the USA. I successfully enlisted his support in making my plans for the Unit's public relations drive and he ('Ray') and his wife Florence ('Flos') visited the Unit. They were a delightful couple who belonged to that Jewish generation who remembered the period of the Depression and the Holocaust years and were devoted to Jewish causes, liberal values, politics and education, and the presentation of scholarly information in a manner that could attract the interest and support of the wider public. Ray told me that I could not expect to succeed in any public relations exercise unless I produced an easily-read pamphlet that briefly summarized the importance of the Genizah. I had also to issue a regular publication that reported on the Unit's progress in both the academic and financial areas. And so were born the pamphlet *A Priceless Collection* and the Unit's newsletter *Genizah Fragments*.

Ray sent me a draft of what he thought should constitute the former and I compiled a draft of what I believed should be included in the latter. I responded to his call for popularity and he to my need for scholarly accuracy. Our partnership in these endeavours was greatly assisted by Meir Persoff of the *Jewish Chronicle* in London, who found time outside his office hours to provide professional assistance with the editing of the newsletter. I would send him the textual and illustrative materials I wished to include and he would plan their lively and attractive layout in a most professional manner. Incidentally, through the connections with Ray Levy, various members of the extended Schechter family visited the Unit to see the manuscripts that their forbearer had brought from Cairo. I should add that Meir also invited me to contribute articles to the *Jewish Chronicle* on many occasions and on sundry subjects. I always found it a challenging and important exercise to describe scholarly findings and ideas in a fashion that would make them readable and comprehensible to the average reader.

Newsletter

Most interesting – even surprising-for me – was the fact that so many serious academics, far from decrying such a 'vulgar' exercise, welcomed the newsletter with enthusiasm from the very first issue, and took the trouble to write to me and say so. In response to the appearance of the first issue of *Genizah Fragments*, distinguished scholars of many disciplines from around the world expressed their approval and wished the Unit every success with its important initiatives. There were even Oxford colleagues who thought it an impressive achievement. Today, almost 40 years later, many humanities departments have similar publications but at that time it was frowned upon by more intellectually purist colleagues. One thanked me for sending him what he classified as my 'piece of propaganda'. I always felt hurt by such barbs and genuinely wondered why so many academics seemed disinclined to welcome the Unit's progress but I learned to swallow hard, ignore the antagonism and power forwards with the Unit's plans. Getting the job done for scholarship as a whole became more important than being popular with a few narrow-minded colleagues.

I must acknowledge that I also learned from all these new experiences in publicity that there was an academic side to the process. Faced by having to explain to non-specialists in simple language and in brief terms the reason why they should support a scholarly project forces the proposers to think closely about precisely what is so important about their work and what are the central elements within it. That helps to prevent one becoming obsessed with the minutiae of compiling footnotes without ever stopping to understand and appreciate the overall historical message and meaning of the data to which they allude.

Taking Stock

By the time that the first newsletter appeared in 1981, there had already been substantial progress in the Unit's achievements. Far from taking 50 years to complete the conservation and much more than one life-career to make a serious impact on the scholarly descriptions and bibliography, as had been predicted by many, there was already a clear indication that the Unit was well on the road to completing many aspects of the physical and scientific attention urgently required by the Cambridge Genizah materials. In the first issue of *Genizah Fragments* I was able to report as follows: 'Among the most remarkable statistics are to be counted the conservation of 100,000 fragments, the processing of 320 microfilms for worldwide distribution, particularly to the USA, Israel and Eastern Europe, the cataloguing of 24,000 biblical fragments, the compilation of a Genizah bibliography consisting of 30,000 items, the numbering of 22,000 unnumbered fragments in the Old Series, and the arrangement of regular lectures, exhibitions and popular articles on the subject of the Genizah.'

In addition to the Leverhulme and Pilgrim Trusts, major donors by then included St John's College, the British Academy (which supported the work of the Unit from 1978 until 1994), the Sherman Foundation, the Sobell Trust and the Tyrwhitt Fund. I also began to cultivate close relations with the American Friends of Cambridge University. If I am not mistaken, it was Gordon Williams who was then the Director of the American Friends and he and I met on numerous occasions in both Cambridge and Washington. I also addressed a large gathering at the Israeli Embassy in Washington D.C. Those meetings resulted in welcome contributions from across the Atlantic. My philosophy at that time, and indeed until my retirement, was to accept every donation, however small, with gratitude and to remain in touch with the donor and to seek an annual renewal. Of course, large sums were important and very welcome but when, in certain years, these proved not to be forthcoming, the Unit's progress could be maintained by way of the smaller and regular gifts.

With regard to the Genizah bibliography, the information gathered by the early 1980s was providing an invaluable source of reference for Genizah scholarship, particularly by facilitating the immediate retrieval of publication details of many of the fragments for any interested scholar. Following a series of discussions with Dr. John Dawson of the University's Literary and Linguistic Computing Centre at the University of Cambridge, the Unit decided to transfer the Genizah bibliography project on to the computer. Laborious tasks such as editing the text and compiling indexes (author, journal, date) could be executed with far greater efficiency by computer, as could chronological and alphabetical sorting. Useful by-products of fast information retrieval included quantitative analyses of the data (for example, who contributed what to a particular journal during a given period), matching dates to periodical volume numbers, and ascertaining the exact percentage of the Collection utilized, as well as the precise number of entries in the Genizah bibliography (to replace approximations). The process was thus under way that would ultimately lead to the publication and the online availability of bibliographical information about every published Cambridge Genizah text.

Conservation

The conservation process that I inherited when I was appointed had been adopted following professional advice from the experts at the British Museum (later the British Library). With the newly-acquired funding, the Library was able to increase the conservation staff from one and a half posts to five full-time posts and thus to ensure a much quicker turnover than before. The process was not an easy one and required much patience and care. The fragments arrived in varying stages of disrepair. Some had been so crumpled and stuck together that considerable time and skill were necessary merely to separate them. The paper fragments, if brittle, dirty or stuck together, were first washed, then floated apart and dried. Much of the paper could be dry cleaned with the aid of brushes and then ironed. Weak or torn sections were repaired.

Vellum fragments were more difficult. Over the years they had become brittle, twisted, stretched and curled, so they had to be relaxed, then dried between blotting paper and boards to remove the creases. Badly damaged fragments were humidified in a sealed container with a tray of water and thymol crystals underneath. Once pliable, the fragment was flattened and dried, using blotting paper and boards. Tears in the vellum were repaired by stitching. The collection was housed in Melinex, a tough, stable film made by ICI. It remains constant over varied temperatures and humidities, inert to most chemicals and is a sparkling, clear film.

Each fragment was enclosed between two pieces of Melinex, sewn round with a zig-zag machine stitch, leaving an air-hole in one side. The fragment was then hand-stitched into position and a label inserted. The completed volumes were taken to their more permanent home in the environmentally controlled stacks behind the Manuscripts Reading Room. All conserved items were microfilmed with copies sent to various academic institutions around the world. A process was also begun for the re-conservation of many of the fragments that had received some cursory physical attention in earlier years but sorely required more up-to-date and efficacious treatment.

Availability and Acknowledgement

On arrival at Cambridge University Library I had been horrified to find that there were some boxes of fragments with the names of individual scholars written on their sides, as if to imply that these individuals had exclusive rights to their contents. In addition, there were boxes in which some scholars had been allowed to rummage to their heart's content until they found what interested them and dismissed the other items as of no interest or value. With the encouragement and cooperation of Eric Ceadel, new rules were set down. No fragments were the exclusive possession of anyone but Cambridge University Library. The Library would no longer allow any scholars access to any unconserved fragments before they had been conserved and microfilmed but, once they had been through those treatments, they would be available to all scholars.

In addition, all books and articles wishing to make use of Cambridge material would be required to give a written undertaking that they would cite the full and accurate class-mark in each instance, make due

17. Eric Ceadel, Cambridge University Librarian, 1967-79 (Cambridge University Library).

acknowledgement to the Syndics of the Library for permission to publish, and send a copy of the publication to the Library. I even published an article decrying the appearance of so many editions, facsimiles and images that lacked such details or arrangements. Scholars around the world were informed of the new arrangements. Most realized the good sense involved and, while perhaps feeling a little inconvenienced, accepted the need for such order and control which could only ultimately benefit all scholarship.

Criticism

Nehemya Allony was not one of those who accepted the new situation. He had been involved with the study of Hebrew manuscripts for many decades and had been the first director of the Institute for Microfilmed Hebrew Manuscripts under the aegis of the Hebrew University of Jerusalem. He had written about the Genizah, had published many fragments, and saw it as his right to continue to do as he had long pleased with the fragments in Cambridge. In fact, when publishing Genizah texts, he often failed to give the accurate class-marks. In response to the new situation, Allony published what was no less than a salacious attack on me and my work at Cambridge in the form of a letter about Cambridge University Library in the Hebrew bibliographical periodical *Yad Laqore* in the summer of 1979. Among the accusations were that I was angling to become the Director of the Jewish National and University Library in Jerusalem, was hindering research, had produced only a brief booklet, had been inaccurate about the numbers of Genizah fragments at Cambridge University Library, and there were some other preposterous claims. All of these strictures were disposed of in a strongly worded and detailed reply by myself that was published in the same periodical late in 1980.

There was one meeting in Cambridge in the late 1970s at which I was also criticized in connection with my work in the Unit. Since my post had been established by both the Library and the Faculty of Oriental Studies, it was my duty to give a report of my progress at the Faculty's annual general meeting in the Michaelmas Term, at which many members of the Faculty were always present. Eric Ceadel was in the chair and called for my report which I delivered, making due reference to the progress achieved in the Unit's various activities. Eric called for comments and questions and an elderly scholar requested the floor. I expected some unqualified praise but was astonished by quite the opposite. He suggested that all the necessary work on the Genizah Collection had long since been completed and that he was therefore at a loss to know what remained for me to do with the fragments. Thinking quickly on my feet, I did not of course embarrass him but said that I was a little unsure of precisely which parts of the work had already been completed before my arrival. If he were to send me a note with such details, I would of course respond as necessary. Needless to say, I heard nothing more from him on the subject and we all assumed that he was beginning to show some unpleasant signs of aging.

Eric also lent me his support in another unpleasant set of circumstances. A scholar from Canada, Ernest John Revell, had been in Cambridge to research the Genizah materials for his work on the history and development of systems of pointing Hebrew in the Middle Ages. He had told me about his personal and unpublished research to date and I had guided him to the relevant parts of the Collection. A few months later, an Italian Hebraist with similar interests, Bruno Chiesa, had asked to see me and, given that he had little English, we had to converse in French. It turned out that he too was working on systems of pointing and so I guided him in the same way that I had guided Revell.

When Revell's work appeared in print, Chiesa wrote an angry letter to the University Librarian, Eric Ceadel, translated for him from Italian into English by a colleague of his in Cambridge. In his letter he accused me of withholding information from him about work that was relevant to his research. Asked by Eric to comment, I explained that I had given Chiesa the same information that I had given Revell but felt that I could not betray the confidence of the latter researcher by providing any details of his unpublished research. That was the end of the matter but it was a lesson for me in how scholars feel free to blame others if they are unaware of all the research in their fields.

VIP Visits

There were a number of distinguished visitors during those first dozen years of the Unit. HRH Prince Philip, Chancellor of the University, included the Genizah conservation department in his tour of the Library. In reply to his questions, I explained how the University had come to possess the collection, its nature and significance, and the continuing work of conservation and research. Lively as ever, he retorted that the survival of so many old items reminded him of the obsession of some older members of his own family never to dispose of any scrap of written text. His Imperial Highness, Prince Mikasa of Japan, himself a keen amateur Hebraist, heard an explanation from me of the collection's importance in the course of his visit to the Library. I especially remember that one of the porters at the front desk of the Library had asked to be excused from attending that day because his brother had suffered terribly in a Japanese prisoner-of-war camp and he could not face the royal visitor.

The Israeli Ambassador, Mr. Shlomo Argov, visited Cambridge for the express purpose of viewing a special exhibition of some of the fragments. I was deeply impressed by his intelligence and his knowledge. Sadly, he was later the victim of a terrorist attack in London which left him disabled for the remainder of his life. The official Chinese delegation of the Ninth International Congress on Archives visited the Library and viewed the special techniques being used to preserve and protect the Genizah material.

Representatives of the media included journalists from *The Times* and the *Jewish Chronicle*, who wrote major articles; news units from BBC TV and ITV, who prepared short films on our work; an interviewer and technician from the Israeli Broadcasting Authority, who prepared an hour-long programme broadcast in Israel; and a reporter from the BBC World Service, who conducted an interview about the Unit's work. Another interview was recorded at the local radio studio and broadcast on the John Dunn Programme on BBC Radio 2. I was astonished at the degree to which a popular presenter such as John Dunn had prepared himself (or perhaps been prepared by assistant staff) with many relevant questions to put to me.

At the invitation of the Jewish Theological Seminary of America, Helen Marmor of NBC in New York produced a film about Schechter's discovery of the Genizah and its importance for reconstructing the lives of the Mediterranean communities in the Middle Ages. The Cambridge research was undertaken by myself and my colleagues in the Unit, who also presented much of the film. Nick Morris and his camera crew spent five days 'shooting' at Cambridge University Library and on location in Cambridge and most of the edited programme consisted of this 'footage'. The hour-long film entitled 'From Cairo to Cambridge' was broadcast on the educational networks in the USA soon afterwards.

One amusing incident springs to mind. When describing the many attributes of Mrs Lewis and Mrs Gibson (who had purchased fragments from their latest visit to the Near East and shown them to Solomon Schechter), I had foolishly alluded to the fact that beauty was not among them. Ms Marmor stopped the filming and gave me a deserved dressing-down for my sexist remark. Next day, I was discussing Solomon Schechter and she stopped the recording in order to ask me to include a description of his attractive red hair. I declined to do so on the grounds that it would be a sexist remark. She demurely concurred and the camera crew, who seemed to me to be male chauvinists to a man, were very pleased with me.

15

A Talented Team
(1973–84)

Cooperative Ventures

It was obvious to me from the start (as had been indicated to me by Professors Goitein and Wieder) that it would be necessary to involve leading academic institutions and individuals from Israel in the work of the Unit. I therefore approached Professor Ephraim Urbach of the Israel Academy and Professor Haim Beinart of the Hebrew University of Jerusalem and explained my plans for the conservation, microfilming and scholarly description of all 32 crates of neglected fragments. I indicated that we needed their endorsement in order to raise funds in Europe and in the USA, as well as their assistance in identifying experts in specific fields who could come and work with me in Cambridge for weeks, or even months, on the sorting, according to subject, of what was stored in those crates. They swiftly arranged to visit me in Cambridge. Together we examined all the Genizah materials in the University Library and during the excellent lunch and warm welcome that Shulie had prepared for them at home on 7 January 1974 (four months after I had taken up my post) we discussed in detail the various ways forward.

As a result of these deliberations, subsequent months saw the arrival of Professors Ezra Fleischer, Israel Yeivin, Malachi Beit-Arié and Yaakov Sussmann, each of whom worked in the Unit on aspects of the sorting process, especially in their areas of specialization. Professor Goitein came in July 1974 and spent a few intensively active days sorting out Judeo-Arabic material. Shulie and I arranged a sherry party in his honour at our home. Also in 1974, I invited my former teacher, Rabbi Dr. Ephraim Yehudah (Ernest) Wiesenberg, Reader in Hebrew and Jewish Studies at University College London, to come for one or two days each week in order to work on the rabbinic fragments. He sometimes stayed over with us at our home and joined the family for some of its celebrations. He was a delightful person and a fount of deep literary and historical knowledge with a gentle personality and a cheerful countenance. He managed successfully to

18. Genizah team, 1981 (Cambridge University Library).

combine deep Jewish piety with traditional rabbinic learning and serious scientific scholarship.

Research Assistance

External funding also soon made it possible to appoint the Unit's first full-time research assistants whose task was to describe the uncatalogued fragments (which meant effectively most of the 200,000 items!) according to their areas of specialization. The task of Malcolm Davis was to prepare catalogues of all the biblical Hebrew fragments, amounting to some 25,000 items. Malcolm was an evangelical Christian with a love of the Bible who knew most of its contents at least in translation but had also completed two degrees in Hebrew studies at the University of Oxford. He felt a personal devotion to the biblical texts and enjoyed his work. He worked at an intense pace and was a loyal, cooperative and pleasant colleague to have in the Unit. Simon Hopkins came as an expert in Arabic to deal with the Judeo-Arabic texts, to make progress with the massive bibliographical project (everything published in 80 years on the Genizah texts), and, later, to describe the unusual items in T-S A45, including the Book of Tobit, the Apocalypse of Zerubbabel and the Scroll of Antiochus.

Simon had studied at the School of Oriental and African Studies in the University of London with Professor Edward Ullendorff, completing his doctorate under the supervision of Professor J.E. Wansbrough, and his preferences and attitudes reflected those of his teachers. He saw scholarship as a pure pursuit, was not greatly enthused by popularization and public relations, and did not mind spending lengthy periods in preparing and publishing highly-detailed papers of linguistic analysis relating to the early history of Judeo-Arabic and its historical development as reflected in the Genizah texts through the eleventh, twelfth and thirteenth centuries. Simon was in the Unit until 1978 when he was appointed (at the age of 28) as professor of Hebrew at the University of Cape Town in South Africa.

Later arrivals from Israel to work on the fragments included Tsvi Groner, whose expertise was in the rabbinic literature of the post-Talmudic period, and Amitai Spitzer, who had worked previously on bibliographical and editorial projects and was therefore assigned to work on the Genizah bibliography. Tsvi's rabbinic education had been in many ways similar to my own and he, and his wife Hava, became close friends with Shulie and me. Avi Shivtiel had been the faculty's first lecturer in Modern Hebrew and had impressed widely with his vast knowledge of Hebrew and Jewish sources, as well as successfully completing with Professor Robert Serjeant an important doctoral dissertation on popular Arabic sayings. As a fine Arabist, Avi came to us in the Unit after his tenure in the faculty had come to an end and he and his wife Elisheva also became close friends with Shulie and me. Sad to relate, both these fine women were destined to succumb to cancer at early ages. Avi, Tsvi and I often exchanged quotes from biblical and rabbinic texts and left those around us far behind in the appreciation of such literature.

Paul Fenton, another fine Arabist with training at the Sorbonne and a period (somewhat incognito!) in Beirut, as well as special competence in the study of Jewish mysticism and medicine, replaced Simon Hopkins in 1978 and did similar work to that of his predecessor for some four years. He also discovered and published a number of intriguing fragments, including one that appeared to describe an unexpectedly affable and warm Moses Maimonides. Paul and his wife Chava were also active members of the local Jewish community in Cambridge and personal friends of Shulie and me.

When we were seeking an expert in the history of Jewish medicine in the medieval Islamic world to continue Penelope Johnstone's work (noted below), Professor Goitein recommended Haskell Isaacs of Manchester.

Haskell had been working for many years as a local family doctor but had also completed a master's degree and a doctorate at the University of Manchester and had jointly published with its Arabist, Derek Latham. Haskell, encouraged by his wife Ruth and his family, came to Cambridge in 1983 and enjoyed a very active retirement, working with us in the Unit and always giving sound and mature advice on personal as well as professional matters. I should add that, as well as regularly entertaining local Jewish students to meals, Shulie and I often had visiting scholars in our home for Shabbat meals while they were on research trips to Cambridge.

Eleazar Gutwirth, an expert on Judeo-Spanish, contributed to that area of research and arranged an exhibition of such material (with an accompanying booklet), while Debbie Patterson assisted with computing, public relations and the planning of the bibliography before later going on to work in the University's development office. Penelope Johnstone was a historian of medicine, especially in the Arab world, and was funded by the Wellcome Trust to come and work on the medical texts. Professor Shirley Lund, who had completed a doctorate at St Andrew's University with Matthew Black and taught at Boston University, laid some foundations for the later, comprehensive work of Michael Klein on the targumic fragments. Rabbi Yehoshua Hutner worked from time to time on the incunables (pre-1501 prints) and Professor David Téné on the linguistic materials.

Menahem Ben-Sasson was a Rothschild Fellow from the Hebrew University of Jerusalem attached to the Unit in 1983-84. He and his wife Ada, a physician, and their children were active members of the Jewish community and close friends of the Reif family. Professor Shelomo Morag, a brilliant scholar of Hebrew linguistics, was a Visiting Fellow at St John's College in 1975-76 and worked on the vocalized Talmudic fragments in the Unit. He and his wife Shoshana, a scholar and intellectual in her own right, were also regular attendees at the Cambridge Synagogue in Thompson's Lane and often ate at our Shabbat table. Geoffrey Khan began his academic career in the Unit in 1983, taking over from Paul Fenton and proving for a decade to be a most industrious Genizah researcher, prolific scholar and friendly colleague. From 1976, my wife Shulie also began to work part-time in the Unit as an editorial assistant. She took on many demanding roles including bibliographer, editor, translator and data processor.

Daily Grind

In addition to all the daily and humdrum activities of a research project, in which they often shared, those in the Unit were primarily concerned with the preparation of catalogues of the Genizah manuscripts. Unlike many large and well-produced codices, Genizah fragments rarely give any clear indication of date, authorship and provenance. Uncovering such data, wherever possible, as well as identifying and describing their content, are challenging activities, demanding wide knowledge, careful analysis, intense detective work and a prodigious amount of patience. Directing such a project became more and more demanding of my time, energy and abilities. Cambridge University Library agreed to initiate a 'Genizah Series' of publications, and the first items, compiled by Simon Hopkins and Malcolm Davis, appeared in 1978 and 1980. Another fifteen volumes, published for the University Library by Cambridge University Press, would duly appear in the subsequent quarter of a century. I read through every one of these, in some cases offering general guidance and some additional comments, while in others I was involved in extensive editorial work.

One visiting professor from Israel told me that my name should be the lead name on all these publications, as was the custom in Israel (and had indeed been so in Germany), and as had been his own practice with his research projects over many years. My reply was that I thought that each of the researchers should receive credit for their own work and that this was especially important for them at the early stages of their post-doctoral careers. Struggling, as the Unit still was, to win the support, recognition and respect that I believed it deserved, we were very gratified by the responses to the appearance of the first volumes in the 'Genizah Series'.

Praise and an Invitation

In London, Raphael Loewe wrote: 'The fact that the scales have at last fallen from the university's eyes is due...principally to the enthusiasm, energy and drive of Dr. S.C. Reif who...has the Genizah in his care'. From the Netherlands came the comments of A.S. van der Woude: 'We sincerely hope that funds may be granted to bring this impressive work to a happy end, since it makes accessible a host of material which otherwise would remain almost unknown to the average biblical scholar.' James Barr in Oxford referred to 'producing order out of what to most people would have looked like chaos'; Mark Cohen in Princeton welcomed 'significant steps forward in the rationalization and publication of the collection'; Alexander Scheiber in Budapest wrote of 'a source of inspiration' for Genizah scholars; while Leon Nemoy in Philadelphia noted 'a capital contribution to our meager knowledge' and 'a profound debt of gratitude'.

It was the same James Barr who almost succeeded in expanding my academic commitments beyond their already unreasonably high levels. I had met Barr at the Society for Old Testament Studies (SOTS) and had known and admired his work since my days of doctoral research in London and early academic teaching in Glasgow. He had been schooled, educated and ordained in my hometown of Edinburgh, had served as a Church of Scotland minister in Tiberias, Israel, and had been professor in various universities, including Edinburgh and Manchester, before taking up a chair in Oxford in 1976. His innovative linguistic approach to the Hebrew Bible had a major impact on its scientific study, forcing many scholars to think again about the theological tendentiousness of many of their theories.

James had taken over responsibility for the planning and production of a new dictionary of biblical Hebrew to replace the well outdated but still widely used *Hebrew and English Lexicon* of Brown, Driver and Briggs that had first appeared in 1906. He was well acquainted with my Genizah work, my publications and my reviews, and asked if he might come and see me when next in Cambridge. I was flattered by his interest and invited him to come to our home in Cambridge, which he did on a dank and dreary Saturday night in December 1974. He explained how things were progressing (or, more accurately, not progressing) with the projected dictionary and asked if I would take over responsibility for the project. I indicated that if I did, the new publication would need to take account not only of the Qumran discoveries but also, to some degree at least, of early rabbinic Hebrew.

The matter dragged on for another three years without resolution and we had a meeting with representatives of Oxford University Press in Oxford in December 1977. I thought long and hard about the offer of involvement but eventually decided that the number of hours in the day, even at my rate of industry, were simply insufficient to permit another such major commitment. Eventually, the dictionary found its rescuer in another member of St John's College, Cambridge, namely, David Clines, who oversaw its production in Sheffield in eight volumes and did sensibly include significant post-biblical material.

Academic and Educational Roles

I welcomed the opportunities that came my way to be an external examiner at the University of Glasgow and at Jews' College, London, was an active member of SOTS and the World Union of Jewish Studies, giving my first paper to the last-mentioned organization, on the topic of the history of

Jewish liturgical research, at its conference in Jerusalem in 1981. I lectured at the meeting of the International Organization for the Study of the Old Testament presided over by Luis Alonso Schökel in Salamanca in 1983, an especially memorable event for me since it was the first time I had been billeted in a monastery. The large crucifix on the wall, and the peep-hole on the door of the room, once used to check if inmates were behaving, were somewhat disconcerting for an observant Jew.

Encouraged by Raphael Loewe, I also served on the Council of the Jewish Historical Society of England (and later became its president). At that time, David Goldstein was in charge of the hebraica at the British Library, and Ronald May had a parallel appointment at the Bodleian Library in Oxford. I thought that it would be a good idea to form a small organization to represent such curators of hebraica and to meet on a regular basis for lectures and discussions. Thus was born the Hebraica Libraries' Group of which I was the convener for the first three years of its existence from 1981 to 1984.

During the winter conference of SOTS held in January 1975 at a conference centre belonging to King's College in Clapham Common, a few of us with special interests in Jewish Studies, led by Geza Vermes of Oxford, arranged an informal meeting at a fast-food establishment near the local underground station and there resolved to set in motion the founding of the British Association for Jewish Studies (BAJS), with Geza as its first president. Within a year or two of its foundation, I became its treasurer and worked closely with Tessa Rajak who was its secretary. I have never been inclined just to go along with a policy that I did not approve and when BAJS chose a route that did not appeal to me I resigned the treasureship. Looking back, I think this was a rather rash decision and I learned over the years to be at least a little more circumspect in how I responded to situations and trends that I did not favour. Expressing active opposition to their decisions is not the best way of making oneself popular with one's colleagues. But, as I have written above, I regarded it (and still regard it) as a matter of retaining my integrity. Ultimately, I seem to have been forgiven (at least by some) since I was elected president of the BAJS in 1992.

Cyril Stein, who was chairman of its governors, enlisted my support for his plans at Carmel College by having me appointed as one of the governors. In that capacity I chaired the head-hunting committee after the departure of Rabbi Jeremy Rosen and the result was the appointment in 1984 of Philip Skelker who did a fine job until the College finally had to close in 1997. Rabbi Abraham Levy established the Young Jewish Leadership Institute for the further education of those who would ultimately play important roles in the Anglo-Jewish community and, at his request, I delivered various courses of lectures to those students over a period of years.

Johnian Jaunts

Once I had been admitted to the University as an MA in 1976, I was asked if I would wish to become as member of St John's College and of course I enthusiastically welcomed the proposal. I thought it would represent another step towards being accepted in the Cambridge academic community as one of their own. It was indeed such a step but only a small one, and there were many more steps that had to be taken before that acceptance became wholehearted and totally effective. Nevertheless, I was able to dine at College expense once a week during term-time and, between 1976 and 1986, I did that on a regular basis. Andrew Macintosh was of course one of my closest contacts in the College and was president of the College from 1995 until 1999.

I sometimes also attended, with John Emerton, the wine circle on Sunday evenings, and marvelled at his ability to remain at the table until most of the bottles and carafes in front of him had been emptied. My capacity for alcohol was nowhere near his and it was astonishing how much more relaxed and coherent he became as the wine took effect. That was certainly the time to hear all manner of otherwise undisclosed gossip. I was also astonished by his ability to ride his bike, admittedly not entirely in a straight line, as he made his way out of the College on his way home. After such an evening, I often chose to make my way home on foot.

It was a real pleasure to come to know some of the prominent members of the College at that period. I remember being aghast when it was pointed out to me in about 1977 that Professor Sir Harold Jeffreys, sitting at high table with us (and known, among other things, for his determined objections to the theory of continental drift and plate tectonics), had been elected to a fellowship in 1914, two years before my mother was born! It was not at all unusual for these College members, especially in humanities, to be plain 'Mr.' since a fair number of them had come to Cambridge in the 1930s and at that time one could proceed from a master's degree to teaching at College and to a fellowship. They researched and published of course but did not necessarily spend time obtaining a PhD. What I found surprising was the degree to which these older and more established Fellows were friendly and welcoming to a newcomer, and (God help us!) a PhD from the University of London, and not Cambridge or Oxford, while the research fellows, there for three or four years, by and large displayed a rather more distant attitude towards one merely enjoying dining privileges. Perhaps they were simply more tied up with themselves and their research and less inclined to welcome non-Fellows into their company.

John Crook, a classicist and an expert in Roman history and law, had been a contemporary of Raphael Loewe but had landed on his academic feet more swiftly and more surely than Raphael had done, having been appointed a Fellow in 1951 and serving as president from 1971 until 1975. He made a point of welcoming visitors and newcomers and would regale you with a wide range of lively anecdotes that made him, as well as you, chuckle and giggle. He had an intense love for the College and its institutions and sometimes when presiding at high table would note that I was present and call me to sit by him (as long as no other Fellows had visitors who should more correctly be accorded that privilege). On one such occasion, he told us about an incident with his father, an army bandsman, at home in Balham, south London. In tones that were in no way hushed, he explained how he had asked his father what 'fuck' meant. Father had explained, but, said John, the confirmed bachelor, 'I had no idea what it meant then and I have no idea now!'

Nicholas Mansergh was then Master and Harry Hinsley President (followed afterwards by Renford Bambrough) but in my rather junior capacity I never enjoyed more than a passing acquaintance with them at that time. Norman Bleehen was from an Orthodox Jewish background, was elected to a chair in clinical oncology, and became a Fellow in 1976. The friendship with him was not only at College but also in the synagogue, which he attended regularly, and encompassed both his wife, Tirza, and Shulie. Having dining rights was a very welcome privilege but in no way comparable with being elected a Fellow. When I had visitors, I often took them to the very twentieth-century University Centre (largely constructed of lumps of unattractive concrete) but it would undoubtedly have impressed them much more to be entertained in a sixteenth-century college.

I recall being told by John Crook that as president he had proposed that the exclusively Christian language of the graces before and after dinner in hall should be adjusted slightly to allow non-Christians to feel included. Strong objection came to the proposal not only from some practising Anglicans but also from the atheists who argued that they did not believe a word of the graces but College institutions should not be altered. As I have already mentioned, Chris Johnson was always friendly and warm towards me. I once mentioned something to do with the seder traditionally held on the first night of Pesaḥ (Passover) and was beginning to explain when Chris told me that he knew all about it since his wife came from a Jewish family.

A similar exchange took place with Frank Smithies, a brilliant mathematician, born and reared in Edinburgh, who had a major influence on the development of functional analysis. He evidently also had a Jewish wife. Frank was a chain-smoker in days when one could smoke in College, and participants in the wine circle were even encouraged to smoke cigars. It was Frank who encouraged me to attend the Junior Book Club where we reported on books read and bid for them at auctions afterwards. I also got to know other Fellows in that context.

Norman Henry and Benny Farmer were Fellows with whom it was a delight to chat as we dined. Benny had come up to St John's in 1934 and had excelled in the field of geography, especially the social geography (as we would today entitle it) of South Asia. Although without a doctorate or a chair (as was not uncommon in those times), he had held his fellowship since 1948 and had been very active not only in widely promoting the academic study of geography but also in numerous College and University committees. Norman Henry, an Aberdonian with a love of tradition, order and good cuisine, excelled in mineralogy and crystallography but made his mark in teaching rather than in publishing research. He would invariably come over to me and start a conversation, sensing intuitively that as a newcomer I might be feeling lonely and even over-awed.

Harry Hinsley, another Fellow from a modest background, became Master in 1979 and I then had some opportunities to chat with him over dinner. Knowing that he had been a major figure in British intelligence during the Second World War, I was once brave enough to ask why the British did not bomb the train tracks to Auschwitz which were ferrying many thousands of Jews to their deaths, when they had control of the skies in the latter part of the hostilities. 'Why should they have done so?' was his counter. 'Well maybe for moral reasons,' I proposed. 'My dear boy,' said Harry, 'decisions of that nature have not been taken on such grounds since the time of Lord Palmerston, in the middle of the nineteenth century'.

But was There an Attractive Future?

Around 1984-85, I wished to clarify whether there was any chance that my academic abilities and accomplishments might ever make me worthy of a fellowship at St John's. I decided that I could ask my good friend Andrew Macintosh that question in a fairly outright manner. He did after all regularly express admiration of my learning (which he often solicited in his research) and was impressed by what I had achieved with the Genizah Collection. I asked the question and he assured me that there seemed to him to be no chance of such an election since such appointments were either of newly-elected professors or of teachers who were needed within the College. I did sometimes dine at College in the subsequent years but with a reduced appetite in every sense.

Despite all my achievements in the Unit and the efforts I had made to maintain a high academic profile, my ambition to win a higher degree of acceptance as a scholar was being fulfilled in the world at large but did not appear to me to be making what I personally would have regarded as genuine progress in Cambridge for a scholar around the age of 40. A lectureship or a readership and a college fellowship were what others enjoyed who had fewer achievements to their name than I, and this rankled with me. I began to put out feelers for jobs elsewhere and even toyed with the idea of going into the bookselling business. To that latter end, I went to London and had a long chat with Erwin Rosenthal's son Tom, then head of the publishing firm Secker and Warburg. He was helpful and made various suggestions. Shulie and I gave the prospect a great deal of thought and finally decided to remain with the devil we knew. I could not rid myself of the firmly-fixed notion that if only I applied myself even more energetically to my projects at Cambridge, due rewards would be forthcoming. Perhaps I was not yet cynical enough about the academic world.

In 1982, I was also approached by Chief Rabbi Jakobovits, Stanley Kalms, the chairman of the Dixon Group, a major electrical retailer, and various other educators and philanthropists who were at that time planning to establish on its own campus to the north-west of London a College of Jewish Studies to provide all manner of higher Jewish education for Rabbis, teachers and the general public. It would effectively be a replacement (although they described it as a continuation) of Jews' College. They proposed that I should take over as Rector of the whole project and offered an attractive package, but only for five years. I thought seriously about it but decided against giving up a tenured university post in Cambridge for a Jewish communal post with an unsecured future.

In 1980 there was an advertisement by the Hebrew University of Jerusalem inviting applications for newly-established lectureships in Jewish studies. As I understand it, the Hebrew University had for long been committed to appointing its own graduates in humanities, especially in Jewish studies, and some of its faculty members realized that this created a kind of incestuous scholarship in some fields. The idea was therefore to try to attract some fresh blood. There were apparently many applications but it was later confided to me that only two scholars had made it through all the procedures and reached the final committee for approval. One of them was Robert Wistrich, an expert in modern Jewish history, who received an appointment and went on to have an illustrious career at the Hebrew University and to excel in the study of modern antisemitism. I was the other.

In a letter dated 6 July 1982, the chairman of the Institute of Jewish Studies, Joseph Dan, updated me on developments and concluded with an optimistic assessment: 'let me express my strong belief that very soon you will join the staff of the I[nstitute of] J[ewish] S[tudies]'. I have heard various rumours over the years about what then occurred. One explanation was that there was considerable disagreement between the Talmud and Hebrew Literature departments about my proposed appointment. Another was that my many articles in numerous fields were interpreted by one major (and mischievous?) academic figure as an indication that I was not an expert in any one of them. Whatever the reason, no appointment was made.

The year after Eric's death, when John Oates was temporarily in charge of the Library, was a difficult one for me not only because he was less enthralled by my work than Eric had been. He was not helpful when I wished to bring a group of Jewish philanthropists to the Library on a Sunday. It may be that he was one of those in the Library who simply did not see the study of Hebrew manuscripts as of central interest to the Library. When the Director of the John Rylands University Library of Manchester, Dr. Frederick Ratcliffe, was being shown around the Library before his appointment as University Librarian in 1980, Oates indicated to him where the Darwin Project and the Genizah Research Unit were located and added that they were not really part of the Library. Two 'jewels in the crown of the Library', as some have called them, but for Oates not really integral to that august institution.

A Fresh Breath of Air

Ratcliffe's arrival at the University Library brought a fresh breath of air for me, as indeed did that of the newly-appointed Deputy Librarian, Reg Carr, who had already worked with Ratcliffe at an earlier stage of his career. Although I had enjoyed an excellent working relationship with Eric, Fred, as he soon permitted me to call him, was a much livelier personality. He had served as an officer in the army and had completed a doctorate in German studies. He greatly appreciated sound scholarship and saw the role of a major research library as one that should encourage research and scholarship to a high level and should generally appoint as librarians those with impressive degrees of academic competence and qualification. A few months before he took up his appointment in Cambridge, he invited me to

Manchester to advise him on what should be done with its important collection of hebraica in general and its Genizah fragments in particular. These fragments had come to Manchester from the estate of Haham Moses Gaster and needed conservation, copying and description. He and I undoubtedly hit it off. We were both direct in our opinions, anxious to succeed in all our projects, efficient and friendly enough personalities to attract support within and outside the University, and committed to research and academic bibliography.

Between 1981 and 1984 I worked assiduously to ensure that Fred became an enthusiastic supporter and encourager of progress in the Unit and he came to appreciate to a considerable degree what was being achieved. He welcomed distinguished visitors and important donors and was happy to arrange admirably catered lunches for them in his room when that seemed appropriate. Sometimes I made a suggestion which he rejected on the spot and I learned to present my case cogently, not to press it, but simply to leave it with him. It was not uncommon for him to call me back some weeks later and ask about that same idea before proposing that we should adopt it. He seems to have needed time to absorb it, in some instances revise it in his own mind, and then to take it on board. I was happy to go along with such a policy and we were rarely at odds.

I do recall that when I grew a beard at around that time he was very disapproving and told me in no uncertain terms, rather like an army officer would have done, to get rid of it. I didn't, and he of course did not pursue the matter. His view was that I should at some stage be promoted to a readership since that would more accurately reflect my scholarship, and that certainly cheered me up and gave me reason for optimism. He took soundings and the consensus of the referees seems to have been that such an appointment would be somewhat premature at that stage. Although I had many articles to my name, I should first publish one or two more books. No account whatsoever seems to have been taken by such referees of the academic value of what I had done in the Unit. I believe that referees some 20 or 30 years later would probably have thought otherwise. It was around that time that a senior Cambridge academic suggested in all seriousness that if only I converted to Anglicanism I would in the future be a strong candidate for the Regius Chair of Hebrew.

Fred was keen to find some way of offering recognition and he came up with the idea of my taking over all the oriental sections of the Library, merging them into one new division and centralizing their administration. As head of that division, I would have responsibility for ensuring its smooth and efficient running and would report directly to him. In this new position, I would be worthy of promotion and he would recommend that I be appointed as Senior Under-Librarian, with a status and salary somewhat similar to that of a reader. That appointment came on 1 October 1984. It was not what I ultimately hoped for but it brought recognition and status, as well as a much better salary. At the same time, it was destined to ensure that my energies were to be employed in even more diverse ways in the course of the subsequent fourteen years.

16

Meanwhile at Home
(1973–84)

Parental Care

While I was busy building a career and developing the Unit into a major international research project, Shulie and the children were also adjusting to their new lives in Cambridge. Shulie was keen to be at home with the children until they were full-time at school but once that stage of life had been reached, she began to look for ways of using her numerous talents and contributing seriously to the meagre income that my University post brought me in the first years at the University Library. She took courses and obtained certificates in book-keeping, typing and computing and also succeeded in completing a course in teaching English as a Foreign Language to students from abroad (EFL). When she also began to assist us in the Unit, she used these qualifications and her other talents in contributing to many aspects of the Unit's activities. She also taught part-time at EFL schools in Cambridge. An additional source of income for the family came from the private lessons she gave in Hebrew and in Judaism to local Jewish children. They enjoyed that experience and recalled many years later the important effect that it had had on them when they wrote letters of condolence to me on Shulie's untimely passing. Whatever jobs she took on, she always insisted on being at home when the children returned from school, a practice that she continued until they had completed high school.

As well as slowly introducing them to reading and writing English, Shulie also taught our children to read and write Hebrew, to understand its grammar, and to read its literature, as well as many of the basics about the observance of Judaism and the importance of the State of Israel. She always prepared well and was an efficient and patient teacher. We were both determined that living in Cambridge should not deny them that sort of education. There were only a handful of Jewish children of their age with whom they could be friendly and that made social matters difficult for them. From about the age of nine, however, they went to the summer and winter camps of Bnei Akiva and they made friendships there that lasted them many years. To recall, Bnei Akiva is a Zionist movement that promotes the settlement of Jews in the land of Israel, a devotion to the Jewish state, and a traditional observance of Judaism. It was a tearful experience for both Shulie and me (especially for Shulie as the mother who had reared them so closely and so devotedly) when we took them to London for the first time and saw them off on the coach that drove them to their first Bnei Akiva camp.

We tried very hard as parents to give our children love, support and confidence, as well as education, and to bring up individuals with a respect for their families, their people and their society, but also with independent minds and a passion for doing excellently well in everything that they undertook and for maintaining high standards of integrity. Only recently, Aryeh reminded me of one of the principles that we enunciated to them. Even when some individuals behaved unkindly to you, the finest response was, wherever possible, to continue to behave correctly towards them. Although evenings and weekends almost always saw me at home with the family, there were times when I was at conferences, on fund-raising trips or giving guest lectures. I knew that Shulie would hold the fort very well but there was always a degree of tension in my mind between my professional and familial commitments. It seemed inevitable for someone with my degree of drive and ambition. If my major efforts were yet to be recognized in the manner I (and numerous others) thought appropriate, was I justifiably denying my wife and family time that was being devoted to the Unit's projects and to my other scholarly endeavours?

Shulie gave lessons to the children in Hebrew and Judaism until they were about ten. At that point she mentioned during one lesson how the renowned eleventh-century Jewish commentator Rashi (Rabbi Shelomo ben Yisḥaq) had explained a certain biblical verse. Aryeh, who had heard many a lecture and Torah interpretation from me over the years, piped up with the comment 'Ah yes, Mummy, but what does Ibn Ezra say about it?' This naughty comment about the twelfth-century Spanish exegete Abraham ibn Ezra (a favourite of mine) prompted a change in the Jewish educational arrangements in our home. Shulie told me the tale that evening and suggested that the time had come for me to take over our children's Hebrew lessons. I consequently prepared a full curriculum of biblical and rabbinic Hebrew that would allow them both to take a Classical Hebrew 'O' and then 'A' Level at their schools and also to become familiar with a fair number of rabbinic texts and some modern Hebrew literature.

We met on Sunday mornings for about three hours of intensive study and were joined by Maurice Roseman, who was of an age with our children and whose parents, Ivan and Lillian, were also traditional Jews and anxious for Maurice to learn more about the Jewish sources. I recall their telling me that poor Maurice used to arrive home totally exhausted each Sunday, and not just from the long cycle ride! I also taught Aryeh his barmitzvah parashah (the pentateuchal and prophetic readings for the Shabbat after he turned thirteen) and we examined together the medieval commentators on those readings. Aryeh and I later studied the Talmud together every morning before he went to school and I to my office. In the winter we would study first and then, when it was light, davend shaḥarit together. In the summer, daylight came much earlier so we could study after prayers.

Family Activities

Both Shulie and I knew from bitter experience what damage could be done by parents (especially fathers) who thought it an important part of child-rearing to stress to their children how junior in status, how lacking in experience and how ignorant they were. The hope of such parents was that this would teach them their correct place within the family and respect for their elders and betters. Such an approach usually had rather more deleterious effects. We did our best to avoid that pitfall of earlier generations and believed that the result would be not only the creation of better-balanced adults but also the maintenance of continuingly close relationships when they had become parents themselves and had built homes and careers of their own.

We usually ate breakfast and dinner together as a family. That gave the children the opportunity of telling us about the day ahead or the day just completed and provided all of us with the chance of discussing all manner of matters that were of importance to each of us. I fear that I took the opportunity of complaining to those who loved me, and those whom I loved, about the frustrations of my professional life and it must have hurt them to see my struggles, to learn how hard I had to work for every achievement, and to hear me complaining that I had not succeeded as much as I should. At the same time, the children knew, and I am sure still know, that families are there not only to enjoy happy occasions together but also to give each other support in challenging times and problematic situations. Such support helps to see one through such difficulties.

Although Shulie generally did the cooking, we always helped with clearing up after meals, after which we would all retire to our work spaces to spend the evening in preparations of various sorts. Sometimes we would watch a television programme together or go for a run or a cycle on the path alongside the River Cam, or take a punt on the river and have a picnic. When visitors came to Cambridge, we walked them around the most attractive parts of a delightful city where trees, lawns, cycle paths and a meandering river seemed to dominate many areas. Aryeh sometimes introduced them, confidently but not always wholly accurately, to the beauties of the more ancient buildings.

On the rare occasions when Shulie was unwell, I did the cooking and the children were amazed that I was able to produce what they liked. If the truth be told, that was no problem since they opted for easy meals, such as fish and chips, which were not very challenging, even for me. On one such occasion, when Shulie was confined to bed with a high temperature and a rather severe bout of influenza, I answered a knock on the front door and made a purchase. The children asked what I had bought and I told them. They ran upstairs to share this intelligence with their mother. A weak voice summoned me to the bedroom. 'What have you done? The children told me that you bought some puppies!' 'Not puppies,' I replied, 'but red paper poppies to be sported on one's lapel in memory of Armistice Day (11 November) and in support of veteran soldiers!'

When the children were still little, and sleeping in two bunk-beds, Tanya above and Aryeh below, we would play some classical music downstairs and they would fall asleep to the strains of Mozart, Tchaikovsky or Mendelssohn. At times, Shulie would play the piano for them, also from downstairs. In addition, we took them to many museums and to some concerts, including '1812' at the Royal Albert Hall in London. Poor little Aryeh had just fallen nicely asleep when the cannons boomed and he jumped with fright. I think we were a little obsessed (or at least I was) with educating them in music, history and sport, as well as in Judaism, and we succeeded in some areas and (inevitably) induced a negative reaction in others. Tanya recently reminded me that, when we had goldfish, we named them 'dag' and 'nuna', the respective Hebrew and Aramaic words for 'fish.' After a visit to the Greek and Roman antiquities, including many statues, in the British Museum, Aryeh gave us a little lecture when we put him to bed: 'A long time ago, people had no heads.' If the children wished to discuss any special problem with me, they knew they had only to come to my study and I would always stop without question what I was doing and pay attention to their needs. I shall never forget hearing from a Cambridge academic colleague that he made an effort to have dinner with his children once a week. When that same colleague was in the final few months of his life, one of his children made an effort to visit him once a year, while two others were allegedly too busy. 'As you sow, so shall you reap.'

During our first year in Cambridge, Tanya was five and Aryeh four. It was about then that I taught both children to ride two-wheeled bikes. I had already taught Tanya and thought I would best leave Aryeh's lessons until he was a little older. Aryeh, however, had other ideas and was determined not to be left behind. So, he too swiftly mastered the cycling technique. Shulie found a wonderful kindergarten called 'The Ace' where she was confident that Aryeh (whom she always regarded as a fragile little boy) could be himself and not have to be regimented or told to do things that he disliked. I believe that he enjoyed the experience. Tanya began infant school at Brunswick across the river Cam but was upset by the number of badly-behaved bullies who did not take their studies seriously. Shulie spoke to the teachers and they agreed that the catchment area on our side of the river and between us and Chesterton Road was a better one since there were many academic families living in what was known as the De Freville estate. Most of their children went to Milton Road Primary School.

Educational Principles and Priorities

Both children therefore began their serious school careers at Milton Road and made excellent progress until the age of about seven. Shulie and I (especially I, if the truth be told) wished to send our children to local schools for ideological reasons and that is why we began their education as we did. Sad to relate, there was soon to be a clash between ideology and educational progress. They enjoyed Milton Road but both of them seemed to reach an impasse at about the age of seven. They had mastered reading, writing and arithmetic, were avid readers of the books I bought them for Shabbat every Friday, and were among the best in their classes. When they seemed to be getting bored, Shulie and I asked the headmistress what was in store for them over the next four years. We were told that they should learn to socialize more. We came home, discussed the matter at length and decided that a sound and demanding education was more important to us than any political ideology. Thus began my gradual but distinct movement away from left-wing politics.

We inquired about the best academic schools in Cambridge and were told that the Perse Girls and the Perse Boys fitted our bill. As each child reached the required age for entrance to these schools, we sent them for the entrance examination. Seven-year-old Tanya told us that it had been a lovely experience that she had enjoyed very much and that she had written a little essay about a rabbits' day out and had finished by writing 'As the bunnies toasted chestnuts over an open fire, they all agreed that it had been day well spent.' We reckoned that she would be accepted and so she was. Aryeh was so bored in his final year at Milton Road that he went around the class doing other pupils' work for them and was sent out of the room for his troubles. Another entrance examination was our proposed solution. In his case, he sailed through all the questions but one. 'If you were born in 1970 (or whatever date they gave) how old would you be today?' Aryeh said that he could not answer correctly because he did not know when the compiler of the test had written that question! He too was accepted. The problem was that we simply did not have enough funds to pay the fees. We mentioned the plan to my parents-in-law, Elly and Muni, the next time we saw them and Muni immediately offered to defray half the cost. That made it possible for us to send them to the Perse Schools. The fees doubled in the course of their school careers and the contribution from the Stekels remained static but as I was given promotions and increases in salary, and Shulie's earnings increased, we managed to keep them in those top two schools until they were ready to enter university.

Both children excelled in the junior houses of their schools and both enjoyed the experience very much. Tanya went on to enjoy the senior school at the Perse for Girls too. She was taught there in no uncertain terms that girls not only could and should achieve every bit as much as boys, but should certainly strive to do even better. The girls were given great confidence in themselves and a sound educational training and Tanya responded splendidly. Of course, not all teachers were superb and likeable but, as I explained to the children, teachers are like all people. There are a few really outstanding ones whom one always remembers and a few inadequate ones, whom one tries to forget; but the majority are hard-working and devoted, even if they are often no more than average.

In the junior school, Aryeh loved his teacher and his headmaster and he greatly enjoyed the sports activities and the drama. He played a major part in a Christmas play put on at school and this led to some good-natured banter from some of our less observant Jewish friends. He did not participate in religious assembly and, when one other Jewish boy arrived, he told him that Jewish boys should stay outside the hall during the religious service. A third Jewish boy chose to take part. As I had always informed the children, one is usually (even if not always, and not by everyone) respected for adhering to one's principles and this was brought home to Aryeh in one incident. Some mention was made of Jewishness and Aryeh responded proudly to the remark. The boy who attended religious assembly then protested that he too was Jewish. His fellow pupils' response was 'No, you are not a real Jew like Reif!'

For Aryeh, the upper school was something of a problem because of our strict observance of the Jewish Shabbat. We went to see its headmaster, Anthony Melville, and he offered no solution other than the suggestion that Aryeh be sent to a Jewish boarding school like Carmel College in Wallingford, near Oxford, to which some of our friends' sons in Cambridge had gone. We were not keen for such a youngster to be away from home and asked whether it might be possible for the other boys or the teachers to help Aryeh to catch up on Monday mornings with the lessons he had missed on Saturdays. Melville was not keen but grudgingly agreed to permit the arrangement. Some helped Aryeh and some did not and, although he received a sound education, he always felt that he was somehow missing something. I shall say more of this, and of the children's teenage years, when I deal with the next period of our Cambridge experience in a later chapter.

When the children were small, I would often come home from the Library for lunch and take them back with me to school afterwards, sometimes on my bike. On one occasion, Aryeh was riding his own little bike ahead of me down a sloping street and shouted to me that he couldn't stop. I pedalled hard, overtook him, and caught him and his bike at the foot of the street. I had started my time at the University Library by driving my MGB car there each day but it soon proved more efficient (as well as gratifyingly cheaper) to ride a bike. I remember how amused Shulie and I were when we first saw all those bike-riders in their seventies and eighties cycling their way around the city. And now that I am myself one of those septuagenarian riders, it is no longer amusing but certainly pleasing.

Jewish Community

I would also walk the children with me to synagogue on Shabbat morning, allowing Shulie to rest for a little longer and to join us later. They both sat with me in the men's section of the gender-segregated Orthodox shool and I showed them how to follow the service. This was an important bonding experience and the children enjoyed the kind attention they received from some of the Jewish undergraduates. We invited many of those to join us for Shabbat lunch at home and that also assisted our children's development. One bright young thing challenged Aryeh, aged about eleven, to a board game and when the guest defeated the young competitor, Aryeh asked for a return match. 'I never play return matches,' said the undergraduate. They then played chess and this time Aryeh won. 'Let's have another game,' said the student. Aryeh's reply was inevitable: 'I never play return matches.'

When University examinations were held on Saturdays, the University agreed to allow observant Jews to take the relevant papers on Sunday morning as long as they were invigilated by a senior member of the University during the time between the Saturday originals and the Sunday replacements. Students therefore stayed overnight with us on those occasions. The only problem was that our standards are created by our environments. The children thought that the students they met, who were mostly *la crème de la crème* who had obtained places and won scholarships at the University of Cambridge, were the norm, and that everyone else was unintelligent, if not stupid.

I chatted to the children about lots of matters as we walked along the river to shool and we experienced the vagaries of the English weather as we did so. One year – maybe 1977 or 1978 – the winter was so cold that the River Cam froze over to a depth of some eighteen inches and we were able to walk on the ice, part of the way to shool. Aryeh learned to lead the singing of one of the last hymns in the service (an'im zemirot) and did it very well. He also recited kiddush, welcoming the Sabbath, at the Friday night dinner table from an early age. Tanya lit candles and said the berakhah (blessing) with her mother on Friday night and held the havdalah candle when we said the ceremonial good-bye to the Shabbat on Saturday evening.

There were many occasions on which Barry and Ros Landy invited us *en famille* to lunch with them at home after shool on Shabbat. That was usually a happy experience although it could be embarrassing when I took my parents with me since my father felt close enough to Ros (he remembered her as a little girl with pigtails in post-war Edinburgh) to tell her what he thought about all manner of things. The chicken was not quite to his taste during one such visit and he said 'Ros, this chicken is not cooked enough.' Such a diplomat. The kids had great fun playing with the Landys' three sons, Aron, David and Josh, in the spacious back-garden and that presented no problem. The long 40-minute walk home was not, however, little Aryeh's idea of Shabbat afternoon relaxation and he grumbled almost all the way about how far it was and how much longer it would take. I soon realized that I could alleviate the torture for him by telling him and Tanya some stories. I invented monsters called 'hobnogidogs' who lived in dark underground passages and did all manner of strange and rather frightening things. That helped the time – and the walk – to pass more pleasurably, or so I hoped. Perhaps I should have written up the stories after Shabbat and offered them to Bloomsbury Books.

We usually had a traditional Shabbat meal on Friday evenings, with chicken soup, oven chicken, roast potatoes and a selection of salads. As a special treat, Shulie would also prepare a delicious apple crumble. As students, she and I had once tasted some wonderful crumble at a vegetarian restaurant in London's West End and I enjoyed it so much that she always prepared such a dessert on Friday nights after we were married. For a number of years I gave some guest lectures at Homerton College, the University of Cambridge's centre for the training of teachers, in its department of religious studies, which was headed by a charming, learned and inspiring lecturer from New Zealand called Jean Holm.

When Jean was compiling a book about Jewish doctrine and practice, she asked if she could spend a Friday evening with us before she completed the relevant chapter. We of course readily agreed and she did so in the summer of 1975. Since there was no Friday evening service in shool we prayed at home and involved her in all our religious activities, explaining the whole procedure as it went. She was well acquainted with Classical Hebrew and was able to participate fairly well, also in the zemirot that we sang at the table in honour of Shabbat, and in the lengthy grace after meals which we all sang all its lengthy way through with great gusto. Jean was thrilled by the experience and told us that she would now be able to write her chapter about the Jewish Shabbat, taking into account all that she had seen and heard.

I cannot now recall whether she sent me proofs for perusal or only a final copy of the book. Either way, her description was accurate except for one detail. She had mentioned the traditional Shabbat meal and its contents and reported that part of the Shabbat tradition was to eat apple crumble on Friday evening! On the subject of Jewish food, I should mention that at that time kosher meat was delivered to our homes once a week by Fachler the Butcher who had his shop in Luton, and that the bread made in the local bakery of Maskells was said by those who knew to be thoroughly in order for observant Jews. Items in the local supermarkets began to be marked as vegetarian and I wrote to the companies and asked about how strict they were in these definitions. It turned out that they complied with vegetarian demands that were by no means less strict that those of observant Jews.

Sabbaths and Festivals

Although the Cambridge Jewish community had been a strong one in the 1940s, with numerous refugees arriving from Hitler's Europe – and indeed from evacuated London colleges – to bolster the small number of local observant students, by the time that we arrived in 1973 the tally was not an impressive one. That same summer, another family, Ron and Thelma Domb and their daughters, Dassa and Debora, came from Liverpool. Ron opened a local dental surgery and Thelma was a professional teacher of what was once called domestic science or home economics but I cannot recall what its more politically correct name was by that year. The girls functioned as leaders of a little local Bnei Akiva for our children and a few others. Ros and Barry Landy had been stalwarts of the Orthodox community for many years and they had sent their boys, Aron, David and Joshua to the Jewish boarding school, Carmel College, that had been established by Rabbi Dr. Kopul Rosen just after the Second World War and was by then in Wallingford. For the first few years, all three families tended to go to their families in London to spend the most important of the Jewish festivals in a more intensive Jewish atmosphere. This was primarily because there was no minyan for the second (extra) day of the festivals observed outside Israel, and also because on the important days of Rosh Hashanah and Yom Kippur a cantor would be brought in and would provide the kind of rather clinical – even heartless – service that none of us three families particularly enjoyed.

Not that we so much enjoyed visiting the Stekels in London either. The children were not that happy away from their own rooms, did not much care for the rich and elegant Viennese cuisine that their grandmother always prepared, and found their grandfather's humour and constant ribbing a little disconcerting. While once sitting in synagogue next to his Grandpa, Aryeh was asked what he thought that the initials MS stood for on Muni's cufflinks. Without hesitation he answered not Meir or Muni Stekel but 'Mr Shlemiel'! To his credit, Muni was highly amused and not at all cross, taking great pride in repeating the story to his synagogal colleagues. We therefore soon resolved *à trois* that we would all stay for the ḥaggim in Cambridge and that we would lead the services ourselves. This was greatly appreciated by all and the little community of observant families grew with the addition (at various points of time) of the Blaukopfs, the Fagelstons, the Romms and the Rosemans, and the arrival of some of my researchers from the Unit, as well as the Freedmans, younger Landy cousins, the Schechters and the Stones. Other couples, such as Brendel and Charles Lang, and Ruth and Haskell Isaacs, even if less strictly Orthodox, joined our festival services and expressed their pleasure at the manner in which they were conducted. Barry Landy, Lawrence Freedman, Paul Fenton and I took it in turns to lead the prayers and Ron Domb sounded the shofar (the ram's horn blown on Rosh Hashanah).

When Barry's father, Harry, and his brother-in-law were in legal trouble over their late father-in-law's bank management, many of his own community abandoned him and he was no longer invited to blow the shofar

for them. Having experienced in the case of Muni Stekel how those who
are close to you when things are going well turn away when there are
difficulties, I felt that Harry should be supported. Ron kindly allowed Harry
to replace him while Ron himself efficiently ran the whole show as a
synagogue beadle (shammas). There were a number of very distinguished
academics in the congregation, among them, Alan and Marilyn Fersht,
David and Hanna Tabor, Erwin and Elisabeth Rosenthal, Norman and Tirza
Bleehen, Eli Lauterpacht and his mother Lady Rachel, Charles Levene, and
Michael and Jeanette Pepper. At one stage there were in excess of a dozen
observant families and we were able to ensure a minyan on all the necessary
occasions. This meant that our children could enjoy a familiar enough
experience of traditional Jewish Sabbaths and festivals that would make it
possible for them to participate without difficulty in the Jewish
communities that they entered when they themselves grew up and
established families and lifestyles of their own. The Dombs, Landys and
Reifs became, and have long since remained, close friends. I began to give
a regular Talmud lesson in my home in 1974 and we covered many tractates
in the course of my decades in Cambridge. The tradition has continued
until the present.

One such Cambridge Jewish experience was remarkable enough to
warrant here the rehearsal of some details. The final day of all the autumnal
festivals is called Simḥat Torah. While there were eight days in the festival
of Sukkot (Tabernacles) in Israel in the early Middle Ages, there were nine
in the Diaspora and the last one needed to acquire an identity of its own. It
was given such an identity in Babylonia in or about the eighth century. Since
the Diaspora custom was to conclude the annual cycle of pentateuchal
readings with Deuteronomy chapter 34 and to begin the cycle again on that
same day with the reading of Genesis chapter 1, a celebration was created
around that synagogal event. Dancing with the Torah, the singing of special
hymns, and the calling to the Torah reading of every male present in the
synagogue (instead of just five, six or seven as on other Sabbaths and
festivals) became characteristics of the day.

On one such Simḥat Torah in the mid-to-late 1970s, the Landys
'invaded' our home just as we were about to eat, and were of course invited
to share our lunch with us. We then all went back to their house for some
cake and fruit and walked on to the Dombs, ready for afternoon tea. Neither
Shulie nor Thelma were ever nonplussed by such unexpected arrivals at
meal-times. It was all such a wonderful success that it became an annual
event. Shulie made the traditional holoptches (cabbage stuffed with
chopped meat) and kigel (baked potato pie) and the other courses were

provided by the Landys and Dombs, and then in later years by others too. I should also have mentioned that imbibing lots of strong drink is another feature of that festival and we piously practised that tradition with great enthusiasm. In fact, some of the younger generation learned how not to drink alcohol when they attempted to follow their parents' example and suffered inevitably unpleasant consequences. When, one year, the number of luncheon guests reached nearly 60, Shulie and I decided that in future it would be the turn of others to provide the festive fare. Some of them duly did so in later years, but (for me at any rate) some of the original magic seemed to get lost along the way.

Ideological Tensions

The growth in the number of Orthodox Jewish families was bound ultimately to lead to a clash with the more established, less committed and larger numbers of local Jews who, while acknowledging their Jewishness, preferred a somewhat lower profile for its expression. They were in many ways more typical of the Anglo-Jewish communities of the day than we more Orthodox families were. They were represented by the Cambridge Jewish Residents' Association (CJRA), while the students who used the synagogue in Thompson's Lane (opposite the Master's Lodge of St John's), where we held Orthodox services, were the Cambridge University Jewish Society (CUJS). Almost all the local Jewish families were members of the CJRA at that time and it ran the usual kind of Sunday morning Hebrew and Jewish classes for its children.

Ramon Phillips was an excellent teacher who was a Reform Jew and who, with a number of others, had been involved in promoting that brand of Jewishness in Cambridge since 1976. Given their majority in that body, the less religiously committed in the CJRA saw no problem in 1979 in offering him the post of headmaster of its Sunday classes while we Orthodox families preferred to have someone who was more traditional in doctrine and practice. They would not heed our strong objections and were determined to press ahead with his appointment. We warned them that if they did so we would resign our memberships and form our own Orthodox organization. They either did not believe us, or did not care, because they went ahead with their plan and we therefore felt obliged to implement our own.

With the help of professional friends in London we drew up a Trust Deed and laid down a constitution for a newly-created Cambridge Traditional Jewish Congregation (CTJC). We avoided the word Orthodox because we felt the need to demonstrate a greater degree of open-mindedness than was (and is) common among some Orthodox communities. In making our legal plans, and in our discussions with the lawyer who assisted us, we were aware that there might at some future date be a group of members who would wish to revert to the kind of wishy-washy Jewishness – as we saw it – out of which we had just voted ourselves. We therefore built in safeguards to our ideals and observance by making the religious practice acceptable to the Orthodox Chief Rabbi in London and ensuring that all decisions were to be made by the Trustees and not by any electoral process. If members wished to have an organization more like the CJRA they could always return to that body and not opt to turn the CTJC into such an organization. It later proved to be a wise and prescient precaution.

With some 50 members, we had a most active and successful existence throughout the years now being discussed, beginning with our formal foundation in 1979. With regard to the synagogue in Thompson's Lane, which was under the control of the CUJS, we drew up an agreement with them and with the CJRA by which we all contributed to the running costs, given that we were all making use of the students' building for our services. The Reform group created its own congregation in 1981 and eventually moved into its own premises in Auckland Road in 2015, by which time we were all on affable terms with each other. The Orthodox services of those years were well attended, efficiently run, especially outside term-time when the CTJC took control. The CUJS's level of competence varied from student generation to generation, at times reaching admirable levels and at others leaving us more than a little frustrated and even cross. But it was their building. On the social side, we were also successful. We organized lectures and debates, quiz evenings, plays (directed by Vic Fagelston), roulette evenings around Purim (usually won by Mrs Priscilla Gee), rambles in the countryside during the Pesaḥ (Passover) holiday (led by Barry Landy), football games of indeterminate numbers out of doors and five-a-side indoors, table tennis competitions and cricket matches. We also produced a bulletin a few times each year in which news of our activities and more general Jewish content were included.

In response to an appeal from some couples for a greater degree of democracy we delegated the day-to-day running of the Congregation to the elected officers and committee, and allowed the committee its own bank account, always on condition, as laid down in our Trust Deed, that the Trustees would approve the accounts and activities at their annual meetings. It was, after all, the Trust that was responsible to the Charity

Commissioners, and the Trustees therefore took their job very seriously. Most of the children of the enthusiastic CTJC members of those early days eventually went off to live in larger Jewish communities where they became active members. I appreciate that there were those who resented what amounted to CTJC's unilateral declaration of independence but I remain confident that it gave us and our children a warm and lively traditional Jewish atmosphere in shool and in our homes that served well to combat the assimilationist trends that were all around us.

Vacations

When the children began to spend summer and winter vacations with Bnei Akiva, Shulie and I were able to get away on our own and by then we could more reasonably afford to do so. In earlier years we holidayed *en famille* in ways that were relatively inexpensive. Whenever we had the opportunity, we took the children to Israel. I was usually doing some work there for the Unit, or lecturing, and my travel expenses were met. We had also built up such good relations with the Israeli academics and institutions that they were often able to provide us with accommodation that was within our means. In that way we were able to spend parts of the summer vacation in different areas of Jerusalem. During our 1979 visit the children even attended school in Rehavia in the centre of the city. Given their polite and orderly education in Cambridge, Israeli primary school was nothing short of a shocking revelation for them both. Tanya just about managed to cope with it while Aryeh was deeply unhappy. But it exposed them to a language and a lifestyle that was later to become their chosen own.

We were waiting for a bus during that visit and, when it drew up alongside, our two little children rushed to the front and were among the first to board. When chided by us, they responded that if you didn't behave in that way in Israel you would be left behind. I tried being polite at a Jerusalem post office and watched as customer after customer pushed ahead of me. Shulie and the kids waited outside and eventually came in to ask what was holding me up. 'British politeness', I replied. In later years the kids also attended summer programmes in Israel but again found it difficult to deal with the lack of order and discipline. When I hosted a group of visiting Israelis at the University Library and showed them some of the Genizah treasures, I had to insist on all sorts of rules in order to safeguard the material and to maintain some form of discipline. They became rather agitated with this degree of control and one of them shouted at me 'Do you think we are in kindergarten, or in the army?' Apparently for many Israelis these were the only two places where order prevailed. I believe that the situation is today better than it was then but progress in such public behaviour takes decades, not days.

For two successive summers in the 1970s we took cheap chalets on the cold and blowy Norfolk coast and self-catered, bringing some items from home and purchasing others at local shops. We had a lot of fun together especially in trying to cope with the cold sea, the powerful waves and the windswept beaches, most of which lacked facilities of any serious sort. The children by this time had learned to be strong swimmers and we allowed them, on reflection rather foolishly on our part, to swim out by a pier. When they were waving to us from there, we waved back, unaware that they were signalling to us by an agreed waving of their arms that they were finding it difficult to swim because of the currents around the pier. Eventually they made it back and gave us a well-deserved dressing down for our failure to be responsible parents.

We also managed to have one trip to Toronto to see my parents and the Bielaks, that is, my sister Cynthia and brother-in-law, Karl, and their family, eventually numbering five boys, Shneur, Gideon and Shlomo joining Yakov and Simcha. They were always most hospitable to us. We thought long and hard about a present for Cynthia and eventually found some miniature cups and saucers in an expensive make of crockery that she could display with some pride in her china cabinet. We thought nothing more of it until we were being interviewed by the Canadian customs. When asked if we were importing any crockery, I said 'No' and Tanya immediately piped up 'Yes you are, Daddy!' It took a couple of minutes to explain to the officer what we had and of course it was perfectly fine but Tanya got a serious lecture afterwards about making that kind of public rebuttal of a parental declaration. Teaching one's children honesty and integrity can sometimes generate complications.

When the children were in their early teens, we took them once to Crete and twice to Portugal. The former visit represented a good opportunity to expose them to the Greek language which they had both started to study at high school. Their, and my, school Greek was sometimes useful but at other times very perplexing for the locals. We hired a little car and made our way across the mountains from Chania in the north to Paleochora in the south. It was then early April and, given the cheerful waves from the residents of the mountain villages, I think we must have been among the first cars to make it across the mountains after the winter snows! Arriving finally at the gorgeous Paleochora beach, the four of us threw off our clothes and dashed into the wonderful sea. While we were swimming, Shulie asked me if I had noticed anything unusual and I merely replied that I was loving the water and the swimming. 'Strange that you didn't notice the nude bathers around us,' she noted with a cheeky smile. Another memory from that Crete visit was Tanya's clash with the local electric supply. Each time she plugged in the hair dryer, everything fused and we had to reset the supply.

Three incidents in Portugal stand out in my memory. One crazy Portuguese driver ferried us around Lisbon with great speed and recklessness, especially when he went around one corner so sharply that one of the back doors flew open on Tanya's side and by some miracle (the car had no seat belts) she did not fall out. Another occasion brought an additional rebuke from our kids. We motored by hired car to the point on the Portuguese coast nearest to Africa, that is the most south-western point of Europe, Capa San Vicente. We had brought with us some salami sandwiches, and had purchased a bottle of cheap wine, that we assured the children would not make us drunk. We sat on the cliff overlooking the sea, spoke about Portuguese explorers and seafarers, and enjoyed our sandwiches and (the adults, that is) our wine. The children claimed that we were tipsy and that was not a wise or welcome state to be in, sitting as we were on the very rocky edge of Europe but we claimed total sobriety and cheerfulness. The children were probably more accurate than we were. One evening we saw some giant sardines being grilled on the barbeque of a fish dealer and decided to have some for supper. Apparently, the hygiene and/or the freshness were not all they might have been since four stomachs expressed their strong displeasure for a number of hours that night.

I was also a visiting scholar at the Oxford Centre in Yarnton and used the opportunity to do some research at the Bodleian Library. We also found a little local lake where we paddled around in our inflatable little dinghy. When it began to leak and to sink, Aryeh demonstrated his powerful instinct for survival by scrambling over the other three family members to get first ashore to safety. Of the trips that Shulie and I took on our own, I recall a working visit in January 1984 to the Brandeis-Bardin Institute in Los Angeles where I was the scholar-in-residence, kindly invited by its director Dr. Ronald Brauner, with whom we had been friendly in Philadelphia. The children were at that time looked after by our visiting scholars from Israel, Ada and Menahem Ben-Sasson.

In addition to smaller gatherings at Brandeis-Bardin, there was one more public lecture on a Saturday evening at which there must have been many hundreds in the audience. I remember the chairman taking an inordinately long time to introduce me and mentioning all sorts of achievements. I could see the restiveness of the audience growing by the second and, when I finally took to the podium, I began by denying all these attributes and (spotting the mature ages of my listeners and wishing to win them over) I said in Yiddish 'Ober ich bin nur a klein yiddele' ('Actually I am only a little Jewish person'). It worked and I won them over. While on a visit in 1982 to Split in Croatia, Shulie and I took a walking tour and, at one point, the guide said to the two of us, 'Come with me, I have something special to show you two.' We obediently followed him up a little alley and a narrow staircase and found ourselves in a superb little Venetian synagogue of the sixteenth century. 'But how did you know we were Jewish?' we asked. 'I know my clients,' he replied.

Batmitzvah and Barmitzvah

There were also happy family occasions to celebrate. It was at the time still not the norm for Orthodox Jewish girls to celebrate becoming batmitzvah (at twelve years old) in a formal religious context but we in Cambridge were able to be a little more innovative than other communities. Tanya delivered an impressive Torah lesson in synagogue at the kiddush following the service and performed in a similar manner again at a Sunday afternoon tea party held in the School of Pythagoras at St John's College. For Aryeh, in February 1983, the synagogue service was more standard and he read the Torah and the prophetic passage with great skill before a packed congregation, including family from around the world and many local friends. On Friday night and at Saturday lunch, Shulie did a marvellous job in catering for some 36 visitors in our tiny house. Quite how they all fitted in – and had enough to eat – was to my mind something of a miracle. On Saturday evening we entertained family and friends to dinner in the rather chilly hall at St John's College and I made sure that high kosher standards were maintained. I had a long chat with the College's helpful Catering Manager and, among other matters, I raised the issue of the crockery. With surprising knowledge and confidence, he lectured me on the laws of kashrut. Although he could of course supply new dishes, there was no problem with used ones since they were of catering quality, thickly glazed and cleaned at a high enough temperature to satisfy rabbinic stringency. Seeing my astonishment, he explained that he had done kosher catering in Toronto for a number of years.

Aryeh and his friends sat at the high table and his grandfather Muni gave an inspiring speech. He said that if you had told any of Aryeh's forebears in Poland that their grandson would one day have a barmitzvah at St John's College, Cambridge, they would have assumed that he must be well on the way to apostasy. Yet, here we were in that College and all able to eat a kosher meal. Tanya had the pleasure of being a bridesmaid at London weddings in 1979 and 1980. The first was at the marriage of Ruth Howard, the daughter of my father's cousin Elsa and her husband Bobby, and the second at the nuptials of the daughter of very dear friends of the Stekels, Eve Dubovie, who herself had been one of Shulie's bridesmaids at our wedding in 1967. Ten years after that 1967 event, we celebrated it at a small dinner party in St John's. In all these instances, the relevant College accommodation had to be booked for me (as a non-Fellow) by Andrew Macintosh or John Emerton, both of whom were always willing to be helpful in this way.

Stekels and Reifs

I should say more about how we connected in those years with the Stekels and the Reifs. Muni and Elly lived only a fairly short car journey (usually just over an hour) from Cambridge so that we were able to see them at least once a month, usually on a Sunday. Since Tanya suffered badly from car sickness in her childhood, the travelling was not very pleasant for her and we had to obtain some medicine that she could take beforehand which usually helped. Elly made her usually grand meals and that was probably a contributory factor in Tanya's troubles. They also visited us in Cambridge and we often took a walk through and around the Colleges. Shulie's grandmother, whom the children called Savta, almost always came with them and she loved walking, especially in such a beautiful ambience.

We were strolling along the Backs (as the areas behind the Colleges are called in Cambridge) in November 1973 when Muni gently raised the matter of my friend Mayer Nissim and indicated that he had been serving as a reservist on the Suez Canal when the Yom Kippur War broke out and was missing in action. I could not believe the news and at first assured him of my confidence that Mayer, with all his talents, would have survived. He then explained that the Israeli Embassy in London wished to know if Mayer had a dentist since they might need X-ray evidence in order to make an identification. It then hit home and Shulie and I were deeply distressed. They eventually located his remains and he was buried in the military cemetery on Mount Herzl in Jerusalem. He left a widow, Ruth, and two young pre-school children. His friends from College days set up a memorial fund and this brought benefits to needy Israeli students of similar background to Mayer's at Ben-Gurion University of the Negev in Beersheba.

As Savta reached the age of 90, she began to suffer from dementia and Elly had to look after her, which was an exhausting business. In the early1980s Shulie and I brought Savta to Cambridge a few times and looked after her so that Elly and Muni could have some respite. It was our first (sadly, not our last) encounter with that problem and it was, to say the least, challenging. In her last year or two, Savta had to be looked after in residential accommodation and Muni could never forgive himself for doing this to his mother. The truth was that he was out all day and it was Elly, herself almost 70, and not he, who had to bear the brunt of the caring. I think it exhausted her. Muni liked to hold forth whenever we were with him and was not keen on anybody stealing his thunder. As long as one bore this in mind, all was well. Early in my academic career, I summarized for him a problematic situation that I was facing and sought his view. He told me how he would deal with the problem but I realized that his proposed solution might be suitable for the business environment but would not work in the academic world. He asked me a few weeks later how I had dealt with matters and, when he heard that I had made a different decision, he told me that if I sought his advice I should follow it, otherwise I should not raise such subjects with him. I learned my lesson.

We were also close at that time to Shulie's brother, Ronnie, and his wife Zsuzsi, and their two children Dov and Yael. We often visited each other's homes. The problem was that Muni made a competition out of his grandchildren's activities and achievements, telling us how wonderful the others were, and telling them similar things about our children. This was intended to keep them all on their toes but all it did was to breed resentment on all sides. Muni, although himself seriously overweight, had an obsession about women being slim (perhaps Shulie and I too?) and Tanya may have been disturbed by this as she was going through puberty. The Stekel grandparents did buy the children gifts from time to time but they in no way spoilt them, since their philosophy of education dictated otherwise. At that time, we had one small black-and-white television and the amount of time that the children were permitted to watch was severely limited. The children complained once – I think it was actually Aryeh – about the lack of a coloured set and a few days later such a set was delivered to our home from the local Robert Sayle (John Lewis) store. Shulie thought it was a mistake, or some sales gimmick, until they showed her that Muni had ordered it and paid for it in London. Shulie and I obviously expressed our warm thanks but we were not greatly pleased with the initiative.

The Reif grandparents visited from Toronto once a year and of course participated in all the family semaḥot (celebrations). I once worked it out that, although they lived thousands of miles away, they actually spent almost as much time with us as the other grandparents did, since they would come for lengthy periods on each occasion, often for three weeks and, in one instance, for more than a month. The problem was that in our tiny house in Manhattan Drive there was so little space. Shulie and I gave them our bedroom and slept on a bed settee in the lounge. This was not very comfortable especially since we always had to be last to bed and first up in the morning. In addition, there was only one bathroom/toilet and that created difficulties in the mornings. I tried to persuade Dad to stay in bed until we four had all finished with our ablutions but Pinḥas was never the easiest person to organize and he resented being subject to any sort of control. Mum and Dad bought presents for us which was very kind but Dad's philosophy was that he would choose the present and you would like it. Otherwise, you were rejecting his generosity.

Before she left her Canadian home for Israel in 1978, my sister Sharron would also come with them. She still had a close relationship with Tanya and Aryeh and they especially enjoyed her being with us. Sometimes, she even came alone and that obviously created fewer tensions than when Dad and Mum were with us. Shulie and I did our best to be good to her and to make her feel at home but we never equalized the relationship with that of our children and that too created problems. While Dad had mellowed somewhat in his fifties and sixties, he seemed to revert in his final years to the short-tempered, anxious and difficult individual that I had known and greatly feared in my childhood. After one visit, during which tensions between Shulie and me increased greatly because I was 'piggy-in-the-middle', between my parents and my spouse, we decided that next time we would find them their own place. We thought they would appreciate and enjoy that but Dad took it as a sign of rejection and a lack of filial respect. We knew that at some stage we would need a larger home and the opportunity came in the summer of 1983.

New Home

We were walking home from supper with friends on a late Saturday afternoon that summer and chose to traverse Parsonage Street on our way to the river and our home across the Brunswick footbridge. We saw in that street a sign offering for sale a small site on which were then located a motorbike courier service and a small workshop for making medieval-style armour, presumably for those who liked to pretend to be medievals in armour. We thought how ideal it would be to have a house there and duly

19. Building the new house in 1984.

made inquiries on Monday morning. The site was for sale at around £26,000 and we realized that this was beyond our means. However, our friends, Thelma and Ron Domb, were also looking for an alternative home and, when offered the chance of sharing the purchase of the site with us, they responded with alacrity.

That is how we came to demolish the existing buildings and build two three-storey town houses, semi-detached, each in quite a different style. With important assistance from Muni and Ronnie in making the financial arrangements, we built our house exactly as we wished and enjoyed it greatly for many years. The architect insisted on repeatedly telling us what he thought we should build, but we consistently held out against his advice, much to his chagrin. The builder, Barrie Rayner, and his partner John, with help from Barrie's retired bricklayer father and his son, Chris, did a fine job and the Dombs and Reifs enjoyed an excellent relationship with all four of them.

We had objections from some of the neighbours which led to a delay in obtaining planning permission but Muni had masses of commercial experience in such matters, and saw us through the difficulties with a combination of wisdom and charm, and a little bullying. Architects and builders have, of course, somewhat different interests and priorities, as was brought home to us by one particular incident. Shulie visited the site almost every day and, when she couldn't do so, I popped by on my home from the University Library. In that way we kept an eye on developments, stage by stage, storey by storey, room by room. When the second floor was almost complete the architect came to check things. Shulie and I stood back as he and Barrie exchanged comments and ideas. Then Barrie said to the architect, 'I don't see anywhere in your plans the inclusion of a metal beam across the ceilings of the second storey to support the weight of the third storey. Shouldn't there be one here', he said pointing upwards. 'Yes, of course; you'd better order one,' said the architect, not a little sheepishly. From then on, he abandoned his efforts to dictate to us the kind of house he thought we ought to be building.

The house was made to provide for all the needs of the four of us and also had a spare room, as well as bathrooms and toilets for visitors. A few weeks after we moved in, I arrived home from the University Library (or maybe it was from lecturing at the Faculty of Oriental Studies) to find Tanya at the door, shedding bitter tears. 'Daddy, Daddy, you'll never forgive me. I have done something terrible.' With that kind of introduction, I was highly relieved to find out that she had not murdered either Shulie or Aryeh, or indeed both of them. Home from school, she had gone into the shower, forgetting that she had put the stopper in the wash-basin and turned on the water to fill it. Needless to say, while she was whiling away the minutes in the shower, gallons of water were pouring on to the bathroom floor on the third storey, and making their swift way downwards through the whole house. We had to wait until it all dried out and ask Barrie to come back and repaint some of the walls. I am glad to say that, somehow, neither Shulie nor I lost it completely over the incident, and Tanya probably learned an important lesson about sinks and showers. Sadly, the house, although much roomier than the previous one, did not solve the tensions between Dad, Shulie and me, but rather exacerbated the situation, as I shall explain in a later chapter.

Two Children or Three?

Both children had lessons in playing musical instruments and Tanya was a natural in this, truly excelling. Her teachers spoke about a possible career but Shulie and I preferred that she should always enjoy her music and not have to depend on it for a livelihood. Her piano teacher was a concert pianist himself and we had to remind him from time to time that we very much wanted Tanya to play for pleasure and not for a living. As a little boy, Aryeh was asked by his grandmother, Elly, what he wished to be when he grew up. He wanted to know from her what made the most money and when she said 'a lawyer, of course', his young mind seems to have been made up. While Tanya greatly enjoyed her music, and performed superbly, Aryeh took to sports and reached good standards in football, cricket, snooker and table tennis. He was also quite a champion at chess when a youngster. Shulie and I were most anxious that they should turn out to be accomplished all-rounders, as well as successful professionals. Tanya could entertain with music at communal events and Aryeh could join me in the various games that we played together with other members of the community. He even played some games of squash with Julius and me, pitting his energy and youth against our experience and maturity.

We always made efforts to do for Sharron at least part of what her parents failed to do. We took the money that Mum had saved for her, and with Ronnie's helpful advice, we invested it well so that she had some funds with which to start her married life. We kept a close eye on her developments and gave assistance and advice when we though they were needed. During our visits to Israel between 1978 and 1982, she would come and visit us and sometimes spend Shabbat or a festival with us. There was one time when she came to us (on her way back from Israel, I think) with a certain kind of air ticket that did not match her needs or plans and I had to go with her to Heathrow and purchase the appropriate ticket.

While we were spending a few weeks in the summer of 1981 in the Old City of Jerusalem, Sharron brought her boy-friend, a brilliant young lawyer called David Elkins, to meet us. When asked my impression, my cautious (of course!) response was that if she did not marry him, she would certainly marry someone like him. She also brought him to Cambridge in November and we took him to a football match, his first experience of this sort, his understanding of 'football' being quite something else. Being a native Californian, he had brought T-shirts and shorts, not ideal clothing for standing watching a game of football in the cold open air of wintry Cambridge. I lent him some more suitable gear for the evening. But he recovered from the appalling quality of Cambridge United's football and became one of the family in March 1982 at their wedding in Jerusalem. Again, Shulie and I did what we thought had not been done by my parents (including some advice about sexuality) and made our financial contributions too. My sometime teacher from Edinburgh, Rabbi Isaac Cohen, conducted the ceremony which was a lively and enjoyable event.

There were just two hitches, one when one of my father's elderly cousins tripped and fell into the wedding cake, and the other when the musicians were paid by David, by his parents and by me, all separately in the full sum of course!

When the new Parsonage Street house was almost finished in August 1984, Shulie and I offered the children the option of either coming with us to the barmitzvah of their cousin, Yakov, eldest son of Cynthia and Karl in Toronto, or going to visit Sharron, who was then living outside Jerusalem in a new development in Maaleh Adumim. They jumped at the chance of being in Israel and visiting Sharron, so we did our trip and they did theirs. Now that she was a mature, married woman and running her own home, she felt that she should try to educate Tanya and Aryeh not to be so dependent on their parents, or indeed on her, but to be a little more self-sufficient. Whatever her motivations, and whatever their response, the children returned to Cambridge somewhat disheartened. Their Sharron seemed not to be quite the adoring aunt that she had been to them for so many years. Family relationships can be complicated, especially when aunts are only a small number of years older than their nephews and nieces. My mother had been an aunt at five to the three children of her eldest sibling Abe, and that relationship too had its ups and downs, further complicated when the Polish soldier, Pinḥas Reif, had arrived on the scene. Relationships, both professional and familial, will also be the subject of a later chapter in the continuing story.

17

Working for Rachel and Leah
(1984–98)

Senior Post

The story is told in the book of Genesis about how Laban managed to have Jacob, eponymous ancestor of the Jewish people, work doubly hard for him by his marriages with Laban's two daughters. Jacob had to labour seven years for Leah and another seven for Rachel. My professional experience in the years now to be discussed in a way matched that of Jacob since I too had to work doubly hard and put in fourteen years of industry, with results that were undoubtedly welcome and successful for the University but sometimes frustrating and disappointing for me.

Now that I was at the head of one of the Library's divisions, I had responsibility for what we then called the oriental sections, including the staff and collections of Hebrew, Arabic, Persian, Turkish, Indian, Chinese and Japanese. This involved academic and non-academic appointees and, taken together with the Genizah Research Unit, which I continued to direct, sometimes meant about 20 colleagues for whom I was responsible to the Librarian. I coped with all that but did not wish to reduce in any way my own researching, lecturing and publishing. My day therefore tended to be a long one. I arose at 05.15 and was regularly in the University Library soon after 07.30. When given a questionnaire to complete for the University, I realized that I was working over 70 hours a week on professional matters. Although I was anxious to make the newly-created division an industrious, successful and well-run part of the Library, I knew that if I reduced my personal academic endeavours, there would never be any opportunity of achieving the kind of major scholarly recognition for which I still craved.

Fred Ratcliffe created a Senior Management Team and I became a member. We met regularly to discuss items that were shortly to be raised by Fred at the Library Syndicate and definitively arranged afterwards. It gave the University Librarian the opportunity of seeing how topics would be addressed, as a kind of practice run for the Syndicate, and in some cases members of the Senior Management Team even made some suggestions concerning minor detail that might have been adopted. Overall, however, my impression was that this was to a large extent management window-dressing and I did not much enjoy it. That was even truer in the later regime of Peter Fox and he was always aware that my patience with these meetings was sorely tried each time. Involvement in making Library appointments was a more stimulating and interesting experience and I was at one with Fred in regarding academic excellence as no less important than library qualifications in deciding who should be appointed.

Fred also involved me in the visits of major figures, including Prince Philip (whom I had met previously) and Princess Margaret. In the case of the latter, we were given strict instructions about how she wished us to behave and how we were to address her as 'Ma'am' and in no other way. She gave the impression of a strong-willed character with a high degree of intelligence and a tendency to be outspoken. When I showed her an item that was linked to Sir Thomas More in the days of Henry VIII, she expressed herself in no uncertain terms (not repeatable) about what she regarded as his disloyal religious commitments. I attended a dinner given by Prince Charles at Kensington Palace to mark the retirement of Chief Rabbi Immanuel Jakobovits. We were a little surprised that we saw nothing of Princess Diana, although we did see Princes William and Harry when they came to say goodnight to their father.

Among visitors, there were numerous ambassadors, including some from Arab states, and I must say that I generally found them to be (in those days) a rather pragmatic and well-informed group. I had to take responsibility for some very wealthy and influential Saudi businessmen and was anxious that we should in no way offend them with regard to what they might or might not eat and drink. When wine and non-halal meat were offered, I suggested that they might not wish to partake but they indicated their view that the religious rules were differently applied away from home. It reminded me of many Jewish families who also eat kosher only at home.

Divisional Character

It took some time for the newly-created Division to develop its own character and to run smoothly. Some staff members were not overjoyed to have me as their divisional head and I had to behave as diplomatically as possible in order to avoid tensions. The retirement of some, and the departure for alternative academic libraries by others, ensured that Fred and I were able to make some good appointments to replace them. The newcomers accepted the divisional situation as it was and made important contributions to the maintenance of the University Library as one of the world's most important holders of extensive 'oriental' materials. Noboru Koyama was responsible for Japanese, Charles Aylmer for Chinese and Craig Jamieson for Indian. Jill Butterworth, who had been at the Library long before I arrived, looked after Hebrew and Arabic. After her retirement, Yasmin Faghihi and Catherine Ansorge took over responsibility for the Near Eastern languages. We had regular staff meetings and I believe that the various linguistic fields benefitted from this kind of corporate management. I tried to create a balance between allowing each area to express itself in its own way and encouraging divisional standards and loyalty.

I think it was during this period that the assessment exercise was introduced for all staff, academic and administrative. I had to interview each member of the Division, including those in the Genizah Research Unit, twice a year and discuss their work with them. The idea was to assess, together, what was being achieved, and what could or should be done differently or possibly better. Frankly, I am not convinced of the efficacy of the system. It did perhaps provide an opportunity for 'a full and frank exchange of views' (as diplomats would put it) and may also have prevented some problems from quietly and determinedly festering. I believe it is fair to say that, partly as a result of the new administrative arrangements introduced by Fred, the efficiency and productivity of those working in the division did, by and large, improve. On the other hand, as far as the assessments were concerned, those who were excellent continued to be excellent and those who might have been less than excellent did not necessarily improve.

As well as submitting such assessments to Dr. Ratcliffe, I also had to provide him with an annual report, and the University Librarian was not slow in pointing to the new divisional achievements within the Library's Annual Report that he compiled for the University. In the latter part of the period now being discussed, the Library was fortunate enough to enjoy the patronage of a wealthy Japanese businessman, Tadao Aoi. He made funds available for the building of a grand new wing, called the Aoi Pavilion, in which all the Japanese and Chinese collections could be housed. It included its own attractive reading room and reference section, as well as some seminar rooms. The formal opening took place in 1998.

My status as divisional head also involved me in numerous other activities, broader than the area of Genizah research, to which I was still centrally and enthusiastically devoted. I made new contacts and attended meetings at the Needham Research Institute for the Study of Science in East

Asia (in Cambridge) and the National Council for Oriental Library Resources (usually in London), later becoming chairman of the latter committee. When chairing, I always indicated at the beginning of a meeting how long I expected it to last and reminded all the members that some of their colleagues had come from outside London and had trains to catch. I concluded the proceedings fairly briskly and did not permit irrelevant or repetitive discussions. After a few such meetings, one of the members remarked that the system was somewhat dictatorial but that he was very pleased with the efficient and expeditious result. When some Hebrew manuscripts from the collection of David Solomon Sasson came the way of the British Government in lieu of estate duty, we made a strong case for their acquisition and six of them were allocated to Cambridge University Library by the Minister for the Arts.

Treasures from among our oriental materials were chosen for display at exhibitions in Cambridge and in London, and plans were being made for the extension of the Library that involved better housing for oriental materials and orientalists. There were also numerous meetings concerning the Library's new Exhibition Centre, formally opened in 1998, and the volume dealing with some of the Library's greatest treasures, *Great Collections*, planned and edited by the new University Librarian, Peter Fox (of whom more anon), and published in the same year. For a number of years, I chaired the student scholarships committee of the Jewish Memorial Council in London and served on Cambridgeshire County Council's Standing Advisory Council on Religious Education (SACRE).

Shulie and I were fortunate enough to be invited to a reception at Claridge's hosted by Shimon Peres, the Israeli Prime Minister of the day (and attended by many leading figures, including Margaret Thatcher), and on another occasion we were able to exchange ideas with the Minister of Education, Kenneth Baker. It was a delight to talk to King Juan Carlos and Queen Sofia of Spain and they were of course especially interested in our Judeo-Spanish literary treasures, including some Genizah fragments. I welcomed Dr. Suleiman Fares, Dean of the Syrian Ba'athist Party's Higher Institute for Political Science in Damascus, and he enjoyed reading an Islamic chancery document of the twelfth century with Geoffrey Khan.

The academic staff in the division were active in raising external funds for their respective areas and this ensured the successful development of all the oriental collections. The Library's Annual Report, published in the *Cambridge University Reporter* of 31 January 1992 summarized the situation: 'One of the purposes of the creation of the Division was to coordinate the diverse and isolated achievements of the various departments into a coherent whole...and to extend and exploit the management structures which had been so successful in the Genizah Research Unit. This has undoubtedly been achieved and the Library can with confidence point to a division which has few equals outside. At the same time, the achievements of the Genizah Research Unit have in no sense been diminished. On the contrary...'

Multi-tasking and Development

I think it is fair to say that there were few periods in my professional life when I was not energetic and productive in one way or another. There are few matters on which I ever found myself in agreement with the Palestinian Professor of Literature at Columbia University, Edward Said (1935-2003), but one statement of his totally resonated with me. In his memoir, he declared: 'I have...no sense of cumulative achievement. Every day for me is like the beginning of a new term at school, with a vast and empty summer behind it, and an uncertain tomorrow before it.' Given my numerous commitments and activities, the 1980s and 1990s were probably the most intense, varied and demanding of my career. That said, I always felt that there was more to achieve, newer projects to champion and fresh ways to prove and improve myself.

I remember mentioning to a senior colleague that I usually got up at around 05.15 and worked most of the day until about 21.30 p.m. 'If that is the case, you are not very organized,' was his retort, 'since you ought to be able to complete your tasks in a normal working day.' I reminded him that if I had chosen to follow that advice, there would probably still be 32 full crates (or perhaps only 28!) of unconserved and unexamined Genizah fragments in the University Library. It would probably also have meant that I would not have been able to do the fund-raising, as well as directing all the research, in those busy years.

The annual budget of the Unit, virtually all of it raised externally, increased to over £70,000, and major funding bodies, including the British Academy, the John S. Cohen Foundation, the Dwek Trust, the Higher Education Funding Council, the Rothschild Foundation, the Sobell Fund and the Wolfson Foundation, became interested and involved in our activities. This was in addition to those foundations, such as the Wellcome Trust, that had already assisted us in earlier years and continued to do so. The connections with the American Friends of Cambridge University flourished and brought in an increasing number of donations and connections.

I met Michael Neiditch of Bnai Brith International in Washington D.C. who offered helpful advice and suggested some useful contacts. There was also a close and helpful relationship with the University's local Development Office, especially when it was directed by Bill Squire from 1988. I had hosted Bill and his wife Sarah at the Library when he was British Ambassador in Israel, and she of course (also a career diplomat) later went on to be a highly successful president of Hughes Hall in Cambridge. I maintained my policy of cultivating personal connections with all donors, whatever the level of their contributions. This not only ensured that there was always some basic financial assistance available to the Unit but was also helpful to our public relations campaign.

That campaign always demanded time, effort and initiative. Many groups came to see the Genizah Collection and numerous 'friends' of the Unit were created in this way. There was always a close relationship with the Embassy of Israel in London, especially through whichever individual was at that time functioning as its cultural attaché. This meant that the Unit was often asked to entertain leading figures of Israeli society who were visiting the United Kingdom. Among those many Israeli personalities whom I met over the years in Cambridge and in Jerusalem were Chaim Herzog, Abba Eban, Yosef Burg, Yitschak Navon, Zvi Gabbay and Chaim Topol.

I involved the Unit's researchers in these activities since I felt that it would be good for them to improve their presentation skills. If I asked them to address some visitors, they would usually do this, at their first attempts, by way of prepared speeches or notes. I encouraged them to make more direct contact with their listeners and I believe that most of them learned how to do this very successfully, an achievement that was certainly not unhelpful to them in their later academic careers. They also worked with me, as did Shulie, on the production of the newsletter, *Genizah Fragments*, as well as the creation of paperweights, tapes, Jewish New Year cards, facsimiles and posters.

The Unit was featured in the flight magazine of El Al Airlines in the autumn of 1997, and the University of Cambridge's alumni magazine *CAM* included an article about my daily routine in its autumn issue of that same year. Raphael Loewe, by then retired from his chair at University College London thought that latter report 'a real qiddush ha-shem', which, if loosely translated, means a 'fine affirmation of Jewish values'. The Arabic weekly, *al-Majalla* even devoted six pages to the Genizah manuscripts in December 1997. There were also radio and television programmes to which the Unit contributed to an increasing degree. I do recall one particular television film in the preparation of which I was asked to explain at length all manner of historical, literary and religious matters relating to Jewish Cairo in the medieval period. I looked forward to seeing myself on the screen when the programme was broadcast. Imagine my astonishment when I appeared for only a few moments while most of my explanatory remarks were conveyed by the presenter, as if they were his own!

A Novelist and Unit Personnel

It had become standard for *Genizah Fragments* to include not only news items but also some summaries of important Genizah research. This achieved important recognition when, in 1993, the editorial board of the *Index of Articles on Jewish Studies* (*RAMBI*), published at the Jewish National and University Library in Jerusalem, agreed to include such articles in its listings. It was very pleasing to be informed that the Unit had been on a short list of five for the Dawson Award for Innovation in Academic Librarianship. In the Unit we never thought we would become an element in the preparation of a piece of contemporary literature. This occurred when a young writer originally from Calcutta, Amitav Ghosh, who was then in Oxford, came over to Cambridge to work in the University Library in 1984. He met Genizah researchers, especially Mark Cohen, Menahem Ben-Sasson and Geoffrey Khan, and used what he learned from them, and from his own gleanings among the rich Genizah harvest then being prepared, in the composition of his fascinating book *In an Antique Land* which was later published in 1992. I became a fan of his work and read with great pleasure various historical novels of his.

The research assistants and associates employed full-time and part-time in the Unit made impressive progress with the description of the fragments and the preparation of the volumes describing them. Their efforts were complemented by the annual presence of senior scholars who, as visiting research associates, gave their attention to areas of the Genizah collection in which they specialized. The arrangement was usually that I found the funding to assist the latter visitors with their expenses and they helped to compile catalogues of some of the fragments.

Having given almost a decade of devoted and productive service to the Unit, Geoffrey Khan was, despite John Emerton's preference for alternative arrangements, deservedly appointed to a lectureship in the Faculty of Oriental Studies in 1992. His work on Judeo-Arabic materials was continued by young scholars Colin Baker and Meira Polliack, who had recently completed their doctorates and would later go on to senior academic posts and noteworthy careers, he at the British Library in London and she at Tel Aviv University. In the mid-1990s, three other researchers joined the Unit and made their mark on its activities. Ellis Weinberger moved from research to the supervision of digitising and typesetting projects, and to the management of the web site, areas in which Douglas de Lacey also made important innovations. I expect that the Unit was at that time generally ahead of the field when it came to cyber innovation.

The primary task of Erica Hunter and Rebecca Wilson (later Jefferson) was the bibliographical project but they both played central and devoted parts in many of the Unit's other activities. Avi Shivtiel, with whom I have always maintained a deep friendship, served as acting director of the Unit while I was on sabbatical in 1996–97 and it was good to work closely again with him. It was Avi who reported in *Genizah Fragments* (no. 35) that the piece about me and my work in the *CAM* magazine (for Cambridge alumni) of Michaelmas Term 1997 had been primarily about the professional aspects, adding: 'Those who know Dr Reif will have to wait patiently for the small talk about childhood memories, hobbies, and juicy anecdotes. The Genizah comes first.'

In the early part of the period being discussed, two of the leading professors from the Hebrew University of Jerusalem, Yakov Sussmann and Yosef Yahalom, spent time with us in Cambridge as senior scholars. Sussmann was preparing his descriptions of all the Talmudic fragments (eventually published in three volumes in 2012) and Yahalom worked on the vocalized Hebrew texts of liturgical poetry from the land of Israel. Their Israeli colleagues, Haggai Ben-Shammai, Yehiel Kara and Oded Irshai, described items in Judeo-Arabic, linguistics, and history, respectively, while Maaravi Perez from the Bar-Ilan University made some interesting identifications among the medieval Bible commentaries of the Genizah. Michael Klein, from the Hebrew Union College in Jerusalem, prepared a volume of targumic fragments and Robert Brody, from the Hebrew University of Jerusalem, a volume on rabbinic items. Both these volumes have proved their worth as seminal reference works.

The younger scholars often needed guidance not only with what they were doing in the Unit but also in the plans they were making for their academic futures. I offered them advice based on the three decades of my own career and they often followed it. I can think of instances when they first rejected it and then later appreciated that they should not have done so. I wrote them references when they wished to move on and always stressed their talents and achievements without in any way exaggerating or misleading the institutions to which they were applying. I believe that my fair and honest recommendations were appreciated and understood so that most of the Unit's researchers achieved, earlier or later, the kind of posts to which they aspired and/or for which they were suited.

Shulie and I did our best to be helpful and hospitable to all the researchers, both in the University Library and in our home. This ensured that we usually developed close personal relationships with almost all the 'family' of Genizah researchers around the world. A few of these relationships even remained close after our retirement, when we were no longer able to offer keys to the Genizah treasures and access to enjoyable stays in Cambridge. One of the most important gatherings of Genizah scholars took place in 1987 when the Society of Judeo-Arabic Studies, presided over by Professor Joshua Blau, held its annual conference in Cambridge and dedicated it to 'Ninety years of Genizah Research at Cambridge.' Fifty international scholars attended and Shulie and I made all the arrangements, including bringing kosher food from London. Only two participants complained about this, joking that they had enough kosher food in Israel and liked to sample other cuisines when outside Israel! I edited the proceedings (officially of course with Professor Joshua Blau) and the volume, containing 21 papers, made its appearance in 1992.

Genizah Series

During those years, the 'Genizah Series', published for the University Library by Cambridge University Press, made a major impact on the scholarly world. Eight volumes, in a variety of scholarly areas, made their appearance and represented many years of devoted work by the researchers in the Unit, as well as, at times, substantial editorial involvement on my part. Co-ordination with the Press was a demanding activity but, in those years, there were still many staff members there who saw their function as the maintenance of high standards of academic publication and of service to the scholarly community. Especially important to me was the fact that the Unit was not only conserving so much new material and making it available to scholars but was also significantly assisting their efforts by offering some basic descriptions of many thousands of fragments.

The project in which I had myself worked closely especially in my early years in the Unit (later ably assisted by a number of the Unit's researchers) was the bibliography and it gave me intense pleasure to see the first hefty volume published in 1989 under the title *Published Material from the*

Cambridge Genizah Collections: A Bibliography 1896–1980. A few months after its appearance, an evening seminar was held at the Ben Zvi Institute in Jerusalem at which four distinguished Jerusalem scholars – Joshua Blau, Ezra Fleischer, Shaul Shaked and Malachi Beit-Arié – explained just how important the publication was and would long continue to be, and I responded. Their remarks indicated just how much of a challenge had existed for researchers in the Unit and how productive their efforts had proved to be.

Hebrew Manuscript Catalogue

The other challenge of those years was the need to complete the task that I had undertaken at the request of Eric Ceadel in my first decade at Cambridge University Library, namely finally producing for Cambridge a catalogue of Hebrew manuscripts similar to those that had long since been composed and made available in all the other major research libraries of the world. I had done some work on this from time to time but in the early 1990s I sat down with Shulie and we planned how we could successfully complete the project without too much more delay. After all, it had by then been more than a century and a half since the Senate had, on 11 May 1825, authorized Dr. Daniel Guildford Wait to compile just such a reference work. Not only had he been the first of a number of scholars who had failed to do so but, in his case, he later also suffered the ignominy of imprisonment for debt.

We knew that in order to complete the description of a thousand Hebrew manuscripts – and to do so in a reasonable time – we would need to be industrious, organized and consistent. We therefore devoted the first two hours of each morning to the project, usually working from when Shulie joined me in the Unit at around 08.30 until we had our coffee break at 10.30. Shulie devised a grid on which there appeared each area of data that needed to be recorded. I held the manuscript in my hand and looked through its contents, sometimes already familiar to me, most times not. Seated at the computer, she issued a list of requests, including, among others: Date? Provenance? Author? Size? Condition? Acquisition? With the help of the earlier work of a number of scholars on the desk before me, my own experience of working with medieval Hebrew manuscripts, and her mastery of the technology, we were able to compile the necessary volume and Shulie then formatted it for the press.

It seemed to me important to have not only descriptions of the manuscripts but also to compose, as an introduction, a detailed history of

Hebrew manuscripts, as well as Jewish interests, at Cambridge from medieval to contemporary times. Herbert Loewe, who had taught Rabbinics at Cambridge in the 1930s, had drawn up a hand-list and I not only made use of this but also included in my volume the introduction that he had compiled for that hand-list. The volume appeared in 1997, included in the publication series of the Faculty of Oriental Studies, and we had a launch party at the University Library attended by the Minister Plenipotentiary at the Israeli Embassy in London, Amiram Magid. *Hebrew Manuscripts at Cambridge University Library* was widely received with acclaim and one reviewer welcomed it as 'the first and worth waiting for catalogue to the Hebrew manuscripts at Cambridge...a model for a printed catalogue of Hebrew manuscripts'.

Personal Research and Publication

All these activities at the University Library notwithstanding, I remained anxious to make an impact in my own personal field of research, that is, in the history of Jewish prayer. During the fourteen years currently being described I somehow found the time to publish over 60 items in scholarly periodicals, or in collections of articles compiled after a conference, or prepared in honour of a retirement. A few of them were about specific periods of Jewish liturgical history and it occurred to me that, if I prepared another five or six chapters dealing with other periods, I could put together a volume on the whole history of Jewish prayer from biblical to modern times. There had been no serious study of the topic that could genuinely be called comprehensive and scientific since the work of Ismar Elbogen in Germany in the first three decades of the twentieth century. I had long felt that such a volume could be of major use, not only to specialists in the field, but to many others, both junior and senior, in the field of academic Jewish studies. While in Jerusalem as a Lady Davis Fellow at the Hebrew University for the first half of 1989, I was able to prepare draft versions of at least two of the required chapters, mainly on the medieval period. My teaching commitment there was not at all heavy and there was ample time for researching and reading at the Jewish National and University Library, as it was then called.

Back in Cambridge, there was inevitably less time to devote to the topic but between 1990 and 1992 I succeeded in writing the remaining chapters concerning developments in the modern and contemporary periods. The volume was submitted to Cambridge University Press for careful and helpful sub-editing (as was still done in those distant days by most reputable publishers) and, with the help of a young and dynamic editor at the Press, Alex Wright, my history of Jewish liturgy, *Judaism and Hebrew Prayer*, duly appeared in 1993. I dedicated it to the memory of my father who had died in 1989. My father-in-law, Edmund Stekel, and the Unit's leading supporter, Cyril Stein, jointly sponsored a reception in a London hotel at which the new work could be welcomed.

In the preface I wrote: 'Of the various books and numerous articles that have appeared over my name in the course of twenty-three years of scholarly publication, none has given me so much satisfaction in its completion as the volume here being prefaced. It has been my ambition for a number of years to offer such an overview of Jewish liturgical history and, given my many other commitments, it has been no easy task to find the time and energy to effect its realization...I can only express the hope that the study proves as useful and acceptable to the student, non-specialist and scholar in its reading as it has proved absorbing and challenging to me in its composition.' The reviews were very gratifying, indicating that I had achieved my purpose and provided what had long been a scientific desideratum. Nahum Sarna at Brandeis University referred to the volume as 'scrupulous and encompassing...informative, erudite, stimulating and intriguing'. A paperback version was published in 1995 and the book is still selling.

Fred Departs and the Genizah Visits Jerusalem

Fred Ratcliffe retired in 1995 and Peter Fox succeeded him. In the months before Peter's appointment a number of the staff at the University Library had suggested to me that I should put myself forward as a candidate. My response to them was that I thought that the electors would be in the market for a librarian with technological interests and competence rather than a scholar of medieval manuscripts. I met one of the electors on a train journey to London and from a gentle sounding out on my part it appeared to me that my hunch was a correct one. On Fred's retirement, I wrote to him, thanking him warmly for his 'wise and generous advice, enthusiastic support and scholarly empathy'.

Peter took up his appointment and was certainly supportive of my efforts. We built up a good working relationship in spite of the fact that our views and interests diverged considerably. Peter had a technocratic approach and was a little impatient of matters that complicated the process of management. He jokingly referred to the Asian languages as the 'squigglies' and felt that no collection in the Library deserved to receive special attention. My approach was a scholarly one and I was impatient of management procedures. I was also especially devoted to the particular needs of the oriental collections in general and the Genizah fragments in particular. We did co-operate on Library matters and often joked about each other's propensities. His succession of deputies – Roy Welbourne, David Hall and Anne Murray (later Jarvis) – were most helpful to me in my efforts for the Division and the Unit.

In 1997 an exhibition to mark the hundredth anniversary of the Genizah and the fiftieth anniversary of the Dead Sea scrolls was mounted at the internationally prestigious Israel Museum in Jerusalem and the Library sent 50 Genizah fragments for display. Peter came to the opening which was attended by many Israeli and international dignitaries. A few months earlier, the wife of the President of Israel, Reuma Weizman, had heard a lecture of mine at Tel Aviv University and had expressed great interest in seeing the Cambridge Genizah *in situ*. As a result, when she and her husband, President Ezer Weizman, visited England in February 1997, they included Cambridge University Library in their itinerary. My impression was that it was Reuma rather than Ezer who was really enthused by these historical documents. Ezer had been a fighter pilot with the Royal Air Force in the Second World War, and then with the Israeli Defence Forces after the establishment of the Jewish state. He was probably keen to go on from the Library to his next visit, to Britain's largest aviation museum in Duxford, some sixteen kilometres south of Cambridge.

Shulie and I were able to spend the whole of that academic year, 1996–97, in Jerusalem, with a few visits to our home in Cambridge and to the Unit. I had been invited to be a professorial fellow at the Institute of Advanced Studies at the Hebrew University and they arranged for us to occupy an apartment in a lovely area called Neve Shaanan, a walk of about fifteen minutes from the Institute and the National Library in Givat Ram. The subject of the Institute's research programme that year was the history of Jewish prayer and I greatly enjoyed my participation. I lectured at many gatherings and various publications resulted from these activities. Shulie worked closely with the Israel Museum staff who were arranging the Genizah exhibition and found that an interesting and demanding experience. Their productive co-operation ensured that the exhibition was a great success and widely covered in the media and that various popular publications, such as *The Genizah News*, were carefully designed and made widely available. An Israeli stamp was even issued to commemorate 100 years of Genizah research and 50 of Qumran studies.

Academic Recognition?

I should now explain the matter of my progress towards personal academic recognition in the 1990s. Soon after his arrival at the Library, Fred Ratcliffe had expressed the view that I should be appointed to a personal readership. Aware that I had by then some 150 published items to my name, he encouraged me to apply in 1990 but the application did not meet with success. I have a suspicion (with some evidence gleaned from various hints made by scholars who knew) that the referees were supportive but not with the degree of intense enthusiasm and urgency that personal readerships and professorships at that time required at Cambridge. The chairman of the Library Syndicate, Derek Brewer, the Master of Emmanuel College, wrote to me about the decision, explaining that such personal promotions were 'extremely difficult to come by' at Cambridge, and that I was 'by the standards applied relatively young'. The application had been considered 'a little premature' but he looked forward to submitting another application after my substantial work on Jewish liturgy had been published so that I could, 'in due course', reach the rank that they would all like to see me hold.

I went to see Professor Brewer at Emmanuel and explained my view that I had been judged as if I were exclusively a teaching officer and that insufficient account had been taken of the academic value of what I had done at the University Library. He was sympathetic but not, of course, critical of the University's methods in this connection. I assured him that I would not apply again for a personal readership but only, 'in due course', for a personal professorship. I was somewhat consoled when a few months later, Henry Chadwick, Master of Peterhouse and an outstanding scholar of theology, asked me to host a leading German scholar researching Hebrew and Aramaic Jewish texts because I was 'one of Cambridge's most distinguished scholars in this general area'.

There were also what I felt to be disappointing results for me at University College London (UCL). A few months before Raphael Loewe retired from his chair of Hebrew in 1984, he and his predecessor, Chimen Abramsky, confided in me that they thought I would be a strong candidate for that post. I had not actually thought about the prospect until they mentioned it. At a reception that I attended at University College, I chatted about the chair to the Provost, but received the distinct impression that their plans for the appointment did not include someone like me. Subsequently, a Jewish historian, and not a hebraist, was appointed.

In the latter part of 1990, UCL advertised a new chair, the 'Jewish Chronicle Chair in Jewish Studies' and invited applications. A number of senior (and highly distinguished) scholars in Jewish studies encouraged me to apply. One wrote declaring me 'tailor-made for the job' and another, undoubtedly the world's leading expert in his field of Jewish Studies, responded to an inquiry from UCL about possible candidates by writing in considerable detail and sending me a copy of his recommendation. What he had written about me to the Provost was very generous and included the sentence: 'His wide knowledge, teaching experience, impressive research publications and boundless energy qualify him to lead the kind of major expansion in Jewish Studies that your distinguished institution appears to be contemplating.' I was not even invited for interview.

It was also at various times during the 1990s that senior academics at three Israel universities approached me about possible appointments in their institutions. They thought of me as an appropriate scholar to direct their libraries and also to teach some of my research interests, much as I was doing successfully at Cambridge. In the UK, one obtained permission to fill a post and then looked for possible personnel. In Israel, one apparently sought a good candidate and then tried to sort out the funding and the administration. I gave guest lectures at those institutions and these were very well received, as were my CV and list of publications. I was of course not a party to why their initiatives came to nothing but I suspect that there were always some individuals in post in each university (as was the case in England) who were not greatly enamoured of the idea of an over-energetic Reif coming and (inevitably) making the kind of changes that might adversely affect their own comfortable arrangements.

Regius Chair

John Emerton was due to retire from his Regius Chair of Hebrew at Cambridge in September 1994 and an advertisement appeared for his post in February of that year. For some months previous to this, John had been working intensely at the Faculty Board of Oriental Studies on influencing the composition of the Board of Electors. He was very keen to ensure that the hebraist chosen would continue the well-established tradition of 'Old Testament' (OT) scholarship, particularly as understood by Protestant Christianity. As a result of his efforts, the board of electors consisted of some who were ordained as Christian clerics and others who could claim little or no expertise in the two-thousand-year history of Hebrew after the Second Temple period.

I made an application and, in four closely typed pages, I summarized my educational background, my research and publications (189 items by then), my achievements in the Unit and my detailed plans for how I would tackle the development of Hebrew if elected. I stressed the need for an appointee to be a hebraist in the broadest sense and not only an expert in the Hebrew Bible within the Christian tradition of OT scholarship. I stated with regard to the Regius Chair at Cambridge that I was 'conscious that the only Jew ever to be appointed to it was a convert to Christianity, Immanuel Tremellius of Ferrara…from 1550 to 1553'. In that connection, I pointed to various developments in related fields that had encouraged a broader interpretation of Hebrew and Jewish studies than had earlier been customary among Christian clerics.

The electors at their meeting in May saw the need to stress the Old Testament aspect of the post and in that area the appointment of my friend and colleague Robert Gordon made the best sense. Perhaps at that stage some foundations were already laid for a broader interpretation of the post since Robert's successor was Geoffrey Khan who had worked with me in the Genizah Unit for ten years before going to a lectureship at the Faculty of Oriental Studies, as it was then called, and could in no way be defined as a scholar of Old Testament, but rather as an outstanding specialist in the detailed analysis of Semitic languages. One of the leading Cambridge

20. Tanya and Aryeh with Shulie and their four grandparents, 1986.

orientalists kindly wrote to me suggesting that I 'must have been disappointed not to have been chosen' and attempting a consolation by praising 'your many and solid contributions to the work of the Faculty and the cause of your subject'. Interestingly, one of the electors to the Regius Chair wrote to me years later reporting that he had made the point at the meeting of the electors that I should be considered for a personal chair.

Personal Chair

I did not sleep well that night but kept waking up and sighing about what I saw as my failure. Later, on considered reflection, I made two decisions in response to that disappointment. The first was to increase my superannuation payments so that I would have enough years to retire from the University by 2006, if I so wished. I had begun my academic career in 1968 so I would in any case have reached the required 40 years by 2008. Additional payments brought forward by two years the welcome possibility of being able to devote the final decades of my active life to my personal research and its publication. The second decision was to apply for a personal chair and I did so from 1995 until 1998, with a break in 1996. In those days, unlike in later times, there were not many personal chairs each year and the limited number had to be spread over all the faculties. Of all the Cambridge academic appointments, only 4 per cent were at that time personal chairs. In the first years of the process, my applications were made through the University Library and I believe that those considering it in the relevant committees of the General Board of the University were not yet willing to accept that anyone outside the teaching offices, however academically successful, should be granted such a privileged promotion.

Somehow, the *creatio ex nihilo* of a whole new area of research, its active promotion and its degree of productivity, and the internal and external ramifications of such novelty were seen as less important than a monograph replete with footnotes. This at least was the case in humanities, if not in natural sciences. From 1996 until 1998, there were many formal discussions in the Regent House about the topic of personal promotions led by Gillian Evans (supported by, among others, David Dumville and Anthony Edwards), and I believe that these ultimately resulted in a broader interpretation. More appointments would henceforth be made on the basis of being academically deserved and would be less financially restricted. I myself contributed to this discussion in a brief speech made in the Senate House on 5 March 1996. I argued that I was not applying that year, that the time had come for change, that those scholars who were not teaching officers should not be disadvantaged in the process, and that the whole system should be more 'equitable, transparent and consistent'.

In a letter of apology for his absence from the launch of my volume *Hebrew Manuscripts at Cambridge University Library*, Fred Ratcliffe praised the publication and my efforts to complete it successfully. It was a matter for real congratulation as well as for celebration. He wrote that he kept looking for my name in the list of personal chairs and was at a loss to understand why my name had not appeared. He added astutely: 'I can only think that it is because you are besmirched with the title of "librarian".'

I applied again for a personal chair in 1997, this time through the Faculty of Oriental Studies, not the University Library, and stated in my application: 'Those who understand medieval manuscript research will appreciate that my task has been neither a routine library one nor a simple matter of editorial supervision. It has been one that could not have been undertaken without the highest standards of original scholarship and intellectual leadership. It is well recognized by experts that it is notoriously difficult to identify, describe and analyse Genizah fragments and that few specialists have the learning and ability to plan and execute research projects and publications. The Genizah Collection ranges over the whole field of medieval Hebrew and Jewish studies and demands high degree of competence in such disparate areas as Bible, Rabbinics, Semitics, Jewish law and Hebrew liturgy, as well as advanced personal research experience in at least some of these subjects.'

For this application, which would take a few months, I undoubtedly had the benefit of scholars in the Faculty who evaluated my work very highly and did not define me narrowly as a librarian. Robert Gordon did all he could to argue my case and, although I obviously do not know the details, I surmise that it was probably to his great credit, and perhaps that also of Richard Bowring, Professor of Japanese Studies and later Master of Selwyn College, that the application was apparently forwarded to the University administration with strong support. Having been disappointed before, I did not hold out much hope. Shulie had gone to Israel to help Tanya with her four little children and I was, on Friday afternoon, 5 June, about to 'shut up shop' and make my way home to prepare my Shabbat meals. Then I recalled that I had not checked my pigeon-hole for the afternoon's internal University mail. I popped down to the Library office and there was indeed a letter stamped 'personal and strictly confidential' that looked as if it might be from the Old Schools, that is, the University offices. On previous occasions it had been a thin envelope with a politely written piece of bad news from the administration. This time, the envelope was much thicker. I wondered.

Tears of Joy

I opened the envelope and found a letter from the Secretary General conveying his delight that the General Board had agreed to propose the establishment of a personal professorship for me and asking me to choose a title for my chair. My eyes filled as I read and reread the message, but this time there were no sighs of disappointment, only tears of joy. Shulie had always checked with me whether in the word 'professor' there were two fs or two ss. I phoned her immediately to Israel and began the conversation by saying that she really must now learn to spell the word professor! I genuinely think she was even more overjoyed than I was. Instead of staying on for another week, she changed her flight to come home and to enjoy the celebration with me. Little Stefan who had informed his mother that he could manage everything on his own, and who had always told himself that he would truly be a success one day, had achieved what had for many years seemed out of reach.

The matter was of course to remain confidential from all except the immediate family and it required much self-discipline to keep it concealed. The formal announcement was finally made at the end of July. I had not been much involved in the College in the 1990s, believing that there would be no serious future for me there. I had helped the Master, Robert Hinde, with his fund-raising efforts in London, but this had not strengthened my College connections in any significant way. In early August, however, I had a telephone call from Andrew Macintosh inquiring whether, if St John's College was minded to offer me a professorial fellowship, I might possibly be willing to accept. I did not need much persuasion and the next stage was to be a meeting with two or three of the Fellows who could chat to me and report back as to my suitability, and then to come and dine with the fellowship. All went well and I was admitted as Fellow early in the Michaelmas Term. Again, I felt my cup was overflowing, another of my pressing ambitions having been fulfilled. It was only a pity that my father and my parents-in-law were no longer with us to appreciate it, and that my mother was suffering from Alzheimer's and therefore not too aware of the significance of the developments. All the sewing she had done until 01.00 or 02.00 in the morning to raise the money to pay my fees at Gillespie's, and my father's engineering efforts repairing coal-cutters and water pumps for the National Coal Board over 500 metres below Newtongrange village, had finally paid off.

John Emerton also thought it long overdue although my impression had been that he had supported my application but not made the kind of major enthusiastic effort required in order to achieve its success. Perhaps it was not so much in his nature to do so for those who were not his students. Be that as it may, he wrote me a charming letter of congratulations in which he expressed the view that, apart from my expertise in the history of Jewish liturgy, none of the success of the Genizah Research Unit would have been possible without my 'breadth and depth of scholarship'. That was most gratifying, given that some earlier ambitions of mine had not matched his own plans.

Even more gratifying was a telephone call to me in Cambridge from Professor Wieder in Jerusalem. Paying compliments to anyone, including his students, was not one of his regular practices. But he had, he explained, telephoned to explain to me how important and remarkable it was that I had been recognized in this way. Waving aside my protestations that I was indeed aware of my achievement, my teacher, who had been a professor at Bar-Ilan University in Israel for a few years, managed to be self-effacing, effusive and offensive at the same time. 'No, no, sir, you do *not* understand! Being a professor at Cambridge is not like being a professor at Bar-Ilan!'

There were many letters of congratulations and there were a number of recurrent phrases such as 'long overdue', 'well deserved' and 'great esteem'. One of the country's most distinguished, and internationally renowned, scholars from Oxford wrote with his 'congratulations on an amply justified promotion which will give much delight'. Looking back now at a very bulky file of such congratulatory notes, I note with a smile those who declined to offer any comment. Perhaps such 'colleagues' would have preferred me to remain at the level of Assistant Under-Librarian so that they could pigeon-hole me as some kind of junior cataloguer. Not long afterwards, when checking a reference, I came across the wonderful statement of Ben Azzai in the Babylonian Talmud (*Yoma* 38a) and thought how appropriate I felt it was to what had finally transpired for me:

אמר בן עזאי בשמך יקראוך ובמקומך יושיבוך ומשלך יתנו לך

'They will call you by your name and they will set you in your place and they will give you what is yours.'

18

Changing Theories of Relativity
(1984–98)

Hosting at Home

If my professional activities during those years saw changing challenges, my personal life over that period was faced with the challenge of changes. The new house in Parsonage Street was the venue for the final visits of the generation most of which was soon to depart this world, and for the transformation of our young teenagers into maturing adults. It was from there that we saw off our children as they started to build their own lives and it was in our Cambridge home that we began to experience the onset of the kind of minor but annoying medical problems that mark one's entrance into middle age, however much one remains loathe to recognize the transformation.

More cheerfully, our three-storey town house was able to accommodate fairly comfortably the little children of the newly-married generation within the family, at first those of my sister, Sharron, and later those of our Tanya and Aryeh. Equally welcome were the opportunities that Shulie and I had to travel on our own and enjoy each other's company, as we had done in much earlier years before familial responsibilities weighed upon us. Happy and less happy memories arise as I think of those years and some of them were important enough to my personal history and development to warrant accounts in greater detail.

Lecturing Abroad

As my scholarly reputation grew, there were numerous opportunities to give lectures and attend conferences in Israel, Europe and North America. As the children matured, Shulie was more often able to accompany me on those trips and it provided wonderful opportunities to see places that we might otherwise have missed. Visits to California introduced us to the multi-lane highways and the smogs of Los Angeles, the beauties of hilly San Francisco, the Berkeley campus and the Golden Gate Bridge, as well as the horror of the prison island of Alcatraz. We also saw Malibu and the Getty Museum and were rather surprised to find in the case of the latter that many items lacked any details of provenance and purchase. When we asked about this, it was whispered to us that some acquisitions may have come in unusual ways. It was thrilling to watch the sailing boats in the beautiful bay of San Diego and to pop over the border into Mexico and briefly visit Tijuana. We learned that New York was totally *sui generis* and had little in common with the other American cities. Going to the theatre and the opera there, as well as sampling its rich choice of museums, walking (while many jogged!) in Central Park and mastering a metro system that is not among the world's cleanest and quietest (contrasting totally with Washington and Toronto where it seemed you could eat off the floors!) – we much enjoyed all these activities.

Visits to Israel were always on our calendar and before the children began to make all their own arrangements, we were able, during a visit by all four of us, to hire a car and to travel around the country. Given so much discussion about Judea and Samaria, or the 'West Bank', as others prefer to call it, Shulie and I agreed that the four of us should visit some of its towns and see for ourselves what they looked like. We drove our small and very hot hired car (air conditioning was not yet compulsory but should already have been) through the Arab-dominated cities of Tulkarem, Jenin, Nablus and Hebron, always with a degree of apprehension. Things were not as calm as they had been in 1970 when my friend Mayer Nissim had taken us on a similar tour, but nor were they yet exploding into the violence of later years. The overall impression that we received was that such cities could easily have been part of Jordan, Syria or Egypt, and had an identity that was far removed from that of the Israeli cities we knew.

Shulie's brother, Ronnie, was active in the Campaign for Soviet Jewry and was keen for us to visit Moscow and meet up with some of the refuseniks. We finally found time to be able to do this in 1987 and the few days we spent in the Soviet Union were both inspiring and frightening. We had been given numerous religious artefacts and Jewish text-books that were desperately sought by the refuseniks and we had to declare that they were all for our own use. Examination by the immigration and customs officials was a dreadful experience and one felt that at any time one might be whisked off to KGB headquarters for interrogation, or consigned to the Lublinianka Prison. We were officially part of a five-day Thomson Tour, and saw some of the Moscow sights, but the arrangement was that we would be met towards lunchtime each day by a refusenik and be taken by the metro to a suburban apartment where I would then lecture on Jewish history and religion and on the Hebrew language to those thirsty for such knowledge.

The questions and comments of the refuseniks were of a generally high standard and the refuseniks were undoubtedly a brave and resilient bunch of people, all inspired by the example of such leaders as Natan Sharansky who had only recently been released and settled in Israel. Some were keen Zionists, others committed to Jewish religious observance, and there were those who simply wished to know more about their Jewish origins that the Soviets were intend on suppressing. With only a few breaks for snacks, I did this teaching each afternoon and evening and we were rarely back in our hotel before 23.00. On one occasion we exited the metro station to find all four exits looking totally identical (by design?) and it took us a few minutes and one wrong turning before we were able to re-orient ourselves and find our hotel. On each floor there was a woman sitting at a table at the end of the corridor to keep an eye on us, and, from the way our cases and possessions had been moved, it was clear that there had been some inspection of those while we were out.

We met many impressive Jews, a large number of whom eventually made it to Israel. On the first day, I was astonished when our contact picked us up and then immediately made a call from a public box to report that he was on his way with us to a specific rendezvous. Wouldn't the KGB be monitoring such calls? 'Yes, of course,' he cheerfully replied, 'but they have so many thousands of calls to check that it will be many months before they get around to listening to this one, and by then you will have safely returned to Cambridge.' The accommodation at the hotel was clean, if fairly basic, but the meals were atrocious. Everything seemed to be some kind of *ersatz* product such as we had not seen in the UK since the 1940s. The eggs were not eggs, the bread was like straw, and the coffee was undrinkable. We were glad that we had brought some snacks with us from the UK.

At breakfast one day we met a Jewish couple from Manchester who were due to leave that day for home. Since we were unable to be in contact with our children, we asked them to telephone and tell them that all was well. Aryeh had been warned to say nothing to anyone about out trip and, when he received their call, he was very careful to give nothing away and to allow them to do all the talking. When the aircraft took off from Moscow, there was an almost audible sigh of relief on the part of many of the passengers.

A brief visit to Heidelberg to lecture at the Hochschule für jüdische Studien, then presided over by Julius Carlebach, was an altogether different kettle of fish, or rather box of asparagus. It was a much more comfortable experience and it was interesting to note the fuss that was being locally made about the imminently expected arrival, and consumption of, the first *weisse Spargeln*. The contrast with Moscow could not have been more sharply drawn. Trips that Shulie and I took without any professional commitments included visits to Toronto for lively family celebrations with Cynthia and Karl, and their five boys, a short visit to the tourist sites of Jordan (including Petra, Madaba and Jerash of course), a week in the Channel Islands and long weekends in Bristol and Bath. The latter was especially exciting for Shulie who was an enthusiastic reader of Jane Austen novels. I was more impressed by the Roman baths than by the Austenian locations and Regency terraces.

During a lecture tour in Washington in 1995, we were advised by a close friend, who had been in Cambridge with us, that one of his colleagues at the National Heart and Lung Institute in Bethesda was married to a woman from a Reif family. It turned out that Harriet and I had the same great-grandparents in Kalusz. What is more, her daughter Laura had hundreds of letters from their eldest son, Avraham (Adolf), who had left Kalusz late in the nineteenth century, and from these we were able to reconstruct the history of their ten children and make connections between their current descendants in the USA, UK and Israel.

Teenager Topics

Although bringing up teenagers always has its challenges, Shulie and I were fortunate to have two youngsters who rarely got into scrapes and were by and large a source of immense pride for us. We felt that we had a good relationship with them both, and could talk to them frankly about most matters. As previously mentioned, Tanya enjoyed all her years at the Perse School for Girls, at both primary and secondary levels, and did outstandingly well. Her only problem was her lack of confidence in her physical appearance. No matter how often I told her how beautiful and attractive she was, it was not until her undergraduate year at Cambridge that she began to believe it. Needless to say, it needed to be others who complimented her and not her father. For his part, Aryeh had not seen the earlier promise of his years at the 'prep' school maintained at the high school of the Perse for Boys. It was especially difficult for him to cope with missing Saturday classes and (like his father before him in teenage!) he did not over-exert himself in his homework or his examinations. Notwithstanding his preference for playing games on a primitive Amstrad computer, he was still among the best in his class. Perhaps his sister's devotion to her studies put him out a little but he was confident that if she could obtain 'A' grades in all her matriculation subjects at 'O' level, he could easily achieve the same. Alas, pride came before a fall and his results, while good, in no way matched those of his sister.

Aryeh's sixth-form years were more enjoyable because he developed a good rapport with the new headmaster, Dr. Martin Stephen, and although he did not work especially hard, he obtained high enough marks in his final examinations to warrant an application to Cambridge. Both children did very well in their Classical Hebrew 'O' and 'A' levels, obtaining among the best marks in the whole country. Shulie and I were proud of them and pleased that our teaching had been productive. Tanya was clearly destined for Cambridge and she was accepted at Queens' College to study Arabic. Her numerous languages at school had included Latin, Greek, German and French and she was a natural linguist. After a 'gap year' with Bnei Akiva in Israel, she loved her years at Cambridge, where she won prizes, obtained two excellent degrees, including first class honours in each of her three undergraduate years (a 'triple first'), and played a major role in the Cambridge University Jewish Society.

Aryeh had, on the other hand, informed us from about the age of sixteen that he had no intention of studying for a degree. It was only with some serious parental determination that we persuaded him not to give up school in order to become a professional snooker player. We reached an agreement according to which he would win a place at Cambridge and would then be able to do what he wanted, as long as it was in some way structured. His first choice of college was Jesus and when asked why he wished to study there he was cheeky enough to reply that they had the best snooker table in the University. Unsurprisingly, they declined to offer him a place but Emmanuel College and University College London did so.

He chose to enrol at a very good yeshivah in Israel with the intention of completing a year or two of talmudic studies and then serving in the army, and perhaps driving a tractor on a kibbutz. Shulie and I always felt more than a little guilty that being resident in Cambridge meant that the children did not have easy access to a lively Jewish social life until their late teens when Tanya was at Cambridge and Aryeh in Israel. They were both keen to earn pocket money in their teens and one summer they worked for the catering department of one of the Cambridge colleges. All went well until they explained that they could work on all other days and times but not on Shabbat. They were promptly sacked by the catering manager. I made representations but to no avail. There was neither sympathy nor understanding.

Engineer Anthony

While Tanya was in Israel, before her Cambridge studies, Shulie and I continued to host Jewish undergraduates for lunch at our home after synagogue on Shabbat. Given that our daughter would soon be one of them, we took a growing interest in those who were to be her fellow students. There was a group of young men who had been to the Hasmonean High School in Hendon, London, and who impressed us. One of them was Anthony Silas, who was reading engineering at Caius College and somehow seemed to be more hard-working, more mature and more self-sufficient than the others. Little did we then know that he would later become our much-loved and highly valued son-in-law. Tanya seemed to us to blossom during her Cambridge studies, not only chalking up numerous academic attainments but also making many friends, both Jewish and non-Jewish, and maturing into a very attractive young woman.

Tanya and Anthony had been friends from her early months in Cambridge but it appears to have taken her a little longer than him to commit. Commit to each other they finally did at the end of September 1990 and they arranged a delightful engagement party for family and friends at Caius College. The children's intentions were declared to us at a dinner party made by Anthony's parents, Helen and Charles, in their London home. The Silas family name had been Saḥayek ('little Isaac') in Baghdad but when they settled in the British Indian city of Calcutta in the late nineteenth century, it had to transform into something that British bureaucrats could more easily deal with. Given the family's Sefardi origins, we joked about camels as dowry and when the children made their announcement, Anthony jokingly presented me with one little cloth camel, which I still have and treasure.

Jewish Wedding at Queens'

Early in 1991 we had to start planning a wedding and Shulie and I, with the young couple, decided that we did not wish to have the standard London Jewish ḥuppah and catering but to have a special Cambridge affair that would more accurately reflect the commitment that all four of us had to the famous academic centre. On 18 August a ḥuppah was set up in the splendid gardens of Queens' College that led down to the river. Rabbi Dr. Abraham Levy and Rabbi Dr. Jeffrey Cohen, both of whom knew the couples and the families very well, officiated at the ceremony, in the presence of about 220 family and friends from all over the UK and from abroad. The catering had of course to be kosher and had to be brought from London. We could not use the kitchens at Queens' and had therefore to arrange a cold fish buffet and to ensure that it arrived late enough not to be spoiled by the warm weather and early enough to have it all set out.

A Cypriot caterer, Michael Andreou, whom I knew from St John's, made all the arrangements but this meant that Shulie and I had to be on hand all the time and ensure that everything was done as we had planned. Aryeh acted very calmly and efficiently as master of ceremonies. When Tanya, looking gorgeous, walked through the College cloisters, there was an audible and appreciative 'Oh!' from the guests and there were Japanese tourists on punts in the river who were videoing the whole thing and would no doubt report back to their friends and family at home about what they probably took to be a typical English wedding.

Having had little joy from our own wedding reception, we did our best to ensure that the couple would have happy memories and I believe that we achieved that. But it has to be said that it was not an easy task and by the end of the day, while almost everyone had gone, and Shulie and I were still clearing up with Michael and the staff he had engaged for us, we felt truly exhausted. We made only one error in our culinary calculations. We had assumed that if we offered five desserts, most guests would have two or three. In fact, a fair proportion of those who served themselves first took all five so that those who were last in line had much less of a choice. An interesting lesson to be learnt.

New Generation

While Tanya had been completing the final year of her BA, Anthony, who had obtained his first degree in engineering a year earlier, had obtained an MA in Jewish Studies at Jews' College and had been working with the Sefardi youth in London. Now the young couple purchased a little Victorian 'two up and two down' in Histon Road, about two kilometres from the city centre, and made it look really charming. Tanya began to study for an MPhil in Arabic and then assisted in the library of the Faculty of Oriental Studies while Anthony found employment as an engineer with Cambridgeshire County Council. They seemed to Shulie and me to be well matched and very happy and it was a great pleasure to see them on a regular basis. I think that Tanya and Shulie became especially close to each other at that time which helped matters when Tanya was having problems becoming pregnant and needed to be reassured that, with some medical assistance, all would eventually be well.

On 7 May 1993, after a fearful few hours of pain, crisis and anxiety on all fronts, Gidon Elia, our first grandchild, and the first great-grandchild for what were by then our two surviving parents, Annie Reif and Muni Stekel, was born at Addenbrooke's Hospital and was duly 'entered into the covenant of Abraham our father'. The young family of three then decided to settle in Israel, and we bade them farewell early in 1994. We were very happy for them but Shulie and I sobbed on each other's shoulders, aware as we were that they were truly making their own life and that both our kids were now geographically distant from us. We felt rather lonely. But by March 1995, the three Silases had become five with the birth of twins, Shoshi and Dani, so that there was even more reason to make regular trips to the Jewish homeland.

Aryeh as Student and as a Soldier

Aryeh too was building a life of his own. In 1988, not many weeks out of high school, he made his way to the renowned Yeshivat Har Etzion, in Alon Shevut, some 20 kilometres south of Jerusalem, beyond Bethlehem, about a third of the way to Hebron. Although we had studied Talmud together, he was by no means at the level of the Israeli boys or the American boys who had studied in yeshivah high schools. He studied hard with a group of UK boys and was thrilled when he was soon invited to join the American group, and, later, the Hebrew speakers. He stayed in touch with us on a regular basis but of course we had no mobile or cell phones at that time and it could at times be worrying, especially since travel to Alon Shevut meant at that time passing by Deheishe Refugee camp where there were always a number of Palestinian 'militants' ready to attack passing Israelis.

Aryeh did return to Cambridge for Pesaḥ and we saw him during our various visits to Jerusalem when we stayed in the apartment that had been purchased by Muni and Elly a couple of years earlier. On Purim we had arranged for him to come and join us after the megillah and were a little troubled when he did not show up. After some hours we finally made contact with a friend of his and, although he loyally did not spell it out too clearly, we could deduce from his remarks that Aryeh had imbibed too much alcohol of too great a variety and that his friends had carried him to his bed where he was sleeping it off!

Early in 1989 Aryeh had decided that he wished to join his fellow yeshivah students who were being enlisted into the Givati Brigade (the Israeli marines) in the summer. If going alone to Alon Shevut was brave, joining the Israeli army as a volunteer and a 'lone soldier' for a year, with no family in the country to take care of him when he had leave, was courageous in the extreme. We visited as often as we could but it was our friends, Ada and Menahem Ben-Sasson, who functioned *in loco parentis* and took great care of him (his appetite and his laundry!) when he had a Shabbat off duties. He had to learn the new Hebrew language of soldiers, put up with what he saw as the illogicality of some military instructions, and even suffer some physical hurt that required a hospital visit. Deeply impressive was the fact that he was chosen to take a course of training as a sniper/sharpshooter.

The lone soldier did receive some minor privileges in those years but nothing near what they were granted many years later. When Shulie was in hospital having a hysterectomy in November 1989, he was allowed to make a phone call to her. In today's IDF climate, he might even have been given leave to come for a few days. We attended as many of his military ceremonies as we could and took great pride in each stage of his advancement, knowing just how difficult it was for him. At the beginning of 1991, when Aryeh had finished his army service and was waiting to commence his University course, the dictator of Iraq, Saddam Hussein, chose to fire Scud ballistic missiles at the Israeli cities that winter in response to the American invasion. Aryeh would send us messages assuring us that he was safe, from a shelter in Jerusalem.

In addition to turning a schoolboy into a maturing young man, the Israeli army also served another (and for us a very welcome) purpose. He began to appreciate that he was more intelligent and more academic than he had previously allowed (and than many other recruits) and he decided that he wished to study law at an Israeli university. With the help of references from the Perse School and from friends who knew him well, he was able to obtain a student place at Bar-Ilan University and to do his degree in law and to qualify as a lawyer, after (predictably) declining to take up his place at Emmanuel College, Cambridge, to read Classics and Law. He was gradually able to write papers in Hebrew and to impress some of his teachers, especially in matters to do with Latin and Greek, as well as correcting the English pronunciation of one professor who was adamant that 'the man on the Clapham omnibus' was travelling to a place called 'Clafam'!

Attorney Aryeh

Aryeh did not care for the purely academic side of law but preferred 'hands-on' activities such as running a law clinic in a poor area of Tel Aviv, and offering the residents some legal advice. When he told his Stekel grandfather that he was keen to buy a car and had the prospect of a good deal, Muni advanced him the money and, on his return to London, claimed reimbursement from Shulie and me. We were not greatly pleased. Not many driving days had passed when he had a serious accident, which virtually wrote off the car. He admitted that he had been driving too fast and that he had skidded off the road but it was a lesson that he had to learn and, to his credit, he absorbed the message and took greater care in subsequent road journeys.

Marriage with Mirit

After his degree he completed his legal training with positions at the Mul-T-Lock company, then with a distinguished lawyer (Adiel Cheshin) in Jerusalem, and with Reuven Borokovsky in Yavne, and learned a great deal from these experiences. He was then able to open his own law office, Reif & Reif, in 2000. While at Bar-Ilan University he had also met a fellow student of law, a bright, dynamic and attractive young woman from Ashkelon by the name of Mirit Hoffman, and they were engaged early in 1994, visiting us in Cambridge for Pesaḥ that year. We met her parents, Haya and Meir, as well as other members of her family, and the nuptial celebrations were fixed for 21 June. These were held in Bnei Braq and were, naturally, typically Israeli. Shulie and I preferred the style we had followed in Cambridge but went along with all the arrangements and developed a friendly relationship with Meir and Haya. Aryeh had some serious worries at the last minute but we put this down to nerves and encouraged him to go ahead.

We were more worried as parents when Aryeh and Mirit seemed to be losing some of the romantic magic a year or two later but again we discounted this as the behaviour of two equally determined and uncompromising individuals. Tanya and Anthony had bought a house in the newly developing city of Beit Shemesh and were soon joined a few hundred metres away by the young Reifs. It was not long until Sharron and David also took up residence in that same expanding city. So, it was now the case that we had a married sister and two married children in Israel, and when we arrived in the late summer of 1996 for a sabbatical year in Jerusalem, they were all there to greet us with placards of welcome. Aryeh had also kindly taken responsibility for purchasing a car on our behalf and we were thrilled to receive the car keys already at Ben-Gurion Airport. Mirit went straight to hospital from there and gave birth to their first child and our fourth grandchild, Nili Avigail, the next day.

Losses Begin

Sadly, but inevitably, such additions to the family were matched by the loss of some of the older generation. I remember well one conversation we had with Muni in the mid-1980s in which he said he felt sorry for me and Shulie because in the coming decade we would probably be mourning the deterioration and passing of our parents. We played it down and invoked the usual Jewish blessing of 120 years but, as it turned out, he was not far wrong. Shulie's much loved grandmother (whom our children called 'Savta') had been deteriorating physically and mentally during the early 1980s. Remarkable as it may seem, even during such deterioration, she could command a conversation in numerous languages. During one of my parents' visits to England, my father addressed her in Polish, in Russian and in Yiddish and she greatly impressed him by being able to respond perfectly well in each. In actual fact, her English, her German and her Hebrew were better than his. Her final few months had to be spent in a Jewish seniors' home where she could receive the nursing attention she needed and she finally passed away in July 1986 at the age of 93. Muni was almost 72 at the time and when we tried to console him by saying that she had led a long life and that he had enjoyed a mother for a greater time than most others, he argued that this made it even more difficult to accept her loss.

King David Court

We should have heard warning bells ringing at this stage about his capacity to deal with such sad events but we put it down to his general tendency to magnify his own problems and minimize those of others. Whatever he said, it gave him and Elly a new lease of life in their early seventies since they could now travel without having to worry about his mother. A few months later we received a call from him to say that they had purchased an apartment in King David Court, in the centre of Jerusalem, next door to the King David Hotel, and were in the process of fitting it all out. To our delight, it was not only very central but also had a parking lot and a swimming pool. They would therefore be able to do what he had always longed to do, that is, to spend much more time in Israel. We, and Ronnie and Zsuzsi, would also be able to use the apartment when the seniors were in England and this excited us greatly. We took advantage of the offer many times in the course of the subsequent six years.

One of these times was in 1989 when I was a visiting scholar, teaching a master's course in Jewish liturgy and doing my own research at the

Hebrew University of Jerusalem for the second semester. We resided in the apartment and even rented a car for part of our stay. In the second half of 1988 I heard from my mother that the doctors were reporting that my father's heart was weakening. He had suffered cardiological problems from 1962 but now the situation was more acute. I therefore took three opportunities of visiting North America to give some lectures and, in each case, travelled via Toronto so that I could visit him and my mother.

Dad's Anger and his Death

The previous years had seen a sad reversal of his personality from the slightly mellower one that had characterized his middle age to the volatile, angry and aggressive one that I had known in my earliest years. Somehow our new house in Parsonage Street made him resentful and he tended to quarrel not only with Shulie and me but with any other members of the family who visited, including even little Yoni, Sharron and David's first child, who had barely learned to walk. The situation reached a dreadful climax in 1985. He had made some adjustment to an item on my desk, for which Shulie upbraided him, and he closed the sliding doors to the balcony in the incorrect way and again this prompted criticism from her. He exploded, went on hunger strike for the remaining days of their visit, and swore he would never again visit our house. He was true to his word.

From Toronto he often added to my mother's letters some angry, bitter and hurtful comments. When I sent him a birthday present, he sent it back to me by return mail, suggesting I give to Muni. When they visited Israel, they would travel via Heathrow Airport in London and we and the children would go and visit them in a hotel which I always booked for them to make their journey more comfortable. I offered profuse apologies for whatever I may have done wrong, tried to reason with him, and begged him not to hurt me in these ways, but he was adamant. Somehow his deep resentment of me, the wife I loved, and my successes, were all too much for him. Short of going back to being a two-year-old and welcoming him and his new regime with open arms and favouring him over my Zeide, there was little I could do.

Strangely, whenever I visited him in Toronto he would rush out and buy gifts for me and for Shulie, as if to demonstrate that he really and truly loved us. I did not follow his example of rejection but accepted these with feigned pleasure. In January 1989, I spent a few days with my parents in Toronto and he seemed much calmer, at least with me, if not with my mother, who was having to tolerate a great deal of anger, abuse and frustration from him. My sister Cynthia drove us to the local bus station from where I could travel to the airport. He put his hands on my head and blessed me with the priestly blessing 'May the Lord bless you and keep you', reciting it in Hebrew, as he and I had done many times in synagogue. He kissed me and, with tears in both our eyes, he added that this would be our last moments together. As I waved to my little Polish soldier Daddy from the bus, I had a gut feeling that he was probably right, and felt miserable all the way to the terminal and during the lengthy flight home.

I was lecturing at a conference in Spain when the news of his hospitalization came to me. I returned to Cambridge and a day later, on Wednesday 8 February, my mother telephoned to say that he had suffered a final and fatal heart attack. Needless to say, Muni seemed, between 1986 and 1989, to have undergone a change of heart about the loss of a parent, telling me that it was only to be expected and that it was the natural way of the world. Ronnie kindly helped Shulie and me to arrange an immediate trip to Toronto where I could sit shiv'ah with my mother, and my sisters, Cynthia and Sharron. Sharron was living in Ginot Shomron in Samaria and had no telephone so it had been a problem to contact her with the news but we had managed to do so and to arrange to meet at Heathrow on our way to Toronto.

On arrival, we went to say goodbye to our deceased father and were upset to see the angry look on his lifeless face. I bore in mind two of Dad's many regular complaints about contemporary Jewish mourning practices. In deference to what I knew would be his wish, I insisted that we did not leave to the graveyard workers the covering of the coffin with earth but followed Jewish custom and had family members and friends complete the task. During the shiv'ah, I did not have a rest period but stayed available all day and until late in the evening, ready to receive all those who paid consolation visits. Dad had recently fallen out with a very good friend, Mayer Holder, and, knowing that Holder often helped to prepare bodies for burial as an act of piety, he made Cynthia swear that Mayer was not be allowed near him if he died first.

It seemed to me significant that the person to whom he was closest in the final months of his life was a young Polish woman called Paulina who had immigrated to Toronto. They chatted intensively and emotionally in Polish (much to my mother's chagrin) and Paulina told us afterwards at the shiv'ah how delightfully correct and traditional his Polish had been, having of course been acquired in the 1920s. I hardly slept that whole week, thinking again and again of my failure to reach any sort of closure with my Daddy and shedding many tears. It was good for me that the subsequent few months were to be spent in Jerusalem. There was a little synagogue opposite King David Court where many of the worshippers were from an eastern European background similar to that of my father and where I led the prayers and said qaddish in his memory very early every morning.

There was also a minyan of Iranian Jews nearby where I could say the afternoon and evening prayers and again recite qaddish. The speed of the former was much to my liking while the latter was so slow that I had to reckon with almost an hour each day. Shulie could not believe the difference in velocity between the two liturgies. The student's synagogue in Cambridge was at that time being renovated and therefore unavailable. On my return to Cambridge in mid-summer, the community helped to arrange prayers in my home as often as they could until the students returned in October when we met every day in one or other of their college rooms. Shulie was always keen to improve her spoken Hebrew and attended an intensive language course (ulpan) during our months in Jerusalem, as well as undertaking some English editorial work for one of the local academic research centres.

Muni's Plans Awry

It is hardly a rarity for husbands to operate under the illusion that they will predecease their spouses and to make arrangements accordingly. Although Muni had serious health problems, he preferred not to know too much about these. Elly was a wise judge of his character and told the family that they should never tell him if he had a terminal illness since he would not be able to accept such a situation, or to cope adequately with it. He had various periods of hospitalization in 1992 and in the summer he made a point of refusing to eat the kosher meals that were ordered for him by the hospital, preferring to eat only the meals that were prepared for him each morning by Elly and transported by her every day to the hospital. It was an exhausting procedure for her and Shulie and Ronnie were more than a little concerned for her health.

Nevertheless, Muni seemed to get better and they went off to Israel in mid-September to spend the Jewish festivals in their King David apartment, planning to return to London early in November. As fate dictated it, Muni would return but not Elly. The Jewish holidays over, they went to see family and friends on Sunday 25 October and got back to Jerusalem in the evening. Aryeh was with them when Elly had a heart attack and he went with them in the ambulance to Shaare Zedek hospital. The situation seemed to stabilize and they came home to daven, to have some breakfast and to bring back some cosmetic items that Elly had requested. Later that morning, she suffered another coronary attack and they were summoned back to the hospital, where they found that she had in the meantime died.

Shulie and I had received the first bulletin at home at around 07.00 and had decided that she would immediately go to Jerusalem to look after her mother. We were working in the University Library later that morning when the totally unexpected and frightful news was conveyed to her. We immediately arranged for her to accompany Ronnie to Israel, where Elly was to be buried near her father in the Nahalat Yitzhak cemetery in Tel Aviv and Muni ordered and paid for a plot for himself beside her. I drove Shulie to London, and Tanya, then a student at Cambridge, came with us in the car to try to console her. As if it was not challenging enough to lose a mother, Shulie and Ronnie then had to put up with a father who was totally distraught. That was understandable in the circumstances but, for the remainder of his life, he refused to be consoled, rejected all attempts, by family and friends, to help him to refashion his life, and totally indulged himself in his own grief and lamented the bitterness of his fate.

Failing to Cope and Giving Up

Shulie used her mother's car to travel a couple of times each week to be with him and we had him with us in Cambridge for many weekends. Elly had left many prepared meals in her freezers in Jerusalem and in London and we thought he would eat these and feel grateful to her. As he expressed it, how could he eat with equanimity what Elly had prepared so lovingly for him now that she was gone? His difficult relationship with Ronnie and Zsuzsi exacerbated the situation and when he found out, from a remark that his doctor accidentally let slip, that he was dying of liver cancer, he simply could not deal with the terminal nature of such a disease.

I persuaded Edmund to co-sponsor a book launch in London in the hope of offering some cheer; sadly without success. He attended Aryeh and Mirit's wedding in Israel in 1994 but even that happy family event did nothing to improve his state of mind. On the contrary, he treated many of those he met with anger and frustration. He determined to sell the Jerusalem apartment because it had been their little home, the warm nest they had shared, and he could not face being there. In addition, he and his companies were experiencing a sharp downturn in their economic fortunes and he simply needed the cash in order to carry on.

On the Shabbatot which he spent with us late in 1994 and early in 1995, Shulie tried to prepare his most favourite meals but he took no pleasure in those and by this time was suffering from acute nausea after each meal, with only limited relief from the medication he was taking. I sat with him listening to his tale of woe and holding the bowl for him when he had those nauseous attacks. For the first time in his life, he began to criticise himself and his role as husband and father. His quarrels with Zsuzsi, and his feeling that Ronnie no longer cared for him, distressed him greatly. He even expressed the wish to cut his son out of his will. Shulie and I felt that this would not be the wisest thing for him to do and talked him out of it. I learned how it was to offer some sort of support to a terminally ill patient and did not then know that this would not be the last time that I had to experience such a role.

Muni had expected to spend Shabbat 25 February with Ronnie and Zsuzsi but he told us that this had not proved feasible so he came to us in Cambridge. He was by this time a broken man in every way and we saw him giving up the fight and the life ebbing away from him. We were booked to go to Israel on Thursday 2 March and this made him worry that he would have nowhere to go the next Shabbat. Shulie assured him that we would take him to Israel with us. We did that but he was no longer alive, having died on Wednesday night. Ronnie told us that he preferred to bury him in London since he himself was not well enough to travel with the body to Israel.

For her part, Shulie was adamant that her father had expressly wished to be buried next to Elly in Tel Aviv and so she and I travelled on the same plane as Muni's body and buried him beside Elly, as he had wished. Ronnie felt unable to come with us and remained in London. Shulie sat shiv'ah in the house of Tanya and Anthony, which Muni had visited when it was just being built, and then helped to look after Tanya, who was by this time in the final month of her pregnancy with twin girls. When Shoshi and Dani were born on 28 March, Tanya, who was very close to Muni and Elly, chose second names for them that would commemorate her two Stekel grandparents, namely, Meira for Meir/Edmund and Esther for Esther/Elly.

Muni and Elly's Will

I returned to work in Cambridge and had long telephone conversations and personal meetings with Ronnie in London. We went together to see the lawyer and were told that the will left the apartment and its contents to Shulie, and a small plot of land in Israel to Tanya, and the property companies to Ronnie and Shulie, to be shared equally between them. Some years earlier, Ronnie had suggested to me during a telephone call that he saw no reason why he and Shulie, as co-executors, could not revise the will in accordance with what they preferred. I had no idea at that time what the will contained but expressed the strong conviction to him that I would never have thought of revising my own parents' wishes in such a way and therefore could not in all honesty recommend to Shulie that she take such action with regard to her parents' will.

When I had at that time discussed this with Shulie, who was also unaware of what the will contained, she had agreed with me wholeheartedly. The situation of the companies at the time of Muni's death was precarious and the property market in London was at a low ebb. Ronnie therefore argued that he had drawn the short straw and that this was wholly unfair. He told me as we walked near Harley Street in London's West End that if we agreed to change the will, and to share everything, he would work to save the companies and would ensure that Shulie would receive some limited income from those, as she had done for many years. If not, it might turn out that she would eventually receive no inheritance at all.

I reported back to Shulie who was with Tanya in Beit Shemesh and suggested that we should not engage in any struggle but simply bow to Ronnie's wishes. Either way, I felt that we were unlikely to see much financial gain. I mentioned what my Zeide had told me about how it was wise never to expect any yerushah (inheritance). Though not at all keen on the idea of thwarting the last wishes of her father and mother, she at first agreed but then spoke to the family lawyer in London who strongly advised her not to agree to Ronnie's suggestion but to fight him over it. I do not know to this day whether the lawyer was offering a genuine (and perhaps misguided) piece of legal advice, or was a party to a scheme to overturn the will.

Be that as it may, Shulie's feeling was that Ronnie had worked with his father in good times and that, according to what her mother Elly had told her, he and Zszusi had derived much benefit from the companies during the profitable years. He should therefore be satisfied with continuing with this role. She was willing to give up her share in the companies and whatever he made from the companies would be his own. She would be content with the proceeds from the sale of the apartment. If I remember correctly, its value at that time was around £140,000. Ronnie undertook to 'use his best endeavours' to ensure that she received such proceeds. Once Shulie had made up her mind which policy she preferred, I worked closely with her and supported her totally.

The subsequent years saw a breakdown of personal relations between us and Ronnie, as well as accusations, angry exchanges of correspondence and threats of legal action of all sorts. Shulie had no stomach for this and was greatly distressed by her brother's reluctance to execute his parents' wishes, by his admission that he had long since lost any affection for Muni, and by his determination that she should in no way benefit while he struggled to deal with the companies' problems. Most of the debts emerged as debts against the personal estate of Muni, essentially the apartment, and most of the assets turned out to be those of the companies. Even the funds that Muni had given Tanya as her wedding present had to be recouped from the personal estate. Ronnie had been the personal and company accountant and was able to explain why this had to be the case. Shulie and I spent about £25,000 of our own money in consulting lawyers in London about the possibility of removing Ronnie as a co-executor.

Aryeh, although only at the beginning of his legal career, was gradually able to assist us in all these struggles and was astonished at the lack of professional competence that we encountered among expensive West End lawyers. When the latter assured us that we had a 70 per cent chance of winning a case against Ronnie, we realized that this meant a 30 per cent chance of losing, and we knew we had virtually to surrender. Aryeh negotiated a form of settlement with Ronnie and we were reimbursed for the legal fees we had incurred. Shulie received about £1,400 as her inheritance, and Tanya inherited the small plot in Israel which she later sold and, to her great credit, shared the proceeds equally with Aryeh.

Ronnie meanwhile rescued what he could of the companies and told me with no small degree of satisfaction a while later that, as a result of his personal efforts, the financial benefit from the properties that remained had been major. I think that the figure he mentioned in one telephone conversation was a very substantial one. If that was intended to hurt us, it compared in no way to the massive distress that Shulie had suffered from the whole episode between 1995 and 2002. It truly depressed and upset her and she could not face the idea of having any sort of future relationship with a brother who, as she saw it, had behaved in such an unfair way towards her, and so disrespectfully towards her father's memory.

Ronnie for his part resented how we presented the story to our family and friends and felt unable at any stage to come to family semaḥot because matters for him remained unresolved. His conditions for a reconciliation involved an admission on Shulie's part that it was all her father's fault, that her father had lied to her, and that Ronnie had been the honest one through the whole episode. Shulie loved her father and always enjoyed a warm and close relationship with him. There was no way that she could agree to such conditions. I cannot say how this contretemps affected Ronnie's well-being but I do feel totally convinced that it had a highly deleterious effect on Shulie's health in the subsequent years.

Mum's Final Years

The story of how I had to deal with my mother during her final years is a very different one, but no less distressing. Her relations with Pinḥas had always been stressful and they were often at loggerheads. She did not have the strength of character to stand up to him but fought back by saying things that only antagonized him more. At the end of his life he expressed the view that she had never really loved him and that after his death she would marry her old 'flame' from half a century earlier in Edinburgh, Leslie Baum. While we were sitting shiv'ah at Cynthia and Karl's home, Mum mentioned more than once that she was now a free woman and could even marry again if she wished. Leslie's wife had died a few years earlier and soon after they began to visit each other. In November 1990, some 20 months after my father's death, Leslie and Annie married in an Orthodox Jewish ceremony in London (as Mum wished) and they settled down in Leslie's small apartment in Ilford, an eastern suburb of London. She lost some surplus weight, dressed smartly and seemed for three or four years to be a happy woman.

Cynthia deeply resented the fact that her mother, who had been so close to her, Karl and their five boys, had apparently washed her hands of them, as Cynthia saw it. Leslie and Mum did visit Cynthia and Karl in Toronto and Sharron and David in Israel but Mum always paid her own way and indeed even lent Leslie money at times. His children ensured that nothing would come her way if she outlived him. We as a family in any event had no interest in encouraging her along such pecuniary lines. Leslie was by this time severely handicapped in his legs and was able to walk only with great difficulty and with the help of walking sticks. But he could still drive so that they were fairly mobile and they often came to visit Shulie and me in Cambridge and also attended Tanya and Anthony's wedding.

In 1995 during a visit we paid to Ilford we noticed that my mother was not producing the kinds of meal that she had once prepared with ease and that she was forgetful, lacking in concentration and often repeating herself. Leslie, for his part, was deteriorating physically but seemed mentally to be coping well. The problem was that he was losing patience with her, especially when she could not respond as he wished when she partnered him in playing bridge. He even took to shouting abuse at her. My Mum's previous claims that everything was wonderful with Leslie now gave way to complaints that people thought Leslie was angelic but that was certainly not the case. It was clear to us in 1996 that my mother needed, or would soon need, some help at home, and her local authority referred her to a psychiatrist to assess her. We went with her and were astonished by the result. A woman who could not remember numbers, names or what she had said a few moments earlier, suddenly responded well to his questions. Afterwards she told us that he was such a nice young man that she had made a special effort to please him. He may have been pleased but Shulie and I certainly were not. Needless to say, she did not qualify for assistance.

The crisis came when Leslie's physical state was so bad that he had to be admitted to a special home for the disabled. We received a call from his daughter telling us to collect Annie immediately, 'as if she was a parcel at a depot', as Shulie put it. We took her home to Cambridge and set up a room for her. Shulie and I had to go to work and we explained to her how to contact us and what she could do at home. But she could not cope at all and even asked me to put her bra on for her. I simply could not bear to do this and Shulie had to oblige. After a few weeks, during which it became clear that we were not successfully dealing with the challenge, Cynthia and I decided that she might be better off in Toronto where there was more family, and we arranged for her to fly from London and to be with the Bielaks.

The Bielaks did their dedicated best for a few months but it became progressively clearer from week to week that she would soon need to be in some sort of special accommodation. She then moved to Israel to be with Sharron, and the Elkins also bravely and devotedly coped for a while. We even took Mum with us to a performance of Swan Lake by the Kirov Ballet in the Sultan's Pool outdoor theatre in Jerusalem. Eventually, however, Mum had to be admitted to a seniors' home in Jerusalem. Even that did not solve the problem because she was by then incontinent and confused and took to wandering around at night mistaking others' bedrooms for her own. She was therefore effectively 'expelled' from there and we had to find an institution that was more specifically suited to those suffering from senile dementia.

Sharron found a wonderful centre in the Elah valley, just a few kilometres south of Beit Shemesh, where she, Aryeh and Tanya were living. Shulie and I, when in Israel, were able to visit every day, or every second day. Tanya would make a point of bringing her Bubbe some rolls that she had baked especially on a Friday and Annie loved that. At first, she participated fully in numerous activities and gradually became accustomed to her new surroundings. The doctors, nurses and other staff were truly dedicated and they loved her, and she them. She spoke regularly to Leslie on the phone, chatted to us fairly intelligibly in the early days there and always loved to see her great-grandchildren and to hear from, or about, her nephews and nieces, especially Doreen and Leon.

Mum had officially made aliyah when she came to live with Sharron and, to their great credit, the Israeli government authorities and services treated her very well and very generously. By the time that I obtained my professorship in 1998, Mum was not really able to appreciate the development. When we told her, she said that she thought I had already been a professor for many years. She was destined to be in the Bet Ha-Elah hospice for another three and a half years, all the time losing more and more contact with reality. By the time that Leslie died around 2000, Mum could not respond very emotionally to the news. She felt sorry about it but it did not seem to touch her deeply.

I found it increasingly distressing to spend time with her, especially when she would ask me why Stefan did not visit her. Gradually she said nothing and looked blankly at us or at her surroundings. She had always been a good person, had looked after her parents devotedly, had run a home, worked as an alteration tailoress to boost our family income, and been a loving mother and aunt. Why did she have to suffer this terrible curse? In 2001 she had a bladder infection and was admitted to Shaare Zedek Hospital in Jerusalem. Sharron inquired whether, given the quality, or lack of quality, of her life, it was necessary to take any medical action. For her pains, she had her head bitten off by the doctor who asked if we really wanted him to kill our mother and self-righteously insisted on inserting a tube through which they could feed the poor woman for the remainder of her sorry existence.

Luckily for her, a few months later she suffered another bladder infection and the doctor at Hadassah suggested that we wait to see whether she herself could begin to fight the infection. If so, he would give her antibiotics the next day. Fortunately for Mum, there was no next day and we buried her in Beit Shemesh on 22 February 2002. Strangely, of the four parents, she had left the most money (about $10,000) and at Shulie's suggestion we used that money to bring my father's remains from Toronto and to bury them next to Mum. What funding remained after that procedure was divided among her grandchildren.

Another Gap

Uncle Abe, to whom I had been very close during my youth, was keen that I should deliver a lecture in Edinburgh. He arranged it and met the fee and expenses, and the community asked him to chair it. That would have been a marvellous event. Alas, on the day, he was not well enough to attend. It did, however, go off well and I and others told him all about it. He took great pride in my achievements. He also set a wonderful example to me of how to deal with old age. As he moved through his eighties and into his nineties, and his devoted wife Dolly died, he exchanged a house for an apartment, then opted for sheltered housing across the street from the synagogue, and finally took up residence in Newark Lodge, the Jewish Old Age Home, as it was then known, in Glasgow. When I rang him there and asked him how it was, he told me he was having a wonderful time. Most of the residents were widows and they would surround him every morning to hear his marvellous fund of stories in English and Yiddish. 'And you know what, Stefan,' he chuckled, 'the wonderful thing is that I can repeat the same stories on a regular basis since they never remember having heard them before.' He died in February 1993 and this left another gap in my close familial attachments.

New Relationships and a *pied-à-terre*

But the family story of the 1990s was by no means all gloom and doom since the three young families were expanding and there were fresh and close relationships to be built between the new generation and us as their grandparents, or uncle and aunt. Not only did we visit them and host them in Israel but they also came to see us in Cambridge. The youngsters loved the spacious house, the extensive common, and the slowly flowing river nearby and, as they got older, the many shops within easy walking distance. We taught them how to ride bicycles and made sure that we had some little bikes for them. We read them stories and poems in English, Shulie in a conventional and instructive fashion, and I in a rather naughtier and more iconoclastic mode. My cousins Leon and Paula, as well as Ronnie and Zszusi before the clash concerning the Stekel will, were also regular visitors. In Israel, Shulie's favourite haunt for entertaining the little ones in the family during the sabbatical year were the Botanical Gardens, which were a few hundred metres from our apartment in Neve Shaanan, and where they could also have an ice cream in the cafeteria.

While in Jerusalem we came to the conclusion that we needed our own *pied-à-terre* in Israel now that we had so many family members to host and entertain. Consequently, in the summer of 1997, we purchased a little apartment in Beit Shemesh where we spent some very happy times between then and 2004. Shulie organized its renovation and furnishings and almost

always stayed a little longer than I could. We made contact with many of
the academics whom we had hosted in Cambridge and most of them took
the opportunity of reciprocating on their home territory. Among those
whom we saw on a regular basis were Shlomit and Yose Yahalom, Ada and
Menahem Ben-Sasson and Anat and Ezra Fleischer, as well as my
'Doktorvater', Naphtali Wieder, and his wife Miriam (Merita).

Prima Donna Behaviour

Neither Fleischer nor Wieder was the kind of individual with whom one
could easily enjoy a warm, relaxed and personal relationship. They were
outstanding scholars who were not only wholly devoted to their industrious
programmes of research and publication but who also carefully cultivated,
in most of their professional connections, that image of correctness,
coolness and mandatory distance that was characteristic of the leading
lights in the central European discipline of *Wissenschaft des Judentums*. I
was fortunate enough to be allowed to approach them more closely than
most others. Shulie and I were often invited to their homes, where their

21. Visit by the President of Israel Ezer Weizman, and Reuma Weizman, Cambridge, 1997
(Cambridge University Library).

wives were especially thoughtful, hospitable and kind. I exchanged lengthy letters with Fleischer for many years and spoke to Wieder by telephone, until his loss of hearing made that a somewhat unproductive and even frustrating activity. That said, one always had the feeling that one's good fortune in achieving such closeness to such scholarly giants could not be taken for granted and might in certain circumstances be reversed.

Some instances of reversal come to mind. In 1990, I was busily engaged in writing some chapters for my book on the history of Jewish prayer when an article by Fleischer appeared in the Israeli periodical *Tarbiz* questioning the broad consensus that obligatory Jewish prayer had gradually developed during the Second Temple period and that liturgical texts were not finalized in the talmudic period. Having talked to colleagues in the field, I realized that nobody in Israel would be willing to challenge Fleischer's historical revisionism and that if I did not do so, it would be accepted as a valid refutation. Bravely, or perhaps foolhardily, I submitted a polite and respectful, but firm, rejoinder to the Jerusalem savant's thesis. I asked a leading Israeli scholar to check my modern Hebrew and he did so, on condition that I did not reveal to Fleischer that he had done so.

Not only did Fleischer immediately reject my views in print but he wrote me a sharply worded letter in which he disclaimed any close and warm relationship between us. I stood my ground and was joined in the challenge by two other scholars, a Canadian and an American, but Israelis who privately agreed with my criticisms were not willing to go on record against Fleischer for fear of what they thought it might do to their careers. It took about three years before we resumed a friendly relationship and reactivated our earlier style of warm, even intimate, correspondence. When I examined an Israeli doctoral dissertation, and recommended the award of the degree, Fleischer asked me if I agreed with everything that was written there. I acknowledged that I favoured some different interpretations but that the candidate had made a good enough case for his theories. Fleischer declared that one had to distinguish truth from falsehood, as one distinguished black from white. We did not fall out over it but perhaps only because I was gentle, even hesitant, in suggesting that my view of scholarship was a little different from his. I did not tell him that I thought his outlook reflected a distinctly nineteenth-century German version of scholarship that was by then outdated.

When Wieder felt the need to put his financial affairs in order, he asked me if my son could do for him what was legally required. I said that I was sure he would do it, without a fee if he wished. 'I am not a schnorrer. I want to pay whatever it costs.' He clearly had no idea of what lawyers charge per hour because when he received the bill, at a standard rate, he telephoned me to claim angrily and loudly that my son wished to take advantage of him, an old man, and to exploit him financially. He was also cross that Aryeh had copied the correspondence to me on the grounds that I had asked him to undertake the task for my teacher. In this case too it took a little while for friendly relations to be restored. To be honest, I believe that this happened only because I did not react angrily to his unwarranted accusations but quietly internalized them. Looking back on these incidents, it seems to me that both these leading academics were in a sense control-freaks who had to have all matters conducted exclusively in their own way. A close friend was astonished that, after the dressing-downs to which I had been subjected, I still wished to maintain relations with them, but I felt that I respected their learning and the influence they had had on me to such a degree that I was willing to swallow some of my pride when necessary.

Although it happened in 2003, this is perhaps the appropriate context in which to mention a clash I had with Edward Ullendorff, after he published a short and rather slight note in the *Journal of Jewish Studies* about the qaddish prayer. Andreas Lehnardt, then a young scholar early in his career, who had written extensively and impressively about the qaddish, chatted with me about Ullendorff's article at a conference and we agreed that it was neither convincing, accurate nor up-to-date. I encouraged him to submit a rejoinder and agreed to check a draft for him. It was duly received and accepted by Geza Vermes, the editor of the *Journal of Jewish Studies* in Oxford.

Vermes must have shared the content with Ullendorff since I received an irate call from the latter in which he accused me of unacceptable behaviour and tried (in my view, unsuccessfully) to argue his position. Why should he be expected to know all the latest literature on the qaddish? I countered that one should not publish if one was not up-to-date with the relevant research and that scholarship should always be allowed to express itself in a frank fashion even if a junior was challenging a senior. We left it at that but Vermes subsequently declined to publish the article, suggesting instead that Lehnardt submit a full study of the *qaddish* for publication in *JJS*. This of course never happened and it saddened me to experience what I saw as an act of academic censorship perpetrated by scholars who ought, in my view, to have known better and should have behaved more professionally.

Being honest about the shortcomings of other scholars is not designed to make one popular with them. I wrote some critical (but polite and fair) remarks about the work of Jacob Neusner and received some rather offensive responses from him. He called me a 'mean, snide, nit-picking know-it-all'. I read the letter aloud to the family at meal-time and the children were highly amused. When asked to sit on an academic appointments committee in London, I was appalled at the chairman's decision to take no account whatsoever of the views I had expressed and I opted not to rubber-stamp the decision but to withdraw from participation. He sent a note to all those involved describing me as 'impossible' and asking them never again to suggest me for anything, 'not even dog-catcher, as the Americans would say'. He was as careless about sending his emails as he was about making academic appointments, and included me in the message.

19

But Pleasures Are Like Poppies Spread
(1999–2006)

Set Fair

As the end of the twentieth century loomed near, the forecast for the future of the Genizah Research Unit and the Oriental Division seemed to be set fair. The annual reports relating to these two departments in the Library testified to admirable progress and major achievements, and there seemed to be less of a struggle to win recognition for their importance. There were often as many as fifteen to twenty staff members to deal with, so that rarely did a day pass without some time having to be spent on a problem, not just professional but also sometimes personal, that one of them had raised. A degree of cohesion and an atmosphere of co-operation now characterized the work of the orientalists and each area enjoyed what I regarded as a fair balance between doing its own thing and playing a part in divisional, and indeed Library, affairs.

Now that there was a new Exhibition Centre in the Library, there were numerous opportunities of displaying items relating to Asian languages, literatures and history. In addition, that part of the Library that included the reading rooms for rare book and manuscripts was renovated and expanded, and the Unit's offices were one of the beneficiaries of the increased space and the modernized facilities. I had the distinct impression that the early animosity towards me in the Library had largely dissipated, perhaps because my divisional work was regarded as part of the Library's daily routine. Given that I was seen to be more involved in such routines, it was as if I could be forgiven for the academic self-indulgence of directing the Research Unit and pursuing personal research. Perhaps the Library staff even began to take some pride in the international reputation that the Unit had come to enjoy. It is also possible that my academic recognition at faculty and college levels made me more self-confident and somewhat less tense. When Peter Fox retired in 2009, Anne Jarvis took over as University Librarian and I enjoyed a warm and encouraging relationship with her for the subsequent seven years. I valued her friendship and she always had appreciative comments to make about my contribution to the work of the University Library. She generously indicated that, as long as she and I were in the Library, there would always be a room, a telephone and a computer available to me.

Another highly successful woman was also a good friend and a supporter of the Unit. Risa Domb, who lectured on Modern Hebrew in the Faculty, was a member of the Unit's Steering Committee, representing the Faculty of Oriental Studies in that capacity. She was an excellent teacher, researcher and organizer and she struggled valiantly and successfully to promote her subject. She did not, however, always enjoy the wholehearted endorsement she undoubtedly deserved. Sadly, she died in January 2007 at the early age of 69 and a memorial meeting was held at Girton College where she had held a fellowship. When, at the reception that followed the meeting, I heard from two senior members of the University just how much they had valued her efforts, I could not resist remarking that it was a great pity that such a high valuation had not always been practically demonstrated during her tenure. Posthumous appreciation (*de mortuis nil sed bonum*) is not an uncommon phenomenon in Cambridge.

Reaping the Harvest

Because the seeds of Genizah research and conservation had been planted over a period of almost three decades, it was now possible to reap regular harvests of various sorts. Fresh fertilization came via the presence in the Unit of such eminent visiting scholars as Efraim Lev in the field of the history of medicine and Gideon Bohak in the area of Jewish magic, and important appointments (some part-time) were arranged (and funded) for Friedrich Niessen, Ben Outhwaite, Leigh Chipman, Nicola Heyes and Mila Ginsburskaya. A joint project on Jewish liturgy was initiated with Uri Ehrlich of Ben-Gurion University of the Negev in Beersheba and this led to the useful mounting online of very important material about prayer texts from the Genizah. Volumes were added to the 'Genizah Series' being published for the Library by the University Press and included two volumes describing Arabic and Judaeo-Arabic items by Baker, Polliack, Shivtiel and Niessen, a second volume of bibliographical references compiled by Erica Hunter and Rebecca Jefferson, and a volume prepared by Shulie Reif and myself entitled *The Cambridge Genizah Collection: Their Contents and Significance*.

The genesis of that volume had been an interesting process. My original intention in the 1970s had been to write an introduction to the Library's Genizah treasures for the 'Genizah Series' but by the late 1990s numerous other activities had interfered with the plans for this. I then decided to respond to Shulie's appeal for a lively and introductory volume that could be read and enjoyed by a much wider readership than that of Genizah specialists. With this latter volume in mind, I changed the nature of the volume intended for inclusion in the 'Genizah Series' and arranged for ten chapters to cover a variety of Genizah topics. Nine of these were based on lectures arranged in the Library in 1995 and in 1998 and given by Genizah specialists, Menahem Kister, Michael Klein, Menahem Kahana, Neil Danzig, Joseph Yahalom, Haggai Ben-Shammai, Paul Fenton, Mordechai Friedman and Joel Kraemer, and these were prefaced by an overall assessment of a century of Genizah research by myself. Shulie did most of the preparation of the volume for publication and it appeared in 2002. In a review in the *Journal of Jewish Studies*, Siam Bhayro wrote: 'The editor is to be congratulated for furnishing us with this truly marvellous collection of essays. Each paper is a joy to read and represents the highest attainment in Genizah scholarship... and Reif's introductory essay certainly demonstrates both the breadth and depth of knowledge accumulated as he has overseen the progress of this field of study'.

22. The award of a Litt.D., Cambridge, 2002.

A Popular Publication

I had started writing the more popular volume in the 1990s, incorporating some earlier articles and composing some new material, and attempting to cover the content and history of the Cambridge Genizah Collections. It had not been easy to find the time to do this but, by 1999, a text was virtually ready. Apart from Shulie's appeal for a broader treatment, major inspiration had come from a successful Manchester businessman, Joe Dwek CBE. Joe, whom I knew from the governing body of Carmel College, had taken a close interest in Genizah research and had helped to fund the Unit. He had for years been pressing me to produce a readable volume. When thanking him in my introduction, I wrote that I owed him 'a deep debt of gratitude for encouraging, even at times cajoling me into completing this volume and for providing not only moral support but also major financial assistance for that purpose through the Dwek Family Charitable Trust'.

Encouraged by some assistance from faculty colleagues, I made contact with Jonathan Price of Curzon Press and, after some lengthy negotiations, the volume was accepted for publication. The condition was that we had not only to give them what amounted to camera-ready copy but had ourselves to plan the smallest details of the layout and the inclusion of all the plates. Shulie, as always, provided invaluable assistance in this and we were delighted with the resultant hardback that emerged in 2000 and was followed by a paperback. Its sales were fairly impressive and it is still going strong, although now part of the book list of the Taylor & Francis Group.

It was particularly pleasing that a review by Menahem Ben-Sasson in the Israeli periodical *Pe'amim* welcomed it for both specialist and broader readerships: 'In spite of its pioneering methodology, its erudition and its richness in primary sources and interpretations, this study is readable and accessible for those in pursuit of information, even if they are meeting the Genizah for the first time.' A launch, sponsored by Joe Dwek, was arranged for the book at the Spanish and Portuguese Synagogue in London, and was graced by the presence of Chief Rabbi Jonathan Sacks and his wife Elaine, as well as a large audience. By that time, two additional grandchildren had been born in Israel, Zaki and Ro'i, and I dedicated the book to all six grandchildren who were then on the scene.

Why Medieval Hebrew?

Although those appointed to chairs in the Faculty of Oriental Studies had not usually delivered inaugural lectures, I discussed the matter with colleagues in the Faculty, in the University Library, and at St John's, and the consensus was that this was a special occasion, given that it was the first time in history that a member of the Library's staff had reached the level of a personal professorship. It therefore seemed appropriate to deliver an inaugural, and St John's would be the best place to do so. Its master, Charles Taylor, had after all worked with Solomon Schechter in 1896–98 to bring the Genizah treasures to Cambridge and had been an eminent hebraist and an expert in the study of Hebrew manuscripts, as well as a keen collector of many medieval Jewish codices.

I thought long and hard about a suitable subject and eventually decided to argue the case for the importance of medieval Hebrew studies, especially of precious manuscripts, and to cite some remarkable examples of texts that are historically instructive. The lecture, entitled 'Why Medieval Hebrew Studies?', was delivered in the College's School of Pythagoras in November 1999 and was attended by a large audience consisting of many major figures from University life, including the Vice-Chancellor, as well as from the Jewish community. As I speculated in my lecture, that very same building may in the twelfth century have witnessed meetings between Christian nobility in need of funds and local Jews willing to provide them. As was its custom, Cambridge University Press published this inaugural in a small booklet format. It consisted of 53 pages and it too was well received by a wide readership.

Some years after I was appointed to my personal chair, I was asked by a visiting American scholar why I had not also by then been elected to a fellowship of the British Academy. He thought my CV and publications by no measure less impressive than those of many Academy Fellows in related areas. He believed that all, or almost all, Cambridge academics with personal chairs had been recognised in that way. I pleaded ignorance of the workings of the Academy and had indeed written a letter to the *Times Educational Supplement* asking why the system could not be more transparent. Indeed, that might have itself been the reason for the apparent black balls. Others who have raised the issue, and who are well placed to understand the way things work at the Academy, have offered their own explanations. One suggested that they were simply afraid of me, another said that petty jealousies influenced such matters, while a third proposed that such elections always required someone who was willing to lead a powerful personal campaign. Future historians of British academe will no doubt judge.

Computing Progress

Progress with research, publication and conservation was by that time a well-established routine but there were exciting new developments with regard to the digitization of the fragments. Douglas de Lacey and Ellis Weinberger had made important strides in this area as well as with the Unit's website but the idea of finding ways of making all the world's Genizah materials available online became a reality early in the new century. A very learned and highly successful Jewish businessman from Toronto, Albert Dov Friedberg, and his wife Nancy, had become interested in supporting Genizah research. In 1998, Friedberg called a meeting in New York of a number of Genizah specialists from around the world and introduced us to Rabbi Reuven Rubelow who managed Friedberg's funding commitments and with whom we were destined to develop working relationships that were also personal and warm. I was happy to participate and my suggestion was that the first task was to digitize all the Genizah collections in the various libraries and museums around the world. My colleagues preferred to advocate the funding of their research programmes and, supported by the consensus, and being at that time also the less expensive option, their view prevailed.

Friedberg recalled this some years later and appreciated that my arguments had been correct but that it had only subsequently become possible to undertake the digitization project at a reduced and reasonable cost, and to the required standard. This task was entrusted to Professor Yacov Choueka, a professor of computer studies at Bar-Ilan University and he turned to the Unit for close involvement in his plans. It was clear that the digitization of all the fragments could be done only if each was given a specific and unique identity, and this necessitated compiling an inventory of all the collections. Shulie set about preparing such an inventory and the work was completed after our retirement by Rebecca Jefferson. Choueka and his colleagues in Jerusalem, including his son Roni, were then able to set in motion their digital production and by 2015 the project had been successfully completed, with the exception of the Russian collections. Yacov Choueka received a variety of awards for his important and fruitful efforts. In the first few years of the Friedberg Genizah project I was closely involved in the work in an advisory capacity and the Unit also had the benefit of generous Friedberg contributions to its budget.

Record Funding

During those final years of the 'Reif era', the Unit was successful in raising record amounts of money so that new research projects could be arranged and fresh personnel engaged. By then, there was a substantial number of regular donors on whose support the Unit could rely, but there were also major awards from Friedberg, Ronald Cohen and the Higher Education Funding Council for England (HEFCE). One of the grants from HEFCE was for a three-year project and the funding amounted to almost half a million pounds. The whole situation in the Unit had never been better and the atmosphere of productivity, industry and success seemed to be enjoyed internally and admired from outside.

There was one couple who had regularly donated a few hundred pounds on an annual basis and whom I had welcomed to Cambridge on a few occasions. I received a call from them about another visit and I invited them to have lunch with me at St John's. Afterwards, we returned to my office where they indicated their wish to offer the Unit another donation. Imagine my astonishment when they reported that a relative had left them money to be devoted to good educational use and they were therefore there and then writing the University a cheque for the Unit's benefit. I was breathless, and almost speechless, when I saw that the cheque was for £85,000. One should never neglect the small givers; they are invaluable in their own right but, in addition, some of them might one day even become major donors. The fund-raising had also become a more major activity in the USA and to that end I worked closely with Cambridge in America, addressed many audiences, and built up a cadre of regular supporters from across the Atlantic. Central to this effort was the involvement of Jim and Mary Ellen Rudolph and Jeff and Gloria Mosseri. Jim had studied at Jesus College in Cambridge and was personally devoted to the University while Jeff's grandfather, Nissim Mosseri, had been closely involved in Schechter's visit to Cairo in 1896-97. Nissim's son Jacques had brought his own Genizah collection to Paris when he settled there between the two world wars.

Mosseri Collection

In 2003 and 2004, the sons of Jacques Mosseri, Claude and Gerard, were anxious to find an appropriate way of dealing with the c.7,000 fragments bequeathed to them by their father. After discussions between them and the Unit, they decided in 2005 that it should be deposited on loan at Cambridge University Library for at least twenty years. During that time, with the aid of substantial funds provided by family and friends, and raised from elsewhere, the detailed description, conservation and digitization of all the fragments, would be undertaken. The ultimate wish of Jacques Mosseri had been that his Genizah collection should find a permanent home in the Jewish National Library in Jerusalem. His sons were adamant that they would under no circumstances give it to Jerusalem in their time.

It was formally agreed that a decision about this would be made at the end of this twenty-year period. Thus, the Cambridge Genizah Collections were again enriched, even if only temporarily, and the feeling in the Unit was that this was a pleasing vote of confidence in its abilities. I reported this fully in *Genizah Fragments*.

Newsletter's Jubilee and Unit's Pearl Anniversary

That newsletter had covered all of the Unit's progress since its first number in 1981 and in issue 50 of October 2005 Rebecca Jefferson wrote a delightful, informative and important summary of its quarter-century of progress. She cited the Library Syndicate's report of 1995 which had noted that 'the newsletter *Genizah Fragments*, which has a large international following of both scholars and lay people, appeared with customary promptness and contained important articles'. For herself, she suggested that the 'success of the newsletter is due in great measure to the spirit of co-operation in which it is produced. In fact, no examples of refusals to write are to be found in the private letters of the newsletter archives, and all are happy with the editorial decisions taken'.

The thirtieth anniversary of the founding of the Unit occurred early in 2004. My plan was to publish a commemorative supplement in the April issue of *Genizah Fragments* and to that end I approached eight scholars, requesting their comments on the Unit's achievements since 1974. Joel Kraemer of Chicago, Judith Olszowy-Schlanger of Paris, Angel Saenz-Badillos of Madrid, Menahem Ben-Sasson of Jerusalem, Philip Alexander of Manchester, Mordechai Friedman of Tel Aviv and Mark Cohen of Princeton were all most generous in their assessments, describing the Unit as a model for other collections around the world, praising the combination of scholarship and fund-raising, and kindly noting that I myself had managed to guide the Unit's work while also actively pursuing my own scholarly interests.

If that was not praise and recognition enough, there was another event which took me entirely by surprise. My squash partner, Julius Lipner, had spun me a yarn about an Indian scholar wishing to meet me at St John's on the afternoon of 10 February, and had arranged to take me to a room where the visitor was waiting to greet me. The whole thing was a ruse and, only as I approached the Wordsworth Room, did it begin to dawn that I had been duped. All the staff of the Unit and the Division, as well as senior colleagues from the Library and the Faculty, with Shulie, Avi Shivtiel and Rebecca Jefferson at the centre, were waiting to welcome me.

Not only had a party been arranged for the thirtieth anniversary of the Unit, and indeed to mark my recently-reached sixtieth birthday, but they had also prepared a booklet, with a cover nicely designed by the Unit's secretary, Sarah Sykes, and with seven articles in my honour, all carefully edited by Shulie to her usual high standards. *The Written Word Remains: The Archive and the Achievement* was introduced by Robert Gordon, and included a paper by Avi on the origin of the word *genizah*, a summary of the Unit's 30 years by Rebecca, a close analysis by Friedrich Niessen of a Genizah fragment relating to elementary education, a report by Efraim Lev on the study of the medical fragments in the Taylor-Schechter Collection, an examination by Ben Outhwaite of the Judaeo-Arabic letters of Solomon ben Judah, and an update by Ellis Weinberger on the Unit's use of the latest computer technology in its work. I was very moved by the whole initiative and astonished (as were all those involved!) that I had somehow failed to be aware of what had been going on in the Unit, virtually under my nose, for a period of some four months.

College Activities

That celebration had taken place in St John's College and, now that I was a Fellow of that august academic body, I participated wholeheartedly and enthusiastically in its activities, involving Shulie whenever it was appropriate. I invited visiting scholars to join me for lunch or dinner and this provided the opportunity of planning future projects with international colleagues. Later, in 2009, I was glad of the opportunity of assisting, in a small way, Tirza Bleehen and the Master in setting up the Bleehen Fund at College, in memory of her husband Norman who had died in 2008. The Fund was set up to encourage researchers in the history of medicine and in matters relating to Hebrew manuscripts. For a number of years, I also played a part in various College committees, the most important of which was the Audit Committee on which I served for four years and latterly chaired. The task of that committee is to give its attention to any matter that its members regard as requiring some close analysis and criticism and to report in detail to the College Council on its findings and recommendations. That was a demanding task and I believe that we did make a number of important suggestions that influenced future policy.

Peter Goddard, the distinguished theoretical physicist, was the Master when I was elected to my fellowship and he had always expressed the intention of serving in this role for no more than ten years. In 2004, true to his word, he crossed the great pond to become Director of the Institute of

Advanced Study in Princeton and the issue of his successor was, as is traditional in St John's, discussed informally for many months beforehand. By then, I felt well enough settled into my fellowship at College to express strong views about it being time to break what had become another College tradition and elect someone who had not been a Johnian for all or most of his career. I made some impassioned speeches at informal meetings and one of the more senior Fellows slowly made his way towards me after one such delivery. 'Yes, Stefan, you are a fine orator, but I fancy that we shall not follow your advice.'

Richard Perham, who had long been a Johnian and had served as President from 1983 until 1987, was subsequently elected and did a fine job for a short time until his required retirement at the age of 70 in 2007. Incidentally, when I retired from my chair in 2006 (of which I shall have more to say shortly), I told him that Shulie and I were planning to spend more time in Israel with our children and grandchildren. He assured me that as long as we kept our home in Cambridge and I spent at least half my time there, it would be in order to retain my fellowship. I greatly welcomed this assurance and it proved to be one of the factors in giving me the strength to cope with the tragic events of the years leading up to 2010.

I do not believe that my views about the Mastership, which were by no means unique to me at College, were buried and forgotten. It has always seemed to me to be the Cambridge way for some innovative ideas to be suggested and discussed at length before being rejected. They then seem to percolate for a while and to bubble up again at a later, and perhaps more suitable, time, when they are somehow no longer regarded as so innovative and even win broad acceptance. Although Chris Dobson had come to Cambridge as John Humphrey Plummer Professor of Chemical and Structural Biology, and indeed to his fellowship at St John's, in 2001, he had been an Oxford man for most of his career. He was nevertheless elected to the Mastership fairly uncontroversially in December 2006. I had introduced him and his wife Mary to the Genizah Collection some time earlier and he had become a keen and welcome supporter of Genizah research and a personal friend. He proved to be a devoted and industrious Master and his early death in 2019 was a great loss for the Fellowship, as well as for his family and close friends.

Once he knew about Charles Taylor's role in the Genizah story and his accomplishments as a hebraist, Chris removed Taylor's portrait 'from the somewhat dubious environment of the gentlemen's cloakroom' in the master's lodge to a place of honour outside his study in that same building. He also noted that the centenary of Taylor's death would be reached in 2008 and he discussed with another Fellow, Norman Bleehen, a leading clinical oncologist, and me, the idea of devoting a day's seminar to the memory of the scholar who had reigned as Master from 1882 until his death and had presented the 'Taylor-Schechter Genizah Collection' to the University in 1898. I undertook the organization of the academic aspects of the seminar and it was held on 2 November 2008, with an audience of about a hundred. The College Library also mounted a splendid exhibition of manuscripts relating to Taylor's life, work and acquisitions.

Ten lectures were delivered that day by a number of specialists in matters connected with Taylor as college man, as mathematician, as pupil and teacher, and as a scholar of rabbinics, and on the subject of the Taylor-Schechter Collection. I myself spoke about Taylor and the importance of the Genizah. It was particularly moving to hear from Raphael Loewe that he was lecturing in the College that he had joined as a student 70 years earlier, in 1938. I edited the papers for publication, adding my account of the seminar, Chris's introductory remarks, an index of names, and plates of some of the items that had been on display.

More Travel, Additional Lectures

During that period, I gave numerous lectures in North America, in Israel, as well as in the UK and other parts of Europe, and in most cases Shulie was able to accompany me. It would be a tiresome exercise (for the reader as well as for me) if I listed all these but there are a few cases which merit attention for a number of different reasons. Being a guest lecturer at the Washington Foundation for Jewish Studies directed by the charming and learned Rabbi Joshua Haberman, often accompanied by his delightful wife, Maxine, gave Shulie and me the opportunity of acquainting ourselves with that splendid city and many of its Jewish, academic and cultural institutions. I think I had to give 22 lectures in a period of a few weeks so it was not a relaxing experience, even if it was certainly a stimulating one. On Shabbat, we attended Kesher Israel, the Orthodox synagogue in Georgetown which included among its regular worshippers some leading Jewish figures, including Senator Lieberman, the novelist Herman Wouk and the writer Leon Wieseltier. I also lectured there on Shabbat and made friends with the Rabbi, Barry Freundel, a fine scholar, teacher and orator who, alas, later became somewhat notorious for some criminal acts of voyeurism, for which he served a prison sentence. We also enjoyed Washington a second time when I was a visiting scholar at the George Washington University in 2004.

Towards the end of 2001, the Unit arranged for the University Library to lend some Genizah fragments to the Spertus College of Judaica in Chicago. Shulie and were able to spend some time in the 'windy city' where I gave a number of lectures, engaged in some important fund-raising activities, and met a number of distinguished scholars in local museums and universities. After one of my lectures, one individual approached me carrying a rather ordinary looking bag, out of which were produced a few original (and, it must be admitted, rather crumpled) Genizah fragments, recently purchased at an auction! Could I possibly identify these for the owner? I agreed to do so and rather hoped that the owner might become a major supporter of the Genizah Research Unit. My descriptions were well received but no major funding was received by way of reciprocation. You win some…

Philly and 9/11

Our time in Philadelphia was also memorable and not only for academic reasons. I was a Visiting Fellow at the Institute for Advanced Jewish Studies in the first semester of 2001-2. The Institute was the successor of Dropsie College where I had taught almost 30 years earlier but had meanwhile become part of the University of Pennsylvania. I very much enjoyed the seminars and the chance to meet, or meet again, and to work with, many scholars and students of Judaica, including those responsible for the Jewish and Hebrew collections at the University, especially Arthur Kiron. The Institute's attractive premises are located in the city centre, near the famous Liberty Bell. We lived in an apartment block a few minutes' walk from there and Shulie would usually stay in the apartment and work on an editorial project she was completing for the Unit, while I made my way to the Institute.

There was a lovely little park nearby and we generally arranged to meet there for a sandwich lunch if the weather was pleasant. On the morning of 11 September, 2001, I arrived in my office to be told that everyone in the building was watching a terrible event on television. We were all aghast to see two hijacked aircrafts being flown by terrorists into New York's Twin Trade Towers. In Israel, the children and my sister Sharron all heard about the attacks and, knowing that we were in historic Philadelphia, and that one of the attacks was in Pennsylvania, they tried to contact us to ensure that we were safe. Telephone connections were impossible and eventually Sharron managed to get an email through to me and I was able to allay their personal fears.

Most Americans were sent home from work that day and I made my way back to our apartment. Shulie was sitting at the table quietly engaged on her editorial work and totally unaware of the dreadful news. We were due to fly home to Cambridge for Rosh Hashanah and had booked an overnight flight on Saturday/Sunday 14-15 September. I had agreed to lead the services as usual in the Cambridge Synagogue, beginning on Monday evening. Of course, flights were almost all cancelled that week and we were told that some might recommence over the weekend and to report on Saturday night to Philadelphia International Airport. The chaos there was nothing short of horrific. Every individual was being searched and X-rayed and every case was being opened and closely examined. All this took hours and by the time we had completed procedures, our flight to London Heathrow had either been cancelled or had left without us. It was not clear; nothing seemed clear. American Airlines was doing its best to get people to their destinations by some means. In our case, they put us on a flight to Chicago on Sunday morning and from there we were 'bounced' on to Boston from where there was an overnight flight, with available seats, to London. We finally arrived at our home in Cambridge on Monday afternoon, just a few short hours before the festival, and my liturgical duties, were due to start.

Soesterberg, Salzburg and the ISDCL

From my earliest weeks in Cambridge I had come to appreciate the importance of the Genizah for the reconstruction of the Hebrew text of Ben Sira and how discoveries had regularly been made, and were still being made, of fragments of codices that had contained medieval Hebrew versions of that work of Jewish wisdom originally written in the second-century BCE. I had also mentioned it in various articles, both popular and scholarly. It therefore came as no surprise when I was invited by Pancratius Beentjes to give a lecture on these discoveries from the time of Schechter until the present at a conference being held in Soesterberg, Netherlands, to mark the passing of one hundred years since the first discovery in 1896. Using slides (in the days before PowerPoint), I did my best to offer a lively and enthusiastic presentation.

I seemed to catch the attention and interest of all the audience, including Friedrich Reiterer of the Paris-Lodron University in Salzburg and two of his doctoral students, Renate Egger-Wenzel and Ingrid Kammer, who had begun a project to prepare a polyglot edition of Ben Sira. Meeting them, as well as Alexander Di Lella, Núria Calduch-Benages, Maurice

Gilbert and Benjamin Wright, kindled a greater interest on my part in the literature of the Second Temple period, especially as it related to the later development of early Christianity and Rabbinic Judaism. A similar conference was held at Ushaw College in Durham, England, in 2001, encouraged by the same scholars, particularly from Salzburg, and arranged by Jeremy Corley, assisted by Renate Egger-Wenzel. As a result of these activities, and the interest in the published volumes of the proceedings of the Soesterberg and Durham meetings, it was decided in 2002 to establish the International Society for the Study of Deuterocanonical and Cognate Literature, based in Salzburg, with Professor Reiterer as its first president, and Renate as its treasurer, and the inaugural conference was held at the St Virgil Centre in Salzburg in July 2003.

Shulie and I went together to that conference. It had started on Saturday so we travelled on Sunday morning and joined them in the middle of the day. We had indicated that we could eat fish or vegetarian but the catering staff at St Virgil did not understand (or sympathize with) our dietary requirements and also thought that it was perfectly in order to use the same serving spoons for everything. After not eating much at the first meal, Shulie found a local supermarket and bought some tinned salmon and tinned tuna and some other supplies. Although Friedrich was the host, Renate, who was by then teaching at Salzburg University and vice-president as well as treasurer of the ISDCL, was responsible for all the arrangements and asked us how our meal had been.

When we told Renate of Shulie's shopping expedition, she indicated that we should not worry and that all would be satisfactory from then on. At subsequent meals we were served our own portions of fish and vegetables, specifically prepared for us in the kitchen. Similar arrangements were made for us when we participated in the next conference held in July, 2005, in Barcelona, Núria's hometown. From then on, I became closely involved in the work of the ISDCL, attending most of its conferences but missing Tübingen 2007 because of Shulie's illness. By then I had already been invited to join its International Advisory Committee, and I ultimately took responsibility for later conferences and workshops in Haifa and at St John's, as well as assisting with the English editing of some of its volumes.

Cairo Visited

Those years also brought the excitement of two visits to Cairo. In the first of these, I was invited by the BBC to come for a day and a half in order to participate in a television documentary being prepared by Peter Jay, its economic correspondent, on the history of money. He was fascinated to discover that the Genizah contained cheques that had been written by Jewish and Muslim merchants in twelfth-century Cairo and he was anxious to interview me about the Genizah and is treasures in the vicinity of the Ben Ezra Synagogue in Cairo. I arrived in the evening, had as pleasant dinner, enjoyed the comfortable hotel and began filming with him at 08.00 the next morning. We worked for most of the day and, needless to say, I appeared for only a couple of minutes in the edited film; but it was something else that I recall with a smile.

We had almost finished all the shots he needed when, late in the afternoon, he remembered that he had been anxious to have some footage of him and me walking towards the synagogue at the start of our day there. He therefore wished to reconstruct the beginning of the day on film. As we began to walk again to the Genizah site, he asked me if it was exciting to be going towards the Genizah synagogue for the first time in my life. I could not resist and replied 'Since we have been filming here all day, it is not at all exciting!' The joke was appreciated by all the crew and we shot it again, this time in the required 'pretence' mode.

The Ben Ezra Synagogue had been restored through the good offices and the generous funds of Edgar Bronfman and his sister Phyllis Lambert and, as part of the building project, it had been decided to set up a permanent exhibition of Genizah facsimiles in a Jewish communal building nearby. Each item had a description in Arabic, Hebrew and English. I had been involved with all the arrangements from the very start and had chosen the fragments to be highlighted in this way. I included one that reported some anti-Jewish behaviour on the part of the local Muslims in the Fatimid period but the Egyptian authorities were not pleased about its inclusion and 'suggested' that, if we wished to continue with the plans, we should omit it. We reluctantly concurred. When all was ready, the leader of the Egyptian Jewish community of the day, Carmen Weinstein, arranged for a launch of the new exhibition centre that involved Israeli and Egyptian diplomats and scholars, and the Israeli Academic Center in Cairo. I was asked to deliver a lecture before the distinguished audience and Shulie and I were accommodated at the famous Shepherd Hotel for the best part of a week.

As is my custom, on the first day I gave a tip of $5 to the chambermaid and she could not have been more helpful for the whole period of our visit. I was told by a local that he was not surprised that she had been so good to us, seeing that my tip was almost equivalent to a week's wage. It was clear that a group of policemen in their white uniforms had been assigned to us, perhaps to ensure our safety but probably also to keep an eye on our activities. Each time we popped out of the hotel to enjoy the evening coolness, or to walk around some of the famous sites in the area, they were there, walking a few metres behind us; and when we needed to cross a very busy highway with lots of lanes in each direction, two of them simply marched into the traffic and raised their hands. Every car screeched to a halt, the locals apparently not keen to argue with their police force.

Media Interest and Meddling

There were many newspaper interviews, and television and radio slots, some of them for non-British productions, in which I and my colleagues in the Unit participated, usually concerning the Genizah Collection. They demanded a considerable amount of time in preparation and in presentation but the publicity they gave to the Unit seemed important to me and therefore, in my view, made the involvement and the effort worthwhile. The results could of course be somewhat different from what we had intended or wished for. One British radio programme was devoted to the theme of 'diaspora' and a producer and a very well-known radio interviewer came to the Library to interview me on the topic of Jewish history. The producer suggested the questions, and the interviewer put them to me.

It quickly became clear to me that the producer's agenda was to prove that the Jews flourished in the diaspora rather than in their homeland. I balanced each question by pointing out that at various stages throughout Jewish history the Jews had been in the land of Israel and had thrived there except when persecuted. I also stressed that the diaspora for its part was not always productive but had brought horrific examples of antisemitism. I thought I had done a good job of balancing the historical account. Of course, when I heard the radio broadcast, all my balance was removed and what remained was supportive of the producer's bigoted agenda. His assistant telephoned me a year or two later to ask me to do another interview and this time I insisted that I should hear the edited version before it was broadcast. She checked with the producer and, as expected, he could not approve this. As expected, I refused to participate.

Sadly, but inevitably, there were respects to be paid to dearly-departed colleagues. Dr. Wiesenberg and Professor Morag had been among the first research associates that I had brought into the Unit and, when they passed away, I wrote obituaries for them recalling the contributions they had made, among many other scholarly activities, to the work of the Unit. For my much-respected *Doktorvater*, Professor Wieder, and for our much-loved colleague, Michael Klein, who had both done stalwart Genizah work, at different periods and in diverse ways, I did a little more. In addition to writing appreciations in *Genizah Fragments*, I spoke at memorial meetings for them in Jerusalem, and, in the case of Professor Wieder, I penned lengthy essays on his life and his scholarship for English and Hebrew periodicals.

After my promotion to a professorship, I took out a subscription to the *Times Literary Supplement* and wrote many letters to the editor on Jewish matters, most of which were published. I was also invited to review some books for the *TLS* on similar topics and I hope that I succeeded in writing those in a style and with content that could be appreciated by the non-specialist. A letter from a fellow Cambridge scholar, Michael Loewe, was published in the *TLS* on 14 October 2011. In it, Loewe stressed that 'the preservation of the material from the Cairo Genizah and the initiation and maintenance of research therein owes much to three men...Charles Taylor... Eric Ceadel...Stefan Reif'. Coming from such an outstanding orientalist, that acknowledgement was deeply appreciated. Years later, I crossed swords with a new editor of the *TLS* about what I saw (and he denied) as fashionable anti-Israel bias, and my relationship with the journal appears to have cooled as a result.

Broader Commitments

In Jerusalem I gave regular lectures on the Cairo Genizah and on the history of Jewish liturgy to the students of Beit Morasha, a centre for academic Jewish studies, founded and led by Professor Benjamin Ish-Shalom, himself an expert on modern Jewish philosophy. The Centre is 'devoted to advancing a vibrant and inclusive vision of Judaism, through cultivating inspired and dynamic Jewish leadership for the State of Israel and the Jewish world' and I enjoyed teaching students from all kinds of backgrounds and with all manner of lifestyles. In London, Rabbi Dr. Abraham Levy, who was an older contemporary of mine at Jews' College, has, over many decades, involved me in his various educational initiatives, arranging for me to lecture to young leaders, students in their 'gap' year and those studying for rabbinic ordination. That has also been an interesting and enjoyable activity.

Writing of such and similar experiences brings to mind a few other events in those years. When lecturing to graduate students at the Freie

Universität Berlin, I noticed how none of them would dare ask a question until their professor had done so. While explaining the Genizah source to Chabad in Oxford it never occurred to me that Shmuel Boteach, who was then running the show there, would one day become a major journalistic personality. It was a treat to meet Prince el-Hassan bin Talal, the brother of King Hussein of Jordan, a man of culture, learning and diplomacy. He was brought to the Library to see some Genizah fragments by Dr. Edward Kessler who had done such stalwart work in establishing a centre for Jewish-Christian relations (later named the Woolf Institute) and whom I had done my best to encourage in the early and difficult days of his splendid project. When meeting HRH Prince Turki al-Faisal, the Saudi Ambassador to the Court of St James, I was unaware that he had been head of the Saudi intelligence agency from 1977 until 2001 and had apparently warned the western powers that something was brewing just before the 9/11 attacks.

Theology

In the final third of my Cambridge tenure, I played a more active role in the activities of the Faculty of Divinity. Apart from sitting on some committees, I also helped to plan courses on aspects of Judaism, as well as giving regular lectures on such topics as halakhah and on the nature of Jewish faith and practice. I particularly enjoyed the lectures I gave for Brian Hebblethwaite and Julius Lipner. The latter had been my squash partner for decades but, after our friend Peter Lipton dropped dead following a game of squash, there was some pressure on us to call a halt. I pointed out that Peter had not died from squash but from an abnormally high level of cholesterol but to no avail. I still miss those games in which we fought so hard, so equally and with such determination, and the loser (slightly more often, it was I) went home a little depressed.

To return to theology, I was asked to be president of the Cambridge Theological Society and took up this role from 2002 until 2004. Unsurprisingly, we decided in committee to devote a number of lectures to Judaism and invited the Chief Rabbi, Jonathan Sacks, the former Principal of Jews' College, Irving Jacobs, my sometime Edinburgh and Glasgow 'chum' Alexander Broadie, and the Rabbi of one of London's largest congregations, my dearest friend, Jeffrey Cohen, to perform, which they all did admirably. I believe that their lectures were interesting and unusual events for the members of the CTS whose topics were usually oriented towards Christianity.

On 30 January 2003 Jeffrey and his wife Gloria joined Shulie and me for dinner at our home after his lecture and were planning to drive home to Stanmore in spite of the heavy snow. They left at 21.45 and returned half an hour later, having got no further than a few hundred metres. The whole of Cambridge was totally gridlocked and we heard on the news that many cars were stranded in the snow on the M11, the main motorway into London. Drivers were advised not to attempt the journey for at least 24 hours. Shulie was in no way troubled and set about preparing for them to be with us for the whole of Shabbat and showing them where to shop for basic items of clothing and cosmetics. I think she even managed to arrange some essential pills for Gloria.

A number of the teachers in the Faculty of Divinity were also members of the Society for Old Testament Study. As we approached the end of the century, I had been a member of the Society for some 30 years and had served on the committee from 1985 until 1989. As an active participant, I had long felt that there were occasional presentations and publications arranged by that Society that troubled some Jewish members, particularly if these latter had an active commitment to Judaism. I therefore welcomed the invitation of my former colleague in Glasgow, Robert Carroll, who was president in 1998-99, to deliver a paper at the winter conference of the Society held in Birmingham early in January. Being Robert, and one who enjoyed upsetting apple-carts, he specifically asked me to be controversial. My subject was 'Jews, Hebraists and "Old Testament" Studies' and I tackled three main issues. Was there a background in Jewish literary culture that matched the modern study of the Hebrew Bible at least in some interesting and valuable, if critically limited, ways? What had been the underlying attitudes to Jews, Judaism and Jewish literature on the part of Christian hebraists over recent centuries? Could it be argued that there were still to be found in current 'Old Testament' studies certain approaches to the subject that left Jews feeling uneasy about participation?

Having cited many examples of what caused such uneasiness, I concluded that these views were a part of the dispossession philosophy of anti-Judaism and anti-Zionism. Such thinking included the desire to replace the Holocaust with broader tragedies and persecutions; to retain exclusively for non-Jews the scientific study of the Hebrew language; to replace the land of Israel with the land of Canaan, Palestine or Syria; to convert the Hebrew Bible, or Torah or Tanakh, into the 'Old Testament'; and to apply the name of Israel (as with 'new Israel') to groups other than Jews. It does not require much imagination to guess that the response, at the meeting, in conversation afterwards, and by way of emails for many weeks, was not wholly enthusiastic. Once again, I probably paid a price for my honesty and my (and Robert's) iconoclastic tendencies, but the questions had to be raised. That the issues have not yet been properly addressed was made clear by Paul Joyce, the president of the Society in its centenary year of 2017. In a paper published in a volume marking that centenary he made reference to my lecture which had appeared in a memorial volume for Robert Carroll (entitled *Sense and Sensitivity*) that was published in 2002.

No Thank You, Twice

Two other incidents that occurred early in 2006 deserve a place in this account of my academic progress during those years. I was approached by representatives of the Jewish National Library in Jerusalem to inquire whether I would agree to my name being put forward as the new director. I indicated that I had no objection to that and to that end I was interviewed by both administrators and academics. As a result, I was asked to come to Jerusalem and discuss terms with Mr. David Blumberg, formerly chairman of the Bank of Jerusalem, who chaired the Library's board of directors. By this time, my son Aryeh was a well-established lawyer and I thought it prudent to take him with me.

The whole discussion went well until we reached the matter of salary. Aryeh had done his homework and knew what the salaries were of those heading comparable national institutions in Israel. We were told that what was being offered was indeed much lower than those but that it was the devotion to the task, and the commitment to work day and night for the Library, that were important, not the financial incentive. We asked for time to think it over and on the way back to Beit Shemesh Aryeh told me, in his words, 'not to touch it with a barge-pole'. We could not help wondering if the chairs of national banks also had to work without appropriate financial rewards. The truth was that Shulie was in any case very ill at that time and I am not sure that I could have taken on the task under such strained personal circumstances.

The other incident concerned a major international award. I cannot recall if all the documentation had already been forwarded by the University on my behalf, or if the process had only just got under way. Whatever the chronology, I received a telephone call from a member of the relevant committee confirming that I was on the short list. He also mentioned, by the way as it were, that his son was applying for a graduate place at St John's and asked if I could be influential. I explained that I was not the one who made the decisions and that it might even be counter-productive if I intervened in any way. A few months later, after I had been informed that the award had gone elsewhere, I received a call from him in which he reported that his son had not been offered a place. He added that I probably knew by then that I was not to receive the award but I should understand that he was 'not the one who made the decision'.

20

You Seize the Flower, its Bloom is Shed (2000–10)

Publications and a Higher Doctorate

During that decade – perhaps partly because of my promoted status and more relaxed mood – I succeeded in producing a stream of publications, adding to my list some 50 scholarly articles for periodicals and anthologies and thirty reviews for academic journals. I also prepared revised and/or expanded versions of 17 articles of mine on Jewish liturgy that had appeared in a variety of contexts over a period of more than 20 years, adding an introduction and extensive indexes. The volume, entitled *Problems with Prayers* was published by de Gruyter in 2006. Another grand-daughter, Naama, had in the meantime been born and I took the opportunity of dedicating the new volume to her and to my mother and my sisters, Cynthia and Sharron, 'the other women in my life'. In a review in the *SOTS Book List 2007*, Jeremy Schonfield welcomed it as an 'important sequel to *Judaism and Hebrew Prayer*' and kindly defined it as 'essential reading' for those in the field.

At the beginning of the century it had been suggested to me by colleagues in the Faculty and in St John's that I had reached the stage in my career when I might successfully apply for a higher doctorate. In Cambridge, such doctorates – in law, science, letters, music, and divinity – were awarded to those who could demonstrate their 'proof of distinction by some original contribution to the advancement of science or learning'. They were generally regarded as the equivalent of a personal professorship. I submitted copies of all my publications and these were sent to distinguished academic referees for their appraisal. I was thrilled to receive notice of the approval of the degree of Litt.D. and was presented by my friend and colleague, Professor Robert Gordon, for the award by the Deputy Vice-Chancellor at a ceremony (called a 'Congregation' in Cambridge parlance) in the Senate House in July 2002.

It was an additional pleasure to have Tanya and her four children with Shulie and me on that occasion, visiting as they were from Israel during the summer break. I should add that the gown is a splendid colour of red and I wear it regularly and proudly to College feasts. I had come to Cambridge at a time when PhDs from what in Cambridge were regarded as such 'parvenu' universities as London were not formally recognized. Although that bias had largely disappeared, one of the more senior Fellows at College who remembered the good old restrictions put his arm on my shoulder and said 'Ah, Stefan, congratulations, now you really are a doctor!'

On the subject of doctorates, I earlier noted how much I had been inspired in my youth by Rabbi Isaac Cohen and Rabbanit Fanny. He had obtained his PhD at Edinburgh University in 1956. In the early 2000s, Shulie and I went to visit them in their Jerusalem home and he asked me to look over a book he was preparing. It was an expansion of some aspects of his earlier research and I felt proud and privileged to contribute in this way to my sometime teacher and inspiration. In the summer of 2005, my good friend Nat Gordon (of some 50 years' standing) and I arranged a dinner at a Jerusalem restaurant to mark the ninetieth birthday of a couple who had made such a central contribution to Jewish life and education in the post-World War Two Edinburgh of our youth. I think that about 40 of his ex-pupils, all by then living in Israel, turned up and there were numerous tributes and delightful responses from both honorands. Rabbanit Cohen remembered most of our families, and especially praised our grandparents who had been stalwarts of the Edinburgh Hebrew Congregation. Rabbi Cohen's book *Acts of the Mind in Jewish Ritual Law* duly appeared but, sadly, he passed away shortly afterwards.

Dreams of Retirement

In the summer of 2005 I inquired of the University's superannuation office about my status with regard to possible retirement and pension. They indicated that by 2006 I would have enough years of work and payment to enable me to retire on a full pension, then equivalent to half of my annual salary. Shulie and I discussed it at length, weighing up the pros and cons. It would be good to enjoy another five years in my appointment and to save some money during that time. On the other hand, we would miss seeing more of our grandchildren in Israel and I would inevitably have less time for writing more books, as I very much hoped to do. We decided to go out 'on a high', when recognition of the Unit's efforts and achievements had reached a record level.

In my farewell editorial in *Genizah Fragments*, I wrote: 'It has been a busy and fascinating thirty-three years and I feel privileged to have been the one to have taken the Cambridge Genizah Collections in some ways almost directly from the nineteenth to the twenty-first century. The current team in the Unit is undoubtedly the strongest and most devoted that the Unit has ever had.' I discussed the possibility of helping the Librarian, Peter Fox, and his deputy, Anne Murray, with the Library's fund-raising efforts on a part-time basis and they agreed to arrange a suitable appointment for me on a professional basis.

Shulie and I were very excited about being able to spend more time in Israel and set about organizing what we would leave in our Cambridge home, where we still intended to spend significant time, and what would better be removed to our second home in Israel. That second home had been an apartment since 1997 but we sold it in 2004 and bought a small semi-detached house, within easy walking distance of all the close family. That house would provide more space for their visits. By way of the engineering skills of our son-in-law, Anthony, and the involvement of Aryeh, 'our son, the lawyer', the renovations and formalities were completed. Shulie spent a good deal of time overseeing all these arrangements while I was busy in Cambridge. On one occasion, the contractor did not attach a door to a new lavatory, arguing that this was not included in the price and was an optional extra! Anthony soon disabused him of such an absurd assumption.

I did manage later to plan a large garden to the rear of the house with a professional gardener. Shulie was keen to have flowering plants to enjoy throughout the year and I was enthusiastic about growing our own fruit. We did both, soon looking with pleasure at the colourful blossoms and blooms, and picking loquats, lemons, oranges, mandarins, apples, pomelos, persimmons and grapes at various times of the year. During one of our visits in 2004, we exercised our right to take out Israeli citizenship which gave us great pleasure, as well as easing our travel in and out of the Jewish homeland. We thought about how our grandparents and great-grandparents who had suffered so many persecutions and indignities in Eastern Europe could have been spared those horrors if only a Jewish state had then existed. We maintained our British citizenship too, since we still intended to spend lengthy periods in Cambridge. All the close family were involved in arranging parties in Jerusalem to celebrate my sixtieth birthday, which we did at the Hyatt Hotel in January 2004, and Shulie's sixtieth birthday at the Inbal Hotel in the autumn of 2005, just before we returned to Cambridge for the new academic year.

Shocking Reality

As Robert Burns put it: 'The best laid schemes o' mice an' men gang aft a-gley.' Our plans were indeed destined to go awry and we were in for the kind of shock that one always dreads but rarely has to face. Shulie and I had been in Barcelona for an ISDCL conference in July 2005, and had taken a short cruise from Haifa in the late summer. During that time, she had complained about pains in her back and we thought they must be the result of some sort of arthritic problem. When the pains did not respond to any kind of pills and began to interfere with her sleeping, we knew we had to check things further. Shulie had an X-ray and our local family doctor sent us to a lung specialist. He asked Shulie about her lifestyle and she told him how she swam, walked and cycled much more than average, was slim and otherwise healthy, and had not lost any weight. Having examined her, he pronounced that we could 'definitely rule out anything sinister'. What we did not know then, but only later discovered, was that the radiologist took a more pessimistic view of what he saw on the X-rays and suggested more tests. It was Shulie's sixtieth birthday on 11 November and we celebrated, just as a couple, by having a splendid tea at Fortnum & Mason in London's Piccadilly, hoping that all would be well.

That was not to be. When the prescribed antibiotics had no effect and the situation did not improve, the radiologist's view began to prevail and it was decided to perform a lung biopsy, a most unpleasant experience for poor Shulie. Even greater unpleasantness was to follow. On Monday 21 November at around 17.00, we saw the specialist once more. He told us that Shulie was suffering from non-small-cell lung carcinoma, that the tumour had been growing for about two years, and that he did not suggest any treatment. He thought that Shulie had about eighteen months to live. He then explained how difficult the previous weekend had been for him, knowing what he had to tell us on Monday. That seemed to us insensitive of him in the extreme. I asked him why he had said that we could rule out anything sinister and he denied ever having said it. These two remarks of his meant that we lost all confidence in him as a professional and we decided that we never wished to see him again. We asked about surgery for the tumour and he replied that he would not himself recommend it but he would refer us to an excellent surgeon who operated in Papworth Hospital, some sixteen kilometres west of Cambridge.

That evening was one of the worst in our lives. A death sentence had been delivered to a woman just turned 60 with everything still to live for, a loving husband and family, and a lively retirement ahead of her. Having updated the children, we tried to continue with our plans for the removal in March but were both distraught. Each time we took out an item from a cupboard or a drawer, Shulie, in tears, would angrily and uncharacteristically throw it aside, telling me that she would not need it any more. She insisted on taking all her certificates, including those for piano playing, and putting them in the pile destined for taking to the municipal 'tip'. We arranged an urgent appointment with the surgeon and he gave us some hope. He thought that he could remove the tumour successfully but would probably have to remove the lung too.

Lung Removal and Kidney Diagnosis

The operation was set for the end of November and Tanya travelled from Israel to join me. After the operation, the surgeon came to tell us that he had indeed removed the lung, and all of the tumour that he could see, and expressed the hope that Shulie would recover and that the prognosis might be better than we had feared. We sat with Shulie all night as she suffered dreadful pains. For a few days we took it in turns to sit by her bedside and she slowly regained strength and was able to come home after about ten days. Tanya then returned to Israel to look after her children and Aryeh came to join us. One of our family doctors popped in from time to time, as did a nurse to deal with the wound, and we gradually recovered some balance and even hoped for the best. I checked all that I could about the disease and, given that the tumour had been over two centimetres in size, there seemed to be little realistic hope. A medical friend pointed out to me that it was inevitable that cancerous cells from the lung would by then have spread elsewhere but that they might be able to deal with those through chemotherapy. He also told me in January that he thought that Shulie ought to be feeling and looking better than she was by then, and that this gave him cause for some worry.

Shulie was suffering from reflux and, since none of the usual pills were doing much to relieve it, the family doctor thought it best for her to see a stomach specialist. We consulted him and, after tests and scans, he assured us that there was no stomach problem at all (wonderful, we thought) but that he had seen something in the scan that might indicate a kidney problem (not so wonderful, we thought). He diplomatically explained that he had no expertise in this but could refer us to a consultant at Hinchingbrooke Hospital, near Cambridge, who was better qualified to judge. After various tests, that specialist reported that the kidney had been affected by the cancerous cells from the lung. It was very unusual for cells to move in that direction but there was no doubt about it since the cells were identical. Again, our hopes were dashed.

He was a very kind and efficient doctor and we asked him if we should have treatment in the UK or in Israel. He told us that Israeli medicine was certainly as good as its British equivalent and we should undergo treatment where we had the most family support. We decided that we could take all the medical data with us to Israel and start the process again there, where the family could be at our side. In November, the lung specialist had asked for a scan that covered only the lung and had therefore missed what was happening in the kidney. Again, it seemed us, this had been a decision wholly lacking in professional care and competence.

Leaving for Treatment in Israel

A few days before we left to celebrate Passover in Israel, our colleagues in the University Library arranged a splendid farewell reception for us both. Peter Fox paid tribute to our work and the numerous gifts that we were given included a slate address-plate commissioned from the renowned

23. Farewell party, Cambridge University Library, 2006 (Cambridge University Library).

Cardozo Kindersley workshop, with the Hebrew words 'mishpaḥat Reif' ('family Reif') engraved in gold, and a bound copy of a commemorative in-house edition of *Genizah Fragments* produced in our honour. This edition was full of witty and amusing comments, as well as some more serious remarks, from colleagues all over the world, as well as generous appreciations of what Shulie and I had managed to achieve in the Unit. I offered our warm thanks to everyone and expressed the hope that, under the new leadership of Ben Outhwaite, the Unit would continue to flourish. Shulie seemed to be a little stronger and more cheerful after this final event in the Unit and was able to make the journey to Israel without getting too much out of breath, although I must say that I remained nervous and apprehensive until we touched down at Ben-Gurion Airport. We knew that after the Passover holiday we would have to make our way to an Israeli hospital and begin the process of arranging additional treatment for her condition.

The Israeli doctors were all honest, stating that her medical situation was not good but at the same time explaining that their policy was to treat cancer as a chronic disease, not a terminal illness, and to provide drugs to keep cancer patients alive for as long as they wished to continue the fight. Unlike the lung specialist in Cambridge, they talked of a number of years. Shulie and I made an agreement with each other that we should together fight on until such time as she thought the battle had been lost and she lacked the energy and will to continue. We fought that fight in Israel from the summer of 2006 until late in 2009. Dr A. was a most efficient and hard-working oncologist who saw as many as 20 patients in a day and always gave them the impression that they were being personally cared for. Dr A. examined all the papers from Cambridge and was deeply impressed by the surgery done in Cambridge on the cancerous lung. Although willing to take Shulie on as his patient, Dr A. suggested that we should try to register with Dr B. who had a major project under way that treated precisely Shulie's cancer with a new drug. In this way Shulie might have a better chance of obtaining the most expensive and up-to-date treatment. Dr B. agreed and obtained the necessary authorisation to include Shulie in the research project and Shulie began the chemotherapy a week or two later.

Many people nowadays are, sadly, well aware of what happens to most patients undergoing chemotherapy. Shulie would have the treatment, feel dreadful, weak and nauseous for a week, start to feel better, and have a few days of virtually normal life before the next round. That was the main problem. The other was having to deal with the bureaucrats and the bureaucracy at the hospital. One had to find parking, which was not an easy task in those days, and we soon decided that we should come at 07.00 in the morning. I took over the management of the procedures in order to relieve Shulie of at least that burden. One had to wait in line with the required blood tests and, with only a few exceptions, the office staff who dealt with you seemed cold and uncaring and made you feel that you were an imposition on them and their colleagues. Having presented and been given the relevant paperwork, one then had to wait until the doctor arrived, checked the test results, and decided whether and when the treatment should be given. If this was approved, one then had again to wait for a nurse to come and take you to a bed and set up the infusion. By the time this was over, we were usually into midday, or the early afternoon.

Shulie was a wreck from the treatment and I was a wreck from the tensions, anxieties and frustrations of the process. There was no point in getting cross since that would mean even less friendly handling by the staff, but keeping calm in such circumstances did not, and does not, come naturally to me. On one occasion, a nurse came with half the usual dose of infusion. I questioned the amount and she told me that she knew what she was doing and not to interfere. Confident as I was, I repeated my question which she did not answer. She did, however, go and check the paperwork and came back with the correct dose but without a word of explanation or apology. When I left after the treatment, I thanked her (as I always did when leaving) and said that I had been surprised that she had said nothing to me after correcting the dose. She shouted at me in Hebrew: 'What do you want? An apology? Ok, I am sorry! Is that better!' I thanked her again in as cool a way as I could, but boiled up inside.

Near Death

After a few weeks of treatment with the new drug, we received a report that the tumour had reduced by 60 per cent and were all greatly elated by this news. The elation was short-lived. Two days later Shulie was in a dreadful state, hardly knew what was going on and was obviously very weak. All this happened in the evening and an emergency doctor came to see her and gave her an injection that seemed to make matters worse. Tanya rushed her to the hospital where she was quickly admitted and went into a coma. I arrived to take over the watch and Aryeh came later when I went home to sleep. Shulie's salt level had reached an acute low and while Aryeh was with her she suffered a frightening seizure. For a couple of days, it looked like we had reached the end.

Next day I asked the doctor in charge of matters in that ward what could be done for her. He seemed to be friendly to another group that was visiting that afternoon and I thought he seemed the sympathetic kind. I did not share the same background as that group and his manner towards me was totally different. He told me in a cold and wholly detached fashion that the brain was probably affected by then and nothing could be done. We were sitting by her bed and Tanya was wiping her forehead with a cool cloth, repeating all the time 'Is that nice, Mummy?' To our utter astonishment, to one of those repeated questions, Shulie opened her eyes and said 'Mmm'. She continued to make progress and was soon home again. Dr B. agreed that she should come off that drug and prescribed something else. So, the chemotherapy continued for about year, during which time Shulie had to undergo radiotherapy for some unwelcome cells in her brain. This required many visits each week for a number of weeks. The treatment was very efficiently carried out and the staff in that department seemed to me more helpful and friendly. I took her for most of these treatments but I was grateful when close members of the family were able to relieve me from time to time.

A Life of Sorts

Shulie and they told me how impressed and surprised they and others were at the amount of patience and concern that I showed. It was not something that came easy to me but I had seen as a child just how lovingly my parents had cared for my Zeide and I felt that this was the correct, indeed the only, way to behave in the case of a loved and loving partner. When Shulie expressed her gratitude, I asked her 'Wouldn't you have done exactly the same for me if I had been the patient?' I even took over kitchen duties, under Shulie's patient guidance, when she did not have the strength to carry out these herself. I had helped my mother in the kitchen as a youngster and had cooked as a graduate student but during our married years my contribution had usually been to wash up dishes and clean the kitchen.

We still travelled together to Cambridge whenever we could, and enjoyed our home there, but sometimes the medical situation meant that I went alone. Whatever we did together, and however weak she felt, Shulie generally managed to remain cheerful and to present a positive front to friends and family. She rarely complained (if so, usually only to me, or together with me) and did her best to participate in numerous activities with friends and family. She especially cultivated and enjoyed close relationships with our grandchildren and even attended regularly an ulpan at which she could improve her spoken Hebrew.

Conference and Festschrift

One trip that we undertook together was in August 2007, a year after her frightful collapse. The Unit had kindly arranged a conference in my honour at Westminster College, a Presbyterian seminary re-established in Cambridge in 1899 thanks to the generosity, vision and drive of Mrs Agnes Lewis and Mrs Margaret Gibson. The conference celebrated the vitality of Genizah studies, to the promotion of which I had of course devoted most of my career. Twenty-one academics from the United States, Israel and Europe delivered papers and we had our meals in the College dining-room beneath the gaze of Agnes and Margaret who had alerted Schechter to their Genizah finds and to a medieval Hebrew fragment that he identified as from the apocryphal book of Ben Sira. I was asked to give an after-dinner speech on one of the evenings and I offered anecdotes and reminiscences, as well as what were to most of the participants somewhat startling revelations about colleagues and events.

The head of the Unit, Ben Outhwaite, together with one of the Unit's researchers, Siam Bhayro, subsequently edited the papers for publication and in his preface Ben wrote that my presentation had been made in a 'typically humorous and pointed manner' and was 'imprinted on the minds of those who had the privilege to hear it'. He explained that it had been preserved for posterity by being included in the volume 'albeit in a slightly expurgated form so as not to invite the interest of members of the legal profession'. Entitled *From a Sacred Source*, the Festschrift was finally published by Brill in 2010, sadly when Shulie was no longer with us to enjoy the volume and the tribute that was also made in it to her.

From 2005 until 2010, I carried on with research, conferences and publication but obviously with a lower level of productivity than had been my wont. It happened on a number of occasions that I had, at a fairly late hour, to cancel lecturing commitments because I felt I myself had to stay with Shulie when her condition seemed critical. I did manage to work with some translators and editors on a Hebrew version of my *Judaism and Hebrew Prayer* which, after a lengthy gestation period, appeared in 2010 and was welcomed by scholars, students and a broader readership. It even merited a fine review in the literary supplement of a leading Israeli newspaper.

As part of my new part-time Library duties I built up some important fund-raising connections, obtained some promises of support, especially after some exhausting visits to North America, made suggestions about the way forward, and helped to entertain important guests. I was also involved, with the University's Vice-Chancellor Alison Richard, in the early stages of winning the support of the Polonsky Foundation. That said, it was a difficult time to raise funds, the whole project obviously required more professional and intensive staff and methods, and Peter Fox and I were aware of this after I had worked with him and with Anne, with the help of Debbie Patterson of the University's development team, for almost three years. I agreed with him that it was time to call a halt to the arrangement.

Doctors and Systems

Early in 2008, a friend who worked in the hospital and knew the doctors and systems very well suggested that, if we had any medical connections in Cambridge, we should perhaps submit all the scans and reports to them and ask for their opinion. I had indeed kept in touch with an oncologist and a radiologist and we still had our BUPA insurance coverage in Cambridge, as well as our Maccabi coverage in Israel. Incidentally, I have to say how generous both health insurances were in providing funding for most of Shulie's treatments. I explained to Dr B. that we still saw these medical personnel when we were in England and sought approval for the suggested course of action. This was forthcoming without any apparent objection or animosity. We saw the Cambridge specialists and they provided a letter in which they suggested that it might be time for a change of treatment.

Shulie and I presented ourselves on our return to Israel for the usual chemotherapy and, once we had been through all the procedures and were waiting for the infusion, I asked to see Dr B. and presented the letter. Despite the approval we had received for the second opinion, Dr B.'s response was an angry one, the chemotherapy was cancelled, and I was virtually thrown out of the office. On our return home, I telephoned Dr A. and told him that we had lost confidence in Dr B. and wished to return to treatment under him. He told me that we could do that but we must seek permission from Dr B. I telephoned Dr B. the next day and was told that we should not be angry with each other and it was only a small difference of opinion and no harm was meant. I explained that Shulie and I could not be expected to have any confidence in a doctor who behaved in this way and, after some discussion, held my ground and we were released again to

24. Sharron, Cynthia and Stefan, 2008.

Dr A. Whenever we saw Dr B. in the hospital from that time onwards we received no greeting whatsoever, only a cold stare or a turn in another direction.

Chemo and Grandkids

The next eighteen months saw a variety of chemotherapy and another bout of radiotherapy. In 2006 we were able to celebrate the barmitzvah of our grandson Gidon and in 2007 the batmitzvah of our twin grand-daughters Shoshi and Dani. For their treats, Shulie and I took Gidon to Venice and the girls to Scotland and had a lot of fun together. Gidon was sure he could guide us in Venice and firmly and confidently took the tourist map into his possession. Of course, we lost our way and laughed about it. We were also upgraded to business class on the trip from Tel Aviv and when the stewardess offered Gidon a tray with a number of choices of drink, he thought that it was polite to take the whole tray! His eyes nearly popped out of his head when we went to the Lido beach and he saw many a female topless sight.

The Scottish trip began somewhat disastrously since we reached Edinburgh in fine time only to find that we had forgotten the girls' suitcase when we left Cambridge early that day. Urgent shopping was undertaken next morning in Princes Street. Near Inverness we visited a museum about the Loch Ness Monster in a place called Drumnadrochit, a name the girls will never forget. The drive home to Cambridge took eleven hours but Shulie did manage to relieve me for a couple of those, and the girls never complained once.

In February 2008 Shulie came with me to Vienna to a conference at the University where her father had once been a law student. One day, we took a tram to Leopoldstadt to see where her parents had lived in the 1930s. But she suddenly weakened that afternoon, and we had to take a taxi straight back to the hotel. In August of that year we celebrated the marriage of our nephew Gideon, Cynthia and Karl's middle son, to Moran. Cynthia was by then very unwell but she managed to do all that was necessary. Shulie also coped well with the challenge. The whole family and many friends were delighted that Shulie and Cynthia, both chronically (and terminally) ill, had been spared to witness such happy family events. The family also took pleasure in the fact that Gideon and Moran had settled in Israel, where they have since then reared a lovely family and been professionally successful.

In 2008, Dr A. received permission to put Shulie on a new drug called Tarceva and the result was amazing. For about eight months she was almost like her old self. The tumour markers were right down, and she felt stronger and more confident. The one very unwelcome side effect was the painful condition of her toes and toenails. This time the treatment offered by Maccabi did not succeed and we had to pay privately for a specialist to do what was necessary to restore her feet to something approaching normal. I made the mistake at that time, when we were living an almost normal life, of checking the known results of Tarceva and was disappointed, but not surprised, to read that the effect was usually not for more than a few months.

Aryeh's Divorce

While Aryeh was with us in Cambridge for Shulie's lung removal at the end of 2005, he confided in us that he was, for a number of reasons, considering divorcing Mirit, and sought our views. We knew that the only possible answer from loyal and loving parents was to say that, whatever decision he finally made, we would stand by him, offering love and support in every way we possibly could. By the summer of 2006, the divorce had been arranged and Aryeh rented a house in Beit Shemesh, a relatively easy walk from us so we could see a lot of him and his three children, Nili, Roi and Naama, whenever they were with him. He cooked for them most efficiently and looked after them to an impressive degree but they were obviously not happy children. He and Mirit had reached an agreement according to which the children would have accommodation in both their new homes and spend half their time with each parent.

It was a very difficult time for everyone, especially those children, and Shulie and I did everything we could to support them. Our relationships with all our grandchildren was a very warm one, as it of course continued to be with our children, and they and we both derived great benefit from the love that we all demonstrated to each other. We often ate meals with each other, especially on Shabbat, and Aryeh became a highly competent cook. Like her mother, Tanya enjoyed entertaining large numbers of guests to meals and she and Anthony always did it to the highest standards.

Final Fun – With Nili

Towards the end of June 2009, Shulie was just about strong enough to undertake another trip abroad and we were keen to take Nili with us as a batmitzvah treat. We therefore arranged to take her to the UK and then to go on to Belgium, where we planned time in Brussels and Bruges. Shulie fell a few days before our departure and cracked a small bone in her wrist but, having consulted the doctors, we decided to go ahead. She wore a sling and that relieved the pain. We took Nili on fun activities in Cambridge and in London and on our final morning in Cambridge we were scheduled to catch a train around noon to King's Cross Station in London and to walk across from there to St Pancras to catch the Eurostar express train to Brussels.

After breakfast, I noticed that one of our appliances had caused a tripping of the fuse in the electrical box and it turned out that our freezer had decided that it was a good time to die. We drove immediately to the nearest freezer store, bought a replacement which Nili and I carried into the back of the car, and transferred the contents of the dead freezer into the new replacement. I recall with great sadness that as we entered the taxi in Cambridge to make our way to the railway station, Shulie looked back at the house that she had loved so much and, sobbing, said 'I don't think I shall see my lovely house ever again.'

We caught our trains and greatly enjoyed our time in Belgium. When Nili offered the adult women her support against some view that I was espousing, I responded with a little Yiddish phrase that she remembers to this day about the little doggie also having something to say ('die kleine Klafte auch hot Epes tsu sogen'). I was due to lecture at an ISDCL conference in the small Dutch town of Kerkrade (on the border between Netherlands, Germany and Belgium) on Sunday 5 July, and to return home on Monday. I was concerned that Shulie would not be able to manage that trip without help and Tanya kindly offered to come to Belgium for the weekend and to see Shulie and Nili safely home a day before me, which she did with great care.

No More Hospitals and Doctors Please

In the final months of 2009 we spent a number of days each week at the hospital where Dr A. was an exemplary doctor and carer. The results all indicated that once again the tumours in her kidneys were growing at a fast rate and Dr A. suggested another, different kind of chemotherapy. As we walked to the hospital car park and in the car on the way home, Shulie reminded me of our agreement that, when she felt she had reached saturation point, we could call off the treatment. She was absolutely sure that she had reached such a point. What she most wanted at that point was to be at home and not to enter a hospital ever again. By that time, she had survived for four years, and not the eighteen months callously predicted by the British specialist. I promised her that I, with the help of the family, would do my best to look after her at home. We did go together to look at a hospice and Shulie kindly said that she could accept being resident there if that was our wish. I could see immediately that she was not at all keen and I therefore vetoed the proposal. When we told Dr A. of our decision and thanked him warmly for all his devoted attention and personal concern, he assured us that he could prescribe other treatments that would keep Shulie alive for a while longer. She was grateful to him but explained that the quality of her life was simply no longer good enough for her to undergo more therapies.

Because the cancer was by then seriously affecting her spine, she was finding it progressively more difficult to climb up and down the stairs from the living room to the bedrooms and to face a similar challenge from our home to the street. I went to a marvellous organization called Yad Sarah and began to borrow all sorts of devices to make things a little easier for her and for us. She hated the idea of a wheelchair but there was soon no alternative. Shulie had always loved the ocean, the beach and the sea breezes and Tanya took her to Tel Aviv for her final visits to enjoy those. Anthony and Aryeh were very helpful in carrying the chair up and down the stairs but that too began to be impractical and we decided that she should spend daytime as well as night-time upstairs.

In January 2010, we set up a table in the spare bedroom where we could eat together and I arranged for our carpenter, Eli Cohen, to build a small balcony leading off that bedroom so that we could wheel her out and she could view her beloved garden and see something of life going on in the nearby streets. Knowing the situation as he did, he gave the project top priority and finished it very quickly for us. Visitors all came upstairs and sat with us either in the bedroom or, in good weather, on the new balcony. I also employed a local woman to help Shulie with some of basic activities such as dressing and washing. With the help of the children and Sharron, I managed a few days in Cambridge to catch up with some academic matters but when I got home the situation had further deteriorated.

Shulie had always told me that her red line would be the inability to make her own way to the toilet. That line had been reached and it saddened her greatly. The oncologists and the oncology nurses had advised us what to do in the final stages if we wished to keep Shulie at home and we followed all their instructions regarding oxygen and the use of morphine patches. We also had support from the health insurance's social worker and visits from Ahuva, the head nurse at our local clinic. She still mentions to me how taken she was by our family's closeness and devotion. On Friday 12 February 2010, I prepared the meals for Shabbat and washed and dressed Shulie in some of her favourite clothes and jewellery. She looked truly lovely. We ate together at the little table and I later managed to get her to bed. It hardly needs stating that, after so many difficult months, we were both truly exhausted.

Last Shabbat Together

Next morning, we again managed to make her look elegant (as she always wished to be) and the children and grandchildren came to visit her on the balcony for kiddush and nibbles. She was not able to eat very much of the lunch I prepared but she did her best to please me. When Shabbat was over and I had made havdalah, she kissed me and thanked me for making such a lovely Shabbat and told me that this would be our last Shabbat together. I dismissed this and said there would still be time together but, knowing her so well, I knew that if she had decided that it was to be so, she would engineer matters to ensure that it was. She had a bowl of chicken soup that I prepared on Sunday and would not eat anything afterwards, taking only some sips of liquid, and requesting morphine patches for the pain.

Tanya, Aryeh, Anthony, Sharron and I looked after her on a twenty-four-hour basis that week. She had previously written farewell letters to every single member of the close family (to be read after she had gone) and, now that she was on her way to join her parents (whose images she claimed at one point to have seen in her bedroom), she saw each one of us independently and said what she felt she had to say. She was finally summoned to her eternal rest at 03.05 on Friday morning, 19 February 2010, 5 Adar in the Hebrew calendar, and as is traditional among observant Jews, we buried her swiftly that same day, before Shabbat, with an attendance of some 200, and with many offering appreciations of her in her various outstanding capacities.

In my offering, I referred to her family background, to our personal love-story and to her numerous talents, especially in editing and preparing texts for publication but also in teaching and inspiring young children. About her priorities, I stated 'Whatever she achieved professionally, Shulie was never in any doubt that her most important, and most loved, role was that of wife, mother and family builder. She loved us all with a great passion and would tolerate no negative comments about any of us. She took great pride in everything that we achieved, quietly knowing (but never needing to trumpet) that it had come about with her direct encouragement and selfless assistance. She wanted each of us in the family to have the same high standards that she set for herself and when we strove to reach such levels, she felt drawn even closer to us, to each and every one in a specially relevant way.'

Ben Outhwaite, to whom I copied my remarks, wrote: 'Your *hesped* text is a wonderful piece of writing; I think that those of us who knew Shulie only a short period of time nevertheless recognise all the qualities you list: She was a lovely person with no side to her; genuinely a pleasure to work with and never perturbed – even in the high-pressure world (and I mean it) of Genizah research.' About a year after her death I compiled a booklet about Shulie, with the help of our grand-daughter, Dani, in which we included all the family eulogies as well as the numerous letters of condolence.

How to cope?

To say that I was distraught would be something of an under-statement. I had, however, seen how angry and bitter Muni had been with everyone after Elly had died and I was determined not to follow his example. During the week of shiv'ah, there was a great deal of support from neighbours, family and friends, but afterwards I had to face the reality. The children offered to stay with me or to have me stay with them but I knew that once again, as I had done from the age of five, I could, and had to, do it 'by myself'. Of course I had the children, my sisters, the grandchildren, and some close friends to help me in the kindest and most considerate ways but going out in the car without Shulie, eating at a table without Shulie, and sleeping in a bed without Shulie, not to mention having to prepare for Pesaḥ without Shulie, or preparing texts for publication without Shulie, were agonizing and tearful experiences.

Like her mother and grandmother before her, she was a very wise woman and she told me on more than one occasion that my academic work would be my salvation, and that I would soon need to function as grandmother as well as grandfather She also assured me that, if her eternal soul could do anything at all to comfort and assist me, she promised that she would arrange it. She also apologized for having to leave me. Apart from that 'apology', she also regretted that she would not be with us to enjoy future achievements and family semaḥot. She was very pleased that Tanya had been appointed to an important government post and that Aryeh had a regular girl-friend. One minor consolation for me as I struggled to cope was the feeling that, if one of us had to endure such loss and such suffering, I preferred that it should be me and not the woman who had been so loved and so loving for more than four decades.

I read and re-read the letter that she had left for me many times in the dark days and months that followed. She told me how much she loved me and she thanked me for over 40 years of happiness, and for giving her our wonderful children and grandchildren, who all adored me. She assured me that they would give me love and support and that I should never feel that I was all alone. We had been a partnership in every sense and she loved me with all her heart and soul. I had been her teacher, guide and shining example. She advised me to live my life as best I could and never to forget that I had been wonderful and adored. She added some deeply moving pieces of poetry and concluded 'I know you will somehow cope – there is no choice.'

In the subsequent months, I just about coped. I continued with all my academic work and spent a good deal of time in Cambridge. I worked feverishly from early morning until late in the evening so that I could retire for the night in a state of exhaustion and not have much energy left for thinking about my loneliness. I did almost all my own cooking and baking. Friends such as Barry and Ros Landy, Jeffrey and Gloria Cohen, and Esther and Shuki Shalev (as well as Sue and Win Robins, Jeanette and Avraham

Persoff, and Sari and Alan Halibard in Israel) were wonderful, and, at St John's College in Cambridge, the Master, Chris Dobson, and his wife Mary, found time in their hectic schedule to sit with me in the master's lodge late at night and converse warmly and sympathetically with me over a glass or two of single malts.

When close family and best friends assured me that I would have the strength to overcome this great loss and to go on with my life, I acknowledged that I might indeed do so and I might still have achievements ahead of me. At the same time, I expressed to them my conviction that my real life was effectively over. I would be travelling through whatever life remained to me 'on automatic pilot' from then on and it would be much less personally and emotionally meaningful than it had once been. For myself, I felt that I merely had to go through the motions until I joined Shulie in the plot that I had reserved beside her in the cemetery. My sister Sharron assured me that I still had an important life to lead and much love still to give. I was not convinced.

21

Still Doing It My Way: Regeneration not Degeneration (2010–19)

Retirement Activities

The beauty of retirement, as I am fond of telling those who have yet to experience it, is that one cheerfully chooses what one wishes to do. One is no longer obligated to shape one's personal activities in accordance with institutional policies, instructions and paperwork that one might find tiresome or misguided. One can simply say no to invitations that involve such dictates from above (as it were) and concentrate on what one finds productive and enjoyable. By way of example, one university invited me as an outsider to chair a committee that was faced with resolving a contentious matter between academics. I took on the task and I was offered my travel expenses. After the meeting, the secretary handed me an envelope and I thought it would contain a cheque or cash to meet those expenses. Alas, no, there were three pages of forms to fill out. I promptly consigned the forms to the waste-paper basket and told the university to regard it as a gift from me. This threw a spanner in the works of the bureaucracy but that was their problem, not mine.

In recent years I have often been approached as an external referee to comment on the suitability of academics around the world for promotion, or of papers for acceptance by a scholarly journal. Since I am almost always busy with research, writing and publication, I respond positively to those individuals and institutions with whom I have, or have had, an active engagement, and to whom I feel a sense of responsibility. Like many (but not all, I fear) of my colleagues, I make every effort to offer a fair and balanced assessment that takes no account of my personal relations or preferences. One of the questions asked by those seeking an informed opinion in a promotion exercise is whether this candidate would receive such a promotion at my university. I always explain how difficult it is (or was?) to obtain promotion at Cambridge and that this is therefore not a good guide for the University of Hotzenplotz in Western Weisnichtvos. I do, however, add that I have checked the list of senior academics at

Hotzenplotz and can say that candidate X is on a par with such colleagues. For whatever reason, I have found that in most cases where I submit an enthusiastic, or at least a broadly supportive, assessment the candidate is subsequently successful.

I should add that the exceptions often have more to do with internal preferences than external assessments. I recall one case in which I was asked to assess six short-listed candidates. I took great care over this and submitted a detailed evaluation of each and placed them in order of scholarly achievement and competence. I was somewhat taken aback when I heard that the candidate whom I had placed fourth was appointed. Perhaps this was a case of what is called in Cambridge 'a safe pair of hands'. A committee knows that the best candidate has her/his own strong opinions, does not agree with the ideology of those who will be his/her colleagues, is not politically correct, or is likely to be too expensive, and it opts for a lesser being who will upset fewer apple-carts. I have also functioned as a consultant, even sometimes being paid for the service, in matters to do with the description, dating and evaluation of Hebrew manuscripts and that has proved to be an interesting and challenging experience. In one case I saved a prospective buyer from committing a large amount of money to what appeared to me to be a fake.

But for an academic, at least, or especially, in humanities, the joy of retirement is that one becomes again primarily what one was when starting one's career, namely, a scholar devoted to increasing knowledge of one's subject in a sound and informative manner, rather than a less than glorified civil servant. In the course of the past decade, I have been able to organize conferences at St John's with the generous financial and administrative assistance of the College, and have edited and published the proceedings of a number of those. When most of the participants at a conference are non-native speakers of English, it is often no easy task to transform what they submit into a reasonably presentable version. I was particularly amused by one such non-native speaker who insisted on twice restoring in the proofs her incorrect English. She then gave me a lecture when we met at a later conference about the correctness of the phrase 'to my opinion' and what it precisely conveyed. I of course ignored her view in the final text for publication and I do not believe that she ever forgave me. During the early and middle years of my career, I participated not only in smaller conferences, which are more productive, personal and collegial, but also in the larger jamborees attended by many hundreds. I now tend to avoid these latter occasions since they sometimes have more than their fair share of mediocrities offering banalities to nonentities.

Filming, Lecturing and Editing

It was fun to work with Michelle Paymar on the production of a film about Genizah research and to watch her successfully develop this project from its earliest beginnings in interviews with me in Beit Shemesh and in Cambridge in 2012 to its international premieres and acclaim in 2018 under the title *From Cairo to the Cloud*. I also enjoyed working with Professor Simcha Goldin in his Diaspora Research Center at Tel Aviv University and functioning as the consultant for some post-doctoral researchers in the history of Jewish liturgy. He and I had planned and arranged a conference in Tel Aviv in 2007 and the papers were published in 2010 under the title of *Death in Jewish Life*, edited by Andreas Lehnardt, Avriel Bar-Levav and myself. The volume examines the degree to which the medieval Ashkenazim were innovative in the area of communal activity surrounding burial and mourning customs. Simcha, Andreas and I established a new series, 'Rethinking Diaspora', published by de Gruyter, under the broader heading of 'Studia Judaica', later with Nahem Ilan as an additional editor.

The Erasmus Scheme that Renate championed in Salzburg and that co-operated with Haifa and Ben-Gurion Universities in Israel provided me with a number of opportunities of giving lectures to students and scholars on medieval Hebrew manuscripts and on the history of Jewish liturgy. Equally gratifying was the two-day 'seniors' seminar' that Renate, Kristin de Troyer and I arranged at Salzburg in 2018. I had long felt that today's students, unlike those of yesteryear (or should I say yester-century) are denied the experience of listening and learning from retired scholars. While we as youngsters gave attention and respect to those who had moved into their senior years, today's educational philosophy appears to be that aging scholars, like aging electrical appliances, should be replaced and binned. We invited Johann (Hans) Maier (Innsbruck), Günther Stemberger (Vienna), Andrew Macintosh (Cambridge) and Tessa Rajak (Reading) to join me in talking about their academic careers and their message to young scholars. The meetings were charmingly and efficiently chaired by Ursula Schattner-Rieser, then in Innsbruck but now in Köln. I believe that the exercise was a blessed one in many respects. Hans was especially pleased and appreciative and that was some consolation for us when he left this world for the ethereal academy a few months later.

A younger scholar of Jewish history and a former Cambridge student, Sara Jo Morris (now Ben-Zvi), is doing a splendid job in Israel in producing, in Hebrew and English versions, a popular but academically sound magazine by the name of *Segula*. She has co-opted on to the advisory board a number of senior scholars and that seems to have done the project no harm whatsoever. I rejoice in taking my place on that board. I was even approached about the possibility of taking on the presidency of an important educational centre in Israel. I met those running the institution but I think that they really wished to have someone who would be more willing than I was to give full-time attention to the project and rightly opted for another scholar. I am not sure that the chemistry would in any case have worked between me and them.

The Famous Genizah

It was also good to see how much more attention was by then being paid to the Genizah. As Tacitus (loosely understood) put it, victory is claimed by all, while defeat is ascribed to only one. Success has many parental claimants while failure is an orphan. The little orphaned Cambridge Genizah which I had fostered, adopted and reared, was gradually recognized as the progeny of many. In his volume, *Sacred Treasure*, published in 2011, Marc Glickman, Rabbi of congregations near Seattle in Washington State, presented the subject in such a lively, entertaining and interesting way, that even those with no interest in history or ancient documents would be hard-pressed not to be excited and enthused. I had provided him with my take on the history of the Genizah and he included some generous references to my work from 1973 onwards.

Although they too had benefitted from my input (and kindly acknowledged the fact), Peter Cole and Adina Hoffman in their *Sacred Trash* told the Genizah story primarily from the 1890s until 1970, paying due tribute to the major actors in the Genizah drama played out during those years and not subsequently. As Adina explained to me, writing about any living scholars in the body of the book would have opened up 'a large can of worms'. For me, that meant that no special recognition could be given to any one Genizah parent without calling into question the claims of all the Genizah's growing band of prospective claimants to that honour. It clearly needed a Solomon in his wisdom to tackle such claims.

College Support

I should put on record the degree to which St John's College has been supportive since my appointment as a Fellow 22 years ago. What I wrote in the introduction to my volume, *Jews, Bible and Prayer*, in 2016, warrants emphatic repetition in the current context: 'I should add how grateful I always am to St John's College, in the University of Cambridge, not only for electing me to a fellowship almost twenty years ago but also for the many generous facilities it has afforded me since then. These privileges have, to no small degree, made it possible for me to continue to be a productive scholar into my retirement years.' The College is one of the few educational institutions I know that continues to accommodate, respect and involve retired scholars and therefore to encourage them to be professionally, socially and intellectually active.

The opportunity to meet local scholars from a large number of disciplines, as well as those who are visiting the College from abroad, is one of the remarkable advantages provided by the collegiate format, and undoubtedly stimulates rather than abandoning those in their senior years. Long may the system survive attempts to weaken or destroy it. As is generally the College custom after a Fellow has enjoyed that status for ten years, I was asked in 2009 to choose an artist for a portrait to be hung in the room behind the Combination Room of the College. I chose Alastair Adams but by the time that we were able to have our first meeting, in April 2010 I believe it was, I had only recently lost Shulie. When I saw the final work a few months later, I remarked that it made me look very sad. The artist's response was that I had indeed at that time been very sad and he had captured this in his portrait.

More Publications

Just as importantly, the past nine years of retirement have witnessed an increased productivity. More conferences, more lectures, more published papers, more editing and more monographs. In his contribution to the special edition of *Genizah Fragments* issued to mark my retirement in 2006, and containing many an amusing comment, a colleague at the University Library, John Wells, cited the Library's Annual Report and the mention of my '37 lectures and conference papers' and mused that retirement might help me 'to press on' for my 'half-century'. I fear I have let him down in that respect. Checking the record, I see that my total number of published items since 2010 has been in the region of 200 and that is only 20 a year and not 50! No matter, it includes two volumes of my research. The first, *Jewish Prayer Texts from the Cairo Genizah*, contained edited, translated and annotated texts of 25 fragments of medieval Jewish liturgy and offered what I believe to be some fresh understanding of the numerous external factors that motivated adjustment in liturgical formulations. In his review in the *Journal of Jewish Studies*, Michael Rand referred to my 'lifetime of work on

Jewish liturgy…spent in active engagement with the Genizah as a concrete trove of manuscript fragments'.

The second volume, *Jews, Bible and Prayer*, was a collection of my papers, most of which had been published in scattered periodicals and collective volumes hither and thither, to which I added one lengthy new chapter. As the title indicated, the chapters dealt with medieval Jewish exegesis of the Hebrew Bible and with a wide variety of liturgical topics. Renate and I were also partners (of which partnership I shall have more to say shortly) in editing *Religious Identity Markers: A Workshop on Early Judaism*; *Ancient Jewish Prayers and Emotions*; together with Jim Aitken, *Discovering, Deciphering and Dissenting: Ben Sira's Manuscripts after 120 years*; and, together with Mike Duggan, *Cosmos and Creation*. The first, third and fourth of these were the result of meetings arranged at St John's College and the second constituted the proceedings of a conference held in honour of my seventieth birthday at the University of Haifa. When asked how I divide my retirement time, I often reply that I spend fifty per cent in Cambridge, fifty per cent in Israel and fifty per cent giving lectures around world. Most hearers appreciate the joke but there are occasionally those who look at me quizzically, wondering why I never mastered arithmetic.

Involvement at Haifa

Mention of Haifa leads me to state how much pleasure it has given me to work with the newly-created Centre for the Broader Application of Genizah Research at the University of Haifa, in particular with its directors Efraim Lev and Moshe Lavee and their impressive academic and administrative team. They have given employment and encouragement to a long list of young Genizah researchers and have demonstrated how innovative and educationally significant their work can be for a wide range of cultural activities. I have played a role in assisting and guiding their efforts, including chairing the Centre's academic committee, and locating some funding sources.

Efraim has ploughed new furrows in the study of Jewish medical history in the Islamic world and Moshe has been highly innovative in the literary analysis of midrashim and in the involvement of a wide range of online enthusiasts in the decipherment of challenging Genizah texts. I have arranged for both of them to spend time at St John's. Efraim spent the whole year of 2003-4 and was a highly popular diner with the Master and Fellows at high table. The then Master's wife, Mary Dobson, is also in the field of medical history and she and Chris welcomed him warmly to the College and the Lodge.

I had met Efraim a few years earlier and heard that despite his best efforts, he had not succeeded in obtaining a full-time tenured post. I advised him to apply, with my support, for a visiting scholarship at St John's College and assured him that this honour, and the publications that would assuredly result from twelve months of intensive Genizah research, would lay the foundations of a solid academic career. I am glad to say that I was not wrong. After his sabbatical in Cambridge, he went from success to success, ultimately being promoted to a full professorship at the University of Haifa and also heading the humanities teaching at the Haifa Technion.

I was thrilled to receive an honorary doctorate from the University of Haifa. In his letter, the president, Amos Shapiro, wrote the award was 'a token of its esteem for your life's work in establishing and preserving the collection of Cairo Genizah documents, in devoting many years to making its contents and research about it available to the public as well as to scholars, and of its admiration of your outstanding academic achievements. You deserve great credit for being a scholar who has been able to combine academic research of the highest standard with advancing, sponsoring and initiating the careers of young scholars, who has contributed in a special degree to academic Jewish studies, and who has, at the same time, been deeply involved in Jewish life in the United Kingdom, as well as maintaining warm connections with your colleagues in Israel. You represent what is finest in Israeli society and deserve the finest honour that the University of Haifa can bestow on you, namely, its honorary doctorate of philosophy.'

Not only were all those closest to me present to see the award being bestowed, but I also had the additional excitement of meeting and/or chatting with the famous Israeli actor Chaim Topol (who, by the way, knew a thing or two about Genizah manuscripts and told me he had some in his library!), and F.W. de Klerk, State President of South Africa from 1989 until 1994, who were among my fellow recipients of the honour. The whole evening was a deeply moving experience for me and those around me.

I have no doubt that Efraim and his colleagues must have played a central role in this generous act of recognition. Efraim is only one of some 20 scholars whose careers got successfully under way via their periods as post-docs in the Genizah Research Unit and then flourished in various centres around the world. He has been the most generous of all those scholars in acknowledging what he owes to the Unit and to myself. Some of the others have on occasion expressed their gratitude but most have generally preferred to concentrate on seeing their academic achievements as their own. I never tire of citing the wife of the famous anthropologist, James Frazer, who consoled him for a certain lack of recognition that he suffered by assuring him that 'such as he, he is – and that suffices'. Rebecca Jefferson once kindly referred to the fact that three scholars who made major impacts on Genizah research all shared the Hebrew name 'Shlomo'. While in no way comparing my contribution to those of the giants, Solomon Schechter and Shlomo Dov Goitein, I feel it to have been an honour to stand on their shoulders and to have advanced the subject in my own way. In Mrs Frazer's words, 'that suffices'.

Gradual Opting Out But Another Festschrift

Soon after my retirement, Ben Outhwaite established a fund in my name and invited friends of the Unit to contribute. The sum raised made it possible for some of my travel expenses to be met and for me to function as a consultant for the Unit. I contributed to *Genizah Fragments* on a regular basis, helped with aspects of the development programme and even laid the foundations for a fund-raising dinner in New York that I would have addressed and that would have brought in as much as $75K to the Unit's coffers. For some reason, the dinner never went ahead.

It gradually became clear to me (from a number of incidents which I shall not enumerate here) that the Unit preferred me to operate at a greater distance. In order to accommodate to such a preference, I turned my attention to the preparation of *Jewish Prayer Texts* and the Unit made available to me financial support for this project, derived from a bequest made by my late teacher, Professor Wieder and his wife Miriam, to support precisely such an academic project. I spent the years 2013 until 2016 on this volume and worked in the room made available to me by Anne Jarvis, without involving myself much in the Unit's day-to-day activities.

There was a progressive disengagement from the Unit during this period and I should perhaps have realized at an earlier stage that this would allow my successors to move matters on in their own way. It is always difficult for those who have established projects *ex nihilo* and devoted their lives to their promotion and success to accept that their departures must mean new methods and fresh priorities. That is especially difficult when, as is often the case, they have a sense (rightly or wrongly) that if they were still running the show, progress would be different, or perhaps even better. The final indication that I no longer had any place in the Unit came with the major Genizah exhibition mounted in the Library's Exhibition Centre in 2017 which covered all aspects of the Genizah Collection except my role in the establishment of the Unit. Indeed, none of the speeches at the opening of the exhibition thought it appropriate to make even a cursory mention of my name.

Soon after Anne Jarvis left the Library in 2016 to take on a similar post at Princeton, I was asked to vacate the room and its facilities that she had promised to maintain for me. By 16 June 2017 I had removed all my belongings to my room at St John's and after 44 years of devoted service I made my exit from the University Library with neither bang nor whimper. By way of consolation concerning my relations with the Unit, I repeated to myself the statement recorded in the Babylonian Talmud in the name of R. Yose, thinking that there might be at least some relevance in it: 'Rather than places bringing honour to individuals, it is individuals who brings honour to places.'

There were, however, still many scholars who generously wished to pay tribute to my academic efforts. At the biennial conference of the ISDCL hosted by Stefan Beyerle in Greifswald in July 2019, I was most pleasantly surprised by the presentation of a volume of essays in honour of my seventy-fifth birthday, edited by Núria Calduch-Benages of Rome, Michael Duggan of Calgary and Dalia Marx of Jerusalem, and specially prepared for the occasion by Albrecht Doehnert of the publishers de Gruyter in Berlin. The impressive Festschrift presented on my retirement had concentrated on Genizah matters and this one was devoted to my other area of special interest, the history of Jewish worship. It was entitled *On Wings of Prayer* and included a preface that made generous reference to my academic achievements, 20 articles by senior scholar from all over the world ('reflecting Stefan's travels as a lecturer and the reach of his publications'), a photograph and a full list of my publications.

Family Love and Partner Love

Turning to the more personal and familial aspects of my life in the first decade of the twenty-first century, I have to acknowledge that the predictions of Shulie, the children and grandchildren, and my sister Sharron, proved to be correct. As is clear from the descriptions of my activities just noted, my work had indeed proved to be my salvation. I had certainly found inner resources of strength to face life's newest challenge. Above all, there was truly much love still to be given and received. Such love was found not only within my wonderfully close and consistently loyal family but also outside it. There are not many individuals who are blessed with the kind of partnership in which there is intense love, powerful support, physical and intellectual excitement, mutual admiration and professional collaboration. Having relished such a relationship with Shulie, I thought that I had enjoyed that one opportunity for such a blessing and looked back on it with gratitude. Astonishingly, Renate was to bring me another such remarkable partnership. As I said at the seventieth birthday dinner arranged for me by the family in Beit Shemesh in January 2014 (at which I was also presented with a wonderful book full of good wishes from the family, friends and public personalities), it must be a rare privilege for a man to have had the outstanding qualities of two exceptional women to see him through the trials, and to share with him the joys that life inevitably brings, and the deepest love.

After almost a year and a half of exceptional sadness, I attended a conference of the ISDCL in Palermo in the summer of 2011 and there I met up again with Renate whom I and Shulie had known from similar meetings

25. With Renate at St John's College, 2017.

in the past. But, during the many hours we spent together in the evenings, while most of the participants went out drinking, I found what was for me a new Renate. Her attractiveness, her intellect, her humour and her sympathetic understanding of my plight drew us closely together and we were soon in an undissolvable partnership. We had a great deal in common and we plumbed the depths of each other's personalities. Of course, we walked, swam, drove, sang, danced and laughed together. We also cooked, baked, feasted, and holidayed, and enjoyed every minute of our shared time. But we also co-operated professionally and assisted each other with our academic projects.

Numerous conferences and publications were the result of our collaborative efforts and I recovered some of the youthfulness I thought I might have lost forever. We also worked together on unravelling the complex Jewish background of Renate's Eastern European family and attended synagogues together in Beit Shemesh, Cambridge and Salzburg. We succeeded in making arrangements to spend time with each other in those three places, and elsewhere, on at least a monthly basis and sometimes even more frequently. What pleased me greatly was the way in which the family and Renate took to each other. Tanya once told me emphatically and definitively that she was wholly convinced that Shulie would never have wanted me to remain alone and would have been delighted that I had found such a suitable helpmate as Renate. And so, the pleasures and achievements of the past few years have been possible through the love generously given and received by Renate in one way, and by my outstanding family in others. When I am in Israel, there is hardly a day when Tanya does not telephone me, and hardly a fortnight or so when Aryeh and I do not meet for a long 'heart-to-heart' over lunch.

Another Set of Grandchildren

Talking of suitable helpmates, I was very pleased that, five years after his divorce, Aryeh found a loving, warm and supportive partner in Rina Joseph and we all danced enthusiastically at their wedding on 2 January 2012. It was Renate's first family celebration and, apart from the terrible musical din that is characteristic of most Israeli weddings, we enjoyed it together. Jewish folk are intense about marking *rites de passage* and indeed all family occasions. Within some six years, I was to become the saba not only of seven young adults but also of four new 'Reiflets', namely, three boys, Yishai, Hillel and Michael and (at last for a patient Rina!) their little sister, Ayala. Unfortunately, they do not live nearby but in Rishon Lezion, near Tel Aviv, where Aryeh and Rina have a lovely, large home, and he has his thriving legal practice, specializing (brilliantly of course) in intellectual property on an international basis. The drive takes about 35 minutes and from time to time I spend Shabbat with them. I also have regular Shabbat meals with Tanya and Anthony and they have extended their attractive home to accommodate their four (+1) children. They too are highly successful professionals and they will all perhaps one day tell their own stories. My children and their spouses are always most supportive and, although I try not to trouble them with too many requests, I know that, if I need their help in any way, they are always willing to provide it unstintingly.

Family Joys and Sadness

Other marriages during those years were those of the children of Sharron and David – Yoni (to Meital), Avital (to Gilad) and Galit (to Itamar) – and it has been exciting to watch them build their own families and lifestyles, and to take pride in their major achievements. Sadly, there have also been two major losses. My sister Cynthia had been ill with a muscular disease which eventually consigned her to a wheelchair. She had fought it valiantly for fifteen years and I took many opportunities of travelling to Toronto to visit her and her husband Karl. My final visit was in October 2015 and I am delighted that Renate was able to join me. Cynthia heartily approved of her and thought we had each made a superb choice of partner. She then deteriorated over the following few months and I could not face the thought of again looking at death in the face. I therefore maintained contact through electronic means. Sharron, more courageously, went to visit and came back totally drained.

Cynthia died in May 2016 and had in her last days asked to be buried near our parents in Beit Shemesh. I, with Anthony's help, made the necessary arrangements, and spent the week of shiv'ah at Sharron's house. Cynthia and I had grown closer again in our middle age and we had spent some European vacations together which gave us all much fun and pleasure. She took with her a part of my earliest life which is now recalled only by my cousins Doreen, Jacqueline and Janis. Another family member who knew about that period was my cousin Leon and we had always been close to him and his wife Paula. He came to Israel for Avital's wedding in March 2011 and we spent wonderful hours together joking and reminiscing. Leon had battled with all manner of physical and mental disease in his final years but usually coped in a very good-natured way. We loved each other like brothers and when I knew he was reaching the final stage I drove from Cambridge to London to see him on a dark and wet Saturday night in the winter of 2016. He chatted as best he could for about 30 minutes and then asked me to forgive him if he went to bed. I helped him into bed and gave him a cuddle and a kiss and he said 'You have always been such a lovely cousin.' I told him that I felt exactly the same way and I said goodnight and goodbye to him for the last time. A few months later I gave a deeply-felt appreciation of him at the unveiling of his tombstone in a North London cemetery.

Saba's Pride

The seven adult grandchildren are now making their own history. My eldest grandson, Gidon, served in the Israeli Army for almost five years as a tank commander and officer, and in August 2018 he married Yiscah Levy, who had herself been an officer in the Air Force. She is a lovely young woman and they are a brilliant match, both now studying engineering at Ben-Gurion University of Beersheva. Dani has finished an even longer stint in the army, also as an officer, and has celebrated her release, like many young Israelis, by travelling in South East Asia. She is now studying linguistics and

26. The Reif clan at Gidon and Yiscah's wedding, 2018.

psychology at Tel Aviv University. Shoshi, after her army service, went to Africa to help poverty-stricken families in Ghana, as well as touring in Ethiopia and South Africa. She is now studying Anthropology and Social Work at the Hebrew University of Jerusalem. The youngest in that family so well reared by Tanya and Anthony, Zaki, is serving as an officer in the Nahal Brigade and hopes to study medicine after his army service as an officer has been completed.

The children of Aryeh and Mirit, equally well brought up, have also made significant progress with their young lives. Nili, who completed her service in the Air Force, has qualified as a tour guide and is studying Psychology and Social Work at the Hebrew University while her brother, Ro'i, has just completed his stint as a commander in the Paratroopers (of red beret fame in Israel too!). Naama is now in the Israeli Army and serves in observation posts that provide essential information for her colleagues. My father who served in the forces for some sixteen years would have been very proud of them all, and I am no less so. It is a wonderful achievement of Zionism not only to build a state but also to take full responsibility for its defence. I am also proud of the fact that every one of those grandchildren knows well how to behave and has a social conscience, as well as a bright and intelligent personality. We have come a long way from the downtrodden existence and dreadful persecutions suffered in Eastern Europe two and three generations ago.

I should not omit to mention all the ways that I interacted with my grandchildren after Shulie's death. I did my best to entertain them in the dining room as well as in the study, as Shulie had said I should. On Pesaḥ, I made them matzabrei (matza fried with egg) and on Sukkot we ate pancakes in the sukkah. Woe betide me if I forget to arrange these occasions even now that they are grown-up. I soon get a message on my smartphone indicating that they are arranging the date that suits most of them best. I also studied traditional rabbinic literature with some of them while I took others to the opera in Tel Aviv. Soon after Shulie died, I met an old friend from my youth at the opera house. He glanced at the pretty young woman with me and I introduced her as a grand-daughter. The next two times it was a different grand-daughter, then it was my sister, Sharron, and later it was Renate. I am sure that he thought I had a whole harem! One of my favourite occasions – now also enjoyed and encouraged by Renate during her visits to Israel – is when we entertain them to kiddush at home on a Shabbat morning. Those who like a single malt are treated to a shot, or rather to a few shots, while the others make do with their favourite cereals and lots of nibbles.

As well as such gatherings in groups, there are also at times individual consultations at which Saba has to listen to frustrations, outbursts, confidences and inquiries and offer what they perhaps believe to be the sage advice of the experienced senior. That has at times included romantic matters and Saba has shared his own tales of a young man finding his way in building human relationships in London. As a barmitzvah treat, I took Zaki and Ro'i to Athens for a few days in the summer of 2011. That provided us with another important period of special male bonding. We climbed hills, viewed the Parthenon, visited the port of Piraeus and enjoyed an excellent hotel. We also exchanged notes about the pretty young women we saw in the hotel pool and around the city and at one point Ro'i confided in me that he was suffering from 'cleavagitis'. I understood and sympathized.

Renate and I took Naama on her batmitzvah treat to Salzburg and Vienna in July 2013. We did all the usual sightseeing but, most importantly for Naama, we also did some shopping. Having seen on our first night in Vienna some items that Naama liked in a clothes shop, by then closed, we returned next morning and began to chat to the owner, I in English and Renate in German. She asked Naama her name, recognized it as Hebrew, and then identified herself as Rachel, also from Israel! We were regally welcomed and obtained our purchases with a substantial discount, or so at least we were told. We also had the unusual, even rare, experience of seeing chocoholic Naama struggling to finish a large piece of rich Viennese chocolate cake, with dollops of schlagsahne (whipped cream). We took her swimming in our favourite Alpine lake, in Höglwörth, some twenty minutes out of Salzburg, but, having dipped herself into the water, Naama screamed at the coldness of it and swore that if she swam there she would assuredly die of a heart attack.

Dad's Shtetel

Having conveyed Naama safely into the protection of an El Al stewardess at Munich airport, we returned to Salzburg and packed for our own journey next morning. We were to visit my father's birthplace, Kalusz, now in Ukraine. The plan was to fly to Vienna and from there to Lviv, where we were to meet my sister Sharron. It was around 07.10 when we received a call from Austrian Airlines that our flight to Vienna at 11.30 had been cancelled and if we wished to make our connection to Lviv we should come immediately to the airport where the aircraft for Vienna was due to leave at 08.25. Thankfully, we were already packed, Salzburg Airport is only twenty minutes from Renate's apartment, and checking-in and security there are quickly negotiated. We were seated on the plane by 08.10!

We made it to Lviv where our driver and guide were awaiting us. We stayed one night in Lviv and the others in Stanislawow (now called Ivano-Frankivsk, after the Ukrainian nationalist Ivan Franko) and visited many small towns (shtetelach) where the populations had once been fifty per cent Jewish. Most of these Jews had perished in the Holocaust and viewing their 'aryanized' homes and destroyed synagogues was a totally harrowing experience. The Kalusz countryside is pretty and fertile and it was moving to find the river where Daddy had learned to swim, the school from which he regularly played truant, the orchards where he, as a poor and hungry orphan, had stolen fruit, and the area where his grandmothers' two houses had once stood. The older and pre-Soviet part of Kalusz is charming and very Habsburgian and we paid our respects at the Jewish cemetery, totally over-grown but at least left standing. Sharron was desperate to find a tombstone with the name Reif on it but I suspected that the family were scarcely wealthy enough to erect such memorials. Since then, the cemetery has been cleaned up and maybe some future visitor will find some Reif tombstones.

When we returned to Stanislawow (I cannot easily call it by the name of a Ukrainian nationalist), we were taken to two infamous sites. The first was where the Jewish ghetto had been and where thousands of Jews had been incarcerated before a proportion of them were slaughtered in a building called Rudolph's Mill. Nazi soldiers of all sorts took turns to rape the Jewish women before shooting them and assigning them to mass graves. With tears in our eyes we recited a memorial prayer outside the building. Most of my father's aunts and uncles left Kalusz in the early years of the twentieth century. Those who went to the United States have progeny there and, in the summer of 2018, we arranged a reunion of the Reifs in London where one of my father's last remaining cousins, Elsa Howard, lives, well into her nineties. There was another reunion in New York in the summer of 2019 which the other surviving cousins, Irving and Eddie, also in their nineties, were able to attend. So, despite the best efforts of many antisemites, there are still some flourishing remnants of the ten children of Lev and Ḥayya Sprintze Reif of Kalusz, Galicia.

In Cambridge

In Cambridge, I maintain a home and a car and St John's College still generously allows me to share a Fellows' set and to participate fully in the

Fellows' activities. I daven and lead the services in the synagogue in Thompsons Lane where I have done so since 1973. I continue to be active as Trustee of the Cambridge Traditional Jewish Congregation, a much weakened body compared to what we had created and nurtured in the 1980s, but we have elected some younger trustees and hope that they will somehow find the strength and the means to continue with the traditional religious practices. In Cambridge and in Beit Shemesh I conduct synagogue services and give traditional rabbinic lessons, to two or three in the former but to twenty times that number in the latter. Health problems associated with seniority are not entirely absent but I do my best to keep fit by exercising, walking and swimming, and am hoping to be busy for at least another decade. Many Fellows at St John's have been active into their nineties so I am hoping that this is an infectious disease.

Parting Shots

When concluding my presentation at the seniors' seminar in Salzburg in 2018, I offered, as an experienced and senior academic, some suggestions to the young researchers who attended. I thought their repetition here might constitute an appropriate peroration.

> Devote yourself to your subject with industry, imagination and enthusiasm. Pursue your own ideas even if major academics disagree with you. You may ultimately be wrong but you have to try.

> There are always fashionable notions in academic life, as there are in all aspects our existence. Do not be tempted to follow these in order to curry favour or cement friendships. Fashion is created by individuals and not individuals by fashion. Maintain your own individuality and create your own fashion.

> If there is a choice between success and recognition on the one hand, and honesty and integrity on the other, maintain your standards of morality. You will ultimately feel better for having done so.

> If patronage by major figures comes your way, it may assist you in your early career but it usually comes at a price. You will always feel indebted to the patron. Think carefully whether you would not rather maintain your independence, even if it does take you longer to climb the greasy academic pole.

Don't be discouraged by judgments of you given by those who might have their own agenda. Scholars are ultimately (usually posthumously) judged by whether their work has made a significantly quantifiable and identifiable difference to a field of study and to the lives of some of those in that field, not whether they have received the most honours.

Take pride in your achievements, especially if they are truly your own. You may not be as good as the best but you have to be what you are and make the most of your abilities.

It was Vauvenargues in 1746 who said that men despise great projects when they do not feel themselves capable of great successes. The form of that sentiment may come in jealousy, cynicism, obstruction and even revenge. Learn to live with those resentments and even smile at them. As Jan Patocka, the Czech philosopher (1907–77) astutely phrased it, 'the real test of a man is *not* how well he plays the role that he has invented for himself, but how well he plays the role that destiny assigned to him.' I am sure his wise remark was not intended to be gender-specific.

And, finally, the comments of a midrashic writer of many centuries ago. He asked why, in Deuteronomy 10:1-2, Moses mentions the original tablets that were smashed as well as the new ones, and why does he imply that both were stored in the same holy ark of the covenant? This is to teach us that when scholars are 'broken', that is, in their advanced years, and no longer running the show, they should still be treated with the same respect as when they were at their peak and wielding academic power. In these days of the disposable society, it is a lesson that should be widely taught and one with which I am happy to conclude my story. As William Wordsworth, who was a student at St John's College Cambridge, indicated, seniority may still allow us to find strength:

> What though the radiance which was once so bright
> Be now for ever taken from my sight,
> Though nothing can bring back the hour
> Of splendour in the grass, of glory in the flower;
> We will grieve not, rather find
> Strength in what remains behind.

Appendix A

The Reif Story

Scene in Galicia

Prussia, Russia and Austria helped themselves to most of Poland-Lithuania in three political partitions of that sorry kingdom at the end of the eighteenth century. The part that was annexed to Austria was the province of Galicia, most of the area stretching from the south-west of Cracow (Cracow was later included) to the territory around Tarnopol, about 120 kilometers east of Lemberg, and southwards for almost 200 kilometres. The western section of the province that was once Galicia is now part of Ukraine and the city of Lemberg, which was called Lwow by the Poles, is now called Lviv by the Ukrainians. The Austrians found themselves with an extra 200,000 Jews after the partitions, a number that expanded to about half a million by the middle of the nineteenth century and represented 10 per cent of the population. Throughout the province, there were many little shtetelech (towns) in which the Jews amounted to almost half of the population, but they also had substantial communities in larger cities such as Cracow, Lemberg, Zolkiev, Przemysl and Brody.

Avner Yehuda Reif, who was known for some reason as Leib (perhaps the name Yehuda was actually Yehuda Leib), was born in 1848 and spent most of his life in and around the area of Kalusz, which is located in the picturesque foothills, fertile farmland and lush forests of the Carpathian mountains. It is set on the left bank of the Lomnitsa River (which runs into the larger Dniester river) and is 35 kilometres to the north-west of what in his day was called Stanislavov and is now known as Ivano-Frankivsk. The large Jewish community of Lemberg was 112 kilometres to the north. The population of Kalusz in his day was about 8,000, more than half of them Jews who ran most of the small businesses there, and the remainder Poles and Ukrainians.

The name 'Reif' (maybe also spelt 'Reiff') was probably adopted or given not many years before Avner Yehuda's time when, as part of the reforms introduced by the Austrian government, Jewish families were told that they had to take surnames and not simply be called by their birth-names and the names of their fathers. The story goes (perhaps only a story) that those who could afford to bribe the relevant official could be 'Goldbergs' while those with less money could manage to be only 'Silberberg' or 'Kupfermann'. Really poor people might end up as 'Katzenellenbogen' (Cats' elbows) or 'Borgenicht' (Never borrow')! 'Reif' means 'ripe' or 'mature' so the family must have had good connections with the authorities when it mattered. Maybe the bureaucrat assigning names threatened to call the family Unreif ('immature') and changed his mind only when his palm was crossed with silver.

Leib and Ḥayya

Because of the Austrian take-over, the culture of Jewish Kalusz was fairly Germanic until the second half of the nineteenth century when, following the general tendency, the Jews showed more interest in adopting a form of Polish identity. Like most Jews, Leib knew German, Polish and Yiddish and seems to have engaged in small trading (money-lending?), sometimes travelling to the towns around Kalusz, such as Chocin, Stryj and Chortkov, or to larger centres such as Stanislavov, and even staying there. Each of these centres, and many others, had pretty squares in which the markets were held and in which the inevitable Austrian-styled town hall and the local chapel were situated. These markets were often dominated by Jewish traders who were supplied by the local Ukrainian peasantry. Leib mentions work in a (locomotive?) factory but it not clear whether as a trader or a worker. My father remembered his grandfather Leib having some electric batteries and a flash-light which greatly impressed the young boy and how cross Pinḥas was when they were denied to him. Though quiet and good-natured, Leib loved nothing more than a good grumble about life, and the conditions in which the Jews lived were certainly harsh. But he and his fellow Jews felt that the situation of Jews under the Hapsburg Emperor, Kaiser Franz Joseph, whom they greatly admired, were not as bad as they were under the Russian Tsar. Attempts were made from time to time to improve the social and political status of the Jews but there were, on the other hand, attacks on the Jews, often inspired by the more fanatic priests of the Roman Catholic Church. For Leib, the most important wishes to express to his grandson in the USA (by correspondence of course, not personally) on his reaching the age of barmitzvah were that he should be a healthy, honest and fine person and a religious Jew who put on tefillin every day. He was thrilled that his son Avraham Yitschak (Adolf) had taught his boy just as he had taught Adolf. Like a Yiddishe Mamme, he offers Adolf, by then in the USA, medical advice: 'You should drink fish oil and stuff your ears with cotton.'

The girl of sixteen whom Leib married in 1870 was altogether a more dynamic character than her husband, who was six years older than her. Ḥayya Sprintze (née Schechter) read German, could herself pen letters in Yiddish in an age when many women were illiterate, had clear ideas of what to expect of her children and grandchildren, and seems to have been resolute in the face of adversity. She wore the traditional sheitel over a shaved head, as was expected of most ḥasidic Jewish women in Galicia at the time, and bore Leib children between 1871 and 1892, but she was not the type to hide herself in the kitchen. Unlike many Jewish women of her day, she took the trouble of obtaining a formal Austrian certification of her marital status. Even as an elderly grandmother, she liked to run the family. She was destined to see all but two of her children leave Kalusz and settle elsewhere in Galicia, as well as in Vienna and New York. It was part of the parental culture of their circles to express severe criticism of their children and disappointment with them but then immediately to move on to warmer and less aggressive statements ('You have totally washed your hands of your parents. Write to us right away if you are already [engaged?]. Regards and kisses'). They clearly thought that this was the correct role of a father and a mother. In various letters to his children, Leib states that he is passing on messages dictated by Ḥayya Sprintze.

Ten Children

It seems that Leib and Ḥayya Sprintze had ten children. Avraham (Adolf), who seems to have been the first to go, as well as Simha (Sigmund), Mendel and Rayzal (Rose), all settled in New York in the early years of the twentieth century while Esther (Erna) and Mayer (Max) moved to Vienna. Berl Hirsh (Bernard, also calling himself Dov Zvi) and Miriam (Mirchik, Mina) who apparently never married, and was a very independent-minded woman, remained in Galicia until she died. I know that there was a connection with an Alfert family (my father remembered a 'Fetter Mikhal/Uncle Michael' who may have been an Alfert) and it seems that Fania married him and bore him children. From Mina's letters we learn that he was thoroughly cruel to her and seems ultimately to have abandoned her. At one point in 1930, Bernard wrote to his siblings asking them to help Mirchik who was unwell and in an impoverished state. Mirchik died young in 1936 (?) while Bernard and Erna and their spouses and families perished in the Holocaust. Sondel stayed at home with her parents and it was she who became the mother of my father, Pinkas, although quite when and how is not wholly clear.

Early Widowhood

Sondel was one of the younger members of the family into which she was born in the mid-1880s. Bernard complains in 1904 that the family's inability to provide a dowry for her has meant that she cannot get a suitable match so she must have then been in her early twenties. What is clear is that Sondel had two children between about 1910-11 and 1915 and the family story is that she married a non-commissioned officer in the Austrian Army whose Hebrew name was Zvi Aryeh (Hirsh Leib) Ha-Kohen and whose surname was evidently Kafka (or, according to one elderly relative, maybe Wassermann) and his family was from Czechoslovakia. My father had an early memory of visiting his father at an army base in Vienna, maybe in 1915, and admiring the blue and red colours of his (dragoon's) uniform. He also had a clear recollection that they lived for a few months in Vienna in an apartment overlooking the Danube canal. He recalled the precise address (Obere Donaustrasse 63) so he must then have been about 4-5 years old. Perhaps the buildings there were owned or rented by the military. His father was summoned to active service on the Italian Front and in 1916 he was reported as missing, perhaps killed in action. Sondel was then an 'agunah' ('a chained woman'), unable according to Jewish law to marry again, because it had not been not proved (by at least one witness) that she was a widow. Broken-hearted and thoroughly miserable (she never seems to have recovered from that), she returned to Kalusz. There she seems to have been in receipt of an Austrian army pension until the end of the First World War. My father thought that his sister Malchik/Malka/Amalya was born very soon after her father's death.

That my father was given his mother's surname of Reif indicates only that, as in many other such cases, a woman in Galicia who married in a Jewish ceremony and received a ketuba was not registered as married by the Austrian authorities. That required a separate (as well as bureaucratic and expensive?) procedure to which most of the women had no interest in subjecting themselves. There is, however, one other conundrum. In a letter dated 25 March 1910, Leib mentions (if I am reading the Yiddish letter correctly) that Sondel is at home with the child, but my father's date of birth was always given as 24 January 1911. He did mention to my mother that this was probably not the actual year but she dismissed this. I therefore suspect that his family made the birthday a later one so that he could at some stage avoid going into the army, as was done for many Jewish boys in the shtetelech.

War Conditions

My father, Pinḥas (Pinkas, officially in his Polish documentation), and his sister Malka had their earliest years in an active war zone. The battles between the Austrian Army and the Russian army took place in and around these shtetelech in Galicia. The famous Yiddish writer Shlomo Anski wrote detailed reports of the events and their impact on the Jewish communities. Whichever army occupied the area immediately took all the food and services that it needed and the Jews suffered terrible deprivation and humiliation. The Austrians regarded themselves as more civilized than the Russians so they bombarded their enemies with pamphlets in Yiddish (and in Hebrew if I remember correctly one I once saw) addressed to the Jewish conscripts saying how much better life was for the Jews under Kaiser Franz Joseph than under Tsar Nicholas, and inviting them to change sides. Whatever the military situation, the Reif family had to make do with potatoes as their staple diet. Whatever else became available was a welcome luxury. Sondel was not very good at coping with life's challenges and looked to her parents, Leib and Ḥayya, to look after things. If that total war situation already seemed a sad one for the family, there was more tragedy still to come.

In the summer of 1917, as part of their looting and pillaging, a group of Russian soldiers attacked the Reif household and demanded that Leib give them the gold watch that he wore proudly on his chest and his other jewellery. The other members of the family were hiding in another house nearby. When he refused, they shot him dead. A neighbour came and told them in Polish that 'Grandpa Leib is no more'. My father remembered being told to ask Zeide for 'meḥila' (forgiveness) for any wrongs he had done him and watching the local chevra kadisha (Jewish burial society) ensuring that every body-part and all the splattered blood were carefully collected for interment.

My father thought that it was the Ukrainian nationalists, under the leadership of Simon Petlyura, that had perpetrated this murder and robbery. But since we know for sure that Leib Reif was killed in July 1917 and that there was exactly at that time a pogrom in Kalusz carried out by recruited soldiers with the encouragement of their Russian officers, it may be that the Russians (Cossacks?) were to blame. Or perhaps Petlyura who killed thousands of Jews some two years later during the brief period of Ukrainian independence, was already inciting antisemitic acts by Ukrainian soldiers at that earlier date.

Wild Thing

So now young Pinḥas had a family of grandmother Ḥayya, mother Sondel, sister Malchek, Auntie Mirchek and no male role model to emulate. Ḥayya ran a kretchmer, that is a kind of inn, near the railway station, and managed to make a reasonable living most of the time. She built an annexe for Sondel and her kids. Needless to say, the young boy was wholly undisciplined and all the efforts of Bubbe Ḥayya to rectify this served little purpose. She tried to beat him, to poke him with a stick when he hid under the bed, but nearing her seventieth year she was no match for her speedy young grandson. He even stole his sister's food off her plate when she looked away for a moment. He, with his one Jewish and two non-Jewish friends, ran riot in many ways. Presumably because of the wars in that area, or because he played truant with his friends, he did not start attending school until the age of 9, when the Polish state was re-established and some order was restored. He and his friends would enjoy a day out by 'borrowing' some bicycles, cycling to the Lomnitsa River and swimming there. Near his home there was a small river, used by the brewery nearby, and it was in that little river that he first learned to swim. Meanwhile, Tante Mirchek had taught him to read and write.

He and his Catholic companion Stefan Bereznicki were always playing tricks on pupils and teachers. They were now being educated in the local school (a grand building in the town centre) as young Poles, who also had to know Russian and Ukrainian very well, and some German, so there were various teachers to deal with. One master always began the lesson by lifting his glasses from the desk and wiping them slowly. Pinḥas and Stefan thought it was a great idea to remove the lenses and watch his surprise when he rubbed his fingers together. They also experimented in the classroom with a primitive explosive device made out of the tops of lots of matches. They were both beaten very severely for their sins by the teacher but by no means mended their ways. As far as Hebrew and Jewish learning were concerned, Pinḥas learned the basic minimum and kept away from the melamed as much as he could because he was always subjected to the meanest corporal punishment.

Pinḥas bred pigeons and they made a terrible mess on the laundry. Since some of them had been stolen and Pinḥas was in trouble with the police about this, his mother solved the problem by taking them to the local shoḥet and giving them to her son for dinner. He first thought that he was eating very small chickens but then the truth dawned and he cried bitterly. There were, and still are, many orchards in Kalusz. Pinḥas climbed over a fence into one of them and ate heaps of large ripe cherries. Obviously, his digestive system could not cope and you can imagine the consequences high in the tree. He was also keen to sample the many 'Kaiserbirnen' (huge pears) on another tree. When the owner caught him at it, the naughty youngster climbed high into the tree. But the owner decided to wait at the bottom of the tree with his dog so Pinḥas tried to make his escape but fell and broke his hand. To his credit, the orchard owner took him to the local 'quack' for treatment. Doctors were an expense that the poor could not afford and so they had to make do with all kinds of folk medicine such as leeches and cupping.

Making a Life and Trying Palestine

That is how Pinḥas spent the first half of the 1920s but then at the age of 14 he was apprenticed to a locksmith. In those days working with hot metal was not just for preparing shoes for horses. It was for making locks, for building gates and fences, for repairing machines, what we would call general metalwork. In German and Yiddish it was called 'Schlosserei'. He loved the work even if he was again the subject of severe bullying. It was fun for the older workers to ask the apprentice to go and fetch a pair of tongs without telling him that they had just been on the fire. Pinḥas quickly learned to beware of such jokes and to be careful of hot metal. But he loved building and repairing things, taking them apart and putting them together. He seemed to have a natural ability to understand how they worked. He recalled many years later how impressed they had all been with anything on which was written 'Made in England'. He completed his apprenticeship by the age of 17. There was a rural path from his home to the railway station and he must have heard and seen the trains that often steamed by. Eyeing those locomotives, he decided that he should leave home and seek his fortune.

His first attempt to do this took him to the east of Germany. He had heard from his mother about a relative there by the name of Leib Jungermann so he made his way to the Jungermann home in Silesia and introduced himself. His middle-aged relative, now called Leo, gave him a change of clothes, arranged a hot bath for the sweaty traveller, fed him well and even gave him 100 marks which, in about 1927, was a great deal of money. But then he sent him packing, telling him not to say anything to the servant about Jungermann's Jewish origins. Instead of going home with his winnings, Pinḥas bought some cloths and cleaning fluid and polished brass door-knobs and plaques and added to his funds. But he was caught by the police (for illegal trading?) and deported back to Poland.

He tried various Zionist movements before opting for Betar, the youth movement of Jabotinsky, and earned his living at the age of 18 by helping prospective settlers to get to the Rumanian port of Constanza on the Black Sea and from there to Palestine. Eventually he himself got to Haifa and was involved in a number of skirmishes with local Arabs. After one such clash, he was arrested by the British and sent to Acre prison where he spent a few weeks cleaning floors, washing dishes and learning some Hebrew and some Arabic before being deported back to Poland.

Soldier, Then Sailor

When wealthy Jewish boys were called to the army, they paid for a poorer boy to go in their place. Some poorer boys avoided the draft by cutting off their trigger fingers. Neither option was employed by young Pinḥas when he was called up to the Polish army in 1930. He packed his little case and made the five-minute walk from his home to the railway station where he faced a long journey of many hours to the training camp for recruits. Bubbe Ḥayya, aged 76, ran after him to give him a large honey-cake that she had made for him and to hug him farewell. He never saw her again. He served for two years and it was in many ways the making of him. He learned discipline, self-reliance and teamwork, and became very strong and fit. Although only 1.57m in height and very slim, he was extremely muscular and took great pride in his appearance. While he was in the forces, his Bubba Ḥayya, who had been sustaining the family in many ways, died and the family then consisted of his sad and rather weak mother, his younger sister, and Auntie Mirchek who was in great difficulties. It will come as no surprise to hear that Pinḥas opted to stay away from the Kalush shtetel and to seek a life elsewhere. A life in the services appealed to him and he joined the Polish Merchant Navy and trained as a naval engineer.

That is how he came to see the world in the 1930s. In his twenties, and at the peak of his fitness and liveliness, he travelled the world with his shipping line. He was highly energetic, loved to poke fun, smoked heavily, enjoyed a good drink, and was a popular and generous companion, except when he lost his temper. He was not very stable in the matter of moods and could, in a matter of seconds, jump from hilarity and joviality to extreme anger and frustration. What triggered the change was not always obvious. He loved the freedom of the life at sea. It was hard work operating in the ship's engine room but there were periods of relaxation and many visits to fascinating places across the globe. He picked up many languages and was willing to try his luck at any of them whenever the opportunity arose. He had an uncanny ability to absorb language, perhaps because he was a good mimic. Of course, all the languages were spoken with Polish or Yiddish accents but that did not deter him. He was never afraid of new challenges or of fresh faces and places.

So what of his Jewishness during those years? His first priority after he joined the army was to get out of the shtetel and build a new life. Initially, this meant taking on a Polish identity, speaking Polish as his main language, and having Polish friends. His Polish was excellent and a few weeks before he died a young female friend who visited him in hospital commented on what a pleasure it was to listen to his charming and polite Polish. But he never denied his Jewishness, his admiration of the Zionist endeavours and his affection for Jewish traditions, and it was through his naval work that he once again drew close to Eretz Yisrael in the mid-thirties, and almost settled there.

The company with which he sailed as an engineer was the Gdynia-America Line and I know for sure that he served on the SS *Polonia* and later on the MS *Batory*, and perhaps at some stage also on the MS *Pilsudski*. He mostly worked on the *Polonia*, of 15,000 tones, with its twin steam turbine engines of four cylinders and 6,000hp, which could accommodate up to 2,000 passengers and steamed from Constanza to Haifa in about three days, making the trip every two weeks. Many Jews making aliyah from Central and Eastern Europe to Palestine, when they were permitted to do so by the British who ruled the Mandate at that time, travelled on the *Polonia* and most of them were unaware that one of the engineers was a Jew. Look at the biographies of famous Jews who settled in Palestine in the mid-1930s and you will see that they often arrived on Pinḥas's SS *Polonia*. I remember meeting one of the directors of Kol Yisrael (the Israeli broadcasting service) in 1960 who was astonished to hear that the boat that brought him to Eretz Yisrael had had a Jewish engineer on board!

The Zionist movement took advantage of this fact and involved Pinḥas in their efforts to get people to their homeland. He brought money and news and was also at times involved in Jewish nationalist activities. Because he was regarded as a Polish seaman it was easy for him to come ashore and he was able to avoid any British suspicion. He somehow always managed to make his way back safely to his ship. All this made him into an ardent Zionist and he was considering settling in Palestine once he had done some more tours of duty and saved some money. He had a Zionist girl-friend who lived on a kibbutz and with whom he spent his leave. The relationship blossomed until she said too much about hating Yiddish ('don't speak to me in that jargon'), and about regarding Jewish traditions as a thing of the past. Pinḥas was now moving back a little towards his origins and these views antagonized him and led to their breaking-up. He never had much patience for secularism or socialism. More than 40 years later, Pinḥas visited Israel in 1979 to see his youngest child, Sharron, who was living for a year on Kibbutz Sde Eliyahu. While walking in the kibbutz one day, he heard a man shout after him 'Pinḥas Hakatan!' ('Little Pinḥas'). Pinḥas turned around and saw a member of the kibbutz who excitedly told that he had not changed a bit. Apparently, this man had been smuggled on a ship during the 1930s as part of the aliyah beit, illegal immigration to Palestine. Pinḥas, who was working on the ship, had helped hide him.

Sailor, Then Soldier

And so it was back to sea, with only occasional visits back to Poland to see his family and to bring them treats from his travels. Life was becoming progressively more difficult for them, with the fascist tendencies of Italy, Germany and Spain also making their presence felt among the Poles and leading to the persecution of its massive Jewish population of three million and the introduction of all manner of discrimination against them. Sondel was having to work in a Jewish-owned factory as well as on the local farms and Malchek was seemingly employed in an office. Pinḥas knew in his heart that he could never settle again in the shtetel but he avoided making final decisions about his life, using the cocoon of his naval service to protect him from the idea of settling down anywhere in particular. Then he worked in engineering for a little while in Danzig and was able to find himself some pleasant lodgings and send money back to Kalusz.

The military situation deteriorated in Central Europe in 1938 and he was called up again to the army. My father told me that he remembered marching into Czechoslovakia with the Polish army and being greeted angrily by most of the population, some of whom emptied the contents of their chamber-pots from their windows on to the marching Poles below. This must have been on 2 October 1938 when Poland played its part, together with Germany and Hungary, in the despicable dismemberment of the Czech republic. It demanded and received under the Munich agreement the 400-square-mile area of Teschen, because it had 100,000 Poles in a population of 240,000. After the army, where he acquired two stripes, he rejoined the Polish merchant navy and was at sea near Stockholm when Hitler took his territorial demands even further and invaded Poland on 1 September 1939.

Another War

I cannot recall which boat he was on when the news came that Poland was being systematically destroyed by the Nazi invaders (was it the ORP *Grom*?) but I know that the crew had a good drink and decided, in their inebriated state, that the Polish army would be in Berlin within days. The way that Pinḥas told the story was that the captain, after talking to his crew – which had at least two Jewish members – decided not to follow instructions to return immediately to Poland but made for the nearest friendly port. Although this is how Pinḥas and the crew saw and heard it, it is possible that the Polish authorities preferred this option since they certainly continued to operate with their ships after the outbreak of the war on the side of the Allies from their new base in London. Be that as it may, Pinḥas Reif found himself in the port of Jarrow, near Newcastle. In the dockyard there, the boat was re-fitted with all manner of weapons, including anti-aircraft guns, and put to sea again. Near Narvik, Norway, they hit some depth charges and the boat went down, with all hands having to evacuate into the sea. Luckily, they were quickly picked up, severely shocked and injured, by a British destroyer, and taken back to England. After a few weeks of hospital care and convalescence, he was again soon in military action.

Pinḥas's story of service as a seaman combined with periods as a soldier was destined to continue. The Poles who handed themselves over to the British were made part of the Allied war effort, usually as a Free Polish Army with its own officers but under overall British control. The same happened to the French and the Czechs who made it to the United Kingdom and wanted to fight against the Nazi invasion of their countries. So it was that Pinḥas became a soldier again and was sent to France to confront the Germans. There were Polish units under General Stanislaw Maczek that fought a brave rearguard action in eastern France and managed to hold up the German progress there, in spite of their poor supplies and outdated equipment. Many were killed or captured and eventually their commanding officers ordered the destruction of what remained and evacuation to the south. My father was apparently part of that, or a related, force and, as well as acquiring some French language skills, was taught how to destroy bridges with TNT to impede the swift German advance. He applied his lessons and watched with amazement and satisfaction as enemy personnel and equipment were blown sky-high.

After some such successes, he was captured by the Germans in the summer of 1940 but prison conditions in the battle zone were not very secure. He and some comrades in arms, now filthy and lice-ridden,

27. Dad in 1942.

managed to cut their way out, dispose of the guards, and soak themselves for relief in the nearest lake. With little or no local French help, he found his way to a neutral Spanish port from where he stowed away on a boat bound for Algiers. He hid in the donkey boiler and once he was discovered earned his fare by working on the boat, something he was well used to doing. In Algiers he was fortunate to find at the port the MS Batory of his own Gdynia-America Line which shipped him back to England! I have a wonderful photograph of my father (I think on his return to England), still in the German boots issued to him when he was taken prisoner, explaining to some senior Polish military how he had escaped. They were astonished at the achievement and look as if they are having a good laugh at his exploits and their successful outcome.

Protecting Scotland

And now he was to be a sapper again, and to use his engineering skills for the defence of the United Kingdom. It was thought likely that if the

Germans were to invade Britain by sea and land they might well do so by way of the Scottish ports, since the crossing from Northern Germany and Denmark was a fairly straight one and would not involve them in the difficult naval challenge of the narrow English Channel. So Polish engineers were given the task of building anti-landing devices and planting mines all along the Scottish coast between Edinburgh and Aberdeen and Pinḥas was assigned work of this nature around the quaint little town of Carnoustie in Angus. He had special training in the dangerous work of laying mines and worked closely in 1941-42 with his Sergeant Czeslaw ('Czeszu') Riszkowski.

The Poles were fairly popular with the locals and an elderly widow called Mrs Ramsey (endearingly called 'Grannie Ramsey' in the area) took a special interest in Corporal Pinkas Reif and made it one of her tasks not only to feed him nice things but also to improve his English. She functioned as a kind of mother-figure for him and there were others in Carnoustie with whom he developed long-lasting and warm friendships. He sometimes forgot that some foodstuffs were rationed and ate more than his share. One occasion, Granny Ramsay told him 'Caw canny with the bu'er, Pinkas' ('Go easy on the butter, Pinkas').

It took him a while to understand the local British customs. Why would anyone want to drink tea with milk if they were not ailing? How could they have snack bars that advertised 'hot pies'? 'Pies' in Polish means dog and he marveled at such a local diet. Why did some Rabbis dress like Christian priests? Was it sensible to buy a dead fish and not choose it while it was still swimming in a tank? What was the purpose of greeting a friend in the street with the statement that it was a lovely day; either it was or it wasn't! As for the Scotswomen grumbling to each other, 'Aye, it's a terrible thing, ye canny git jam', or declaring 'Isn't it a braw day for the washin', that was totally beyond him. Waiting in queues was a custom that never appealed to him and when told that the items he wished to buy were 'rationed' he refused to co-operate and replied 'Me no Russian; me Polish'! But he worked on his English, helped by his Carnoustie friends.

The Polish army had its share of Jewish recruits and officers but there was always a degree of antisemitism, especially among the upper military echelons, that was waiting for an opportunity of revealing itself. Pinkas Reif was in charge of a training a group of recruits ('that little bastard' was what one of them called him!) and therefore felt that he had a certain degree of authority and seniority. When an officer instructed him rather rudely to go and go and fetch a sack of potatoes for him, he explained angrily that he was a non-commissioned officer and not a recruit and that was not something he was prepared to do. The officer angrily retorted in Polish 'Shut your

Jewish mouth, you impassioned little Jew!' and was for his pains promptly knocked off his feet by the impassioned little Jew. Officers and men had to pull him off and handcuff him. Some Polish officers who sympathized with the Nazis were in Rommel's German army in North Africa in 1942. When they were defeated, they were offered the option of joining the Free Polish Army in the UK. It is possible that my father's assailant was such a Nazi sympathizer, then working with the other side but still antisemitic. Be that as it may, a court-martial followed at which Reif was allowed to keep his stripes and continue to contribute to the war effort but was promised that when he returned to free, democratic Poland after the war, he would be duly punished. Under his breath, Reif told the presiding officer in Yiddish where he might kiss him and where he might ultimately lie. There was no meddling with such a hothead and he often allowed his bad temper to dictate the progress of his life rather than vice versa.

Meanwhile, in Kalusz

Needless to say, he heard nothing from his family in Poland and could only guess and worry about their fate. What had happened was that the Nazi-Soviet pact had allowed Russia to invade the east part of Galicia, including Kalusz. Many of the Jewish men were taken off to the depths of Russia. This seemed like a terrible fate at the time but in fact saved the lives of many. Those who remained had to learn to live under Soviet occupation and its many restrictions on Jewish communal life but that seemed less bad to them than subjugation to the Nazis. As long as they co-operated with the Soviets and their policies, the Jews of Kalusz could survive, much to the chagrin of many of the local Ukrainians and Poles. Malchek worked in the offices of the local Soviet government and was able to keep the family going between 1939 and 1941.

The Nazis broke their pact with the Soviets in the summer of 1941 and marched into Kalusz in July. With the help of local Ukrainian nationalists, they murdered many Jews and took their property. One Jewish family who survived later reported that the Ukrainians had raped and murdered Malchek, and Polish Catholic neighbours told my father after the war (in a letter) that his mother had been confined to the local ghetto where she had died of starvation on 28 July 1942. She was therefore spared deportation to the Belzec concentration camp which was the fate of those who still remained alive by that time. These neighbours were the family of Pinḥas's friend Stefan (who was killed in a torpedo attack by a U-Boat) and they tried to bring food to Sondel but to no avail. Bernard and Mina Reif and their family also perished in Galicia as did Erna, her husband Moshe and her family, and Max and his wife Regina in Vienna. Max had got to Italy and written to his brothers from Milan in February 1940. But he felt that he had to return to Vienna and try to rescue his wife and little boy and thus they all perished. Their older children Elsa, Lori and Fritz had left in 1939 and found refuge in the United Kingdom and in Palestine. So, if we assume that Fania had also perished by then, there were at the end of the war only four survivors of Leib and Ḥayya Sprintze's original family of ten. But that, sadly, is a fair proportion compared to many other Polish Jewish families.

If Only He Knew

But Pinḥas, although he was in general aware of Nazi persecution of the Jews, knew nothing yet of his family's fate in 1942 and could only assume the worst. Militarily, he and his fellow Polish soldiers were left much to their own devices and were expected to plan and execute all the necessary plans for the defence of the Scottish coast. He was therefore kept very busy but there were periods of leave when Jewish soldiers, sailors and airmen from Polish as well as other nationalities were able to make contact with local Jewish communities. There was a social club in Edinburgh for Jewish servicemen and servicewomen where they could meet each other as well as members of the local Jewish community, have a drink, smoke and snack and dance together. On one occasion in 1942, Pinḥas went along to the club, in Duncan Street, Newington, I think it was, and tried to chat to a friendly young girl of eighteen, called Debbie Rabstaff. He was having difficulties in being understood and apologized for his poor English, explaining that Yiddish was his mother tongue and he could express himself in that language (or Polish) much more efficiently. Debbie said that she knew almost no Yiddish but that she had an aunt called Annie, her father Abe's youngest sister, who was fluent because she chatted to her parents in Yiddish. It was arranged that next time Pinḥas had some leave he would come to the club and Debbie would ask Annie to come and meet him and converse with him in Yiddish. Corporal Pinkas Reif of the Free Polish Army in the UK had little inkling that his life would soon change completely as a result of such a meeting.

Courtship and Marriage

And so it was that in the latter part of 1942 and the early part of 1943, Pinḥas and Annie (Ḥayya) began to go out on dates. They conversed in

Yiddish but Annie was adamant that he should learn English so she tried as much as possible to teach him. With his wonderful ear for languages Pinhas was soon reading and writing as well as talking English. Of course, most of the time he was on military duty and he could only snatch short periods of leave during which he could see Annie. But he never wasted a moment even while on duty, and in the evenings, with the help of an English-speaking comrade in arms, he composed letters to Annie. These letters soon became love letters as the couple began to appreciate that they were very attracted to each other. During one evening together, Pinhas asked in his broken English 'Hayya-le, do you mean serious, or are you making from me a fool?' Annie assured him that she greatly enjoyed being with him and she hoped their relationship would continue to be successful. They each came to the relationship with a different perspective. Pinhas loved the atmosphere in her home, chatting with her parents in Yiddish, eating their traditional Jewish cooking that reminded him of home in Kalusz, and attending synagogue whenever he could with Reb Aharon. Now in his early thirties he was searching again for a home, and even for a more traditional life-style, things that he had lived without for over ten years. Aharon and Sarah Mahla loved him and thought him a fine yiddisher boy, with a heimishe background like themselves, an Eastern European. Annie knew that he was totally different from the local boys she had previously dated. In one way, that worried her, but from another perspective she was excited by it. He was always immaculately clean and tidy, he had a cheeky sense of humour, he was passionate about everything he did, and he could face any new situation without fear. He therefore complemented her to a large degree and gave her security and deep love, and she knew that she needed those. She also could tell soon after they started to go out together that he would make a wonderful lover. She was very attracted to him physically but she was not sure if she loved him as much as he seemed to love her. What perhaps tilted the balanced for her was the fact that he got on so well with her parents, who did all that they could to encourage the young couple.

By Pesah 1943, part of which they spent in the Rapstoff home, they had decided to get married and they tentatively fixed the date for Lag B'Omer, 33 days after the hag. They were now ready to be man and wife and the arrangements were made for the wedding. At that stage, as they later confided to their children, they could no longer resist the temptation of sleeping together, believing that they would be married within about a month. But the local Rabbi, Dr. Salis Daiches, was not so easily convinced that he could arrange a ketubah for Pinhas, given that he knew nothing about him. He knew the Rapstoff family very well but who was this little Polish soldier and what was his background? He summoned Pinḥas to attend an interview and he asked him all sorts of questions about Yiddishkeit and about the shtetl and about his family and their traditions. Pinḥas was never the most patient of people in tense situations and he finally exploded. 'Rabbi Daiches, I shall let down my trousers and show you how Jewish I am, and that should satisfy you!' he shouted. Rabbi Daiches calmly replied that this would prove nothing and he required witnesses to testify to Pinḥas's Jewish status. Jewish colleagues in the army were drafted in for that purpose and eventually Rabbi Daiches was satisfied but by this time the wedding had had to be postponed and could now take place only on 15 June 1943. The couple were distraught since by then it seemed that Annie was pregnant. But the wedding finally took place and Annie used all her savings to cater a reasonable celebration and meal, all of which she prepared herself with some assistance from other members of the family. She was happy, as were her parents, but the other members of the family were a little more parochial in their tastes. They saw Pinḥas as a Pole, a foreigner, a soldier – and they were convinced that he would abandon her and return to Poland after the war. So the atmosphere was not so warm and in any case Pinḥas spent much of the day in tears, missing his mother and sister, and without the presence of a single guest who was even a distant relative of his. But at last they were man and wife and after a few days leave, and a mini-honeymoon at Granny Ramsey's home in Carnoustie on the Fife coast, he was back at his engineering work with the Polish sappers on the east coast of Scotland.

Arctic Convoys

The officer whom Pinḥas had once struck down made some inquiries and soon found that Pinḥas had served in the Polish Merchant Navy for a number of years during the 1930s. So he had found a perfect way of taking revenge for being knocked down by this hot-headed little Jew. The British had agreed to send supplies, mostly obtained from the USA, to the Russians who were fighting a desperate war against the Nazis and were greatly in need of food and equipment. One of the ways of providing such assistance was to send heavily laden ships from the UK to the northern ports of Russia such as Murmansk and Archangel. The voyage, which took about twelve days, would begin in Liverpool or in Loch Ewe in Scotland, would stop for supplies in Iceland, and then continue across the Arctic Sea to Russia. The German enemy was determined to stop this supply route and used its aircraft, warships and submarines to attack the convoys at every available opportunity. Although the supply ships were escorted by British destroyers, as many as a quarter of them sometimes went down in the frozen Arctic waters, with heavy loss of life. The British asked for ships and crews to be manned by the many Poles who had joined the allies to fight the German invaders of their country, especially those with naval experience.

Pinḥas, recently married, was ordered to report for duty as a marine engineer on the SS *Krakow*. He was thrilled to be serving again at sea, an experience he had always found exhilarating and challenging. He enjoyed taking care of the massive engines that powered the boats and he loved the seamen's intense feelings of camaraderie. But he soon realized that the Arctic convoys brought more misery than pleasure to all those involved. He saw ships going down and crew members dying in the icy waters. He felt great compassion for those drowning but knew that, if they slowed down in order to attempt a rescue, they would also be easier targets for the enemy hunters. So it was with tears in his eyes that he followed the captain's instructions for 'full speed ahead'. On returning to Edinburgh on one occasion he heard that the son of one of the local kosher bakers had perished on one of the convoys. It troubled him all his life to think that he may have sped past that young man as he lay dying in the water.

He had enjoyed a brief few days of shore leave with his heavily pregnant wife at home during Ḥanukah late in 1943. He was very amused by the fact that she had a great craving for potato latkes and could not get enough of them. Then she would suffer nauseous attacks. When the little baby inside her could later make his own dietary choices, he abhorred latkes and perhaps his mother had given him good reason to do so! Pinḥas was assured by the family that they would somehow get the message to him of the impending birth of his first born and he was soon off again on one of his nerve-wracking tours of duty at sea. Meanwhile Annie had left her parents to cope as best they could for the moment and had moved in with two of her own generation. She got on very well with her brother Yosef's wife Lily and adored their son, Leon, who was by then six years old. Lily had decided that Yosef – known in the family as Joe and now in the army – should better be called John and she also suggested that Pinḥas should become Peter. Annie took to using that name but among his Polish and Jewish colleagues he was still known as Pinkas or Pinḥas. Lily's younger sister Yehides (Judith or Ada) also moved into Jordan Lane where John and Lily rented an apartment and young Leon was delighted to be spoiled not only by his Mum but also by two aunts, both of them also on their own. Whenever he went out with his Auntie Annie everyone thought that he was her son, given that he looked more like her than like his own mother. Indeed, one of Pinḥas's friends warned him not to court Annie because he was sure that the little boy he had seen walking out with her was her son!

Pinḥas's next voyage began in January 1944 and reached its destination at the end of the month, a harrowing sixteen days of storms at sea, dodging many German attacks, and seeing others reap their cruel harvest of those ahead or behind them in the convoy. But Pinḥas had exciting news awaiting him when he landed in Reykjavik, the capital city and main port of Iceland. Lily had been true to her word. She had gone to the General Post Office in Edinburgh on Sunday 23 January and sent a telegram to Pinkas Reif at the military address give to her, which was 'S.S. Krakow, Harbourmaster, Queen Quay, Belfast'. Since only immediate family were allowed to make use of this facility, she signed herself not 'Lily Rabstaff' but 'Lily Reif'. The message read 'Have already wired. Annie had a son on Friday. Both well'. Pinḥas told his two closest friends among the crew, one Jewish and one not, and they decided that they should go ashore, buy a bottle of whisky, and celebrate. The three finished the whole bottle and were so drunk that they attracted the attention of some patrolling British military policemen who soon escorted them back to their ship. When told the reason for the celebration, they agreed not to press charges against the three jolly seamen.

Annie had had a difficult birth and had little strength to organise the brit milah but her father Aharon was happy to undertake this religious duty and to stand in for his absent son-in-law. Pinḥas had said before he joined his ship that he left it to Zeide to choose a Hebrew name as long as it was not Shneur Zalman since so many of the family were already named for the founder of Chabad. He had also said that if it were a boy he would like him to be called Stefan since his childhood friend from Kalusz, Stefan Bereznicki, had recently met his death as a result of a German torpedo and Pinḥas was anxious to immortalize him in some way. Calling to mind two relatively distant family members of his son-in-law who had passed on, Aharon named the eight-day-old baby boy Shlomo Qalman. The local hazan and shochet, Berl Zucker, was also a mohel and a good friend. He carried out the procedure and the boy was admitted to the covenant of Abraham our Father. Annie had preferred the name Karl but was overruled by her serving husband. The little boy's birth certificate recorded his names as 'Stefan Clive'.

Appendix B

The Rebtsov Story

Family Prayer-book

In Russia about 150 years ago very few of the Jewish community were able to afford their own books containing the yomtov davening. To own your own maḥzor was a sign of success and wealth. So, we may assume that Yosef ben Yehuda Yitschak Vinakourov, unlike many of the poor Jewish folk around him, was doing well financially because I have in front of me as I write the Ḥasidic maḥzor that he used on Rosh Ha Shanah and Yom Kippur. Since it was published in 1868, he appears to have bought it soon afterwards. To ensure that nobody in shool helped himself to it when he was looking in another direction, Yosef used a little stamp, probably something like a signet ring, on which his initials had been engraved, to mark his ownership of the maḥzor in ink on various pages. Interestingly, the initials are in Russian script and read 'EB' which is equivalent to 'YV'. Around them appears his Hebrew name.

The family were Ḥasidim and they lived in an area of Russia that was not too distant from the city in which the Lubavitch or Chabad sect thrived. When, around the year 1846, Yosef was arranging a marriage for his daughter Ḥayya Sarah, he naturally looked for a Ḥasidic family. The choice fell on Shneur Zalman Rebtsov. His family's customs and their pronunciation of Hebrew, as well as their style of leining and davening, were very similar to those of Chabad but the family tradition is that they were Tsefase Ḥasidim, seemingly called after the town in Turkish Palestine that we now know as the Israeli city of Tsefat (Safed). Groups of Russian Ḥasidim had emigrated to Eretz Yisrael a few decades earlier and had suffered from terrible poverty, disease and persecution. Those who had survived had returned to Russia so perhaps some of those early Zionists were among the ancestors of Shneur Zalman. Given that Shneur Zalman was given by his father, Shmuel Yisrael, the name of Shneur Zalman of Liady, the founder of Chabad, there can be little doubt that the family felt itself close to Chabad. To understand which period of history we are discussing, it should be noted that Shmuel Yisrael personally knew Jews who had experienced the invasion of Russia by Napoleon.

Shneur and Ḥayya Sarah

Shneur Zalman Rebtsov was a very intelligent man with energy and ambition but there was little outlet in Russia at that time for talented Jews (trades and professions were very restricted to them) so he made do with learning the craft of a tailor, knowing that this talent was something that he could take with him wherever he might go and be sure of making a living. His father-in-law, Yosef Vinakourov, must have grown to like his son-in-law Shneur Zalman Rebtsov because he passed on the large maḥzor to him at some point.

Russian Responses

The shtetelech in which the Vinakourovs and the Rebtsovs lived were not far from White Russia, Lithuania, Ukraine and Poland and had become part of Russia only towards the end of the eighteenth century when Tsarist Russia, together with Prussia (later part of Germany) and the Austro-Hungarian Empire had divided up Poland among them. Jews had lived in Poland since about the tenth century, and in large numbers since the sixteenth century, and had been the middle men between the Polish nobility on the one hand and the local peasants on the other. There is more about this arrangement in the previous chapter.

The Russians were not, to put it mildly, greatly enamoured of the many Jews who came under their control as a result of their conquest of parts of Poland and they limited them to certain areas (called the Pale of Settlement), forbidding them to live in some of the larger cities such as Moscow. Occasionally the Tsars or their political leaders would decide that they needed to blame someone for one misfortune or another so they would point their fingers at the Jews and would encourage their soldiers or local ruffians to attack their little communities. The Russian Orthodox Church of the time often spoke of the Jews as 'Christ-killers' so there was widespread hatred of them among the non-Jewish population. In such attacks or pogroms, some Jews were killed, some were severely wounded, women were not infrequently raped, and property was burnt and looted.

There was also a scheme for sending in troops, usually Cossacks, to a shtetel, grabbing young boys and carrying them off for army service. One of Shneur Zalman's three brothers (or was it an uncle?) suffered just such a fate and nothing was heard of him until many years later when the family were told that he had distinguished himself in the army. He had died and the epaulettes from his uniform were sent to his relatives. That is one of the many stories that my Zeide told me as a small child. Like all his generation, he often spoke of 'a mohl in der heim', how it once was in the 'homeland' of Eastern Europe, usually with some warmth, in spite of what they had suffered there.

Forests and Farms

So where were these shtetelech where the Vinakourovs and the Rebtsovs resided, busy with trading and with tailoring, and maintaining strictly orthodox Jewishness? The tradition is that they were from Suraz and Starodub. On a map of Russia you will see that these shtetelech (some 55 kilometres from each other) are not far from the main road that travels the 275 kilometres from Bryansk in the north east (itself almost 400 kilometres south of Moscow) to Gomel (sometimes pronounced Homel) in the south west, now in the independent country of Belarus but part of Tsarist Russia in the middle of the nineteenth century . When Zeide spoke about his area of Russia he always referred to the largest city as Chernigov which is another 100 kilometres to the south of Gomel. Perhaps Chernigov was the administrative capital of the province. Possibly some of the Rebtsov family records are there or in Gomel.

The area is one of small towns, forests and farming with many rivers, the largest of which are the Iput (Snov, Sudast?) and the Sozh. The language spoken at home was of course Yiddish but Russian was also known. Zeide Aharon's Russian was better than his English even after living half a century in the United Kingdom. The men could read and write Yiddish but the women were often left illiterate if their fathers preferred them to attend to domestic matters.

Introducing Young Aharon

The eldest son of Shneur Zalman and his wife Ḥayya Sarah was Aharon, born in 1870, and there were other siblings, one of whom was Noah who emigrated to the United States and settled on the north west coast in Tacoma, in Washington State. He or a close relative of his visited us when I was a little boy and my Zeide Aharon was still alive. They were talking in Yiddish about his reputation in the family and when my Zeide admitted that he had always had the philosophy of putting off until tomorrow whatever needed to be done today, they corrected him: 'not until tomorrow, until the day after tomorrow' ('nisht morgen, uber morgen'). There was also a sister, I think, called Gittel, as well as three brothers.

We have to remember that in those days, before the widespread use of anaesthetics and the existence of antibiotics, it was not uncommon for young people to die of medical conditions that would today be operable or treatable with drugs. When Zeide was still a boy, his mother Ḥayya Sarah complained of terrible stomach-aches and within a few days had died. Perhaps she had a perforated appendix that turned to peritonitis. The tragedy of losing their mother was compounded for the young family by the remarriage of their father. The woman he chose was the widow Sarah Basson (née Hordonov) who already had two children by her first marriage who would go on to produce ten grandchildren for her. With Shneur Zalman, she had four more children. One of them was called Devora Lea, after the daughter of the first Chabad rebbe. Sarah Basson Rebtsov always ensured that major attention and concern were directed by Shneur Zalman and herself not to the children and grandchildren of his first wife but to those of her replacement.

Aharon's Step-mother

Family tradition has it that Ḥayya Sarah's children occupied a different house, or part of the house, and that there was a fire in that part of the house that led to the death of three sons. The rumour among the Rebtsovs was that the step-mother had engineered the whole thing. The Rebtsovs among themselves always referred to the second wife of Shneur Zalman not as Sarah but as 'die makhasheyfe', 'the witch', and deeply resented her.

Young Aharon was not like his father, although he did have a similar reputation for being a wonderful tailor. He lacked ambition, had little interest in making money, and was a kindly and gentle soul. Whenever asked to express a preference for one thing over another, he would reply in Yiddish 'Ich hob a dayge', meaning that he didn't mind either way. He did have a foul temper as a young man but he told me that he had learned from one experience never to indulge that weakness. He had once become so angry that he threw a pair of those massive scissors used by tailors down on to the cutting table so powerfully that they bounced back on to him and cut his arm deeply. That was his excuse for never again taking anything too seriously. He showed me the scar. He loved his ḥevra, whether in the workshop or in shool, and would rather spend time with them, davening, joking or telling stories, than devising ways of making anything more than a paltry living. He was a lively spinner of tales and always enjoyed a good chuckle. He always had a great sympathy and admiration for those Jews who had gone to Turkish Palestine and, later to the British Mandate there, to rebuild the Jewish homeland and he encouraged the family (naturally, in a quiet and gentle way) to raise funds for them.

But Was He Good Enough For Sarah Maḥla?

When, at some point in the 1890s, Aharon had to take a wife, he found one who came from Zlynka, a smaller town than what he was used to but one that was much nearer the larger city of Gomel than his birthplace of Surazh, some 80 kilometres to the north east. Sarah Maḥla Varanovski's family regarded themselves as more 'up-market' and more intelligent than the Rebtsov tailoring family. The father Avraham Lipa and his wife Ḥayya thought that their daughter could do better but she seems to have fallen in love with the tall and erect Aharon with his reddish hair, blue eyes and his cheerful and relaxed character. The family of Varanovski were in some way related to the Hordonovs from whom Sarah Bassin hailed. Perhaps she arranged the introduction.

Sarah Maḥla was herself not pretty and maybe she had worries about who might seek her hand. Her parents were not thrilled by the match and never quite forgave their daughter for urging them to accept it. They thought, rightly, that she herself was cleverer than Aharon and again rightly, that he would not be very good at making a living. They themselves lived well and they were apprehensive about what Aharon could do for their daughter. The family saga talks about the ownership of orchards which may have brought the Varanovskis a good income.

I know of at least four children of the Varanovskis who were, unlike the Rebtsovs, of dark hair and complexion, smaller, rounder and with fairly prominent noses. There was one brother, I think called Yosef, who became involved with one or other of the revolutionary movements that operated against the Tsarist regime at that time. The Russian government had passed anti-Jewish laws in 1882 (known as the 'May Laws'), restricting Jewish settlement, business, property ownership and education, and some Jews had decided that positive, and even violent, action was required. Like many young firebrands, Yosef Varanovski was swiftly made to 'disappear' by the secret police and the family heard no more of him.

Sarah Maḥla's younger sister was called Rachel and they had a baby brother called Hirsh. Hirsh was still being breast-fed when his mother died and by that time my Bubbe, Sarah Maḥla, was herself a mother (I think the year was 1893) and she managed to feed him as well as her own baby. Brother Hirsh (who later called himself Harry) and sister Rachel both eventually made their way to the United Kingdom and the Varanovski family's reputation for brilliance reached its peak when Rachel's son, Abe, became Regius Professor of Medicine at the University of Glasgow and highly distinguished in the medical profession. At one point, Zeide Aharon was called for some form of Russian military service. He told me that he had to do some basic training. He proved himself to be an excellent marksman and, according to his explanation, it was this success that led to his early return home.

A Voyage to London

Whether because of the fear of more military service, or the outbreaks of antisemitism that were becoming more frequent in Russia, especially after the May Laws, Shneur Zalman decided to emigrate to London, bringing with him Aharon and Sarah Maḥla and their children, as well as his second wife and her family. A statement quoted in the name of the Russian Tsarist statesman, Konstantin Pobedonostsev, said that a third of the Jews would be converted, a third would emigrate, and the rest would die of hunger. He clearly saw no room for the continued existence of vibrant Judaism in Russia!

In about 1898, the Rebtsovs, who became Rapstoffs in the process of that emigration (later changed by some to what they thought of as the more 'anglicized' form of Rabstaff), settled in the East End of London and Shneur Zalman set up a tailoring workshop in which his son Aharon also worked. Aharon left industry and intensity to his father and was content to wait until the day came when his father would pass on and he would inherit his business and the assets. He warned me at an early age never to wait for family inheritance because that had been one of his own mistakes. He failed to take account of the influence and power of his step-mother who seems to have ensured that whatever was coming from her husband's estate came to his second family and not his first. Shneur Zalman arranged things for his workers and they all relied on him.

Scotland Beckons

An uncle told me once that a local family, who established a kosher wine business in Brick Lane in the East End of London towards the end of the nineteenth century, at one point received financial support for their project from Shneur Zalman. You have to remember that workers in the 'shmatte' trade worked for long hours and that those who had remained religiously observant had their prayers and meals together and formed a strong and well-knit hevra. Shneur Zalman was the leading figure in his hevra and when early in the 1900s a strike of tailors made it impossible for him and his work-shop to continue operating without attracting violence from the angry strikers, he did not wring his hands in horror and bewail his fate but made alternative plans. He saw that the British Army needed tailors to make uniforms in Edinburgh so he successfully applied for the contract and moved his whole workshop up north.

Aharon and Sarah Mahla followed, as you would have expected them to do. They had had a difficult time in London, never being able to pay their rent and therefore having to flit from one abode to another. Sarah Mahla, my Bubbe, had nine live births but only six survived into adulthood. Two had died in infancy in Russia, one from a chest infection and another in what seems to us a strange accident. The Russian winter was so cold that they sometimes placed babies on the top of the still-warm stove at night so that they could remain warm. One baby was too lively for its own good and fell from the stove to its death.

Tragedy and Poverty

An even greater tragedy occurred in London when Sarah Mahla was having her sixth child in hospital in the East End of London. It must have been just before the family moved north to Edinburgh in about 1906. Hayya Rivka was their little daughter who was at home looking after her younger brothers while Bubbe was in hospital, having the baby who was given the name of Binyamin. Zeide was perhaps at work or maybe in shool. At any rate Hayya Rivka was drying her hair in front of the open fire when her night-dress caught fire. She was rushed into the same hospital where her mother was giving birth. The rumour went around the hospital that a beautiful young girl called Hayya Rivka with golden locks had been brought in badly burnt and had succumbed to her injuries and when Bubbe heard the story she was distraught and cried out 'Dos is mein Hayya Rivka!' ('That is my daughter Hayya Rivka!') From then on she suffered badly with her nerves, with terrible headaches and with hallucinations. Little wonder.

But there was no time for self-pity. A new home had to be set up, tailoring had to be done, and shool activities had to be supported. Aharon and Sarah Mahla now had three sons, all born in London, and named Avraham (Abe), Mordechai (Maxie) and Binyamin (Benny) and another three children were born to them in Edinburgh. They were Yosef (later called John by his wife, Lily), Buni (Bessie) and (my mother) Hayya

(Annie), who was born in 1916. The family lived in what was effectively a little ghetto of impoverished Jewish tradesmen in Richmond Street, a short walk from the busy commercial centre of town but very far away from its affluence and success. 'Happy land' was the ghettos' nickname but it was neither happy nor their land. And yet somehow most of those poor Jewish immigrants produced children and grandchildren of whom they could be proud, not only for their achievements but also for their values.

Aharon earned very little and there were many mouths to feed so Sarah Maḥla would think of ways to supplement the family income so that her children would not go hungry. One scheme was to make boiled sweets at home and then sell bags of them to the local schoolchildren for a half-penny each. Another was to buy beigels at the bakery from the early-morning batch, fill them, and sell them to those rushing off to work, for their breakfast or their lunch. Whatever her poverty, she never refused to help those many beggars who appeared at her door, both Jewish and non-Jewish. She would often invite them in and sit them down to a meal. Bubbe had to do everything herself at home and in those days the processes of washing clothes, cleaning floors, baking and cooking were in no way mechanically aided. An uncle remembered the revolution when one neighbour acquired a metal grater (a 'ribeisen' in Yiddish) and everyone in the tenement took turns to borrow it. Zeide Aharon did not seem to take much interest in domestic matters. He did always look immaculate, however, and it must have been difficult for those who saw him strutting proudly in Princes Street, with his self-tailored three-piece double-breasted suit, bowler hat, heavy overcoat and cane, to believe the level of poverty in his home.

Somehow, Sarah Maḥla ensured that there was food on the table and she always served Aharon first and gave him the best part of the meal. She excelled in preparing scrumptious meals, often from potatoes, cheap meat or fish, and damaged fruit and vegetables which could be obtained without much expense. She made a cholent on Shabbos and my mother, Ḥayya, remembered that as the youngest of the family it was her job to go and collect it on Shabbos morning. The local baker, who was also of ḥasidic stock like Zeide Aharon, was very near the tenement blocks were the poor Jewish immigrant families lived, each crammed into two or three damp and bug-infested rooms. His ovens were still hot after he had baked the challah for Shabbos so the local families placed their cholent there overnight to cook for many hours and to acquire its distinctive shabbosdik taste and smell.

Tatte und Kinder (A Dad and His Kids)

In such close and cramped conditions, there were of course tensions between the siblings, especially between Yosef and Binyamin who had a particular dislike of each other. Yosef saved up money from his work as a tailor's presser and managed to buy himself a suit. One day he was due to take a girl out for the evening so he carefully pressed his suit and hung it up in the bedroom that he shared with his brothers. When he got home, it was gone! Having only sweaty working clothes, he could not go out on his date. His brother Benny had decided that his need that evening was the greater one and had 'borrowed' the suit. When he returned the brothers came to blows and I do not think that Yosef ever forgave his sibling for the enforced loan.

By 1916, Avraham (Avremel as his mother called him) had had enough of such domestic conditions and decided to join the British Expeditionary Force fighting in France. He had never seen a birth certificate and could only guess how old he was. He had been working as a tailor for some six years so he thought he could argue that he was eighteen and old enough to fight for his country. Many years later, after much searching in official records, he located his birth certificate and it turned out that he had started work at 10 and become a soldier at 16! He experienced the terrible situations in the trenches and saw many colleagues killed or wounded. He wrote long Yiddish letters to his parents describing, in so far as the censor allowed, what he was suffering. Finally, his own luck did not hold out and he was wounded and almost choked to death by mustard gas. In the confusion of the war, the news did not get back to his unit that he had been hospitalized and he was posted as 'missing in action, presumed killed'. That message was sent to his parents. Imagine their shock and horror. No definite news, no body, no funeral or shiv'ah. But imagine what greater shock Sarah Maḥla experienced when her Avremel turned up on the doorstep some weeks later, on sick leave from his unit! Having survived more action later in France, he married and set up his own home soon after completing his army service.

That became the story of all the siblings. In the 1920s and 1930s they each left home, most of them having trained in some aspect of the tailoring business, and found a partner, leaving only my mother, Annie (Ḥayya), as the baby of the family, to look after her parents as they became older and unwell. While the Rapstoff home, with Aharon running religious matters, remained traditionally orthodox, none of those setting up their own home followed his example. They had not been educated by him in Jewish

28. Stefan's Mum, Annie (seated) with two friends, about 1933.

matters, had opted to follow their friends and adopt a more British (actually in many ways Scottish) way of life, and felt that their father had not set them much of an example with regard to how a wife should be treated and how a home should be run. But most of them remained warm towards many aspects of the Jewish traditions. They visited their parents for the festivals and expected all the customs to be kept there, as they always had been.

Hardly surprising to say, Zeide Aharon was not regarded by his children as much of a success as a parent. But his relaxed manner, his gentleness and his warmth made him a very much loved Zeide to all his twelve grandchildren, from Hanna ('Nan') who was born in 1921 to Cynthia who was born in 1947. (Sharron came on the scene after he had died.) They loved to come and visit him, to sit on his knee, to be tickled by his beard and to hear his tales of what once was. He expressed only love and never any criticism so that they always came back for more. As adults, they all remembered the joy of visiting Zeide Rapstoff and had the fondest of memories of him. It was Zeide Aharon who gave most of them their Hebrew names and, needless, to say, Shneur Zalman figured prominently on the list.

What of the Girls?

In the late 1920s Annie's elder sister Bessie (Buna) had a terrible experience as a fourteen year-old. She was either raped or sexually abused and became pregnant as a result. She never divulged the name of the man responsible for this cruel act but members of the family had their suspicions that he might have been a family member well known to her. It seems that same member of the family later assaulted Ḥayya and even his own daughters. Aharon could not cope with the shame of it so he sent her to London for the birth. He was soon informed by letter that Bessie had given birth to a beautiful boy, and that there would be no problem finding a couple to adopt him. His response was to ask her sister Annie to write to the London correspondent and to arrange for Bessie to come home and guiltily carry the responsibility of rearing the child herself. He then arranged a marriage for her at the age of 17 with a young man who had been brought up in the Glasgow Jewish Orphanage, and brought her back to Edinburgh. The marriage produced seven more children for her but it was never a happy relationship. She never cared much for her husband and although he seemed often to be besotted with her, he had a very unstable character and would often resort to drink and to aggressive behaviour.

In 1918 Shneur Zalman died and his second wife, the 'mechasheyfa', rewarded his generosity to her and to her children by erecting what was then a very expensive and impressive headstone at the cemetery in Piershill. It is in a most prominent position, just as you enter the Jewish part of the complex, and anyone arriving there will soon see her tribute to 'Solomon Rapstoff'. One of my mother's earliest memories was of earning a halfpenny from her step-grandmother. The old lady was virtually blind and wanted to go regularly to visit the grave of her husband. So, she asked Annie to hold her hand and take her on the tram-car, or on two tram-cars as the journey required, all the way to Piershill. There she would stand by the tombstone and cry bitter tears while little Annie waited for her and for her limited monetary reward. If, for any reason, her step-grandmother was displeased with Annie, she would lock her in a dark cupboard. Poor Annie was forever afterwards terrified of sleeping alone in a totally darkened room and would recall her fear when later dealing with her own first-born.

Being the youngest in the family, Annie was never far from her mother's apron, always hanging on to her, as though her life depended on it, as it probably did. Like all her elder siblings, she remembered being sung to sleep by her mother with Russian and Yiddish lullabies. The Rapstoffs of course, and all the impoverished but warm and friendly neighbours around them, spoke only Yiddish to each other which created something of a problem when Annie went to the local school at the age of five. She spent the first few days in a terrible state of misery, not understanding a word. But one kindly teacher had pity on her and made sure that within a few weeks she was chatting in as Scottish a dialect as all her chums. Another teacher was less kind. She told Annie that she should not be wearing rubber shoes in the winter and that she should change her dress when it got dirty. Poor Annie did not know how to respond. She only had one dress and shoes were beyond the family budget. She learned from Abe's wife, Dolly, to wash out her dress in the afternoon and dry it in front of the fire so that it would be ready for the next day. Luckily, she did not meet the fate of her sister Ḥayya Rivka in London some fifteen years earlier.

What Did Zeide Enjoy?

Shneur Zalman's eldest son, Aharon, continued to work as a tailor in different workshops with a succession of colleagues but his heart was in Jewish matters. He tried his hand at being a Jewish bookseller and supplier of Jewish items. He prepared for individuals and for families lists of the dates in the civil calendar on which the yahrzeits for their close relatives would occur. He started to make one of those on a piece of parchment for display in the synagogue but never completed it. I have it here on my desk. He loved to re-bind books, especially siddurim, as they disintegrated. He had a great deal of patience and an artistic eye for such things and he might well have succeeded. He had the contacts, people trusted him and liked him, and he knew enough of Jewish matters to enable him to function in those ways. He had just one problem. He provided all the services without ever having any guarantee of receiving payment. Many promised him that they would settle their bills but they somehow forgot. And being Aharon, who was always putting things off until tomorrow, he did not chase them up, and therefore found himself losing money instead of making it.

He loved to be part of his Eastern European Ḥasidic ḥevra. Edinburgh had in Graham Street what they called an 'Englische shul' with all the formalities that went with it. Top hats for the officials, clerical gowns for the Rabbi and the ḥazan, silk tallitot, an English sermon and a concern for decorum. It had very few observant congregants and was not to the liking of Aharon and his friends. That was all a little too much like a church in their eyes. They preferred a little shtiebel near their homes in Richmond Street where they could, in their large and yellowing woollen taleisim, run things in a less formal and more personal way, doing the davening and leining themselves, blowing the shofar and dancing a Kossatski (a Cossack dance) after having a good schnapps on Simḥat Torah. When they needed someone who could read and write English, they would turn to the younger generation and for some years Uncle Abe functioned for them in this way, as a sort of communal secretary.

Jewish Immigrants and Scottish Gents

There were a number of such little synagogues in Edinburgh attended by those who had been born in Eastern Europe. Rabbi Dr. Salis Daiches, from a Lithuanian rabbinic family but with a modern academic education and a deep knowledge of German philosophy, was much more of a central European intellectual than the kind of rebbes and rabbonim that the immigrants were used to. When in 1918 he became the Rabbi of the 'Englische shul' he and those who ran that congregation thought that it would be a good idea to unite all of them in the one larger synagogue that they were planning to build. But the immigrants were stubborn and liked their traditional set-up. For them, if a Rabbi was a Doctor it showed that the congregation was sick! It was those immigrants who tried to provide a living for Rabbi Rabbinowitz whose son, Louis, later became Chief Rabbi of South Africa and a leading Zionist. On one occasion they even collected enough money among themselves to arrange for someone who had been recommended to them as a wonderful ḥazan to come and lead the prayers on Rosh Ha-Shanah and Yom Kippur. This would attract even more members, they thought, and strengthen their feelings of uniqueness and independence. Alas, it brought about their undoing.

The ḥazan was a great success but Rabbi Dr. Daiches though that there was something suspicious about him. He made intensive inquiries and found out that the man's brother had been a member of a Christian congregation in Eretz Yisrael. He had apparently converted to Christianity at some stage. Needless to say, major publicity was given to this and the little ḥevra that had engaged him was made to look very foolish. They never recovered from that incident and neither they nor the other groups could withstand the trend of the 1920s towards one united 'Hebrew Congregation'. By the time the new synagogue was built at 4 Salisbury Road in 1932, they had all come under its umbrella. They were never very pleased with the new set-up and felt no warmth towards Rabbi Dr. Daiches. But they formed the core of the daily minyan, morning and evening, and among them there was always a yahrzeit, a shiur and a Yiddish joke. They also made sure that the less fortunate among themselves were assisted whenever and however they need it. But on Shabbat and the ḥagim in Salisbury Road it was the top hat and the silk tallit that held sway.

Better Conditions

After over 20 years in the Richmond Street 'ghetto', with Jewish bakers, butchers and grocers all nearby, Aharon and Sarah Maḥla, with the two children still at home, Yosef and Annie, moved into a brand-new apartment at 2 Prestonfield Terrace, about two kilometres further south. The building, consisting of six apartments, three on each side, stood at the end of an attractive public garden, and had a kind of architectural independence from the streets and buildings around it. The new residents claimed on good authority that they had been chosen for this new Edinburgh Corporation public housing project because they had been exemplary tenants. So, it seems that, unlike in London, they had paid the rent in Edinburgh. From the outset, the neighbours knew that the family was Jewish and Aharon was never seen without his hat or without the large black yarmulka, built up to a height of about 5 centimetres with a button on each side, that he had made for himself. He was able to take a leisurely fifteen-minute walk to shul on Shabbat and ḥag, or catch a bus, for 3-4 stops, to get him there during the week.

For most of the 1930s it was my Mum, Annie (Ḥayya) who looked after her parents, Joseph having also married. She left school at 14, where she had been among the brightest in the class, and – surprise, surprise – was sent to the tailoring firm of Katz to learn to be a tailoress. There she assiduously served her apprenticeship and eventually earned a reasonable wage. The problem was that Mr. Katz did not always have the money to pay his staff. He was addicted to gambling (or was it drink?) and only when his wife intervened were his workers finally paid. There was always a worry as to when one might get one's wages. Although he himself never worked on Shabbat (and this caused difficulties with some firms), Aharon's children all felt that they had to do so in order to make a tolerable living and to keep their jobs. Annie too followed suit.

Annie Steps Out

For entertainment, there were many youngsters of her own age and she made her own clothes and went out with them in groups or in foursomes to dancing, to cinema ('the pictures', as they called it) and to variety shows at the local theatres. They also ventured on holiday as far as the Isle of Man, 27 kilometres south of the Scottish coast, half way to Ireland. She had a succession of boyfriends from Edinburgh and from Glasgow, which had a much larger Jewish population and was only an hour away by train. In her late teens she had a good mind, pleasant features, a nice shape and a very kind character. Though she tended to leave initiatives to others (much like her father), she was hard-working, reliable and enjoyed socializing. But for one reason or another it did not click for any of her young men, nor for her. She also constantly had at the back of her mind that her parents were getting older and less able to take of themselves. Her mother was prone to neurotic attacks of one sort or another and gradually, towards the end of the 1930s, she found that she had to take responsibility for running the household.

War Times in Scotland

She used to tell me with great emotion the story of Sunday 3 September 1939. She was sitting in the living room of their home with Aharon and Sarah Maḥla listening to the radio when Prime Minister Neville Chamberlain made his historic speech. The British had asked the Germans for an assurance that they would immediately withdraw from Poland, which they had invaded two days earlier, or a state of war would exist between Britain and Germany. The absence of such an assurance meant that the two countries were now at war. Not knowing what this might mean for them, and recalling what had happened in the Great War not much more than two decades earlier, she and her parents sobbed at the news.

They had to ensure that not a chink of light could be seen through their windows and she and her father set about arranging this 'black-out'. But her mother, as her mental state deteriorated, forgot from time to time the purpose of these covers and would go to the windows and remove them. This was a reportable offence and gave Annie and Aharon many a worrying moment. Once the war got truly underway in 1940 and 1941, young women were asked to report for war duties. They could join the army or do some civilian job that released men for that purpose.

Annie became a bus conductress for Edinburgh Corporation Transport and learned a great deal about life beyond the warm Jewish household.

Lucky for her, her driver Jimmy Meikle (the two jobs were separate at that time) was very supportive. If she saw that the bus was full, she would ask those standing at the bus-stop to wait for the next bus. But sometimes that led to shouting, to abuse or to attempted violence against her by those desperate to get home or to get to work, and some of them would force their way on. At this point, Jimmy would stop the engine and come around to the platform at the back of the bus and use his big frame and loud voice to settle matters down. He would not move the bus until only the officially permitted number of passengers was on board. Those who had already boarded the bus at previous stops inevitably lent their support.

It was convenient for the other members of the family that they had Annie there in Prestonfield Terrace with their parents and perhaps they were not overly anxious to see her married. She herself had not found Mr. Right and she began to think that she never would. She kept busy with her work and her household duties and continued to socialize with her Jewish contemporaries. But by 1942 the Jewish community was enlarged not only by the addition of more refugees but also by the regular visits of Jewish soldiers, sailors and airmen who were engaged in war work or had their bases nearby. Ḥayya Rebtsov (aka Annie Rapstoff) had little inkling that her life would soon change completely as a result of such visits.

Select Index of Names

Lightning Source UK Ltd.
Milton Keynes UK
UKHW021326210521
384126UK00006B/161